Ruin the Sacred Truths (1989)

Poetics of Influence (1988)

The Strong Light of the Canonical (1987)

Agon: Towards a Theory of Revisionism (1982)

The Breaking of the Vessels (1982)

The Flight to Lucifer: A Gnostic Fantasy (1979)

Wallace Stevens: The Poems of Our Climate (1977)

Figures of Capable Imagination (1976)

Poetry and Repression (1976)

Kabbalah and Criticism (1975)

A Map of Misreading (1975)

The Anxiety of Influence (1973)

*The Ringers in the Tower: Studies in
Romantic Tradition* (1971)

Yeats (1970)

Commentary to *The Complete Prose and Poetry of
William Blake* (1965)

Blake's Apocalypse (1963)

The Visionary Company (1961)

Shelley's Mythmaking (1959)

The
DAEMON
KNOWS

SPIEGEL & GRAU

NEW YORK

The
DAEMON
KNOWS

Literary
Greatness
and the
American
Sublime

HAROLD
BLOOM

Published in the United States by Spiegel & Grau, an imprint
of Random House, a division of Penguin Random House LLC,
New York.

SPIEGEL & GRAU and the HOUSE colophon are
registered trademarks of Penguin Random House LLC.

Photo of Walt Whitman on p. 20: Mathew Brady. Photo of
Emily Dickinson on p. 150: © Three Lions / Getty Images.
Photo of Mark Twain on p. 298: courtesy of The Mark Twain
House and Museum. Photo of Wallace Stevens on p. 344:
© Corbis. Photo of T. S. Eliot on p. 344: © George Douglas /
Picture Post / Getty Images. Photo of William Faulkner on p. 404:
Carl Van Vechten photograph by permission of the Van Vechten
Trust. Photo of Hart Crane on p. 404: The Metropolitan Museum
of Art, Walker Evans Archive, 1994 (1994.255.75) © Walker Evans
Archive, The Metropolitan Museum of Art.

LIBRARY OF CONGRESS CATALOGING-IN-PUBLICATION DATA
Bloom, Harold.
The daemon knows : literary greatness and the
American sublime / Harold Bloom
pages   cm.
Includes index.
ISBN 978–0-8129–9782–8 (hardback : acid-free paper)
ISBN 978–0-8129–9783–5 (eBook)
1. American literature—History and criticism. I. Title.
PS121.B594 2015
810.9—dc23   2014040844

Printed in the United States of America on acid-free paper

www.spiegelandgrau.com

987654321

FIRST EDITION

Book design by Barbara M. Bachman

For my wife, Jeanne

———

and for John T. Irwin

and the outrageous Bricuth

Authentic tradition remains
hidden; only the decaying [*verfallende*]
tradition chances upon [*verfällt auf*]
a subject and only in decay does its
greatness become visible.

—GERSHOM SCHOLEM,
Ten Unhistorical Aphorisms
on Kabbalah

.

Contents

The
DAEMON
KNOWS

Why These Twelve?

THIS BOOK IS ABOUT THE DOZEN CREATORS OF THE AMERICAN SUBLIME. Whether these are our most enduring authors may be disputable, but then this book does not attempt to present an American canon. For that I can imagine alternative choices such as Edgar Allan Poe, Henry David Thoreau, Edith Wharton, Theodore Dreiser, Edwin Arlington Robinson, Willa Cather, Ernest Hemingway, F. Scott Fitzgerald, William Carlos Williams, Marianne Moore, Ralph Ellison, and Flannery O'Connor, without including later figures.

Yet my own selection seems more central, because these writers represent our incessant effort to transcend the human without forsaking humanism.

Thomas Weiskel, my friend and former student, who died tragically in a vain attempt to save his little daughter, left as memorial his seminal book *The Romantic Sublime* (1976). "A humanist sublime is an oxymoron" is his cautionary adage. Do my twelve masters of the sublime confirm Weiskel?

The American Sublime of Ralph Waldo Emerson and Walt Whitman is knowingly self-contradictory. You could not be a self-created Adam early in the morning with no past at your back, in 1830 or in 1855, even in the American vein.

Weiskel gave a pithy account of what the literary sublime asserts:

The essential claim of the sublime is that man can, in feeling and in speech, transcend the human. What, if anything, lies beyond the human—God or the gods, the daemon or Nature—is matter for great disagreement. What, if anything, defines the range of the human is scarcely less sure.

Except for T. S. Eliot, none of my twelve believed in God or the gods, and when they spoke of "Nature" they meant the American Adam. An Emersonian vision, the American Adam is the God-Man of the New World. He is self-created, and if he ever fell it was in the act of initial creation. What lies beyond the human for nearly all of these writers is the daemon, who is described and defined throughout this book.

The common element in these twelve writers—albeit covertly in Eliot—is their receptivity to daemonic influx. Henry James, the master of his art, nevertheless congratulates his own daemon for the greatest of his novels and tales. Emerson was the family sage for the James clan, including Henry James, Sr., as well as the novelist and the psychologist-philosopher William, whose essay "On Vital Reserves" is a hymn to the daemon.

I have paired these twelve figures in juxtapositions of no single pattern. I begin with Walt Whitman and Herman Melville because they are the Giant Forms (William Blake's term) of our national literature. *Moby-Dick* (1851) and the first *Leaves of Grass* (1855) have the aura and resonance of the Homeric epics and in that sense share a primacy among all our imaginative writers.

Exact contemporaries in time and space, Whitman and Melville must have passed each other often on the streets of New York City, and both attended the same lectures of Emerson but had no interest in each other. Whitman had read the early *Typee* yet nothing more. Melville, without a public from *Moby-Dick* on, resented Whitman's self-advertisements and the little shreds of notoriety they gathered.

I have avoided direct comparisons between *Moby-Dick* and *Leaves of Grass* except in a few places, though they might be redundant, since Melville and Whitman inaugurate the American fourfold metaphor of night, death, the mother, and the sea that has become perpetual for us.

Ralph Waldo Emerson and Emily Dickinson met when he lectured in Amherst and stayed for dinner and overnight at her brother's home next door. Her references to him in her letters are wistful and humorous, while her poems offer a sly critique of him. I bring them together here because he is her closest imaginative father, as Walter Pater was Virginia Woolf's.

What they share are powers of mind surpassing any others in our literature.

The relation of Nathaniel Hawthorne to Henry James is one of direct influence and so I bring them close together, in a way James would have disliked. I interpret all four of Hawthorne's major romances but fewer of the tales than I should for want of space. Emerson, Hawthorne's walking companion, deeply contaminates Hester Prynne and Hawthorne's other heroines, and his mark is as strong on Isabel Archer and James's later women protagonists. The ghostly Henry James, as in "The Jolly Corner," also emanates from Hawthorne.

Mark Twain and Robert Frost have little in common despite their mutually concealed savagery, but they are our only great masters with popular audiences. Both dissemble and move on two levels, implying deeper meanings to only an elite.

With Wallace Stevens and Thomas Stearns Eliot, I turn to an intricate interlocking: a polemic conducted by Stevens against Eliot. The eclipse of *Harmonium* by *The Waste Land* doubtless displeased Stevens, yet the personal element was minor compared to the opposition between a naturalistic humanism, akin to Sigmund Freud's, and a virulent neo-Christianity. There are greater depths in the conflict. Both Stevens and Eliot were Whitman's progeny; this proved a discomfort yet also an impetus for the seer of *Harmonium* while it was totally denied by Eliot until his closing years, when Whitman, Milton, and Shelley were allowed back into the Eliotic canon.

William Faulkner and my lifetime favorite, Hart Crane, are placed here side by side since each forces the American language to its limits. I contrast these titans implicitly, and I hope subtly, in their authentic shared tradition of American precursors. The only begetters they have in common are Melville and Eliot, to whom Faulkner could add Hawthorne and Mark Twain. Crane's formidable lineage includes Whitman and *Moby-Dick*, Emerson and Dickinson, Stevens and Eliot, and a panoply of other American poets from William Cullen Bryant and Edgar Allan Poe through William Carlos Williams.

Whitman, our national poet, calls out for an answering greatness. Of all classical American writers, Melville uniquely features the contours of a possible sublimity. What is the American Sublime and how does it differ from British and Continental instances? Simplistically, the sublime in literature has been associated with peak experiences that render a secular version of a theophany: a sense of something interfused that transforms a natural moment, landscape, action, or countenance.

America, the Evening Land, favors more drastic sublimities than Europe, abrupt splendors such as Dickinson's "certain Slant of light" or Stevens's auroras. Both are illuminations of discontinuity; at first reading, Wordsworth in the Lake Country and Shelley at Mont Blanc are more traditional than they or we are. True, Shelley and Wordsworth have broken from the immense literary cavalcades beautifully explored in my favorite work of modern critical scholarship, *European Literature and the Latin Middle Ages* (1953) by Ernst Robert Curtius, which traces a profound continuity moving all the long way from Homer through Goethe. The critic William Hazlitt remarked that Wordsworth seems to begin anew, on a tabula rasa of poetry. But though there is a gap, certainly, between Goethe and Wordsworth, it is hardly a dumbfounding abyss. Both are Shakespeare-haunted, an anxiety compounded for Wordsworth by Milton. Shelley, as classical as Goethe, had the triple burden of anxiety of influence from Shakespeare, Milton, and Wordsworth. A High Romantic English poet joins Homeric tradition not by choice but by contingencies of lasting and personal ambitions, whereas the greatest American Romantics—Whitman and Melville—necessarily have a very different relation to the tradition of European literature.

Emerson mediated literary tradition for Whitman. Melville, with no mentor, worked out his own relation to Shakespeare, Milton, and Shelley, as well as to Cervantes, Hawthorne, Emerson, and most darkly the Bible. Whitman's complex metric stems from Hebrew parallelism, and the Quakerism of his youth governs the stance and form in *Song of Myself,* yet Melville is the more Bible-soaked. Shadowed by Jonah and Job, *Moby-Dick* is the American book closest in cadence to the King James Bible, at least until Cormac McCarthy's Melvillean *Blood Meridian.*

It is difficult to foreground Walt Whitman. We cannot always rely on his own statements as to what he read. He and Emerson, he proclaimed in 1855, had their subsequent difficulties, best summed up however by Whitman finally affirming: "loyal at last." Mutual gratitude does not always culminate in such vital relationships, and it cheers me that it did.

For a few years Hawthorne was Melville's close friend, so his is not analogous to Emerson's role for Whitman. Still, he is the daemonic muse for *Moby-Dick,* while *Leaves of Grass* 1855 locates the daemon in one aspect of a tripartite Whitman, which I will discuss later. Emerson, Dickinson, and Hawthorne were New Englanders, while Melville, Whitman, and Henry James were more or less New Yorkers. Mark Twain emerged from the Mississippi landscape, while Robert Frost moved from California to New England. Eliot, of New England ancestry, came out of St. Louis to study at Harvard and to end as a Londoner, while Stevens emanated from Bucks County, Pennsylvania, east to Harvard and then on to his life in Hartford, Connecticut. Notoriously, Faulkner invented his own county and state in the Yoknapatawpha saga, which has now replaced Mississippi; Hart Crane, a child of Garretsville, Ohio, emulated Whitman and Melville by transmuting himself into the epic poet of New York City. He seems now the last transcendentalist poet of the American Sublime and the absolute conclusion to daemonic tradition in our literature. American poetry did not end with him, yet something glorious may have departed that cannot be renewed.

The two American writers I love best are Walt Whitman and Hart Crane, and the bridge of *The Daemon Knows* leaps from *Song of Myself* to Crane's *The Broken Tower.* At eighty-four, I can only write the way I go on teaching, personally and passionately. Poems, novels, stories, plays matter only if we matter. They give us the blessing of more life, whether or not they initiate a time beyond boundaries.

Daemonic Preludium

O UR TWO MOST AMBITIOUS AND SUBLIME AUTHORS REMAIN Walt Whitman and Herman Melville. Whitman creates from the powerful press of himself; Melville taps his pen deeply into the volcanic force of William Shakespeare.

American Shakespeare for the last two centuries has been a prevalent obsession, a more nervous and agile relationship than the bard's cultural dominance in Britain. Emerson remarked that the text of modern life was composed by the creator of *Hamlet*. *Moby-Dick,* Shakespearean and biblical, relies upon Ahab's fusion of aspects of Macbeth and of Lear. Consciousness, an ordeal in Emily Dickinson, Henry James, and William Faulkner, shares the quality of that adventure in self that is the Shakespearean soliloquy.

Charles Olson, poet and seer, pioneered the study of Shakespeare's influence upon *Moby-Dick*. Others have expanded his recognitions, and there is more to be apprehended; *Macbeth, King Lear, Antony and Cleopatra,* and above all *Hamlet* reverberate throughout Ahab's odyssey. Is *Moby-Dick* a revenge tragedy? Only as *Hamlet* is: not at all. Prince Hamlet rejects Shakespeare's play and writes his own. Does Ahab accept Herman Melville's epic? The great captain composes his fate, and we cannot know his enigmatic creator's intentions any more than we comprehend Shakespeare's.

I first read *Moby-Dick* in the early summer of 1940, before I turned ten. My sympathies were wholly with Captain Ahab, to some degree because the Book of Job—and William Blake's designs for it—were engraved deep within me. More than seventy years later, I teach the book annually and my judgment has not swerved. Ahab is as much the hero as Milton's Satan in *Paradise Lost,* or Macbeth. You can call them all hero-villains, but then so is Hamlet. I weary of scholars neighing against Ahab, who is magnificent in his heroism. Would they have him hunt for more blubber? His chase has Job's Leviathan in view, a quarry representing Yahweh's sanctified tyranny of nature over man.

Moby-Dick is an ecological nightmare; so are we. Melville's cause is not save the whales but strike the sun if it insults you and strike through the white pasteboard mask of all visible things at God, who has degraded you. Ahab has passed through Parsee Manichaeism and arrived at an American gnosis, ruggedly antinomian. Yes, Ahab is a dictator who drowns his entire crew with him, except for Ishmael. What would you have? Yahweh's Leviathan cannot lose; should Ahab yield to Starbuck, who informs him that he only seeks vengeance on a dumb brute? The Promethean captain ought to abhor himself and repent in dust and ashes? Write your own tale then, but it will not be Melville's.

Moral judgment, irrelevant to *Moby-Dick* and to Shakespeare, would have provoked Dr. Samuel Johnson not to countenance Ahab nor to finish reading more than a page or two. From the best of opening sentences on, the White Whale remorselessly voyages to a heroic conclusion. Except for Starbuck and Pip, the *Pequod*'s company votes for its marvelous catastrophe. Ahab is possessed, but so are they (Ishmael included). As leader, their captain finds his archetype in Andrew Jackson, who represented for Melville and others the American hero proper, an apotheosis of the politics of one who characterizes the American Dream. From lowly origins he ascended to the heights of power and brought into sharper focus what is still American nationalism.

Denying Ahab greatness is an aesthetic blunder: He is akin to Achilles, Odysseus, and King David in one register, and to Don Quixote, Hamlet, and the High Romantic Prometheus of Goethe and Shelley in another. Call the first mode a transcendent heroism and the second the persistence of vision. Both ways are antithetical to nature and protest against our mortality. The epic hero will never submit or yield.

Such uncanny persistence is dangerous to all of us. We do not wish to rise crazily with Don Quixote, to plot and counterplot with Hamlet in poisoned Elsinore, to serve under doomsayer Ahab in the *Pequod*. But how can the reader's sublime be better experienced than with Cervantes, Shakespeare, or Melville? Only the self-named "Walt Whitman, an American, one of the roughs, a kosmos," is comparable to Captain Ahab in the United States. Ahab and Whitman are our Great Originals, our contribution to that double handful or so among whom Falstaff and Sancho Panza, Hamlet and Don Quixote, Mr. Pickwick and Becky Sharp take their place.

IN THE EDITION OF *MOBY-DICK* I RECOMMEND TO MY STUDENTS, THE Norton volume edited by Hershel Parker and Harrison Hayford, the novel runs to four hundred large pages. I share the students' sentiment that the novel's division into one hundred thirty-five short chapters and an epilogue enhances its effectiveness. Ahab does not enter until Chapter 28, after what I tend to call the Ishmaeliad, a beautiful hundred-page induction still fresh and humorous a century and a quarter after its initial publication. From Chapter 28 on, it is Ahab's saga, not Ishmael's. The total quest abounds in contradictions since Ishmael, though a winning narrator at securing our favor, is unreliable. Like Huck Finn, he charmingly lies merely to keep in practice.

Paul Brodtkorb, in his *Ishmael's White World* (1965), terms the narrator a relativist, which is a good starting point. Go a touch beyond and call Ishmael the Shakespeare implanted—by Shakespeare—within Melville. A comedian of the spirit, detached from irony, Ishmael gives *Moby-Dick* what Marlow failed to give *Lord Jim* and his other Conradian narrative assignments—a stance capacious enough to enfold all genres. Like its prototype, *Hamlet, Moby-Dick* is a Poem Unlimited.

Shakespeare is the burning fountain out of which emanate all High Romantics: British, German, American, Russian, and the whole earth. Melville is American High Romantic, a Shelleyan divided between head and heart, who held against Emerson the sage's supposed deficiency in the region of the heart. Melville is the most Shakespearean of our authors. Like Macbeth, Ahab desires to pull down everything over him, and in Hamletian mode the lord of the *Pequod* too cries aloud: "Strike through the mask" so that "let be" indeed shall be "finale of seem."

It misleads to call Ahab's a metaphysical quest, unless the metaphysics is embedded in Western religious formulations: Zoroastrian, Judaic, Christian, Islamic. Ahab is a tormented Job who fights back and will not accept the tyranny of Leviathan. His struggle has its roots in Job:

> Canst thou draw out leviathan with an hook? or his tongue with a cord *which* thou lettest down?
>
> Canst thou put an hook into his nose? or bore his jaw through with a thorn?
>
> Will he make many supplications unto thee? will he speak soft *words* unto thee?
>
> Will he make a covenant with thee? wilt thou take him for a servant for ever?
>
> Wilt thou play with him as *with* a bird? or wilt thou bind him for thy maidens?
>
> Shall the companions make a banquet of him? shall they part him among the merchants?
>
> Canst thou fill his skin with barbed irons? or his head with fish spears?
>
> Lay thine hand upon him, remember the battle, do no more.
>
> —JOB 41:1–8

From childhood, I have wondered why Melville's "Extracts" prefacing *Moby-Dick* omit this most relevant of passages. Instead, he quarries Job for:

> Leviathan maketh a path to shine after him;
> One would think the deep to be hoary.

More appositely, he gives a grand prophecy from Isaiah:

> In that day, the Lord, with his sore and great and strong sword, shall punish Leviathan the piercing serpent, even Leviathan that crooked serpent; and he shall slay the dragon that is in the sea.

I take it Melville strikes obliquely. God's nasty boasts concerning his kingship over all the children of pride would have seemed too direct a provocation. The same care manifests in Chapters 41 and 42, "Moby Dick" and the magnificent "The Whiteness of the Whale." In Chapter 41, a single reference to Job inaugurates the strong last paragraph:

Here, then, was this grey-headed, ungodly old man, chasing with curses a Job's whale round the world, at the head of a crew, too, chiefly made up of mongrel renegades, and castaways, and cannibals—morally enfeebled also, by the incompetence of mere unaided virtue or right-mindedness in Starbuck, the invulnerable jollity of indifference and recklessness in Stubb, and the pervading mediocrity in Flask. Such a crew, so officered, seemed specially picked and packed by some infernal fatality to help him to his monomaniac revenge. How it was that they so aboundingly responded to the old man's ire—by what evil magic their souls were possessed, that at times his hate seemed almost theirs; the White Whale as much their insufferable foe as his; how all this came to be—what the White Whale was to them, or how to their unconscious understandings, also, in some dim, unsuspected way, he might have seemed the gliding great demon of the seas of life,—all this to explain, would be to dive deeper than Ishmael can go. The subterranean miner that works in us all, how can one tell whither leads his shaft by the ever shifting, muffled sound of his pick? Who does not feel the irresistible arm drag? What skiff in tow of a seventy-four can stand still? For one, I gave myself up to the abandonment of the time and the place; but while yet all a-rush to encounter the whale, could see naught in that brute but the deadliest ill.

Ishmael goes deeper, in his famous meditation on the whiteness of the whale:

Though neither knows where lie the nameless things of which the mystic sign gives forth such hints; yet with me, as with the colt, somewhere those things must exist. Though in many of its aspects this visible world seems formed in love, the invisible spheres were formed in fright.

But not yet have we solved the incantation of this whiteness, and learned why it appeals with such power to the soul; and more strange and far more portentous—why, as we have seen, it is at once the most meaning symbol of spiritual things, nay, the very veil of the Christian's Deity; and yet should be as it is, the intensifying agent in things the most appalling to mankind.

Is it that by its indefiniteness it shadows forth the heartless voids and immensities of the universe, and thus stabs us from behind with the thought of annihilation, when beholding the white depths of the milky way? Or is it, that as in essence whiteness is not so much a color as the visible absence of color, and at the same time the concrete of all colors; is it for these reasons that there is such a dumb blankness, full of meaning, in a wide landscape of snows— a colorless, all-color of atheism from which we shrink? And when we consider that other theory of the natural philosophers, that all other earthly hues—every stately or lovely emblazoning—the sweet tinges of sunset skies and woods; yea, and the gilded velvets of but- terflies, and the butterfly cheeks of young girls; all these are but subtile deceits, not actually inherent in substances, but only laid on from without; so that all deified Nature absolutely paints like the harlot, whose allurements cover nothing but the charnel-house within; and when we proceed further, and consider that the mysti- cal cosmetic which produces every one of her hues, the great prin- ciple of light, for ever remains white or colorless in itself, and if operating without medium upon matter, would touch all objects, even tulips and roses, with its own blank tinge—pondering all this, the palsied universe lies before us a leper; and like wilful travellers in Lapland, who refuse to wear colored and coloring glasses upon their eyes, so the wretched infidel gazes himself blind at the monu- mental white shroud that wraps all the prospect around him. And of all these things the Albino whale was the symbol. Wonder ye then at the fiery hunt?

The trope of the intransigent blank, an ultimate image of our Ameri- can selfhood, survives from two prime English prototypes, Shakespearean and Miltonic. In Shakespeare, the blank is the center of a target, perhaps evoking the mark forever missed, the hamartia of Athenian tragedy, as when Kent cries out: "See better, Lear, and let me still remain / The true

blank of thine eye." Milton, invoking the Holy Light at the commence-
ment of *Paradise Lost,* Book III, laments: "Presented with a universal
blank / Of Nature's works to me expunged and rased, / And wisdom at
one entrance quite shut out."

The Shakespearean blank becomes Emily Dickinson's and Hart Crane's;
Milton's engenders a chain or sequence of dramatic images that goes from
Samuel Taylor Coleridge and William Wordsworth, Percy Bysshe Shelley
and Robert Browning, into the American procession of Emerson and
Whitman, Hawthorne and Melville, on to Wallace Stevens, who was
haunted by the terrible whiteness I remember first when I brood again
upon his poetry: "Here, being visible is being white, / Is being of the solid
of white, the accomplishment / Of an extremist in an exercise." Walking
the bare beach at twilight, the old poet, illuminated by the great glare of
the auroras, "turns blankly on the sand."

The United States, considered as a final Western culture, never was a
blank to be filled. Emerson in the optative mood might desire to be a man
with no past at his back, but he knew better. Shakespeare and Michel de
Montaigne were always with him. Of the eleven other spirits appreciated
in this book, only Faulkner's was unaffected by the dialectical prophet of
the American Newness. Hawthorne, the sage's silent walking companion,
might seem antithetical to Emerson, yet he had to be aware that his Hester
Prynne, worshipping only the god within herself, stemmed from the selfhood of "Self-Reliance." The James family, raised by their Emersonian
father, accepted their heritage, with reservations by Henry yet fewer by
William. Whatever Henry's distinctions, his Isabel Archer is as Emersonian
as Hester Prynne in her determination to face destruction rather than re-
linquish her soul's right to choose—however bad the choice—while Ahab
restores self-reliance to an original daemonic wildness.

A subtler freedom attends Emily Dickinson, whom I regard as a heretic
from the Emersonian religion, which exalts whim over trust and faith.
Walt Whitman, Waldo's most eminent disciple but an expander of self-
reliance into a solar trajectory, takes the "real Me" as dusky daemon and
brother, just as Dickinson uncovers a sufficiency in the single hound of her
own identity.

Melville found his daemon in the image of the Handsome Soldier, a
memory of his shipmate Jack Chase, most famously reincarnated as Billy
Budd. In *Moby-Dick,* the Handsome Sailor was to have been a counter-

force to Ahab in the guise of Bulkington, who is introduced to us in the
splendid Chapter 3, "The Spouter-Inn":

> I observed, however, that one of them held somewhat aloof, and
> though he seemed desirous not to spoil the hilarity of his shipmates
> by his own sober face, yet upon the whole he refrained from making
> as much noise as the rest. This man interested me at once; and since
> the sea-gods had ordained that he should soon become my ship-
> mate (though but a sleeping-partner one, so far as this narrative is
> concerned), I will here venture upon a little description of him. He
> stood full six feet in height, with noble shoulders, and a chest like a
> coffer-dam. I have seldom seen such brawn in a man. His face was
> deeply brown and burnt, making his white teeth dazzling by the
> contrast; while in the deep shadows of his eyes floated some remi-
> niscences that did not seem to give him much joy. His voice at once
> announced that he was a Southerner, and from his fine stature, I
> thought he must be one of those tall mountaineers from the Allega-
> nian Ridge in Virginia. When the revelry of his companions had
> mounted to its height, this man slipped away unobserved, and I saw
> no more of him till he became my comrade on the sea. In a few
> minutes, however, he was missed by his shipmates, and being, it
> seems, for some reason a huge favorite with them, they raised a cry
> of "Bulkington! Bulkington! where's Bulkington?" and darted out
> of the house in pursuit of him.

The parentheses indicate Bulkington's role as *Moby-Dick*'s secret
sharer, a Chekhovian pistol Melville chooses not to fire at Ahab. A natural
leader, Bulkington alone could have turned his shipmates from the mono-
maniacal quest. Instead, he is swept away with the others and is awarded
the beautiful elegy of "this six-inch chapter," 23, "The Lee Shore":

> Some chapters back, one Bulkington was spoken of, a tall, new-
> landed mariner, encountered in New Bedford at the inn.
>   When on that shivering winter's night, the *Pequod* thrust her vin-
> dictive bows into the cold malicious waves, who should I see stand-
> ing at her helm but Bulkington! I looked with sympathetic awe and
> fearfulness upon the man, who in midwinter just landed from a four

years' dangerous voyage, could so unrestingly push off again for still another tempestuous term. The land seemed scorching to his feet. Wonderfullest things are ever the unmentionable; deep memories yield no epitaphs; this six-inch chapter is the stoneless grave of Bulkington. Let me only say that it fared with him as with the storm-tossed ship, that miserably drives along the leeward land. The port would fain give succor; the port is pitiful; in the port is safety, comfort, hearthstone, supper, warm blankets, friends, all that's kind to our mortalities. But in that gale, the port, the land, is that ship's direst jeopardy; she must fly all hospitality; one touch of land, though it but graze the keel, would make her shudder through and through. With all her might she crowds all sail off shore; in so doing, fights 'gainst the very winds that fain would blow her homeward; seeks all the lashed sea's landlessness again; for refuge's sake forlornly rushing into peril; her only friend her bitterest foe!

Know ye now, Bulkington? Glimpses do ye seem to see of that mortally intolerable truth; that all deep, earnest thinking is but the intrepid effort of the soul to keep the open independence of her sea; while the wildest winds of heaven and earth conspire to cast her on the treacherous, slavish shore?

But as in landlessness alone resides the highest truth, shoreless, indefinite as God—so better is it to perish in that howling infinite, than be ingloriously dashed upon the lee, even if that were safety! For worm-like, then, oh! who would craven crawl to land! Terrors of the terrible! is all this agony so vain? Take heart, take heart, O Bulkington! Bear thee grimly, demigod! Up from the spray of thy ocean-perishing—straight up, leaps thy apotheosis!

Ishmael is and is not Melville, by turns, yet this is his author's true voice of feeling. "Apotheosis" unites Bulkington and Ahab, demigods as shoreless as the authentic divinity of the wickedly spotless book.

As a boy of ten, I was puzzled and intrigued by Bulkington, whose sparse presence in the epic is comprised by my two quotations. Apotheosis of what? I wondered. Mountain man and whaler, Bulkington is the Heracles of the *Pequod,* the shipmate who adds a finer tone to the voyage. He has an erotic aura first suggested in conversation to me by Camille Paglia, whose *Sexual Personae* (1990) I had the honor of mentoring, though Paglia, sprung full-grown from Athena, scarcely needed any aid. She attributed "the novel's operatic gigantism" to "its force of *sexual protest*" against what William Blake named the Female Will, the matrix of night, death, the mother, and the sea that Walt Whitman celebrated and longed to enter.

Bulkington is the epic's hidden daemon, Melville's secret muse. He is to the author what Queequeg was to Ishmael and may be a surrogate for Nathaniel Hawthorne, to whom *Moby-Dick* is dedicated "in token of my admiration for his genius." But Bulkington, the helmsman as the *Pequod* plunges out of port, becomes a kind of Virgilian Palinurus, the lost pilot of a voyage whose only object is elusive and deadly beyond all measure.

MELVILLE'S ADMIRER FAULKNER ENVISIONED HIS DAEMON AS CANDACE Compson, the heroine of *The Sound and the Fury,* who grows out of and merges with a personal series of younger women who served Faulkner as muse-mistresses. Caddy never speaks, but her brother Quentin is sexually obsessed with her, while her poor idiot brother Benjamin in some deep way carries her image in what remains of his mind, and her brother Jason obsessively despises her. Faulkner loved her best among all his women characters and remarked that she represented the younger sister he never had.

Wallace Stevens, who like Melville and the young T. S. Eliot was unhappily married, pursued his daemonic self in the fabulous "interior paramours" of his major poems. Eliot, who had abandoned Emily Hale and had lost his friend Jean Verdenal to an early, heroic death, created haunting images of infinitely gentle, infinitely suffering, mostly feminine wraiths. The Orphic Hart Crane, heir of all these, celebrated his Handsome Sailor Emil Opffer in *Voyages* and brilliantly found his bride in *The Bridge,* where a "steeled cognizance" imperishably is hymned.

My mentor and friend Kenneth Burke remarked to me that Crane mentioned the bridge/bride kenning to him in conversations. Bridal imagery abounds in Crane's brief epic, lending a poignance: "And see'st thy bride immortal in the maize!" And yet Orpheus is Crane's archetypal bridegroom, questing to rescue his beloved from the shades. Dionysus and

Orpheus fuse together in ancient Greek religion, a mingling renewed in *The Bridge.*

Of the twelve writers upon whom this book centers, the unchurched Hart Crane is the most deeply religious, more in the vitalistic mode of D. H. Lawrence than of the pious T. S. Eliot, uneasy neo-Christian. It is an oddity that Crane, with only his mother's Christian Science at his origins, is a kind of natural Catholic by temperament and acute sensibility. *The Bridge* hymns a god unknown, yet the overtones of its yearnings are conditioned by El Greco's *Agony in the Garden,* Crane's favorite painting.

In *The Tunnel* section of *The Bridge,* a descent to the Virgilian inferno Avernus, Crane invokes the New York City subway as "the Daemon," probably taking the word from the discussion of Dionysus in Walter Pater's *Greek Studies.* Initially there is rich strangeness in this identification, since Crane favors Dionysus as his path to poetic vision but not to the infernal. Yet ambivalence has to mark the American Sublime: Think of Melville, Whitman, Eliot's *The Waste Land,* Faulkner's doomed landscapes. A selfhood endlessly aspiring to freedom from the past is bound to resist actual overdeterminations that bind us all in time.

We are at last bequeathed to an earthly shore and seek memorial inscriptions, fragments heaped against our ruins: an interval and then we are gone. High literature endeavors to augment that span: My twelve authors center, for me, that proliferation of consciousness by which we go on living and finding our own sense of being.

I.

WALT WHITMAN *and*
HERMAN MELVILLE

Foregrounding the Giants

———

Walt Whitman and Herman Melville abide as the giants of American literary tradition. Their vaunting overreach is not matched until Hart Crane and William Faulkner, each equally ambitious in scope and drive, assault the frontiers already extended outward by *Moby-Dick* (1851) and the first three *Leaves of Grass* (1855, 1856, 1860).

Rich as North American literary culture became—at least before the twenty-first century—it brought forth no peers of Dante and Cervantes, Montaigne and Shakespeare, Tolstoy and Joyce. Only *Moby-Dick* and Whitman in his half-dozen major poems—*Song of Myself, The Sleepers, Crossing Brooklyn Ferry,* and the three elegiac meditations (*Out of the Cradle Endlessly Rocking, As I Ebb'd with the Ocean of Life, When Lilacs Last in the Dooryard Bloom'd*)—suggest Tolstoyan resonances. Søren Kierkegaard found in Shakespeare "the resonance of the opposite." All twelve writers centering this book share in that antithetical strain. It is not that Whitman and Melville possess it more deeply than Emerson, Emily Dickinson, or Henry James, but I do not hear in them the sea crying out, as we listen to the earth calling aloud in Tolstoy.

Yet Melville and Whitman have little else in common. Walt was interested in *Typee* but nothing by Melville after that, and the defeated seer of *Moby-Dick* rather resented whatever notoriety the self-promoting Whitman achieved. I doubt he ever read a line of *Leaves of Grass*.

Foregrounding Dante and Shakespeare depends upon intricate infer-rings. Their direct precursors, Guido Cavalcanti and Christopher Marlowe, were major poets, but the authors of the *Commedia* and of *Hamlet* and *King Lear* are beyond all simplicities of inheritance. Certainly there was an anguish of contamination. The *Inferno* places Cavalcanti's father and father-in-law among the damned and poignantly allows the father anxiously to question the Pilgrim: Why is it Dante rather than Cavalcanti who makes the Divine Journey? Kit Marlowe haunts Shake-speare, though scarcely in style and hardly in the creation of personalities. The art of achieving rhetorical power over an audience was bequeathed by Marlowe to his contemporary Shakespeare, who might not have seen its possibilities without this apprenticeship to the dramatic oratory of Tamburlaine, the Guise, Barabbas, and Doctor Faustus.

Foregrounding Whitman and Melville is difficult, because of the radi-cal originality of *Leaves of Grass* and *Moby-Dick*. Emerson, Walt's only begetter, evoked considerable resistance from Melville, who attended the sage's New York City lectures and annotated his essays. Melville's am-bivalence led to his satirizing Emerson as Plotinus Plinlimmon in *Pierre* and as Mark Winsome, savaged in *The Confidence-Man*. Ahab and Ishmael nevertheless are partial Emersonians, while Hester Prynne and Isabel Archer are his daughters. Only Southerners, from Poe to Faulkner and Robert Penn Warren, have been immune from the Concord contagion.

Though Emerson rubbed his eyes to puzzle out "the long foreground somewhere" of *Leaves of Grass* 1855, nobody was unlikelier to probe in-ferential origins. A man without a handle (the complaint of Henry James, Sr.), Emerson was skilled in the art of slipping away from categories and persons alike. His greatness allowed for a singularity that could thrill to the commonplace and that enabled Walt, the child who went forth. What-ever Whitman looked upon, he became. Melville massively resisted so promiscuous a cavalcade of identifications.

AHAB IS A HARD TRANSCENDENTALIST:

Hark ye yet again,—the little lower layer. All visible objects, man, are but as pasteboard masks. But in each event—in the living act, the undoubted deed—there, some unknown but still reasoning thing puts forth the mouldings of its features from behind the unreasoning mask. If man will strike, strike through the mask! How can the prisoner reach outside except by thrusting through the wall? To me, the white whale is that wall, shoved near to me. Sometimes I think that there's naught beyond. But 'tis enough. He tasks me; he heaps me; I see in him outrageous strength, with an inscrutable malice sinewing it. That inscrutable thing is chiefly what I hate; and be the white whale agent, or be the white whale principal, I will wreak that hate upon him. Talk not to me of blasphemy, man; I'd strike the sun if it insulted me. For could the sun do that, then could I do the other; since there is ever a sort of fair play herein, jealousy presiding over all creations. But not my master, man, is even that fair play. Who's over me? Truth hath no confines.

Walt, confronted by sunrise, now and always could send forth sunrise from himself. Melville, opposing titan, would strike at and through the sun as another pasteboard mask. *Moby-Dick* is our national countersublime and *Leaves of Grass* the American Sublime, incarnated in a book that is also a man. That man cannot be confused with Walter Whitman, Jr. He is Hermetic Man, poised over the abyss of death and sleep in a precarious balance before falling outward and downward into the sea of space and time.

Whitman had encountered the Hermetic Speculation, the second-century C.E. secular gnosis, in George Sand's novels, though his taste for Egyptian antiquity might have guided him anyway to the doctrines of "Thrice-Greatest Hermes." Hermetic Speculation came out of Alexandria, proclaiming itself as ancient Egyptian wisdom, and deceived Renaissance Europe, though "deceived" itself is deceptive. Hermetism, like Christian Gnosticism, expressed the spirit of religiously eclectic Macedonian and Roman Alexandria, a fecund "Jewgreek is greekjew" (James Joyce) hybrid.

American literary selfhood, or the American Religion, participates in a gnosis. The American androgyne (*Song of Myself*'s protagonist) is not part of the creation and fall but emanates from the prior abyss, foremother and forefather invoked by transfigured Captain Ahab, electrified by the corposants, Saint Elmo's fire:

"Oh! thou clear spirit of clear fire, whom on these seas I as Persian once did worship, till in the sacramental act so burned by thee, that to this hour I bear the scar; I now know thee, thou clear spirit, and I now know that thy right worship is defiance. To neither love nor reverence wilt thou be kind; and e'en for hate thou canst but kill; and all are killed. No fearless fool now fronts thee. I own thy speechless, placeless power; but to the last gasp of my earthquake life will dispute its unconditional, unintegral mastery in me. In the midst of the personified impersonal, a personality stands here. Though but a point at best; whencesoe'er I came; wheresoe'er I go; yet while I earthly live, the queenly personality lives in me, and feels her royal rights. But war is pain, and hate is woe. Come in thy lowest form of love, and I will kneel and kiss thee; but at thy highest, come as mere supernal power; and though thou launchest navies of full-freighted worlds, there's that in here that still remains indifferent. Oh, thou clear spirit, of thy fire thou madest me, and like a true child of fire, I breathe it back to thee."

(Sudden, repeated flashes of lightning; the nine flames leap lengthwise to thrice their previous height; Ahab, with the rest, closes his eyes, his right hand pressed hard upon them.)

"I own thy speechless, placeless power; said I not so? Nor was it wrung from me; nor do I now drop these links. Thou canst blind; but I can then grope. Thou canst consume; but I can then be ashes. Take the homage of these poor eyes, and shutter-hands. I would not take it. The lightning flashes through my skull; mine eye-balls ache and ache; my whole beaten brain seems as beheaded, and rolling on some stunning ground. Oh, oh! Yet blindfold, yet will I talk to thee. Light though thou be, thou leapest out of darkness; but I am darkness leaping out of light, leaping out of thee! The javelins cease; open eyes; see, or not? There burn the flames! Oh, thou magnanimous! now I do glory in my genealogy. But thou art but my fiery father; my sweet mother, I know not. Oh, cruel! what hast thou done with her? There lies my puzzle; but thine is greater. Thou knowest not how came ye, hence callest thyself unbegotten; certainly knowest not thy beginning, hence callest thyself unbegun. I know that of me, which thou knowest not of thyself, oh, thou omnipotent. There is some unsuffusing thing beyond thee, thou clear spirit, to whom all thy eternity is but time, all thy creativeness mechanical. Through thee, thy flaming self, my scorched eyes do dimly see it. Oh, thou foundling fire, thou hermit immemorial, thou too hast thy incommunicable riddle, thy unparticipated grief. Here again with haughty agony, I read my sire. Leap! leap up, and lick the sky! I leap with thee; I burn with thee; would fain be welded with thee; defyingly I worship thee!"

I resume this intricate rhapsody for close commentary later in this chapter but emphasize now how strenuously it manifests what has been called our Native Strain. The American Sublime in Melville, Whitman, Emerson, and Hart Crane relies upon extraordinary hyperbole—not an exaggeration but an untamed casting, in which the images of *voice* break and scatter ashes and *sparks*. Whitman calls this the breaking of the tally. In Melville, we hear it marvelously in the lament of Urania (quite possibly Margaret Fuller) that ignites *After the Pleasure Party*:

> For, Nature, in no shallow surge
> Against thee either sex may urge,
> Why hast thou made us but in halves—
> Co-relatives? This makes us slaves.
> If these co-relatives never meet
> Self-hood itself seems incomplete.
> And such the dicing of blind fate
> Few matching halves here meet and mate.
> What Cosmic jest or Anarch blunder
> The human integral clove asunder
> And shied the fractions through life's gate?

That Gnostic anarch-archon cleaving asunder of the cosmic androgyne shies Aristophanic fragments (women *and* men) through the gate of human birth. Call this Melville's breaking of the vessels, akin to Emerson's "there is a crack in everything God has made." Intransigent Ahab is the truest daemonic Emersonian, unlike Melville, who loved the Concord sage's deep diving yet dissented from what he took to be an affirming force. Seventy years of deeply reading Emerson make me wary of any account of him that neglects his powers of thinking by and through negations.

Disputes between anyone—even Melville and Emerson—are hard to sustain; Waldo will not rest for long in any one stance or proposition. Polymorphic, he proclaims that a foolish consistency is the hobgoblin of little minds. He is large, contains multitudes, and likes seeing them escape containment. He was the perfect reader for *Leaves of Grass* 1855.

Imagine what the then-twelve-year-old Henry James, already a deep reader, could have made of Whitman's inaugural self-presentation. A decade later, James wrote an absurd review of *Drum-Taps,* demonstrating a total refusal to actually *read* the poet he later came to regard, rightly, as our nation's finest. At twenty-two, James skipped over such magnificences as *Reconciliation* and *Vigil Strange I Kept on the Field One Night,* while devoting himself only to what he dismissed as bardic pretensions. The *Lilacs* elegy for Lincoln was not in the edition that James saw, but I doubt he could then have absorbed it, though he came to love the threnody and to chant it with what Edith Wharton and other rapt auditors termed an organ's resonance. Probably he was disturbed by the homoeroticism already emergent in his own nature.

I have pondered for decades Emerson's wonderful initial receptivity toward Whitman and have come to believe that the sage's daemon recognized itself in his shamanistic godson. Could anyone else then in America or in the world have been that perceptive? In a long lifetime of championing new poets at first reading, I have attempted to emulate Emerson, but only because he broke the new road for American pragmatic criticism.

In my life, the comparable experience began on my tenth birthday, when I found *The Collected Poems of Hart Crane* in the Melrose branch of the Bronx Public Library. I had never seen any reference to Crane, but I opened the book at the *Atlantis* conclusion to *The Bridge* and was transformed by invocatory splendor:

> O Thou steeled Cognizance whose leap commits
> The agile precincts of the lark's return . . .

What I construed of this or the rest of Hart Crane seventy years ago, I cannot recall. Yet the drive, rhetoric, syntax, and flight beyond limits overwhelmed me, precisely as my initial reading of Christopher Marlowe had been a transport to the sublime. More than that, Crane's image of voice permanently altered my sensibility and sent me back to the Shakespeare of *Venus and Adonis* and *The Rape of Lucrece,* as to Marlowe, George Chapman, and the earlier, pre-conversionary T. S. Eliot.

HAD I BEEN BORN IN 1899 rather than 1930, I would have been an earlier champion of Crane and perhaps would have known or tried to meet him. There is a curious wonder in discovering the undebatable art of a living writer, as I did with the works of Wallace Stevens, Elizabeth Bishop, John Ashbery, A. R. Ammons, Alvin Feinman, and Henri Cole, among the poets, and Tony Kushner's *Angels in America.* The experience grows rarer, but it may be that in my eighties I am less open to fresh splendors.

Falling in love seems the aptest analogue to the first discovery of aesthetic glory. For a time, all perspectives shift and demarcations become ghostlier; sounds, keener; vistas democratize. Teaching is nearly akin. In the third week of a new semester, the students I have taught in prior years begin to seem refreshingly stranger, illuminated by the group of recent young women and men who so rapidly become familiar. To be four times their age renders the classroom a phantasmagoria at moments, in which I seem the Button Moulder from *Peer Gynt* or a grotesque emergent from *Faust: Part Two.* I lead a discussion on Falstaff, whose years I now match, or on Walt Whitman in the final Mickle Street phase, worn out by the sufferings of thousands whom he had nursed yet holding fast to the still-powerful press of his sole self, a single separate person.

Perhaps all that Whitman shared with Shakespeare, Goethe, and Henrik Ibsen was an implicit insight that the self was a necessary fiction, an illusion so desired that leaves of grass would sprout from the barren rock of being. A smoky taste flows but then ebbs in our reception of agonies as one of Walt's changes of garments. Rancidity gathers, though it does not fall, and our self-vividness grows less bright. We turn blankly and discover that no direction is at home in us.

Certain mornings in midwinter my wife asks me: Why at eighty-four continue teaching full-time? It is fifty-eight years since first we courted but fifty-nine since I commenced full-time teaching in the Yale faculty. I mutter that I fear breaking the longest continuity of my life. Is that my deeper motive? What can I know? The daemon only knows how it is done.

What remains to be done? Talking with my wife, our friends (the few surviving), my students, is endless and necessary yet insufficient. Yet what would suffice? Shadows of the Evening Land are rarely daemonic Shadows of Ecstasy. Daemons have their ranks and their rebellions against subordination, with the difference that they cannot be conquistadores; their place in the hierarchy always returns to confine them.

Emersonian American self-reliance is daemonic, as are American self-influence and American self-overhearing. Does that depart from the Shakespearean paradigm of influence and overhearing? The American malaise differs from a grand passage in *The Anatomy of Melancholy*, taken by my personal daemon, Angus Fletcher, as epigraph for his superb *Allegory: The Theory of a Symbolic Mode* (new edition, Princeton):

'Tis no disparagement to be a stranger, or so irksome to be an exile. The rain is a stranger to the earth, rivers to the sea, Jupiter in Egypt, the sun to us all. The soul is an alien to the body, a nightingale to the air, a swallow in an house, and Ganymede in heaven, an elephant at Rome, a Phoenix in India; and such things commonly please us best, which are most strange, and come farthest off.

The newfound America of Emerson and Whitman, of Melville, Hawthorne, Dickinson, and their few imaginative peers, is inhabited by American Adams and fiercely American Eves, from Hester Prynne through Isabel Archer on to Willa Cather's lost ladies. Neither strangers nor exiles, they celebrate what is most familiar and near at hand. Our prime celebrant, Walt, is also our greatest elegist for the self, for the daemon errant in time's wastages.

In ancient Greece, daemonic power, thought to be passed along through the gods, molds cognitive cadence and form. After Emerson, American makers themselves daemonize. Hart Crane's *The Bridge* measures its song, fusing Eliotic-Jacobean dark rhetoric with Whitmanian enlargements of vista and aspiration. Grandly, the consequence represents the utmost achievement of the sublime mode in our America, akin to Whitman's *Sea-Drift* elegies, *Moby-Dick*, Dickinson's ambivalent transports, Stevens's *The Auroras of Autumn*, Eliot's *The Dry Salvages*, Faulkner's *As I Lay Dying*.

Foregrounding the twin titans of our literature, Whitman and Melville, should trace lineaments of the giants emergent in sublime theories (really speculations) that inform such daemonic heroes as the Walt Whitman of

Song of Myself—"an American, one of the roughs"—and Captain Ahab. The cavalcade would commence with the Alexandrian Longinus, the French neoclassicist Nicolas Boileau, and the British Joseph Addison and David Hume. Edmund Burke, in his brilliant youth, published a treatise in 1757 that influenced Kant, the major theorist of the sublime. Emerson inevitably fathered the rather different American Sublime, particularly by his rhapsodic essay "Self-Reliance."

The Longinian-Burkean-Kantian Sublime can be judged as an excursion into the psychological origins of aesthetic magnificence. Samuel Johnson, king of Western literary critics, remained always a Burkean apprehender of the sublime as vast and awesome. Emerson radically internalized the European Sublime by attaching it to "the God within" the American self. Rather than rehearse again the difficult dialectics of American Sublimity that I worked through in *Poetry and Repression* (1976) and *Agon* (1982), I refer curious readers to these books and condense here to solar intensities that oppose Whitman to Melville, Wallace Stevens to T. S. Eliot.

"It is for that the poet is always in the sun" is a Stevensian affirmation, Platonic and pagan and thus alien to Eliot, who yearned for neo-Christianity well before he half-persuaded himself to have attained it. Whitman, ghostly father alike of Stevens and of Eliot, gloried that now and always he could send forth sunrise from himself. Captain Ahab's vaunt—"I'd strike the sun if it insulted me"—marks the difference between the Lucretian Whitman and the Gnostic Melville.

WALT WHITMAN

An Induction

MY LIFELONG CRITICAL HERO SAMUEL JOHNSON TAUGHT ME TO VALUE biography over history, even as I emulate his voracity at devouring histories. Emerson, a later idol, said there is no history, only biography. Johnson thought we owed everything to Shakespeare, for where else can the commonwealth of imagination turn?

The labor of the authentic critic, Johnson reflected, improved opinion into knowledge. He did not need to ask: What precisely is *literary* knowledge? We arrived later and are morosely skeptical of what can be known in the living labyrinth of literature.

Sequentially, the greatest literature is more a pageant than a history. I rather wish us to see it as a baroque dramatic celebration, spectacular alike for its pomp and its covert achieved anxiety, a mystery play with the disciplined imagination as dying god.

Literary critics avoid pomp, lest they be seen as pompous. The three inventors of criticism were Aristophanes, Aristotle, and the pseudo-Longinus, acclaimed by Ernst Robert Curtius as the inaugural literary critic. Aristotle had his lyrical aspect, and I agree with Heinrich Heine that there is a God and his name is Aristophanes, who visited divine wrath upon Euripides for challenging Aeschylus.

Myself a Longinian critic since early youth, I rejoice at all strong transports of sublimity, from Aeschylus and the first Isaiah, through Shakespeare and Milton, and on to Friedrich Hölderlin, Giacomo Leopardi, and Shelley. Longinus found the sublime in Moses and Sappho, delightful bedfellows, and I emulate him by obeying Shelley's observation: The function of the sublime is to persuade us to end the slavery of pleasure.

Etymologically, the word "pageant" goes back to the medieval mystery play. Lord Byron marches his heart's pageant across Italy and Greece, hoping for the pomp of death in battle, proper for a descendant of the royal Stuarts of Scotland. His mystery play *Cain* holds up splendidly when read—though I was once offered a performance in my honor at an Athenian amphitheater and sadly had to judge it unplayable.

I read and teach Whitman's *Song of Myself* as a mystery play, with Walt palpably playing the Christ. Together with *Moby-Dick,* it is the sublime of American imaginative literature, yet I would not desire either work to be mounted upon a stage, except as pageants, spectacular celebrations, positive and negative, of our American Sublime. I think of Whitman and Melville, in their relation to the contemporary United States, as our resource akin to Isaiah's prophecy:

> And a man shall be as a hiding place from the wind, and a
>   covert from the tempest;
> as rivers of water in a dry place, as the shadow of a great
>   rock in a weary land.
>
> —ISAIAH 32:2

We have a need to heal violence, whether from without or from within. Our strongest writers—Emerson, Whitman, Melville, Dickinson, Hawthorne, James, Twain, Frost, Stevens, Eliot, Crane, and Faulkner, among others—can meet that imaginative poverty and help protect the individual mind and society from themselves. I now have come to see *that* as the highest use of literature for our way of life.

Only Walt Whitman, of all our titans, professedly comes to us as a healer. His heroic service was performed as an unpaid volunteer nurse and wound dresser, comforter of maimed, sick, and dying soldiers in the dreadful Civil War hospitals of Washington, D.C. Yet that vocation flowered from the first *Leaves of Grass* (1855), where the poem of Walt Whitman an American, later titled *Song of Myself,* concluded by inviting us to what Stevens would come to call a cure of the ground, and of ourselves, in the predicate that there is nothing else:

> I depart as air . . . I shake my white locks at the runaway sun,
> I effuse my flesh in eddies, and drift it in lacy jags.
>
> I bequeath myself to the dirt to grow from the grass I love,
> If you want me again look for me under your bootsoles.

You will hardly know who I am or what I mean,
But I shall be good health to you nevertheless,
And filter and fibre your blood.

Failing to fetch me at first keep encouraged,
Missing me one place search another,
I stop some where waiting for you.

What could a reader gain by having these luminous lines historicized? Walt, more than any other poet, pulls you close to him, face-to-face. Such a gesture defies our refusals to confront greatness directly.

Whitman is not one of the poets extraordinary for cognitive power, such as Shakespeare, Blake, or Dickinson. His still-undervalued art abides in nuance, indirection, gesture, subtle evasiveness, insinuation, ineluctable modalities of the visible, the signature of all things that he summons us to come and see. Shamanistic shape-shifter, Hermetic androgyne, he indeed is prelapsarian Adam, early in the morning of what has become our Evening Land.

I never question why I constantly reread, teach, and write about Shakespeare—there is no God but God, and his name is William Shakespeare—whereas I wonder incessantly why Walt Whitman has been an obsession for me ever since I suffered a dreadful middle-of-the-journey crisis in 1965, now almost a half century ago. The indubitable aesthetic eminence of Whitman in itself does not provide an answer. More even than Emerson and Melville, Hawthorne and James, Dickinson and Twain, Frost and Eliot, Stevens, Crane, and Faulkner, Walt is our gift to world literature: He *is* the poem of our climate. And yet the mystery of his fascination still puzzles me.

Kenneth Burke chuckled when I first brought this up to him sometime in the 1980s. "Harold," he remarked, "Walt has hold of you precisely because you do not write poems." I could not follow Kenneth then and still am baffled. Burke composed weird poems abundantly and mailed them to me in batches. I have never wanted to write a poem but only to read as many strong ones as I could apprehend. Whitman summons us to be both poets and readers. *Crossing Brooklyn Ferry* addresses us as readers who *will* come later, and I emerge from each experience of it more confirmed in my lifelong vocation as a reader. Perhaps Kenneth meant that Whitman uniquely calls the reader-in-a-reader into more life.

The influence of a reader's mind upon itself is akin to searching for the labyrinthine ways in which that most copious of all minds, Shakespeare's, influenced itself. Fourteen consecutive months sufficed to compose *King Lear, Macbeth,* and *Antony and Cleopatra.* Something abandoned Shakespeare after that furnace of terrifying tragedy came up at last. I have ventured to name this "inwardness," but that word is insufficient. Recoiling from the abyss, the dramatist gave us Coriolanus and Timon, Leontes and Prospero, all of them light-years outward from Lear and Edgar, Macbeth and Cleopatra. The inventor of Falstaff and Hamlet, Rosalind and Iago, is a Montaigne-like humanist but well on his winding path to nihilism. Beyond nihilism is the Gnostic abyss, our foremother and forefather, dwelling place of Lear, Macbeth, and Cleopatra. The name for that emptiness in ancient gnosis was the *kenoma,* habitat of Timon, Coriolanus, and Leontes. Prospero stands apart: Enchanted islands are domains not to be quarried betwixt outwardness and inwardness.

The reader transmembered by Hamlet becomes precursor to Macbeth's auditor and then suffers the madness of Leontes, rather in the mode of Faulkner longing for the death of Captain Ahab to be his own:

> . . . a sort of Golgotha of the heart become immutable as bronze in the sonority of its plunging ruin . . .

That catches Ahab's alienation from his crew and would fit his precursors Hamlet and Macbeth. Leontes scrambles up out of that bronze sonority at enormous cost to himself and to others. The influence of Hamlet's devastating mind upon itself is echoed by the downward and outward effect of Macbeth's proleptic imagination upon itself. Paul Valéry was fascinated by the influence of his own mind upon Valéry, which we can read throughout his major poems. We are neither Shakespeare nor Valéry, but all of us suffer the mind's force and violence upon ourselves.

Samuel Johnson spoke of our "hunger of imagination" and conceded that Shakespeare alone assuaged that dangerous prevalence. Perhaps Shakespeare helped Johnson avoid madness, a function he has served for me whenever I waver in my own perilous balance. My late acquaintance

Jack Bate reminded us that the mind, for Johnson, was a ceaseless activity that could not be allowed to idle.

ANYONE WHO WRITES BOOKS FOR WELL OVER A HALF CENTURY IS LIKELY to believe that one work in particular is a neglected child. Of my own more than forty volumes, I regard that waif as *The American Religion* (1992, 2006). I recall touring the South and Southwest throughout 1986–1991, lecturing upon American poetry while visiting whatever churches were kind enough to allow me to attend services. Many sorts of esoteric Baptists and wild Pentecostalists were warmly receptive, and so were the Mormons, though necessarily they could not admit me to their temples.

Brooding upon the highly original stances of Emerson, Whitman, Melville, and Dickinson had been my starting point, but my wonder-wandering among rather less articulate American Religionists changed my way of thinking about the United States. The rise of the Tea Party did not surprise me, because I had encountered its origins on my journey a quarter century before our dismal national election of 2010. I listened closely to hundreds of American knowers, who in one sense knew nothing yet in another way knew everything, because they were all the subject and the object of their own quests. Alone except for and with a very American Jesus, each was beyond belief and dwelled in a solitude that only the resurrected Jesus could share.

Hearing them discourse, in and out of their divine assemblies, taught me that the American Jesus suffered no crucifixion and experienced no ascension. Instead, he manifested himself only in the forty days he spent with disciples after his resurrection, and for Mormons, Pentecostalists, and independent Baptists, he sojourned still in their America, walking and talking with them. Because of that, some told me they were already resurrected and would never die, while nearly all affirmed they had heard him speak, and quite a few had seen him.

The sincerity and evident amiability of so great a cloud of witnesses was equal to anything I have encountered. You don't need a third ear to apprehend such testimony, but comprehension is an ongoing quest for me still. What might be called the natural religion of our America has little to do with historical, received European Christianity. Seventeenth-century

Enthusiasm mingles with discords of ancient Gnosticism and shamanistic Orphism in our Native Strain.

What has this to do with the influence of any American critic's mind upon itself? I have learned to shrug off historicist overdeterminations, because they cannot account for aesthetic and cognitive splendors. Their contextualizations blur more than they illuminate. Yet as readers, writers, and teachers, our authentic context is the myriad countrymen and -women who live in a daily reality that is mostly not at all our own. Socioeconomic reductions of their stance help only in a limited way. Karl Marx is irrelevant to many millions of them because, in America, religion is the poetry of the people and not their opiate.

The function of literary criticism at the present time cannot be to struggle with this Moby Dick of the American spirit, yet awareness of it should be part of our common ordeal of consciousness. I love Whitman's poetry and wish I could say, with him: "Whoever you are, now I place my hand upon you, that you be my poem." But we cannot proclaim to another person that you be my interpretation.

Literary love has more to do with Plato or Saint Augustine than with Homer or the Bible. Perhaps it has most to do with Dante and Shakespeare. We fall in love when very young, as Dante did with Beatrice. My earliest memory of a similar experience goes back to an afternoon when I was seven or eight, playing in the snow with other children. I cannot recall the name of the little girl who suddenly caught my spirit, yet in the semi-wakefulness just before dawn, three-quarters of a century later, I sometimes see her face again with startled vividness, framed in the hood of her winter jacket.

Falling in love in Shakespeare's modes comes later, from what we now call adolescence onward. The sense of wonder remains pervasive, but the attendant wound differs. Freud's suggestion was that the hurt was the reactivation of the narcissistic scar, itself inflicted by having lost the parent of the gender opposite of one's own to the other parent. That is the love of the Song of Songs, as strong as jealousy and death.

American Religionists, when I questioned them, frequently said that falling in love was affirming again Christ's love for each of them. In such a labyrinth of idealizations I get lost, lacking the thread that might lead to an escape. Yet if our night journey is to meet an exit, we need the poet of our climate to cut it for us. Whitman stops somewhere waiting for us.

WALT SINGS OF WHAT HE HEARS AND SEES MORE OFTEN THAN OF WHAT he knows, but his proclamations of knowledge can be overwhelming. Authority is sanctioned not least by the breathtaking descent beneath the bottom limits of being:

> And mossy scabs of the wormfence, and heaped stones, and
>   elder and mullein and pokeweed.

How can I improve my opinion regarding that sanctioning into *knowledge*? One thinks of Samuel Beckett: "Ever tried. Ever failed. No matter. Try again. Fail again. Fail better."

Walt failed better. *Song of Myself,* like Hart Crane's *The Bridge,* fails only as "American epic" gives a new meaning to "failure." Melville's Ahab fails in his quest; so does Twain's Huckleberry Finn, if American heroic quest be judged by Old World criteria. American literary criticism, be it by Emerson or Kenneth Burke, is a new mode that is on vacation from the work of interpretation. It may fail, but no matter. It will try again.

In an outrageous failure, Walt's dreadful 1871 *Song of the Exposition,* written for hire and recited at the fortieth National Industrial Exposition of the American Institution in New York, the American bard chides the Muse to "Cross out please those immensely overpaid accounts, / That matter of Troy and Achilles' wrath," and migrate instead to the United States, in order to celebrate a society little different from our plutocratic shambles a hundred forty years later. But at his strongest, Whitman was able to overwhelm his reader with an unprecedented *immediacy:* "Whoever you are, I fear you are walking the walk of dreams . . . Whoever you are, now I place my hand upon you, that you be my poem." I again solemnize these secretive syllables, and as a critic ask myself: Who else has pursued me as Walt pursues? Shakespeare, whether in sonnets or onstage, lets it be. Like Hamlet, he does not need our love.

Famously, John Keats thought we hate poetry that has a design upon us, but Whitman rejected Keats's Negative Capability, an irrelevance to Walt's powerful press of Myself. Yet, watching childbirth, he transmembers the midwife in a line Keats might have admired: "I recline by the sills of the exquisite flexible doors." Uncanny at his frequent best, Walt still can be absurd in overidentifying, thus inviting the fury of D. H. Lawrence, whose anguish of contamination by our national poet was titanic. In his famously outrageous book *Studies in Classic American Literature,* Lawrence wrote:

> "Whoever you are, to endless announcements—"
> "And of these one and all I weave the song of myself."

Do you? Well, then, it just shows you haven't *got* any self. It's a mush, not a woven thing. A hotch-potch, not a tissue. Your self.

Oh, Walter, Walter, what have you done with it? What have you done with yourself? With your own individual self? For it sounds as if it had all leaked out of you, leaked into the universe.

Post mortem effects. The individuality had leaked out of him.

No, no, don't lay this down to poetry. These are post mortem effects. And Walt's great poems are really huge fat tomb-plants, great rank graveyard growths.

All that false exuberance. All those lists of things boiled in one pudding-cloth! No, no!

I don't want all those things inside me, thank you.

I cite Lawrence because his zestful intemperance enchants me. You need to love a poet and poem before your appreciation can transcend the accidents of your own nature. But it is time to be Bloom and not Lawrence and read Whitman as closely as he deserves. I need a brief text and have chosen one of the rare late returns of his genius, *The Dalliance of the Eagles,* composed in 1880, when the poet was sixty. He had never seen eagles mate and relied on a description given to him by his disciple and friend, the naturalist John Burroughs:

> Skirting the river road, (my forenoon walk, my rest,)
> Skyward in air a sudden muffled sound, the dalliance of
>   the eagles,
> The rushing amorous contact high in space together,
> The clinching interlocking claws, a living, fierce, gyrating
>   wheel,

Four beating wings, two beaks, a swirling mass tight grap-
pling,
In tumbling turning clustering loops, straight downward
falling,
Till o'er the river pois'd, the twain yet one, a moment's lull,
A motionless still balance in the air, then parting, talons
loosing,
Upward again on slow-firm pinions slanting, their separate
diverse flight,
She hers, he his, pursuing.

An astonishing vision, in just ninety words or so; I prefer this to Gerard Manley Hopkins's *The Windhover* and William Butler Yeats's *Leda and the Swan,* both of them experimental sonnets. Hopkins loved and feared Whitman, while Yeats rather nastily disliked the American upstart, dismissed in *A Vision* with weak misunderstanding. Writing to Robert Bridges in 1882, the Jesuit poet remarked:

> . . . I always knew in my heart Walt Whitman's mind to be more like my own than any other man's living. As he is a very great scoundrel this is not a pleasant confession. And this makes me the more desirous to read him and the more determined that I will not.

To describe the ministering angel of the Washington, D.C., Civil War hospitals as a very great scoundrel is breathtaking, yet the textual evidence of Father Hopkins's own poems indicates a wider and deeper reading in Whitman than he acknowledged.

Walt's verbs, like his erotic attachments, are largely intransitive and tend toward adverbial status. In *The Dalliance of the Eagles* you confront: "skirting," "rushing," "clinching," "interlocking," "living," "gyrating," "beating," "swirling," "grappling," "tumbling," "turning," "clustering," "falling," "pois'd," "parting," "loosing," "slanting," "pursuing." That makes eighteen verbal forms, all but one or two intransitive. One-fifth of this fierce lyric's words mount together into what seems desire without an object, though the coupling that is the poem describes a mutual passion fulfilled.

Angus Fletcher observed that "To read Whitman aright, we have to remain perpetually intransitive, like the vast majority of his middle-voicing verbs, his verbs of sensation, perception, and cognition." Sixty years of friendship with Fletcher lead me to call that the Fletcher Principle and to apply it also to Dante, Shakespeare, Shelley, Hart Crane, and many other great poets. As a teacher, I urge myself and others to remain perpetually intransitive, like the Jesus of the very Whitmanian Gnostic Gospel of Thomas, who proclaims: "Be passers-by."

Walt is always passing us by, waiting somewhere up ahead. This evasion ought to be at odds with his shocking, startling immediacy, yet it fuses with it. Any strong poem, whether by Hopkins or Yeats, Bishop or Ashbery, eludes our drive to objectify it, and Whitman is no more ill-assorted than his compeers. At eighty-four I wonder why poems in particular obsessed me from childhood onward. Because I had an over-emotional sensibility, I tended to need more affection from my parents and sisters than even they could sustain. From the age of ten on, I sought from Moyshe-Leyb Halpern and Hart Crane, from Shakespeare and Shelley, the strong affect I seemed to need from answering voices.

The Dalliance of the Eagles finds me by its only apparent refusal of affect: The poem hesitates between its vista of "a motionless still balance in the air" and subsequent "separate diverse flight." Walt only rarely stands still, yet hesitation, as his disciple A. R. Ammons wrote, has its own rewards.

The intransitive verb "hesitate" is related to the Latin for "holding fast," Whitman's "motionless still balance in the air." We do not think of Walt as we recite this poem: What it celebrates and sings is not "myself" but the Lucretian way things are, though implicit magnificence remains its burden. We see and hear not the American Sublime but a particular encounter, vividly represented for its own sake. John Ruskin admired Whitman's powers but feared the poems were compromised by excessive personality. He would have made an exception for this strenuously impressionistic vista, where the personality of Walt Whitman, an American, one of the roughs, is conspicuously absent.

No poem, Paul Valéry remarked, is ever finished. Rather, the poet abandons it. That certainly is Whitman's customary praxis, and so *The Dalliance of the Eagles* must be a sport. Yet Whitman's art intimates that both the dalliance and its representation are fragments torn from the astonishing trope: "leaves of grass." John Hollander splendidly caught some of the enigmas of that title:

Its title was—and remains—as deeply problematic as its appearance. Are the leaves literally the pages of books—not "those barren leaves" that Wordsworth's speaker wanted shut up to free the reader for the texts of nature, but pages that were paradisiacally both green and fruitful? Or are they rather metaphors for the poems, here not the "flowers" of old anthologies, but green with newness? Are they the leaves that, broadcast by the wind, served the Cumaean Sybil for her prophetic pages? Are they revisions of the oldest poetical leaves of all, those figurations of individual lives in Homer, Virgil, Dante, Milton, and Shelley, and is the grass likewise also that of all flesh mown down by death in Isaiah and the Psalmist? Are they *leavings*— residues of the act of "singing," departures for worlds elsewhere that are always regions of here? And in what way are the leaves-pages *of* grass: made of, about, for, authored by? "Leaves of Grass"—hard words, putting body, life, text, presence, personality, self, and the constant fiction of some Other, all together.

As a mixed trope, "leaves of grass" is virtually inexhaustible. Raised as a Bible-reading Quaker and a follower of the circuit-riding dissident Elias Hicks, Whitman remembered the transmutation of a trope from Isaiah in the First Epistle of Peter 1:24:

For all flesh is as grass, and all the glory of man as the flower of grass. The grass withereth, and the flower thereof falleth away.

With this, Whitman compounded the fiction of the leaves: Homer analogizing the generations of leaves to those of humankind; Virgil's recently dead souls troped as autumnal leaves, humanized by the stretching forth of their hands, longing for the farther shore of the living; Dante's damned souls falling away over the dark water as the autumnal leaves fall. The later developments of this image in Milton, Coleridge, and Shelley also are transumed in Whitman's title, a compost he will yield to his involuntary disciple Stevens in *An Ordinary Evening in New Haven*:

The mobile and the immobile flickering
In the area between is and was are leaves,
Leaves burnished in autumnal burnished trees

And leaves in whirlings in the gutters, whirlings
Around and away, resembling the presence of
    thought,
Resembling the presences of thoughts, as if,

In the end, in the whole psychology, the self,
The town, the weather, in a casual litter,
Together, said words of the world are the life of the
    world.

I need a greater text than *The Dalliance of the Eagles* and give Walt at
his grandest in *Song of Myself*:

A child said, *What is the grass?* fetching it to me with full
    hands;
How could I answer the child? I do not know what it is any
    more than he.

I guess it must be the flag of my disposition, out of hopeful
    green stuff woven.

Or I guess it is the handkerchief of the Lord,
A scented gift and remembrancer designedly dropt,
Bearing the owner's name someway in the corners, that we
    may see and remark, and say *Whose?*

Or I guess the grass is itself a child, the produced babe of the
    vegetation.

Or I guess it is a uniform hieroglyphic,
And it means, Sprouting alike in broad zones and
    narrow zones,
Growing among black folks as among white,
Kanuck, Tuckahoe, Congressman, Cuff, I give them the
    same, I receive them the same.

And now it seems to me the beautiful uncut hair of graves.

Tenderly will I use you curling grass,
It may be you transpire from the breasts of young men,
It may be if I had known them I would have loved them;
It may be you are from old people, or from offspring taken
    soon out of their mothers' laps,
And here you are the mothers' laps.

These beautiful lines, endless to meditation, epitomize the poem and the poet at the heights of artistic control over his vision. How to convert my ravishment by this into knowledge? An Epicurean materialist, and not at all a transcendentalist, Whitman believes that the *what* is unknowable and denies he is the answerer. Yet his figurative guesses, or tropings, are florabundant: the green flag of his hopeful disposition, God's flirtatious handkerchief, the babe of nature, a uniform hieroglyphic, and, best of all, in the most Homeric of native American similes: "the beautiful uncut hair of graves."

One wonders if Whitman remembered that line as he consoled the maimed and dying soldiers in Washington, D.C., in the closing years of the Civil War. Heroic pathos yields to the homoerotic tenderness that follows, comprehending young and old, mothers and untimely dying children, and then mounts into a biblical sublimity, in a passage Hemingway must have pondered, since his characteristic voice—evenly weighted, usually precise, emotionally deferred—is both anticipated and surpassed by it:

This grass is very dark to be from the white heads of
    old mothers,
Darker than the colorless beards of old men,
Dark to come from under the faint red roofs of mouths.

Biblical parataxis is enhanced here by monosyllabic diction. The only disyllables are "very," "mothers," "darker," "colorless," and "under." The grass—"very dark," "darker," "dark to come"—all but blackens in this vista. In 1855, Whitman has gone ahead of any surrealism and stops somewhere waiting for it. Stare at a flourishing meadow with Whitman in mind, and contemplate the beautiful uncut hair of old mothers in a kaleidoscope or riot of colors: green, black, white—a white not the colorless all-color of Melville's whiteness of the whale but a redemptive white, because its life is ongoing. Knowledge of and in Whitman at his flood tide is authenticated by what he calls later in the poem a "Me going in for my chances, spending for vast returns."

How can the critical receiver convert those returns to her own? I read Walt and become, in Hamlet's words, a wonder-wounded hearer, even as I am when reading Shakespeare. Whitman sustains the comparison, as do Cervantes and only a few others. Shakespeare birthed scores of people, Cervantes but two, and Whitman only the one, but Sancho, the Sorrowful Knight, and Walt are among the everliving, with Falstaff, Hamlet, Cleopatra, and so many more in the dramatist unlimited.

Knowing Don Quixote, Falstaff, or Walt is hardly an option. It is seeing face-to-face. If I say Walt knows me face-to-face as I do him, is that a critical turning? Figuration certainly is involved: You and I, like Whitman, wish to be taken literally but have to be taken figuratively. Walt cries out to embrace and be embraced, but all *his* couplings were intransitive, in the sadness of reality.

A century and a half after his heroic hospital service, Walt is an American legend, our unanointed redeemer figure. Transvaluation of Old World Christianity is absolute in Whitman, even as it wavers curiously in Melville. Whitman is the evangelist of our American religion, where everyone can say with him, "I am the man, I suffered, I was there." Lincoln was assassinated on Good Friday, which prompts a poem in Melville's *Battle-Pieces and Aspects of the War,* but Walt's *Drum-Taps* and *Sequel to Drum-Taps* culminate in the *Lilacs* elegy, where all Christian ritual is rigorously excluded.

Is the release of enormous energy and ambition akin to the conversion of opinion into knowledge? One thinks of the occult vitalism of Honoré de Balzac and of the surge that is *The Pickwick Papers. Leaves of Grass* 1855, contemporary with Balzac and Charles Dickens, is matched only by *Moby-Dick* as the New World's explosion into a mode of solar cognition. The American difference is in Whitman's and Melville's *immediacy.*

A critic's knowledge, in my experience, is a kind of gnosis, an Alexandrian mode in which the knower also is known. Self-awareness in Montaigne's tradition becomes secular gnosis in Paul Valéry, who declined to separate the aesthetic from any other mode of consciousness. All acts of knowledge fuse in the Valéryan poem.

The poetic mind of Walt Whitman is obviously antithetical to that of Paul Valéry. And yet the affinities between Montaigne and Emerson are palpable and were appreciated by Friedrich Nietzsche. Walt also compounds aesthetic consciousness with self-awareness but in the American grain—beautifully isolated by Kenneth Burke, with whom I walked around the Battery while we chanted Walt in unison. Kenneth can set the table for us:

> In sum, Whitman would programmatically make all days into a kind of permanent Saturnalian revel, though celebrating not a golden age of the past, but rather the present in terms of an ideal future. And, in poetically personalizing his program, he "promulges" democracy in terms of a maternal allness or firstness and fraternal universality ambiguously intermingling in a death hug that presents many central problems for the patient pedestrian analyzer of The Good Gray Poet's terminology.

"Death hug" reflects the Burkean persuasion that Walt's "entire scheme was based upon an ideal of all-pervasive and almost promiscuous Union." It is perhaps excessive of me to go on juxtaposing Whitman and Valéry, but I have a beast-in-view. Composing prose poems, the French master felt again an angel's weariness and quested for the source of intellectual desire in his first conscious apprehension of the world. Whitman, in his stunning 1855 long poem belatedly titled *The Sleepers,* makes much the same night journey into the abyss of the mind.

Emerson and Nietzsche, Whitman and Valéry deprecated mere memory and its tiresome prolongation of ancient enmities and resentments, of systems that are the mind's violence against itself. Famously, Valéry remarked that "reading is a military operation." Whitman certainly was not a poet of Valéry's Young Fates or of cemeteries by the sea, but I would argue that his formalism exceeded Valéry's precisely because he was the stronger poet of the two. Wallace Stevens, who venerated Valéry, might have scoffed at my contention, yet it is not Valéry who swims just beneath the surface of Stevens's poems and rises up to break through when he is not summoned. Here is Stevens in *Notes Toward a Supreme Fiction:*

The weather and the giant of the weather,
Say the weather, the mere weather, the mere air:
An abstraction blooded, as a man by thought.

This evokes the magnificent vision of Walt in which Stevens surpassed
Federico García Lorca and Hart Crane:

In the far South the sun of autumn is passing
Like Walt Whitman walking along a ruddy shore.
He is singing and chanting the things that are part of him,
The worlds that were and will be, death and day.
Nothing is final, he chants. No man shall see the end.
His beard is of fire and his staff is a leaping flame.

—LIKE DECORATIONS IN A NIGGER CEMETERY

At once Yahweh, Moses, and Aaron, the American bard proclaims here
against finalities. Try to conceive of Stevens envisioning Paul Valéry striding upon the heights of the graveyard by the sea, blindly staring at its un-
dulations, pitched betwixt vacuous mortality and fiery space, an
unendurable airlessness. In his most famous poem, the Gallic seer regards
the sun of the south suspended at noon, while in Stevens's poem, Walt
Whitman, an American, one of the roughs, beholds in the far south the
sun of autumn passing, while he walks by the water's edge, singing and
chanting death and day, intimate partitions of his consciousness. So deep
is the poetic mind of Wallace Stevens that he has (perhaps unknowingly)
placed Paul Valéry and Walt Whitman in a giant agon, which the French
child of Stéphane Mallarmé and Arthur Rimbaud, of Victor Hugo and
Charles Baudelaire, cannot win. Go down to the waterline and you are in
Walt's domain, where only he can triumph.

Yet where am I, worn-out ancient exegete, in this conflagration of three
great poets? All the splendors of Valéry's *The Marine Cemetery*, Whitman's *Out of the Cradle Endlessly Rocking*, and Stevens's *The Auroras of
Autumn* depend upon their *finding* me, to employ a critical trope of Samuel Taylor Coleridge. Valéry and Stevens help form my critical mind, and
yet the presence of Walt Whitman overwhelms me, possesses me, as only

a few others—Dante, Shakespeare, Milton—consistently flood my entire being. What Leo Spitzer called "clicks" as he read, in Old Bloom become a transport to the sublime.

Without vision, criticism perishes. The American Sublime, a precarious mode even when opening to glory in the age of Emerson, seems a mockery in 2015. And yet the poet of our climate and our moment, the noble John Ashbery, subtly revives it:

> The one who runs little, he who barely trips along
> Knows how short the day is, how few the hours of
>   light.
> Distractions can't wrench him, preoccupations forcibly
>   remove him
> From the heap of things, the pile of this and that:
> Tepid dreams and mostly worthless; lukewarm fancies, the
>   majority of them unprofitable.
> Yet it is from these that the light, from the ones present here
>   that luminosity
> Sifts and breaks, subsides and falls asunder.
> And it will be but half-strange, really be only semi-bizarre
> When the tall poems of the world, the towering earthbound
>   poetic utterances
> Invade the street of our dialect, penetrate the avenue of our
>   patois,
> Bringing fresh power and new knowledge, transporting
>   virgin might and up-to-date enlightenment
> To this place of honest thirst, to this satisfyingly parched
>   here and now,
> Since all things congregate, because everything assembles
> In front of him, before the one
> Who need only sit and tie his shoelace, who should remain
>   seated, knotting the metal-tipped cord
> For it to happen right, to enable it to come correctly into
>   being
> As moments, then years; minutes, afterwards ages
> Suck up the common strength, absorb the everyday power

And afterwards live on, satisfied; persist, later to be a source
    of gratification,
But perhaps only to oneself, haply to one's sole identity.

—Finnish Rhapsody

"Perhaps" and "haply" are delicate apotropaic gestures, but "only to
oneself . . . one's sole identity" renders this another *Song of Myself.* Emerson spoke of "the great and crescive self," and Whitman manifested it
with what I find to be a touchstone for American Sublimity in *When Lilacs
Last in the Dooryard Bloom'd:*

In the dooryard fronting an old farm-house near the
    white-wash'd palings,
Stands the lilac-bush tall-growing with heart-shaped leaves
    of rich green,
With many a pointed blossom rising delicate, with the
    perfume strong I love,
With every leaf a miracle—and from this bush in the
    dooryard,
With delicate-color'd blossoms and heart-shaped leaves of
    rich green,
A sprig with its flower I break.

Six lines of what might be termed "plain radiance" find their only transitive verb in the very last word: "break." Walt breaks the tally, his defining
synecdoche, in the sprig of lilac he will throw upon Lincoln's funeral cor-
tège as it slowly departs Union Station in Washington, D.C., to begin a
long journey through many cities to rest at last in Springfield, Illinois.

Inevitable phrasing—my criterion for the highest poetry—is a difficult
matter for criticism to expound upon, since "inevitable" here is itself a
trope dependent on aesthetic experience. In old age, doubtless still infused
by Nietzsche-as-genealogist, I begin to believe in what might be called his
poetics of pain. He taught that memorability was heightened by suffering:
a hard doctrine, but akin to Shelley's notion that the sublime persuades us
to abandon easier pleasures for more difficult engagements. In this severe

vision, the slavery of pleasure yields to what lies beyond the pleasure principle. Is then the inevitability—for me, anyway—of Walt's dooryard
fronting an old farmhouse and the lilac bush so commonly growing there
more of a difficult pleasure than it seems? Is my opinion that this is so an
act of knowledge, and in what sense of knowing?

Is becoming wise an act of knowledge? For Nietzsche, the greatest
thoughts were the greatest actions. Thinking in and through metaphors,
Shakespeare gives us persons who act with titanic self-destructiveness, incarnate sublimity: Lear and Macbeth, Hamlet and Othello, Antony and
Coriolanus. Whitman's metaphors include what John Hollander called
his "hard ordinary words," terms that are charged by Whitman with an
accent entirely his own: among them "drift," "passing," "vista," "lilac,"
"leaf," "grass," "sea," "star," and many more. Keats's nightingale and
Shelley's skylark are not more tropological than Whitman's mockingbird
and his hermit thrush. A poet who equates his soul with the fourfold metaphor of night, death, the mother, and the sea is thinking figuratively as
fiercely as did the Hermeticists and the Kabbalists.

Meaning, to be human, starts as memory of a fecund variety of pain.
To inaugurate meaning, rather than merely to repeat it, you cultivate an
illness that is oxymoronic, a pathos that is already play. Falstaff and Walt
meet in this arena and find words for what is alive in their hearts. Against
trauma we *need* Falstaff and Whitman, solar vitalists abounding in desire. Better than Nietzsche's Zarathustra, they realize a fresh dimension
to the primordial poem of mankind, because each creates a fiction of the
self that becomes a poem in our eyes. Meaning is voicing, and images of
voice become tropes of knowing. "We can know only what we ourselves
have made," proclaimed Giambattista Vico, the eighteenth-century Nea-
politan philosopher, and Falstaff and Walt know the selves they have
forged.

I recall writing, long ago, that any new poem is rather like a little child
who has been stationed with a large group of other small children in a
playroom, where there are a limited number of toys and no adult supervision whatsoever. Those toys are the tricks, turns, and tropes of poetic
language, Oscar Wilde's "beautiful untrue things" that save the imagination from falling into "careless habits of accuracy." Oscar, who worshipped and twice visited Walt during an American tour, charmingly
termed criticism "the only civilized form of autobiography." I have aged

not, alas, into Wilde's wit but into a firm conviction that true criticism recognizes itself as a mode of memoir.

Poets and critics alike seek to convert opinion into knowledge, but this means opinion in the legal and not the public sense. What is it you know when you recognize a voice? Hart Crane's extraordinary images of voice, whether a broken tower or a vaulting bridge, undo my expectations, even after more than seventy years of reading and knowing him. At eighty-four I lie awake at night, after a first sleep, and murmur Crane, Whitman, and Shakespeare to myself, seeking comfort through continuity, as grand voices somehow hold off the permanent darkness that gathers though it does not fall. Frequently, I modulate to Stevens:

> Likewise to say of the evening star,
> The most ancient light in the most ancient sky,

> That it is wholly an inner light, that it shines
> From the sleepy bosom of the real, re-creates,
> Searches a possible for its possibleness.

Out of the Cradle Endlessly Rocking

OF WHITMAN'S SIX MAJOR POEMS—*SONG OF MYSELF, THE SLEEPERS, Crossing Brooklyn Ferry, Out of the Cradle Endlessly Rocking, As I Ebb'd with the Ocean of Life,* and the *Lilacs* lament for Lincoln—I am least attached to *Out of the Cradle,* yet I choose it here as proof-text for the improvement of Walt's image of voice into knowledge. Mockingbirds, like robins and sparrows, can be backyard denizens, but they are uniquely imitative—indeed, mockingly inventive—of the birds they drive away. In Walt's wake, the late Mona Van Duyn wrote an agile poem called *Mockingbird Month.* I quote the first four of seven stanzas:

> A pupa of pain, I sat and lay one July,
> companioned by the bird the Indians call "four hundred
> tongues." Through the dark in the back yard by my bed,
> through the long day near my front couch, the bird
> sang without pause an amplified song "two-thirds
> his own," books told me, "and one-third mimicry."

Gray charmer, "the lark and nightingale in one,"
unremitting maker of music so full of wit
and improvisation, I strained by night and light
to hear the scientists' record: "In ten minutes
he mimicked thirty-two species." I counted eight
(even I) variations on cardinal's song alone.

Cock of the neighborhood, his white flashes of wing
and long distinguished tail ruled the bushes and boughs,
and once, enchanted, I saw him walk past my house,
herding, from three feet behind, the neighbor's nice,
cowardly cat. He controlled without any fuss
but took little time off. Most of our month he sang.

The sticky wings of my mind began to open.
No mere plagiarist, a Harold Bloom singer,
he leaned on, but played with, robin or jay or
starling or whippoorwill. I began to prefer
him and house and hurting to the world outdoors.
Both art and art-lover attend to what may happen.

The lovely Native American name for the mockingbird, "four hundred
tongues," will outlast "a Harold Bloom singer," but Van Duyn's appreciation of natural misprision is an apt starting point for considering Walt's
forlorn singer:

Out of the cradle endlessly rocking,
Out of the mocking-bird's throat, the musical shuttle,
Out of the Ninth-month midnight,
Over the sterile sands and the fields beyond, where the child
    leaving his bed wander'd alone, bareheaded, barefoot,
Down from the shower'd halo,
Up from the mystic play of shadows twining and twisting as
    if they were alive,
Out from the patches of briers and blackberries,
From the memories of the bird that chanted to me,

From your memories sad brother, from the fitful risings and
    fallings I heard,
From under that yellow half-moon late-risen and swollen as
    if with tears,
From those beginning notes of yearning and love there in
    the mist,
From the thousand responses of my heart never to cease,
From the myriad thence-arous'd words,
From the word stronger and more delicious than any,
From such as now they start the scene revisiting,
As a flock, twittering, rising, or overhead passing,
Borne hither, ere all eludes me, hurriedly,
A man, yet by these tears a little boy again,
Throwing myself on the sand, confronting the waves,
I, chanter of pains and joys, uniter of here and hereafter,
Taking all hints to use them, but swiftly leaping beyond
    them,
A reminiscence sing.

What an astonishing artist Whitman is, in this opening of what he called his "curious warble"! Rightly admired by a host of superb readers, from Algernon Swinburne to Leo Spitzer, the poem enhances the tradition of odes celebrating the incarnation of the poetic character: William Collins, Wordsworth, Coleridge, Shelley, Keats, Lord Alfred Tennyson, Browning, and Yeats figure in that genre's story, and Whitman swerves it to an American variant developed later by his descendants Wallace Stevens and Hart Crane. Walt's swerve compounds the poet's calling with his fourfold trope of night, death, the mother, and the sea, and with his intransitive eros, whose authentic object can only be death.

Twenty-two lines in a rocking shuttle delay their clarification until "I, chanter of pains . . . A reminiscence sing." Whitman had his own personal Audubon in his disciple John Burroughs, who mediated for him the hermit thrush of the *Lilacs* elegy and the mockingbird. What *Out of the Cradle* deliberately omits is the salient quality other poets emphasize when this allusive singer is celebrated. Randall Jarrell, in his *The Mockingbird*, concludes:

Now, in the moonlight, he sits here and sings.
A thrush is singing, then a thrasher, then a jay—
Then, all at once, a cat begins meowing.
A mockingbird can sound like anything.
He imitates the world he drove away
so well that for a minute, in the moonlight,
which one's the mockingbird? which one's the world?

Walt's solitary singer does not imitate the world. I taught myself a half century ago to ask of any poem or Shakespearean drama: What precisely does this leave out to make it the beautifully expensive torso it is? I regard the question as Kierkegaardian, in the spirit of his *Either/Or*'s rotation method, which took its epigraph from Aristophanes, where a chorus chants:

You get too much at last of everything: of sunsets, of cabbages,
    of love.

Whitman hints that we get too much at last of allusiveness, yet his poem, like all strong writing, knows better. The apotropaic gesture is what counts for Walt: As outsetting bard, he intimates his difference from prior celebrants of the poet's calling. Knowingly, he invents what Paul Fussell named the American Shore Ode, in distinction from what M. H. Abrams calls the Greater Romantic Lyric, his term for poems such as Wordsworth's *Ode: Intimations of Immortality* and the odes of Shelley and Keats. Abrams's student, I rejoice that he is still active in his hundred third year, and I long ago based my accounts of the High Romantic crisis poem, British and American, upon my mentor's clearing of the ground.

The question arises: Why, then, did Whitman choose the mockingbird, when he so deftly turns aside from its characteristic agon with all rival songsters? Though he and Tennyson admired each other and corresponded amiably, Walt seems to have regarded the laureate as a mockingbird of genius, a kind of greater Henry Wordsworth Longfellow. And yet I hear Lord Tennyson in the magnificent finale of the *Lilacs* lament for Lincoln:

Yet each to keep and all, retrievements out of the night;
The song, the wondrous chant of the gray-brown bird,

And the tallying chant, the echo arous'd in my soul,
With the lustrous and drooping star with the countenance
    full of woe,
With the holders holding my hand nearing the call of the bird,
Comrades mine and I in the midst, and their memory ever
    to keep, for the dead I loved so well,
For the sweetest, wisest soul of all my days and lands—and
    this for his dear sake;
Lilac and star and bird twined with the chant of my soul,
There in the fragrant pines and the cedars dusk and dim.

Here, as elsewhere at his best, Whitman is a true mockingbird. Walt's image of voice, which he names the "tally," is a comprehensive trope that I seem to have been explicating nonstop since 1965 and that defies simplistic reductions. Whitman chose as epigraph for his *Death Bed Edition* of *Leaves of Grass* (1891–92) a brief poem he first printed in 1876:

Come, said my Soul,
Such verses for my Body let us write, (for we are one,)
That should I after death invisibly return,
Or, long, long hence, in other spheres,
There to some group of mates the chants resuming,
(Tallying Earth's soil, trees, winds, tumultuous waves,)
Ever with pleas'd smile I may keep on,
Ever and ever yet the verses owning—as, first, I here
    and now
Signing for Soul and Body, set to them my name,
                    Walt Whitman

Elsewhere he wrote of tallying the greatest bards, an act appropriate for the American Homer. Let us say, then, that he tallied the mockingbird in his agonistic drive to establish an American poetry upon the Emersonian preference for voice over text. For me, he remains the single instance of the American variant on Johnson's quest to convert opinion into knowledge. Knowledge of what? If, as Epicurus insisted, the what is unknowable, Walt's knowledge is a personal gnosis, in which the knower himself is known by whatever can be known.

I gladly turn from the Hermetic to the sweetly ridiculous, following a suggestion of Angus Fletcher, whose curious universal knowledge has inspired me since we first bonded in 1951. At this point in writing I phoned Angus out in Albuquerque, and he referred me to Whitman's auditory sense of rhyming internally within rhyme: here, "rocking" with "mocking." Wonderfully, Angus invoked the American popular ballad "Listen to the Mockingbird," composed in 1855 by one Septimus Winner, writing under the pseudonym of Alice Hawthorne. It was one of Abraham Lincoln's favorite songs and was madly popular during the Civil War. Walt certainly knew it and presumably enjoyed hearing the Hutchinson Family Singers performing what is really rather poor stuff. I give the first stanza only:

> I'm dreaming now of Hally, sweet Hally, sweet Hally;
> I'm dreaming now of Hally,
> For the thought of her is one that never dies:
> She's sleeping in the valley, the valley, the valley;
> She's sleeping in the valley,
> And the mockingbird is singing where she lies.

Note only that, like Whitman's solitary singer, this pop mockingbird has been denatured and chants in its own pathetic voice.

HOW THIS CRITIC THINKS, WHAT I LOOK FOR WHEN I READ, AND ULTImately what I project on a text is a critical method only because I believe there is no critical method except yourself. As women and men of letters, we ought to share in a vision in which the highest literature becomes our way of life. Whitman had no poetic method except his self, though I should say "selves," as there are three of them: "myself, Walt Whitman, an American, one of the roughs," and also "the real Me" or "Me myself," and the nearly unknowable "my Soul." His vision was what he called *Democratic Vistas,* and here I again need another personal mentor, Kenneth Burke, who suggested that Whitmanian vistas are future possibilities, results to come through the spiritualization of our nation's wealth. Imagine Whitman contemplating Mitt Romney's spiritualization of *his*

wealth and you can be thankful that our national poet, who suffered the first Gilded Age, is not here to experience the even more vicious second one.

That excursus merely brings the rough Walt up to date, though I cannot perform the conjuring channels to Whitman invoked by Fernando Pessoa and Federico García Lorca, by D. H. Lawrence and Hart Crane, by Wallace Stevens and Jorge Luis Borges.

The point of view for my life's work as a literary critic, such as it was and is, founds itself upon the Whitmanian vista and on the Falstaffian vitalism, both of them beyond me yet beckoning on as the Blessing, which means "more life into a time without boundaries." Emerson remarked: "What we are, that only can we see." At eighty-four, I see by glimpses yet behold feelingly. Only authentic painters, writers, composers, sculptors improve their beholdings into knowledge. Dr. Johnson thought genuine critics also could improve their opinions into knowledge. Much depends, in our belatedness, upon persuasively redefining "opinion." The critics in Anglo-American tradition who still find me include Johnson, William Hazlitt, Ruskin, Emerson, Pater, Wilde, and, in my own lifetime, William Empson and Kenneth Burke. That is only eight and omits Coleridge and Matthew Arnold, both of whom make me impatient, and T. S. Eliot, whom as critic I abominate. Charles Augustin Sainte-Beuve, Valéry, and, above all, Nietzsche go on informing me among the Continentals. Nietzsche's poetics of pain, as I would call it, fuses memory and knowledge, since, however resourceful and willing, we cannot will backward.

I cannot, with Nietzsche and with Pater, believe that life can only be appreciated as an aesthetic phenomenon. But I wish to believe that, and perhaps Judaic tradition blocks me from it. Wisdom needs to be added to aesthetic splendor and cognitive power as the three stigmata or criteria of knowledge or value. But where except in Shakespeare are all three to be discovered consistently? More of Nietzsche than even he realized is quarried out of the quests and questionings of Prince Hamlet.

And yet Nietzsche as educator is beyond just another Dionysian enlightener; sublimely, he is a genealogist of the imagination, curiously similar to Kierkegaard as a master of repetition in a dialectical mode. This wish to transfigure the trauma of forgetting by repetition is contaminated by redemption theology in Kierkegaard but not in Nietzsche, who urged us, Just one step more and forgive yourself everything, so that the drama of fall and redemption will be enacted in your own soul.

Nietzsche is not the fountain of our will; Emerson is. The sage of Concord taught that voice, not text, is America's mode of self-knowing. Walt Whitman, tallying his sonorous image of voice, fulfills Emerson, as Nietzsche's Zarathustra could not. Walt is for me the American difference, which I keep attempting to improve into knowledge.

Leaves of Grass | 1855

——

SONG OF MYSELF

WHAT WE CALL SONG OF MYSELF, IN THE FORM FIRST READ AND ACCLAIMED by Emerson, was a single text of thirteen hundred and sixty-two lines, without section divisions. A reader now needs to revive Emerson's shock of recognition when beholding the opening lines:

> I Celebrate myself,
> And what I assume you shall assume,
> For every atom belonging to me as good belongs to you.
>
> I loafe and invite my soul,
> I lean and loafe at my ease . . . observing a spear of
>   summer grass.

As an epic opening, this was unique. To "celebrate" is to launch a festivity, proclaim a hero, rejoice in a Eucharist, display praise. All this for "myself"? To "assume" is to take upon oneself, as in a rule, to put on a garment, to feign, to avoid self-justification, above all to receive another person into association. You—the reader, whoever she is—is so received by Walt Whitman. His credentials are a Lucretian-Epicurean universality, shared atoms, and his insouciance: a loafer, a leaner, at ease, observing what is most worth beholding, a spear of summer grass.

A "loafer" was even more a term of reproach in 1855 than it is now in 2015. Walt is idle and unitary, at leisure to address us. His prophetic word is anti-apocalyptic: "But I do not talk of the beginning or the end." Inception is perpetual; perfection is now and in America.

Authority in classical terms meant augmenting the foundations. Walt's authority, his call, is different. It is daemonic and emanates from his "Me myself," which he defines by indirection:

> Apart from the pulling and hauling stands what I am,
> Stands amused, complacent, compassionating, idle, unitary,
> Looks down, is erect, bends an arm on an impalpable
>   certain rest,
> Looks with its side-curved head curious what will come
>   next,
> Both in and out of the game, and watching and wondering
>   at it.
>
> Backward I see in my own days where I sweated through fog
>   with linguists and contenders,
> I have no mockings or arguments . . . I witness and wait.
>
> I believe in you my soul . . . the other I am must not abase
>   itself to you,
> And you must not be abased to the other.
>
> Loafe with me on the grass . . . loose the stop from your
>   throat,
> Not words, not music or rhyme I want . . . not custom or
>   lecture, not even the best,
> Only the lull I like, the hum of your valvèd voice.

The "real Me" or "Me myself" is an androgyne, whereas the persona Walt is male and the soul female, her images being night, death, the mother, and the sea. An authentic difficulty for the reader arrives with the questions of abasement between the soul and "the other I am." To abase is to degrade in rank or to lessen in esteem. Why inevitably do the soul and the daemon, Whitman's genius, tend to degrade each other?

The revelation making possible the breakthrough that is *Leaves of Grass* 1855 was neither mystical nor psychosexual. It was the invention of the mask "Walt Whitman, an American, one of the roughs, a kosmos," who could not reconcile his soul and his true self and so took up the middle ground between them.

I recall conversations with Gershom Scholem in Jerusalem and New Haven, during which he discoursed upon his conviction that Whitman was "an intuitive Kabbalist." When I reminded the sage that Whitman knew nothing about Kabbalah, he observed the palpably Hermetic elements that present the poet as an Adam-God hybrid, like the Adam Kadmon of Kabbalah. As usual, Scholem was right: Whitman had derived, from reading George Sand, a rough notion of the Hermetic Corpus. The rest was the work of the daemon, who is excluded from the highly metaphoric embrace between Walt and his soul:

> I mind how we lay in June, such a transparent summer
> morning;
> You settled your head athwart my hips and gently turned
> over upon me,
> And parted the shirt from my bosom-bone, and plunged
> your tongue to my barestript heart,
> And reached till you felt my beard, and reached till you held
> my feet.

Literal-minded scholars can read this as though "my barestript heart" is the Whitmanian phallus. That is reductive and neglects what might be termed the inspired gymnosophistry that calls forth the epic's first grand epiphany, a testimony in the mode of the Quaker meetings the boy Whitman attended with his father, a follower of Elias Hicks. It seems to me a little inadequate that this Hicksite spiritual declaration be provoked by an exuberant act of fellatio:

> Swiftly arose and spread around me the peace and joy and
> knowledge that pass all the art and argument of the earth;
> And I know that the hand of God is the elderhand of my
> own,
> And I know that the spirit of God is the eldest brother of
> my own,
> And that all the men ever born are also my brothers . . . and
> the women my sisters and lovers,
> And that a kelson of the creation is love;
> And limitless are leaves stiff or drooping in the fields,

And brown ants in the little wells beneath them,
And mossy scabs of the wormfence, and heaped stones, and
    elder and mullen and pokeweed.

Chant this aloud to others and yourself, for it is one of the glories of
Whitman. The three final lines, extending his love to what most of us regard as the bottom of creation's scale, are unique to the greatest celebrant
of the American Sublime.

The stunning fantasia on the grass follows, but I turn to the title *Leaves
of Grass* before proceeding to that poetic triumph, since Whitman's title is in
itself a difficult poem. Kenneth Burke and John Hollander taught me how to
read Whitman's perpetual title. Burke found it too rich for any single conclusion, while Hollander pondered the rich ambiguities of the title's "of."
Wallace Stevens attempted to subsume Shelley and Whitman in his poem
The Rock, in what he named "the fiction of the leaves." That trope passes
from Homer and Pindar through Virgil and Dante on to Edmund Spenser,
Milton, and Shelley, before Whitman fuses it with Second Isaiah 40:6–8:

The voice said, Cry. And he said, What shall I cry? All flesh *is*
    grass, and all the goodliness thereof *is* as the flower of the
    field:
The grass withereth, the flower fadeth: because the spirit of
    the Lord bloweth upon it: surely the people *is* grass.
The grass withereth, the flower fadeth: but the word of our
    God shall stand for ever.

In March 1842, Whitman attended Emerson's lecture on "Nature and
the Powers of the Poet" in New York City and heard the sage remark: "All
things are symbols. We say of man that he is grass." Leaves are pages in a
book and, due to Shelley's *Ode to the West Wind,* also words quickening
a new birth.

One offers multiple conjectures as to what the trope "leaves of grass"
might be made to mean. In the Homeric fiction of the leaves, each stands
for a single mortal life falling away. Isaiah's metaphor is transposed by
Whitman, who invests more heavily in grass-as-flesh than in leaf–as–
mortal span. His title is not *Grass of Leaves,* because that "of" means
both "concerning" and "consisting of."

We tend to call Whitman's descriptive lists "catalogs"; Emerson jokingly called them "inventories." Rhetorically, they are synecdoches: part-for-whole substitutions that tend to become antithetical completions, Whitman's most characteristic trope. Walt puts the world together again with images of voice, his "tallies":

> The blab of the pave . . . the tires of carts and sluff of
>   bootsoles and talk of the promenaders,
> The heavy omnibus, the driver with his interrogating
>   thumb, the clank of the shod horses on the granite floor,
> The carnival of sleighs, the clinking and shouted jokes and
>   pelts of snowballs;
> The hurrahs for popular favorites . . . the fury of roused
>   mobs,
> The flap of the curtained litter—the sick man inside, borne
>   to the hospital,
> The meeting of enemies, the sudden oath, the blows and
>   fall,
> The excited crowd—the policeman with his star quickly
>   working his passage to the centre of the crowd;
> The impassive stones that receive and return so many
>   echoes,
> The souls moving along . . . are they invisible while the least
>   atom of the stones is visible?
> What groans of overfed or half-starved who fall on the flags
>   sunstruck or in fits,
> What exclamations of women taken suddenly, who hurry
>   home and give birth to babes,
> What living and buried speech is always vibrating here . . .
>   what howls restrained by decorum,
> Arrests of criminals, slights, adulterous offers made,
>   acceptances, rejections with convex lips,
> I mind them or the resonance of them . . . I come again and
>   again.

Wonderful as this is, how does he accomplish it? Partly by the dominance of the auditory over the visual: blab, sluff of bootsoles, talk, clank, shouted jokes, hurrahs, mob fury, flap of litter, sudden oath, echoes, groans, exclamations, vibrating speech, howls, erotic offers made, accepted and rejected, resonances of a metropolitan litany. Whitman tallies voices and not urban visions, unless and until he can render them a little hard to see.

Vision returns in the extraordinary lunar parable of twenty-eight young men swimming together while they are spied on by a twenty-eight-year-old virginal woman:

> Twenty-eight young men bathe by the shore,
> Twenty-eight young men, and all so friendly,
> Twenty-eight years of womanly life, and all so lonesome.
>
> She owns the fine house by the rise of the bank,
> She hides handsome and richly drest aft the blinds of the
>   window.
>
> Which of the young men does she like the best?
> Ah the homeliest of them is beautiful to her.
>
> Where are you off to, lady? for I see you,
> You splash in the water there, yet stay stock still in
>   your room.
>
> Dancing and laughing along the beach came the twenty-ninth
>   bather,
> The rest did not see her, but she saw them and loved them.
>
> The beards of the young men glistened with wet, it ran from
>   their long hair,
> Little streams passed all over their bodies.
>
> An unseen hand also passed over their bodies,
> It descended tremblingly from their temples and ribs.
>
> The young men float on their backs, their white bellies swell to
>   the sun . . . they do not ask who seizes fast to them,

> They do not know who puffs and declines with pendant and
>   bending arch,
> They do not think whom they souse with spray.

In one sense, "she" is the moon, yet that only starts an appreciation of this splendor. I am puzzled here again by the redundancies of a current school of homoerotic scholars, who urge a reading in which the young woman fades away to be replaced by the poetic speaker himself, rendering matters politically correct. Nothing in the text justifies the argument of the generally astute Michael Moon: "The nature of the exchange that takes place midway in the passage might be interpreted as the speaker's appropriation of the woman's position for his own. Leaving her standing at her window, he passes from one of its sides to the other on the energy of her desire." Why, then, is she in the poem as Whitman composed it? What happens to the wonderful pathos of her unacted desires, a quality in which Whitman here resembles the *Mariana* lyric of Tennyson? Remove the young woman as twenty-ninth bather and you mar the poem.

Like all great poets, Whitman is omnisexual in most of his strongest work. In this aspect he needs to be read as we read Shakespeare's sonnets, except that he lacked both the Fair Youth and the Dark Lady. Keep in mind always his declarations that he is "maternal as well as paternal, a child as well as a man" and "I am the poet of the woman the same as the man." I again recall provoking resentment by dubbing the American bard "a male lesbian," much as Shakespeare was when writing the sonnets.

Two hundred and forty lines farther on and Walt himself becomes one with the twenty-ninth bather:

> You sea! I resign myself to you also . . . I guess what you mean,
> I behold from the beach your crooked inviting fingers,
> I believe you refuse to go back without feeling of me;
> We must have a turn together . . . I undress . . . hurry me
>   out of sight of the land,
> Cushion me soft . . . rock me in billowy drowse,
> Dash me with amorous wet . . . I can repay you.
>
> Sea of stretched ground-swells!
> Sea breathing broad and convulsive breaths!

> Sea of the brine of life! Sea of unshovelled and always-ready
>   graves!
> Howler and scooper of storms! Capricious and dainty sea!
> I am integral with you . . . I too am of one phase and of all
>   phases.

He is the moonlike woman of the nonexistent twenty-ninth phase and also the twenty-eight male bathers of the lunar cycle. Wallace Stevens parodies Walt in *Notes Toward a Supreme Fiction* as the Canon Aspirin's sister, who attires her twenty-eight children—the days. As always in Stevens, the Whitman parody is uneasily wrought, since the poet of *Notes* identified the evening sun with his intimidating precursor. Whitman's principal power fascinated Stevens and Hart Crane, as it should us, whenever the voice that is great within Walt rises up:

> Through me many long dumb voices,
> Voices of the interminable generations of slaves,
> Voices of prostitutes and of deformed persons,
> Voices of the diseased and despairing, and of thieves and
>   dwarfs,
> Voices of cycles of preparation and accretion,
> And of the threads that connect the stars—and of wombs,
>   and of the fatherstuff,
> And of the rights of them the others are down upon,
> Of the trivial and flat and foolish and despised,
> Of fog in the air and beetles rolling balls of dung.
>
> Through me forbidden voices,
> Voices of sexes and lusts . . . voices veiled, and I remove
>   the veil,
> Voices indecent by me clarified and transfigured.

These lines hammer me like those utterances of Macbeth's that break into him from some higher realm of eloquence. What shall we make of the uncanny voices in Whitman?

For Walt, they were a sublimity larger than location. "It is not every day," Stevens remarked, "that the world arranges itself into a poem."

Whitman wanted that daily transformation, even though he could not bring it about. No man, no woman, can live in a continuous secular epiphany, though it is the enabling fiction that made possible *Song of Myself.*

At moments, Whitman is so strong that we do not desire to argue the fiction:

> The heaved challenge from the east that moment over my head,
> The mocking taunt, See then whether you shall be master!
>
> Dazzling and tremendous how quick the sunrise would
>   kill me,
> If I could not now and always send sunrise out of me.
>
> We also ascend dazzling and tremendous as the sun,
> We found our own my soul in the calm and cool of the
>   daybreak.
>
> My voice goes after what my eyes cannot reach,
> With the twirl of my tongue I encompass worlds and volumes
>   of worlds.

This is the American Sublime properly in place, centering upon the image of voices, the tally, "the twirl of my tongue" that can encompass volumes of worlds, "keeping tally with the meaning of all things."

The cost of this confirmation is steep and results in two severe crises, the first autoerotic:

> Mine is no callous shell,
> I have instant conductors all over me whether I pass or stop,
> They seize every object and lead it harmlessly through me.
>
> I merely stir, press, feel with my fingers, and am happy,
> To touch my person to someone else's is about as much as I
>   can stand.
>
> Is this then a touch? . . . quivering me to a new identity,
> Flames and ether making a rush for my veins,

Treacherous tip of me reaching and crowding to help them,
My flesh and blood playing out lightning, to strike what is
    hardly different from myself,
On all sides prurient provokers stiffening my limbs,
Straining the udder of my heart for its withheld drip,
Behaving licentious toward me, taking no denial,
Depriving me of my best as for a purpose,
Unbuttoning my clothes and holding me by the bare waist,
Deluding my confusion with the calm of the sunlight and
    pasture fields,
Immodestly sliding the fellow-senses away,
They bribed to swap off with touch, and go and graze at the
    edges of me,
No consideration, no regard for my draining strength or my
    anger,
Fetching the rest of the herd around to enjoy them awhile,
Then all uniting to stand on a headland and worry me.

The sentries desert every other part of me,
They have left me helpless to a red marauder,
They all come to the headland to witness and assist
    against me.

I am given up by traitors;
I talk wildly . . . I have lost my wits . . . I and nobody else
    am the greatest traitor,
I went myself first to the headland . . . my own hands carried
    me there.

Whitman's notebooks indicate that the starting point for his emergence
as the persona Walt Whitman was "I went myself first to the headland."
This extravagance, or wandering beyond limits, places you upon a prom-
ontory from which you cannot scramble back unaided.

Overtly autoerotic and at moments grotesque, the poetic power of this
obscures the unresolved conflict between Whitman's mask or persona—
the rough "Myself" of what became the poem's title—and his daemon or
"real Me," an interior paramour or muse. Like its major descendants—

T. S. Eliot's *The Waste Land*, Hart Crane's *The Bridge*, Wallace Stevens's *Notes Toward a Supreme Fiction*, William Carlos Williams's *Paterson*, Conrad Aiken's *The Kid*, A. R. Ammons's *Sphere*, John Ashbery's *A Wave*—*Song of Myself* is an internalized quest-romance, whose antecedents include the long English Romantic tradition of falling in love with the poet's failure. That tradition goes from Wordsworth's *The Excursion* and Coleridge's nightmare *Rime of the Ancient Mariner* on through Shelley's *Alastor* and Keats's *Endymion* to Browning's ruined questers and the daemonic defeats of poets by their antithetical muse in Yeats.

The professed program of *Song of Myself* is American democracy, just as Hart Crane's *The Bridge* wants to affirm American imaginative potential against *The Waste Land*. Yet the actual drama of Whitman's and Crane's brief epics has little relevance to myths of America. Walt's authentic drive is self-integration, which he discovers he can never achieve, while Hart's search is for a bridal fulfillment that could never accommodate his uncompromising nature. Both great poets lived and died without ever finding an answering voice. Whitman's eros, like his verbs, remained intransitive; Crane created a new rhetoric of negations and made himself the most difficult American poet of true eminence down to our own day, in a different sense from Whitman, rhetorical rather than misleadingly direct.

There is no question here of self-deception: Both *Song of Myself* and *The Bridge* know and intimate the irreconcilable rift betwixt daemon and project. Whitman is not tormented by this, as he had a blessed calm in his nature. Crane, a Pilgrim of the Absolute, like Shelley and Byron, knows only what Melville had Ishmael call "the tornadoed Atlantic of my being."

Though *Song of Myself* will end in earliness and strength, this freedom results from voluntary disintegration: "I effuse my flesh in eddies, and drift it in lacy jags." *The Bridge*'s much more violent coming/spent is Crane's Orphic *sparagmos*, or rending apart by the Dionysian women.

Whitman's deeper crisis in *Song of Myself* results from an anxiety of lost identity:

> I become any presence or truth of humanity here,
> And see myself in prison shaped like another man,
> And feel the dull unintermitted pain.

For me the keepers of convicts shoulder their carbines and
    keep watch,
It is I let out in the morning and barred at night.

Not a mutineer walks handcuffed to the jail, but I am
    handcuffed to him and walk by his side,
I am less the jolly one there, and more the silent one with
    sweat on my twitching lips.

Not a youngster is taken for larceny, but I go up too and am
    tried and sentenced.

Not a cholera patient lies at the last gasp, but I also lie at the
    last gasp,
My face is ash-colored, my sinews gnarl . . . away from me
    people retreat.

Askers embody themselves in me, and I am embodied in them,
I project my hat and sit shamefaced and beg.

I rise extatic through all, and sweep with the true gravitation,
The whirling and whirling is elemental within me.

Somehow I have been stunned. Stand back!
Give me a little time beyond my cuffed head and slumbers
    and dreams and gaping,
I discover myself on a verge of the usual mistake.

That I could forget the mockers and insults!
That I could forget the trickling tears and the blows of the
    bludgeons and hammers!
That I could look with a separate look on my own
    crucifixion and bloody crowning!

I remember . . . I resume the overstaid fraction,
The grave of rock multiplies what has been confided to
    it . . . or to any graves,

The corpses rise . . . the gashes heal . . . the fastenings
  roll away.

Quaker by upbringing, Whitman could never bear seeing himself as an
asker or beggar. Overextended in this great passage, he becomes a crucified redeemer—Walt, not Jesus—and then is resurrected. His new life will
sustain him for the rest of the poem.

So rich are the next three hundred lines that I must keep myself to the
observation that Whitman justifies his resurrected vaunt: "I troop forth
replenished with supreme power." That plenty of the world and of the self
achieves a magnificence in *Song of Myself*'s closing passage:

The past and present wilt . . . I have filled them and emptied
  them,
And proceed to fill my next fold of the future.

Listener up there! Here you . . . what have you to confide to me?
Look in my face while I snuff the sidle of evening,
Talk honestly, for no one else hears you, and I stay only a
  minute longer.

Do I contradict myself?
Very well then . . . I contradict myself;
I am large . . . I contain multitudes.

I concentrate toward them that are nigh . . . I wait on the
  door-slab.

Who has done his day's work and will soonest be through with
  his supper?
Who wishes to walk with me?

Will you speak before I am gone? Will you prove already too
  late?

The spotted hawk swoops by and accuses me . . . he complains
  of my gab and my loitering.

I too am not a bit tamed . . . I too am untranslatable,
I sound my barbaric yawp over the roofs of the world.

The last scud of day holds back for me,
It flings my likeness after the rest and true as any on the
    shadowed wilds,
It coaxes me to the vapor and the dusk.

I depart as air . . . I shake my white locks at the runaway sun,
I effuse my flesh in eddies, and drift it in lacy jags.

I bequeath myself to the dirt to grow from the grass I love,
If you want me again look for me under your bootsoles.

You will hardly know who I am or what I mean,
But I shall be good health to you nevertheless,
And filter and fibre your blood.

Failing to fetch me at first keep encouraged,
Missing me one place search another,
I stop some where waiting for you.

Poets like Stevens and Crane, readers like myself, are invited to a formidable agon by the American bard at his most urgent: "Will you speak before I am gone? Will you prove already too late?" Containing multitudes yet self-contained, Walt touches apotheosis as a redeemer, inviting us to accompany him on the road to Emmaus, anticipating *The Waste Land*'s neo-Christian *What the Thunder Said*.

The promise of good health rings with special force for me, going from one illness or accident to another at eighty-four. Yet any among us, young or old, hale or faltering, respond to Walt Whitman's generosity:

I stop some where waiting for you.

THE SLEEPERS

AFTER *SONG OF MYSELF*, THE GREAT POEM OF THE 1855 *LEAVES OF GRASS*
is *The Sleepers,* which needs to be read in that text because Whitman mutilated it in revision. No poem since Wordsworth is more original than
Song of Myself, unless it be *The Sleepers,* a unique alternation of phantasmagoria and vivid naturalism.

Several times in the late 1970s, Kenneth Burke and I gave dialogue-
lectures, quite unrehearsed, before audiences. Kenneth would ask: "What
was the poet trying to do for himself or herself *as a person* by composing
this particular poem?" I modified this to: "*as a poet.*"

Song of Myself marvelously presents the fictive "Walt Whitman" self and
the evasive "real Me" or "Me myself," a dialectic developed further in *Out of
the Cradle Endlessly Rocking* and *As I Ebb'd with the Ocean of Life.* In *The
Sleepers,* Whitman's purpose as a poet is to achieve a sense of his soul, which
is always menaced by night and the sea and so can lose any clear identity. In a
great insight, the poet sleeps and dreams that a new form can merge death
and the mother with night and the sea. Only in the dream can Walt discover
his otherwise unknowable soul. As an Epicurean materialist, Whitman quests
for the unknown *whatness* of nature while knowing it cannot be found.

"The soul knows only the soul" is Emerson's aphorism. In *The Sleepers,* there is only one rather flat passage that specifically mentions the soul
(lines 166–173), but the entire poem redefines the soul as the shifting
boundary between opposing forces—death and the mother confronting
night and the sea, until the mother harvests it all. At its strongest, *The
Sleepers* stands with the best of Whitman, yet the poem is oddly uneven.
After a powerful opening in which the poet wanders through the night, the
poem conceals itself as though it desires to be coaxed out. Still, the impact
of the opening would be difficult to match:

> I wander all night in my vision,
> Stepping with light feet . . . swiftly and noiselessly stepping
>   and stopping,
> Bending with open eyes over the shut eyes of sleepers;
> Wandering and confused . . . lost to myself . . . ill-
>   assorted . . . contradictory,
> Pausing and gazing and bending and stopping.

How solemn they look there, stretched and still;
How quiet they breathe, the little children in their cradles.

The wretched features of ennuyees, the white features of
    corpses, the livid faces of drunkards, the sick-gray faces of
    onanists,
The gashed bodies on battlefields, the insane in their strong-
    doored rooms, the sacred idiots,
The newborn emerging from gates and the dying emerging
    from gates,
The night pervades them and enfolds them.

The married couple sleep calmly in their bed, he with his palm
    on the hip of his wife, and she with her palm on the hip of
    the husband,
The sisters sleep lovingly side by side in their bed,
The men sleep lovingly side by side in theirs,
And the mother sleeps with her little child carefully
    wrapped.

The blind sleep, and the deaf and dumb sleep,
The prisoner sleeps well in the prison . . . the runaway son
    sleeps,
The murderer that is to be hung the next day . . . how does
    he sleep?
And the murdered person . . . how does he sleep?

The female that loves unrequited sleeps,
And the male that loves unrequited sleeps;
The head of the moneymaker that plotted all day sleeps,
And the enraged and treacherous dispositions sleep.

I stand with drooping eyes by the worst-suffering and
    restless,
I pass my hands soothingly to and fro a few inches from
    them;
The restless sink in their beds . . . they fitfully sleep.

The earth recedes from me into the night,
I saw that it was beautiful . . . and I see that what is not the
    earth is beautiful.

I go from bedside to bedside . . . I sleep close with the other
    sleepers, each in turn;
I dream in my dream all the dreams of the other dreamers,
And I become the other dreamers.

Whitman did not read William Blake until 1876, when Anne Gilchrist, the widow of Blake's first biographer, came to America. Of all Whitman's poems, *The Sleepers* most resembles Blake in its assured visionary confidence and the sweep of its phantasmagoria. The largest difference between the poets is in Whitman's personal shamanism, since he moves through the night as a healer. Walt's major trope is synecdoche: "And I become the other dreamers." This allows him a delightful sequel; he is not *at* a dance but *is* the dance of being itself:

I am a dance . . . Play up there! the fit is whirling me fast.

I am the everlaughing . . . it is new moon and twilight,
I see the hiding of douceurs . . . I see nimble ghosts
    whichever way I look,
Cache and cache again deep in the ground and sea, and
    where it is neither ground or sea.

Well do they do their jobs, those journeymen divine,
Only from me can they hide nothing and would not if they
    could;
I reckon I am their boss, and they make me a pet besides,
And surround me, and lead me and run ahead when
    I walk,
And lift their cunning covers and signify me with stretched
    arms, and resume the way;
Onward we move, a gay gang of blackguards with mirth-
    shouting music and wild-flapping pennants of joy.

Who or what are those "nimble ghosts"? Divine journeymen like the sprites bossed by Ariel in *The Tempest*, they are elemental beings or daemons whom Whitman employs for a public festival or triumph. An extraordinary passage invoking the Song of Songs then becomes one of Whitman's glories:

> I am she who adorned herself and folded her hair
>   expectantly,
> My truant lover has come and it is dark.
>
> Double yourself and receive me darkness,
> Receive me and my lover too . . . he will not let me go
>   without him.
>
> I roll myself upon you as upon a bed . . . I resign myself to the
>   dusk.
>
> He whom I call answers me and takes the place of
>   my lover,
> He rises with me silently from the bed.
>
> Darkness you are gentler than my lover . . . his flesh was
>   sweaty and panting,
> I feel the hot moisture yet that he left me.
>
> My hands are spread forth . . . I pass them in all directions,
> I would sound up the shadowy shore to which you are
>   journeying.
>
> Be careful, darkness . . . already, what was it touched me?
> I thought my lover had gone . . . else darkness and he are
>   one,
> I hear the heart-beat . . . I follow . . . I fade away.

I set aside the ideologues who read this somehow as being a homoerotic encounter. Whitman's woman, like the Song of Solomon's, waits in a dark secret place for a truant lover, yields to him, and then accepts a substitute for him. Her receptivity preludes a passage Whitman omitted after 1855:

> O hotcheeked and blushing! O foolish hectic!
> O for pity's sake, no one must see me now! . . . my clothes
>   were stolen while I was abed,
> Now I am thrust forth, where shall I run?
> Pier that I saw dimly last night when I looked from the windows,
> Pier out from the main, let me catch myself with you and
>   stay . . . I will not chafe you,
> I feel ashamed to go naked about the world,
> And am curious to know where my feet stand . . . and what
>   is this flooding me, childhood or manhood . . . and the
>   hunger that crosses the bridge between.

> The cloth laps a first sweet eating and drinking,
> Laps life-swelling yolks . . . laps ear of rose-corn, milky and
>   just ripened:
> The white teeth stay, and the boss-tooth advances in
>   darkness,
> And liquor is spilled on lips and bosoms by touching glasses,
>   and the best liquor afterward.

Why remove this eloquent vision of sexual annunciation? The compounding of the phallic "boss-tooth" with the ancient banquet in which lust and hunger alike are gratified is too poetically zestful to have been abandoned without aesthetic loss. Whitman in *The Sleepers* arouses more anxieties than he could assuage:

> I see a beautiful gigantic swimmer swimming naked through
>   the eddies of the sea,
> His brown hair lies close and even to his head . . . he strikes
>   out with courageous arms . . . he urges himself with
>   his legs.
> I see his white body . . . I see his undaunted eyes;
> I hate the swift-running eddies that would dash him head-
>   foremost on the rocks.

What are you doing you ruffianly red-trickled waves?
Will you kill the courageous giant? Will you kill him in the
    prime of his middle age?

Steady and long he struggles;
He is baffled and banged and bruised . . . he holds out while
    his strength holds out,
The slapping eddies are spotted with his blood . . . they bear
    him away . . . they roll him and swing him and turn him:
His beautiful body is borne in the circling eddies . . . it is
    continually bruised on rocks,
Swiftly and out of sight is borne the brave corpse.

The courageous giant in his middle prime has to be the thirty-six-year-old poet, fearing destruction by the mothering sea. Shipwreck follows and then yields to an image of George Washington lamenting the men he lost at his Brooklyn debacle, a grief not redressed by his tavern farewell to his officers.

At the halfway point of *The Sleepers* the poem intensifies, a heightening I might have thought unlikely. But Walt kindles his fourfold trope of death, night, the mother, and the sea.

His mother begins the second half in a poignant episode of lesbian longing:

A red squaw came one breakfasttime to the old homestead,
On her back she carried a bundle of rushes for rushbottoming
    chairs;
Her hair straight shiny coarse black and profuse
    halfenveloped her face,
Her step was free and elastic . . . her voice sounded
    exquisitely as she spoke.

My mother looked in delight and amazement at the stranger,
She looked at the beauty of her tallborne face and full and
    pliant limbs,
The more she looked upon her she loved her,
Never before had she seen such wonderful beauty and
    purity;

She made her sit on a bench by the jamb of the fireplace . . .
    she cooked food for her,
She had no work to give her but she gave her remembrance
    and fondness.

The red squaw staid all the forenoon, and toward the middle
    of the afternoon she went away;
O my mother was loth to have her go away,
All the week she thought of her . . . she watched for her
    many a month,
She remembered her many a winter and many a summer,
But the red squaw never came nor was heard of there
    again.

Whitman's sexual complexity transcends any homoerotic reduction: His intransitive eros is diffuse and universal. So is his ambivalent vision of the national stigma of black slavery. A soft Abolitionist, he yet harbored a dread of black vengeance, pungently expressed in the other passage removed from *The Sleepers* after 1855:

Now Lucifer was not dead . . . or if he was I am his sorrowful
    terrible heir;
I have been wronged . . . I am oppressed . . . I hate him that
    oppresses me,
I will either destroy him, or he shall release me.

Damn him! how he does defile me,
How he informs against my brother and sister and takes pay
    for their blood,
How he laughs when I look down the bend after the
    steamboat that carries away my woman.

Now the vast dusk bulk that is the whale's bulk . . . it seems
    mine,
Warily, sportsman! though I lie so sleepy and sluggish, my tap
    is death.

Whitman had read no Melville, so this was independent of *Moby-Dick* or of the later tale "Benito Cereno." Memorable and rightly reflecting the poet's disturbance, why was it deleted?

This Leviathan black Lucifer is more an ontotheological matter than a sociopolitical concern. The speaker's menacing tap of death is very different from the mothering death *The Sleepers* will offer at its close. It is a nightmare; what does it reveal about Whitman, poet and man?

The clearest clue is the total change in *The Sleepers* after this excised outburst. For seventy lines the poem flows on with gathering serenity and certitude until the shamanistic Walt is wholly restored. Without having encountered Blake, Whitman beholds a Blakean phantasmagoria:

> The sleepers are very beautiful as they lie unclothed,
> They flow hand in hand over the whole earth from east to
>   west as they lie unclothed;
> The Asiatic and African are hand in hand . . . the European
>   and American are hand in hand;
> Learned and unlearned are hand in hand . . . and male and
>   female are hand in hand;
> The bare arm of the girl crosses the bare breast of her
>   lover . . . they press close without lust . . . his lips press
>   her neck,
> The father holds his grown or ungrown son in his arms with
>   measureless love . . . and the son holds the father in his
>   arms with measureless love,
> The white hair of the mother shines on the white wrist of
>   the daughter,
> The breath of the boy goes with the breath of the man . . .
>   friend is inarmed by friend,
> The scholar kisses the teacher and the teacher kisses the
>   scholar . . . the wronged is made right,
> The call of the slave is one with the master's call . . . and the
>   master salutes the slave,
> The felon steps forth from the prison . . . the insane
>   becomes sane . . . the suffering of sick persons is
>   relieved,

> The sweatings and fevers stop . . . the throat that was
>   unsound is sound . . . the lungs of the consumptive are
>   resumed . . . the poor distressed head is free,
> The joints of the rheumatic move as smoothly as ever, and
>   smoother than ever,
> Stiflings and passages open . . . the paralyzed become
>   supple,
> The swelled and convulsed and congested awake to
>   themselves in condition,
> They pass the invigoration of the night and the chemistry of
>   the night and awake.

Coming after the Lucifer vision, one line here is disturbing: "The call of the slave is one with the master's call . . . and the master salutes the slave." One wonders what Whitman's first admirers—Emerson and Thoreau—found in that sentiment?

Always strongest at the start and end of his chants, Whitman surpasses himself as he concludes:

> I too pass from the night;
> I stay awhile away O night, but I return to you again and
>   love you;
> Why should I be afraid to trust myself to you?
> I am not afraid . . . I have been well brought forward
>   by you;
> I love the rich running day, but I do not desert her in whom I
>   lay so long;
> I know not how I came of you, and I know not where I go
>   with you . . . but I know I came well and shall go well.

> I will stop only a time with the night . . . and rise betimes.

> I will duly pass the day O my mother and duly return to you;
> Not you will yield forth the dawn again more surely than
>   you will yield forth me again,
> Not the womb yields the babe in its time more surely than I
>   shall be yielded from you in my time.

Night and the mother are allied with the universe of death, the sea. Wallace Stevens and Hart Crane at moments assert the power of the poet's mind over the universe of death, yet they learn to follow Whitman's subtle passivity in poems like *The Owl in the Sarcophagus* and the *Voyages* sequence. Walt sets the limit for his major inheritors even as he breaks the new road for them.

Leaves of Grass | 1856

CROSSING BROOKLYN FERRY

SKILLED READERS FROM THOREAU TO KENNETH BURKE HAVE REGARDED the "Sun-Down Poem" of *Leaves of Grass* 1856 as Whitman's masterpiece. By any standards *Crossing Brooklyn Ferry* is superb, though I recall telling Burke that, almost by definition, no other poem in American literature could match *Song of Myself.* As a brief epic, it stands with the vastness of *Moby-Dick* and the full-length *Huckleberry Finn, The Scarlet Letter,* or *The Portrait of a Lady.* For originality, nothing matches *Song of Myself,* yet *Crossing Brooklyn Ferry* comes close. Both pull the reader in close to the poet, face-to-face.

The biblical trope "face-to-face" reverberates because Moses sees Yahweh that directly and yet is not consumed. Jacob at Peniel wrestles with one of the Elohim (perhaps the angel of death) in a nocturnal confrontation, while Paul, in Corinthians 13, attempts transumption both of Moses and Israel (Jacob) in another vision of seeing face-to-face.

Walt, though, begins by seeing the setting sun face-to-face. His fellow passengers, homeward bound to Brooklyn, blend into one another and into passings of the future in a visionary New York City. The poems of my native city are remarkably varied, yet the most eminent are by Whitman and Hart Crane, who was cognizant that Brooklyn Ferry had been replaced by the Brooklyn Bridge. I grew up reading side by side the *In New York* poems of the marvelous Moyshe-Leyb Halpern—the Yiddish Baudelaire—and Hart Crane's overgoing of T. S. Eliot's London in *The Bridge.* Whitman came for me just after them and I learned gradually that, surfaces aside, he is an even more difficult poet than Hart Crane, not in texture but in initially deceiving the reader.

Crossing Brooklyn Ferry is an ineluctably subtle modality of the visible edging toward making the visible a little hard to see. Stevens chides Eliot for lacking that gift and follows Whitman in this praxis, just as Elizabeth Bishop is shadowed by the Hartford seer in her own fusions of the seeable and unseeable.

Whitman's relationship to the American Luminist painters has been much studied, yet I do not consider Walt a product of the sensibility of his own time. Genius or the daemon is rare and of its own age. Blake said it well: "Genius is always above its Age."

The daemon gave Whitman in 1856 the sudden gift of addressing the reader with an astonishing directness:

> Whoever you are, now I place my hand upon you, that you
>   be my poem,
> I whisper with my lips close to your ear,
> I have loved many women and men, but I love none better
>   than you.

Seeing face-to-face in the Bible is hazardous yet can be triumphant. *Crossing Brooklyn Ferry* redefines immortality more radically than *Lilacs* will. Walt interprets his readers-to-come by an advanced authorial reading through which they merge. We will be his survivors.

The fusion is made possible by a diffusion of Whitman akin to the close of *Song of Myself* but more intricate:

> The impalpable sustenance of me from all things at all hours
>   of the day,
> The simple, compact, well-join'd scheme, myself
>   disintegrated, every one disintegrated yet part of the
>   scheme,
> The similitudes of the past and those of the future,
> The glories strung like beads on my smallest sights and hear-
>   ings, on the walk in the street and the passage over the river,
> The current rushing so swiftly and swimming with me far
>   away,
> The others that are to follow me, the ties between me and them,
> The certainty of others, the life, love, sight, hearing of others.

To be disintegrated but part of the scheme leads on to the poem's central formulation:

> I too had been struck from the float forever held in solution,
> I too had received identity by my body,
> That I was, I knew was of my body, and what I should be I
>   knew I should be of my body.

The sublime borders the grotesque here: Reality is an Epicurean emulsion until the self identifies with its own body, which is its fate. A consistent metaphysical materialism allows for no freedom except the knowledge of the body's priority. Freud's "anatomy is destiny" comes to mind.

Section 6, one of Whitman's darkest, works through the consequences:

> It is not upon you alone the dark patches fall,
> The dark threw its patches down upon me also,
> The best I had done seem'd to me blank and suspicious,
> My great thoughts as I supposed them, were they not in
>   reality meagre?
> Nor is it you alone who know what it is to be evil,
> I am he who knew what it was to be evil,
> I too knitted the old knot of contrariety,
> Blabb'd, blush'd, resented, lied, stole, grudg'd,
> Had guile, anger, lust, hot wishes I dared not speak,
> Was wayward, vain, greedy, shallow, sly, cowardly,
>   malignant,
> The wolf, the snake, the hog, not wanting in me,
> The cheating look, the frivolous word, the adulterous wish,
>   not wanting,
> Refusals, hates, postponements, meanness, laziness, none of
>   these wanting,
> Was one with the rest, the days and haps of the rest,
> Was call'd by my nighest name by clear loud voices of young
>   men as they saw me approaching or passing,
> Felt their arms on my neck as I stood, or the negligent
>   leaning of their flesh against me as I sat,

Saw many I loved in the street or ferry-boat or public
   assembly, yet never told them a word,
Lived the same life with the rest, the same old laughing,
   gnawing, sleeping,
Play'd the part that still looks back on the actor or actress,
The same old role, the role that is what we make it, as great
   as we like,
Or as small as we like, or both great and small.

Whitman directly alludes to *King Lear*'s Edgar and may also be recalling Psalm 139. Disguised as Tom O'Bedlam, Edgar pretends to previous sins: "hog in sloth, fox in stealth, wolf in greediness, dog in madness, lion in prey."

The self-accusations of Whitman are darkly eloquent, but are they persuasive? Very subtly, Walt combines Edgar, who becomes a reluctant king at the end of Lear's tragedy, with King David of Psalm 139. Whitman condemns himself for playing false roles that then reprove him. In a rare moment of erotic truth-telling, he admits his failure to respond to the advances of young men. David in Psalm 139 proclaims that he is "fearfully and wonderfully made," thus tracing his identity to God and not—as does Walt—to the body. Yet each, unlike the desperate Edgar (who at last turns heroic avenger), fuses praise and trepidation in regard to the divine—Yahweh for King David; his own body for Walt Whitman.

Prophetic of William Carlos Williams, the poem's resolution comes through its exaltation of things seen: Whitman's "dumb, beautiful ministers." I myself believe that Wallace Stevens was even more deeply Whitmanian when he wrote to his friend Williams in *Notes Toward a Supreme Fiction*, ". . . the first idea is an imagined thing." But then Williams must have known that while Whitman—as befits our incarnate Supreme Fiction—raises appearances to the sublime, these manifestations are tallies:

Appearances, now or henceforth, indicate what you are,
You necessary film, continue to envelop the soul,
About my body for me, and your body for you, be hung our
   divinest aromas,
Thrive, cities—bring your freight, bring your shows, ample
   and sufficient rivers,

Expand, being than which none else is perhaps more
  spiritual,
Keep your places, objects than which none else is more
  lasting.

You have waited, you always wait, you dumb, beautiful
  ministers,
We receive you with free sense at last, and are insatiate
  henceforward,
Not you any more shall be able to foil us, or withhold
  yourselves from us,
We use you, and do not cast you aside—we plant you
  permanently within us,
We fathom you not—we love you—there is perfection in you
  also,
You furnish your parts toward eternity,
Great or small, you furnish your parts toward the soul.

The tonalities of Lucretius are far away from this, yet the doctrine is his Epicureanism. Atoms are our working reality, lasting and spiritual, presided over by gods who are indifferent to us. "Free sense" ensues from the swerve, or *clinamen,* a limited but still enabling fiction of the soul. "We fathom you not" is sound Epicureanism, as was "The what is unknowable."

For Whitman, the soul was unknowable except by the dark process described in *The Sleepers* after night and death are reconciled with the mother and the sea. *Crossing Brooklyn Ferry* is a luminous, uniquely original poem with an anxiety at its edges: "We use you, and do not cast you aside—we plant you permanently within us." Are use and perpetual planting reconcilable? What is used in reality will at last be used up. That seems to be why Whitman's poetry declined after 1865.

Ultimately, I read *Crossing Brooklyn Ferry* as a daemonic parable that gets beyond Whitman's apparent designs, whether we take those as an aesthetic transcendentalism or a metaphysical materialism similar to a conflict between Shelley's heart and his head. A daemonic intensity pervades Edgar playing the part of Tom O'Bedlam. Though he is heretofore a gentle and gullible young man, Edgar's betrayal by Edmund activates a genius for histrionic disguise and for a torrent of preternatural eloquence,

both in verse and in prose. Whitman, echoing Edgar, plays the part of
Walt Whitman, an American, one of the roughs, and is abashed by the
part when he looks back on himself.

The poem's final exaltation of appearances has some questionable aspects despite its rhythmic drive and considerable eloquence of diction.
Why are the Minute Particulars, as William Blake might have termed
them, or "appearances," able to indicate what you are? As "appearances,"
what is the warrant for their avoidance of dissimulation?

Whitman—who knows this—makes the strong reply: "About my body
for me, and your body for you, be hung our divinest aromas." In Walt's
psalm, the body is God, an affirmation that the poet who composed the
139th Psalm of David would have assigned to Yahweh's enemies.

The reader will recall Whitman's biblical obsession with perfumes
from the second section, *Song of Myself,* through to the aroma of the lilacs. G. K. Chesterton, before his conversion to Roman Catholicism,
fiercely defended the American bard from accusations of egotism by re-
marking that Whitman, like Jesus Christ, testified to the potential divinity
of humankind.

Leaves of Grass | *1860*

A WORD OUT OF THE SEA

WHAT NOW IS TITLED *OUT OF THE CRADLE ENDLESSLY ROCKING* WAS
in *Leaves of Grass* 1860 included as the even more powerful *A Word Out
of the Sea:*

> Out of the rocked cradle,
> Out of the mocking-bird's throat, the musical shuttle,
> Out of the boy's mother's womb, and from the nipples of
>   her breasts,
> Out of the Ninth Month midnight,
> Over the sterile sands, and the fields beyond, where the
>   child, leaving his bed, wandered alone, bareheaded,
>   barefoot,
> Down from the showered halo,

Up from the mystic play of shadows, twining and twisting
    as if they were alive,
Out from the patches of briers and blackberries,
From the memories of the bird that chanted to me,
From your memories, sad brother—from the fitful risings
    and fallings I heard,
From under that yellow half-moon, late-risen, and swollen
    as if with tears,
From those beginning notes of sickness and love, there in
    the transparent mist,
From the thousand responses of my heart, never to cease,
From the myriad thence-aroused words,
From the word stronger and more delicious than any,
From such, as now they start, the scene revisiting,
As a flock, twittering, rising, or overhead passing,
Borne hither—ere all eludes me, hurriedly,
A man—yet by these tears a little boy again,
Throwing myself on the sand, confronting the waves,
I, chanter of pains and joys, uniter of here and here-after,
Taking all hints to use them—but swiftly leaping beyond them,
A reminiscence sing.

In the British eighteenth-century poetry of sensibility, this vision of the outsetting bard is termed the "incarnation of the poetical character," a reference to the brilliant and frenzied William Collins poem *Ode on the Poetical Character.* Whitman takes his stand centered among Collins, Coleridge, Shelley, and Wallace Stevens in *Mrs. Alfred Uruguay.* Collins celebrates a "rich-hair'd youth of morn," who modulates into the youth of "flashing eyes" and "floating hair" of Coleridge's *Kubla Khan.* Shelley becomes that youth in his *Hymn to Intellectual Beauty.* Walt, the self-proclaimed "outsetting bard of love," ecstatic "with his hair the atmosphere dallying," the wind wafting his bare head, prophesies the youth in *Mrs. Alfred Uruguay,* "no chevalare and poorly dressed . . . arrogant of his streaming forces," who gallops down Mrs. Alfred Uruguay's mount of vision, passing her as she plods on, riding her patient, sad donkey. "I fear that elegance must struggle like the rest," she says, resplendent in velvet and proclaiming: "I have wiped away moonlight like mud."

Stevens, defensively wary of his prime American forerunner, cannot enter the elegy season without evoking Walt's words out of the sea. Powerful as is the press of Whitman, his effect is enhanced, upon Stevens and ourselves, by his secure place in the hidden tradition of one of Western poetry's salient themes: the power of the poet's mind over a universe of death. From Homer through Virgil, Dante, Spenser, Milton, Goethe, Wordsworth, and their European progeny, this strain of imaginative concern mutated into the American difference of Emerson, Whitman, Melville, Dickinson, Frost, Stevens, Eliot, Hart Crane. To what extent is, in Wordsworth's sense, the poet's mind lord and master, her outward sense the servant of its will? In Shakespeare, Hamlet's seven soliloquies give us the most capacious instance of an agon between creative mind and old night, abyss at once foremother and forefather. Origin—associated with the figure of the mother—for life's sake, Nietzsche urged, needed to be held apart from end by utilizing the image of the father. A grand irony in Nietzsche and Kierkegaard, as in *Hamlet* before them, this whimsical hope drowns with Ahab and the *Pequod*.

For Stevens, this immersion was the enterprise of *The Idea of Order at Key West*, a Whitmanian meditation upon transcending the daemon of the sea. The girl walking the water's edge, singing her own poem as she strides, is the poet's daemon defying and transcending the genius of the sea. Forging her song word by word, she superbly asserts power of mind: "For she was the maker." At poem's end, Stevens ironically reproves a Gallic anti-Romantic critical contemporary, a stand-in for Eliot or Allen Tate:

> Ramon Fernandez, tell me, if you know,
> Why, when the singing ended and we turned
> Toward the town, tell why the glassy lights,
> The lights in the fishing boats at anchor there,
> As the night descended, tilting in the air,
> Mastered the night and portioned out the sea,
> Fixing emblazoned zones and fiery poles,
> Arranging, deepening, enchanting night.
>
> Oh! Blessed rage for order, pale Ramon,
> The maker's rage to order words of the sea,
> Words of the fragrant portals, dimly-starred,

And of ourselves and of our origins,
In ghostlier demarcations, keener sounds.

Fernandez cannot know, because the High Romantic illumination masters night and the sea, though not death and the mother. Ramon's is a wounded rage *for* order; Stevens's—like Whitman's and Keats's—is the poet's rage *to* order by boundaries rendered less confining, cognitive music yet keener: Walt's word out of the sea, Keats's charmed casements, songs of ourselves, returns to origins still hidden in the American Sublime.

Here is Stevens on the dangerous Walt, writing in *Nocturne* in 1955:

> I suppose that you think of Whitman as one who lived in Brooklyn. But that was a totally different Brooklyn from the Brooklyn of today. I always think of him as one who lived in Camden and rode around Philadelphia on open street cars. If he was up front he would be lounging with one foot on the running-board. If he was in back he would have both feet on the rail.

The lounging tramp-poet, man on the dump, was hardly an ideal for Stevens, yet I quote again the most exalted passage the Hartford seer composed:

> I
>
> In the far South the sun of autumn is passing
> Like Walt Whitman walking along a ruddy shore.
> He is singing and chanting the things that are part of him,
> The worlds that were and will be, death and day.
> Nothing is final, he chants. No man shall see the end.
> His beard is of fire and his staff is a leaping flame.
>
> II
>
> Sigh for me, night-wind, in the noisy leaves of the oak.
> I am tired. Sleep for me, heaven over the hill.
> Shout for me, loudly and loudly, joyful sun, when you rise.

Section II is purer Whitman than even D. H. Lawrence ventured in the wonderful *Whales Weep Not!* Lawrence, son of Nottingham, is truly the child of Whitman and Melville, instigators of his heroic vitalism.

But let us return to the first strophe of *A Word Out of the Sea*. Readers have noted how brilliantly Whitman sustains his opening sentence for twenty-three lines. Is this a rhythm of gradual awakening or something very different, delaying recall so as to elude consciousness of mortality: "the word stronger and more delicious than any"? The bereft male mockingbird, the poet's "dusky daemon" or true self, pragmatically is outwhispered by the sea in another American Great Defeat. Whitman gives precedence to his own songs as well the most vital among his progeny.

Roy Harvey Pearce, who edited a very useful edition of the 1860 *Leaves of Grass,* remarked to me decades ago on his conviction that it was the crown of Whitman's work, of "now" in the fullest sense: "sheer givenness," power as *potentia,* something ever more about to be. Hart Crane, contrasting William Carlos Williams to Whitman in a letter, found both poets "too casual" yet emphasized the undersong in their common progenitors.

But with Whitman, there is a steady current—under or overtone—that scarcely ever forsakes him. And a rhythm that almost constantly bespeaks the ineffable 'word' that he has to speak. This 'tone,' assertion, or whatever—emerges through all the paradoxes and contradictions in his work. It doesn't try to be logical. It is an 'operation' of some universal law which he apprehends but which cannot be expressed in any one attitude or formula. One either grasps it or one doesn't. When it comes out in a thing like the first 'paragraph' of *Out of the Cradle Endlessly Rocking* it is overwhelming. The man is both distant and near:

> This is the far-off depth and height reflecting my own face;
> This is the thoughtful merge of myself, and the outlet again:

Here are the closing lines of the 1860 *Out of the Cradle:*

> Which I do not forget,
> But fuse the song of two together,

That was sung to me in the moonlight on Paumanok's
    gray beach,
With the thousand responsive songs, at random,
My own songs, awaked from that hour,
And with them the key, the word up from the waves,
The word of the sweetest song, and all songs,
That strong and delicious word which, creeping to my feet,
The sea whispered me.

Transvalued here, the whispered word "death" is not literal death our death but a trope for awakening to poethood. A few years ago I gathered a volume of "last poems" (*Till I End My Song*), from Spenser to our moment, and noted that strong poems are composed against death, though not against dying. That Lucretian distinction is vital to Walt, who followed Epicurus through the tutelage of Fanny Wright. In Lucretius, the image of freedom is the *clinamen,* the sudden swerve of the atoms falling outward and downward from the sea of space and time into our cosmos. Whitman's *Sea-Drift* elegies are swerves into the outsetting bard's new freedom. Liberation from what bindings?

Pearce emphasized Whitman's discovery and acceptance of limits in *Leaves of Grass* 1860. Having been brought so far by language, Walt came to realize he could go no further unless he ventured beyond language, which would be the death of poetry. For Pearce, that realization was Whitman's greatness. When I agreed and remarked to him that the Hermetic Walt mostly fails after 1865, precisely because he loses all sense of limits, I was surprised by the rejoinder, which blamed the decline instead upon prophetic ambitions.

Prophetic poetry, from Isaiah through Blake and Shelley to Geoffrey Hill, is a difficult mode, and Whitman certainly has a central place in its hidden traditions: How does one detach him and his achievement from a vision of the United States itself becoming the perfect poem? We know that, to use Emerson's phrase, the cost of confirmation for him was very steep. Emerson rapturously proclaims that in our highest moments we become a vision. Walt's raptures can be startling, though often enough they do not persuade even him.

Moby-Dick (1851) and *Leaves of Grass* 1860 are spiritual autobiographies in the American mode of Emerson's vast journals, Thoreau's *Walden,* and Poe's outrageous *Eureka,* his reply to Emerson's *Nature.* Being American, the daemon tells his own story yet indirectly, the growth as much of the poet's personality as of the mind. Ethos was the daemon for the ancient Greeks, but in Shakespeare's invention of the human, as in that of his American followers, pathos is the daemon, the hidden potential of awakened personality.

In *Leaves of Grass,* all drama is internalized. Whitman divides into three—self, real Me, soul—and they argue it through. *Moby-Dick* has diverse players: Ahab, the White Whale, Ishmael, Queequeg, Starbuck, Stubb, Fedallah, Pip, and the rest of the *Pequod*'s crew. In Shakespearean terms, Walt amalgamates Hamlet, Falstaff, *Lear*'s Edgar; Ahab fuses Macbeth, Hamlet, Lear. Is Ahab, Ahab? as Ahab himself asks. Is he agent or the dark double Fedallah, mystic Parsee harpooner? Is Ahab, Melville? No Melville scholar says so, but of course he is, only as Hamlet is Shakespeare's capacious consciousness, Macbeth his prophetic imaginations, Falstaff his god of life, more life. Ahab is Herman Melville's daemon, his genius, his prolongation of Job's rebellion that we miscall patience. In a letter to Hawthorne, he wrote, "I have written a wicked book, and feel spotless as the lamb." Spotless as a lamb, Melville freed himself by writing a wicked book, the American marriage of heaven and hell. Can quest-romance, however dramatic, achieve tragedy? Is *Hamlet* tragic, or is it too unlimited for that mode?

T. S. Eliot's "word out of the sea" emerges in *The Dry Salvages,* a return of Whitman into the third section of *Four Quartets:* a more chastened Walt than the elegist achieved throughout *The Waste Land.* That was Whitman in *Lilacs,* but these lines of Eliot's measure themselves by the metrical contract of *Sea-Drift,* where the ocean of life ebbs:

> The menace and caress of wave that breaks on water,
> The distant rote in the granite teeth,
> And the wailing warning from the approaching headland
> Are all sea voices, and the heaving groaner
> Rounded homewards, and the seagull:

Eliot has been lacquered over by hagiographical exegesis, by the proponents of the myth of the Great Western Butterslide, as my late friend and former mentor Northrop Frye memorably termed it. For acolytes like Allen Tate and Cleanth Brooks, Helen Gardner and even Frank Kermode, a much more considerable figure, Eliot was the prophet who proclaimed the onetime existence of a great blob of classical and Christian butter that started to melt in the later seventeenth century, slid down Enlightenment and Romantic slopes, and at last superbly congealed in *The Waste Land.*

As a young scholar-critic in the period 1957–77, I was a Romantic Revivalist, furiously battling to restore many great writers to the canon: Spenser, Milton, Blake, Shelley, Browning, Tennyson, Emerson, Whitman, Thomas Carlyle, Ruskin, Pater, Wilde, Swinburne, Lawrence, Stevens, Hart Crane, and others. Many if not most of these had been exiled by Eliot and his churchwardens. When I was a child, my ear had been ravished by Eliot's poetry, but his criticism—literary and cultural—dismayed me. At eighty-four I have calmed down: My warfare is accomplished, my grudge ebbing with the ocean of life. The prose Eliot still displeases me; I have just read through three enormous volumes of his letters and my ancient fury almost revives. His scorn for Emerson is so ill-informed that some personal bias has to be noted in it.

With some poets, Shelley and Whitman particularly, sorrows of family romance activate Eliot's defensiveness. Shakespeare, everyone's resource, had a mixed effect upon Eliot: He preferred—he said—*Coriolanus* to *Hamlet,* a weirdness unworthy of refutation, and he echoed Shakespeare both overtly and involuntarily, a general phenomenon. At his best, early and late, Eliot's incantatory style achieves a difficult rightness that only Hart Crane could transume, to very different purposes. Allen Tate, whose poems blended Eliot and Tate's close friend Crane, told me at one of our several uneasy meetings that "Hart's problem was the impossible project of extending Walt Whitman's stance in Eliotic cadences." I recall murmuring that the result was not problematic but triumphant, as Eliot may have concluded when Crane published *The Tunnel,* the descent into Avernus in *The Bridge.*

Eliot shares a later chapter of this book with Stevens, who was always amused to a subtle pugnacity by his younger and more famous rival. But both poets conducted a lifelong agon with the American bard of the *Lilacs* elegy, *The Sleepers,* and the *Sea-Drift* monodies, much as Crane's *The Bridge* strove with *Crossing Brooklyn Ferry, Song of Myself,* and *Passage to India.* Crane's loving contest was open; Stevens's and Eliot's struggles with

Whitman were deeper. Of the major American poets, only a few were immune to Whitman: Dickinson, Frost, Moore, Bishop, Warren, James Merrill. The others, in very different ways, are of his lineage: Robinson Jeffers, Ezra Pound, Williams, Ammons, and Ashbery, as well as Eliot, Stevens, Crane. The now-undervalued Edwin Arlington Robinson celebrated Whitman's force but not with the intimacy of poetic family romance.

AS I EBB'D WITH THE OCEAN OF LIFE

A WORD OUT OF THE SEA, THE 1860 VERSION OF THE POEM THAT BECAME *Out of the Cradle Endlessly Rocking,* is the founding paradigm of what the late Paul Fussell taught me to call the "American Shore Ode," a beach meditation that Whitman gave us as an answer to the High Romantic "crisis ode" of Coleridge, Wordsworth, Shelley, and Keats. Wonderful instances in our now-rich poetic heritage include Whitman's own *As I Ebb'd with the Ocean of Life,* Stevens's *The Idea of Order at Key West* and *The Auroras of Autumn,* Eliot's *The Dry Salvages,* Hart Crane's *Voyages,* John Wheelwright's *Fish Food* (an outrageous tribute to Crane), Bishop's *At the Fishhouses* and *The End of March,* James Wright's *At the Slackening of the Tide,* Ammons's *Corsons Inlet,* and Amy Clampitt's *Beach Glass.* Whitman's *As I Ebb'd* and Crane's *Voyages* perhaps win the palm, but *A Word Out of the Sea* invents the mode in genre: metamorphic, elegiac, recording the incarnation and then the withdrawal of poetic vocation.

"The outsetting bard of love" relies upon "the dusky daemon aroused," yet that arousal provokes the mothering sea's fatal response:

> Answering, the sea,
> Delaying not, hurrying not,
> Whispered me through the night, and very plainly before
> daybreak,
> Lisped to me constantly the low and delicious word Death,
> And again Death—ever Death, Death, Death,
> Hissing melodious, neither like the bird, nor like my
> aroused child's heart,
> But edging near, as privately for me, rustling at my feet,
> And creeping thence steadily up to my ears,
> Death, Death, Death, Death, Death.

That fivefold "Death" reflects Whitman himself making a fifth with
night, death, the mother, and the sea. The outsetting bard of love is transformed into the Evening Land's poet of death. Keats's "Do I wake or
sleep?" may have had an effect upon Walt's simultaneous awakening to
love and to death. My surmise is that Whitman, late in 1859, fled his initial
full homoerotic encounter. The darker, magnificent companion-rival, *As I
Ebb'd with the Ocean of Life,* carries that implicit burden, given here in its
1860 version:

> Elemental drifts!
> O I wish I could impress others as you and the waves have
>   just been impressing me.
>
> As I ebbed with an ebb of the ocean of life,
> As I wended the shores I know,
> As I walked where the sea-ripples wash you, Paumanok,
> Where they rustle up, hoarse and sibilant,
> Where the fierce old mother endlessly cries for her castaways,
> I, musing, late in the autumn day, gazing off southward,
> Alone, held by the eternal self of me that threatens to get
>   the better of me, and stifle me,
> Was seized by the spirit that trails in the lines underfoot,
> In the rim, the sediment, that stands for all the water and all
>   the land of the globe.
>
> Fascinated, my eyes, reverting from the south, dropped, to
>   follow those slender winrows,
> Chaff, straw, splinters of wood, weeds, and the sea-gluten,
> Scum, scales from shining rocks, leaves of salt-lettuce, left
>   by the tide;
> Miles walking, the sound of breaking waves the other side
>   of me,
> Paumanok, there and then, as I thought the old thought of
>   likenesses,
> These you presented to me, you fish-shaped island,
> As I wended the shores I know,
> As I walked with that eternal self of me, seeking types.

As I wend the shores I know not,
As I listen to the dirge, the voices of men and women
   wrecked,
As I inhale the impalpable breezes that set in upon me,
As the ocean so mysteriously rolls toward me closer and
   closer,
At once I find, the least thing that belongs to me, or that I
   see or touch, I know not;
I, too, but signify, at the utmost, a little washed-up drift,
A few sands and dead leaves to gather,
Gather, and merge myself as part of the sands and drift.

O baffled, balked,
Bent to the very earth, here preceding what follows,
Oppressed with myself that I have dared to open my
   mouth,
Aware now, that amid all the blab whose echoes recoil upon
   me, I have not once had the least idea who or what I am,
But that before all my insolent poems the real Me still
   stands untouched, untold, altogether unreached,
Withdrawn far, mocking me with mock-congratulatory
   signs and bows,
With peals of distant ironical laughter at every word I have
   written or shall write,
Striking me with insults till I fall helpless upon the sand.

O I perceive I have not understood anything—not a single
   object—and that no man ever can.

I perceive Nature here, in sight of the sea, is taking advantage
   of me, to dart upon me, and sting me,
Because I was assuming so much,
And because I have dared to open my mouth to sing at all.

You oceans both! You tangible land! Nature!
Be not too rough with me—I submit—I close with you,
These little shreds shall, indeed, stand for all.

You friable shore, with trails of debris!
You fish-shaped island! I take what is underfoot;
What is yours is mine, my father.

I too Paumanok,
I too have bubbled up, floated the measureless float, and
    been washed on your shores;
I too am but a trail of drift and debris,
I too leave little wrecks upon you, you fish-shaped island.

I throw myself upon your breast, my father,
I cling to you so that you cannot unloose me,
I hold you so firm, till you answer me something.

Kiss me, my father,
Touch me with your lips, as I touch those I love,
Breathe to me, while I hold you close, the secret of the
    wondrous murmuring I envy,
For I fear I shall become crazed, if I cannot emulate it, and
    utter myself as well as it.

Sea-raff! Crook-tongued waves!
O, I will yet sing, some day, what you have said to me.

Ebb, ocean of life, (the flow will return,)
Cease not your moaning, you fierce old mother,
Endlessly cry for your castaways—but fear not, deny
    not me,
Rustle not up so hoarse and angry against my feet, as I
    touch you, or gather from you.

I mean tenderly by you,
I gather for myself, and for this phantom, looking down
    where we lead, and following me and mine.

Me and mine!
We, loose winrows, little corpses,

Froth, snowy white, and bubbles,
(See! from my dead lips the ooze exuding at last!
See—the prismatic colors, glistening and rolling!)
Tufts of straw, sands, fragments,
Buoyed hither from many moods, one contradicting
    another,
From the storm, the long calm, the darkness, the swell,
Musing, pondering, a breath, a briny tear, a dab of liquid or
    soil,
Up just as much out of fathomless workings fermented and
    thrown,
A limp blossom or two, torn, just as much over waves
    floating, drifted at random,
Just as much for us that sobbing dirge of Nature,
Just as much, whence we come, that blare of the cloud-
    trumpets;
We, capricious, brought hither, we know not whence, spread
    out before You, up there, walking or sitting,
Whoever you are—we too lie in drifts at your feet.

Of the five major poems flanking *Song of Myself,* what we now call *As I Ebb'd with the Ocean of Life* seems to me, in my old age, grander even than *A Word Out of the Sea, Crossing Brooklyn Ferry, The Sleepers,* and the *Lilacs* elegy for Lincoln. This original is stronger than the smoother version Whitman came to favor and is a worthy answer to Shelley's *Ode to the West Wind,* its covert agonist. Shelley's tropes—the dirge of the dying year, the dead leaves, each like a little corpse, the blare of the cloud-trumpets of prophecy, the poet lying in drifts at the feet of the gods of the storm—are appropriated by Whitman forty years after the English revolutionary poet addressed the elements.

"Elemental drifts!," the first line of *As I Ebb'd,* is a worthy title, and I will employ it here. "Impress," in the second line, takes every range of meaning in the word, and "As I ebbed with an ebb of the ocean of life" repeats "an ebb" for a more Whitmanian rhythm than the shorter, later version. By changing to "Held by this electric self out of the pride of which I utter poems," Whitman lost much of the powerful pathos of "Alone, held by the eternal self of me that threatens to get the better of me, and stifle me," with its hint that the eternal self is the real Me or Me myself, and not the fiction of rough Walt the American. The restored contrast vivifies the Jobean spirit that trails in the lines underfoot, the accusing daemon that haunts the lines of the poem and in the sand.

Stand back from *Elemental Drifts!* and you can behold a more original design than in *A Word Out of the Sea*. The metaphors stem from Western tradition, as mediated by Shelley's *Adonais,* a fierce ode to "the breath whose might I have invoked in song," but their patterning is more daemonic than ever before. Musing in an autumnal twilight the beach-walker encounters his dusky daemon, the other self or personal genius, who has come only to mock him. Hart Crane's *Passage* in *White Buildings* and Stevens's masterwork, *The Auroras of Autumn,* inherit Whitman's scenario, as does Eliot's *The Dry Salvages*.

The "thought of likeness" may be old, as reflected by Joyce's Stephen Dedalus recalling Jakob Boehme's "signatures of all things I am here to read." Whitman employs it with radical newness since his signatures, the types he seeks, are purely daemonic, agencies for reproving his own failures in freedom. Beckett's motto—"Fail better!"—catches Walt's spirit, bowed certainly though unbroken:

> As I wend the shores I know not,
> As I listen to the dirge, the voices of men and women
>   wrecked,
> As I inhale the impalpable breezes that set in upon me,
> As the ocean so mysteriously rolls toward me closer and
>   closer,
> At once I find, the least thing that belongs to me, or that I
>   see or touch, I know not;
> I, too, but signify, at the utmost, a little washed-up drift,
> A few sands and dead leaves to gather,
> Gather, and merge myself as part of the sands and drift.

> —*As I Ebb'd* (1860)

The 1867 revision omits "At once I find, the least thing that belongs to me, or that I see or touch, I know not." This canceled line in itself falters, an instance of what the late Yvor Winters called "the fallacy of imitative

form," his name for loose, sprawling poetry—which is how he regarded
Whitman's work in general. My personal relations with Winters were cor-
dial; I shared his delight in Edwin Arlington Robinson and admired his
early friendship with Hart Crane. But on Crane, Whitman, Emerson, and
Stevens, we had to cease discussion, as each aggrieved the other. An admirable critic in other respects, Winters had no use for what Crane called
"the logic of metaphor," tropological thinking, without which Shakespeare is inconceivable.

Self-revision in Whitman generally retreats from his own rhetoric of
colors and forms into ineffective gestures of Tennysonian emulation. But
the superb struggle between the 1860 and 1867 versions, both of which
follow, does show both gain and loss in revision:

> O baffled, balked,
> Bent to the very earth, here preceding what follows,
> Oppressed with myself that I have dared to open
>   my mouth,
> Aware now, that amid all the blab whose echoes recoil upon
>   me, I have not once had the least idea who or what
>   I am,
> But that before all my insolent poems the real Me still
>   stands untouched, untold, altogether unreached,
> Withdrawn far, mocking me with mock-congratulatory
>   signs and bows,
> With peals of distant ironical laughter at every word I have
>   written or shall write,
> Striking me with insults till I fall helpless upon the sand.
>
> O I perceive I have not understood anything—not a single
>   object—and that no man ever can.
>
> I perceive Nature here, in sight of the sea, is taking advantage
>   of me, to dart upon me, and sting me,
> Because I was assuming so much,
> And because I have dared to open my mouth to sing at all.

(1860)

O baffled, balk'd, bent to the very earth,
Oppress'd with myself that I have dared to open my mouth,
Aware now that amid all that blab whose echoes recoil upon
    me I have not once had the least idea who or what I am,
But that before all my arrogant poems the real Me stands
    yet untouch'd, untold, altogether unreach'd,
Withdrawn far, mocking me with mock-congratulatory
    signs and bows,
With peals of distant ironical laughter at every word I have
    written,
Pointing in silence to these songs, and then to the sand
    beneath.

I perceive I have not really understood any thing, not a single
    object, and that no man ever can,
Nature here in sight of the sea taking advantage of me to
    dart upon me and sting me,
Because I have dared to open my mouth to sing at all.

(1867)

"Striking me with insults till I fall helpless upon the sand" is far less effective than the high art of "Pointing in silence to these songs, and then to the sand beneath." In a brilliant afterthought, the beach-walker confronts waves and daemon with a copy of *Leaves of Grass* in his hand (presumably the second edition, 1856), again equating poetic lines and windrows (in either spelling). In the other significant change, Whitman cuts "Because I was assuming so much," which is a loss because it undoes the superb confidence manifested in *Song of Myself:* "And what I assume you shall assume."

Walt's most direct confrontation with his daemon (real Me, or Me myself) yields the bitter self-parody of "mock-congratulatory signs and bows." And yet this yields also an exquisite pathos almost Shakespearean:

You oceans both! You tangible land! Nature!
Be not too rough with me—I submit—I close with you,
These little shreds shall, indeed, stand for all.

Was Walt right to eliminate the following three lines from the later versions?

> For I fear I shall become crazed, if I cannot emulate it, and
>   utter myself as well as it.

> Sea-raff! Crook-tongued waves!
> O, I will yet sing, some day, what you have said to me.

True, they break the beautifully subdued mood of the reconciliation with the father. But his desperate need of continuing to compose poetry has its own poignance, less in dignity perhaps but more in urgency. How infrequently Walt entertains the thought of madness!

For me the high point of all Whitman comes in one tercet:

> I throw myself upon your breast, my father,
> I cling to you so that you cannot unloose me,
> I hold you so firm, till you answer me something.

I think back to carrying my younger son in my arms, when he was just past a year in age. He held me so tightly that I hardly knew how to set him down safely or transfer him to another person's grasp. I could not bear to detach him by mere force and became abashed whenever it became necessary.

There is great pathos when Whitman writes: "Touch me with your lips, as I touch those I love." It is worth recalling here that, except in his apotheosis as wound dresser and comforter of the maimed and dying soldiers, Walt's eros was intransitive: "To touch my body to someone else's is about as much as I can bear."

Elemental Drifts! concludes familiarly for the reader with what will become essentially the text of *As I Ebb'd with the Ocean of Life*, beginning with "Ebb, ocean of life, (the flow will return,)" and ending with "Whoever you are—we too lie in drifts at your feet." (See pp. 95–96.)

Shelley's *Ode to the West Wind* haunted Whitman and Wallace Stevens alike. The "little corpses" return to Shelley's dead leaves, "each like a corpse within its grave," and "that blare of the cloud-trumpets" recalls Shelley's "the trumpet of a prophecy." Both Whitman and Shelley were

Lucretian materialists, and Whitman invokes the Epicurean gods at the close: "You, up there, walking or sitting, / Whoever you are."

Against that divine indifference, Shelley offers a secular apocalypse, as he leaps from the advent of autumn to "If Winter comes, can Spring be far behind?" Whitman places a more modest hope in a marvelous modulation from "Up just as much out of fathomless workings" through "Just as much for us" on to "Just as much, whence we come."

THE TWENTY-TWO-YEAR-OLD HENRY JAMES, IN HIS ATROCIOUS REVIEW of Whitman's *Drum-Taps,* ridiculed the 1865 version of *Starting from Paumanok.* Future master of the American novel, he never read the 1860 *Leaves of Grass,* where the poem's stronger text leads off the volume as *Proto-Leaf:*

> Free, fresh, savage,
> Fluent, luxuriant, self-content, fond of persons and
>   places,
> Fond of fish-shape Paumanok, where I was born,
> Fond of the sea—lusty-begotten and various,
> Boy of the Mannahatta, the city of ships, my city,
> Or raised inland, or of the south savannas,
> Or full-breath'd on Californian air, or Texan or Cuban air,
> Tallying, vocalizing all—resounding Niagara—resounding
>   Missouri,
> Or rude in my home in Kanuck woods,
> Or wandering and hunting, my drink water, my diet meat,
> Or withdrawn to muse and meditate in some deep recess,
> Far from the clank of crowds, an interval passing, rapt and
>   happy,
> Stars, vapor, snow, the hills, rocks, the Fifth Month flowers,
>   my amaze, my love,
> Aware of the buffalo, the peace-herds, the bull, strong-
>   breasted and hairy,
> Aware of the mocking-bird of the wilds at daybreak,
> Solitary, singing in the west, I strike up for a new world.

James might have liked it no better than the later version, but then he would have exposed himself as blinded by extra-poetic prejudice. For fifteen lines Walt delays meaning, until the revelation of "Solitary, singing in the west, I strike up for a new world." It stuns me in the manner of *The Dalliance of the Eagles* and *Vigil Strange I Kept on the Field One Night.* Whitman, when most at one with his poetry, indeed is "Free, fresh, savage, / Fluent, luxuriant, self-content." Who else is, among our greater poets? Dickinson comes closest and the cunning Frost after her, but not Stevens, Eliot, or Crane—all of them Whitman-haunted.

"Tallying, vocalizing all" is uniquely Walt's work. Again Dickinson, among our poets, verges on that scope, but who else could dare the universal? Emerson (though in the other harmony, prose) and Melville in the miracle of *Moby-Dick* are of such amplitude, but who else? Of the novelists, Henry James aspired to Balzacian scope and variety. There is (though critics are now reluctant to say so) something forlorn in the master invoking the lesson of Balzac; no one could remark, as legend has it Baudelaire said of Balzac, that in James every janitor is a genius. There is Balzacian energy in James, but it has the stigmata of the American Sublime, what Stevens was to term "the stale grandeur of annihilation."

The American Negative, a vision of how dangerously minimal life can be, despite Whitman, knows little of Balzacian energetics, except perhaps in the later Mark Twain. There is a grand negation in *our* Balzac, Faulkner, though the comparison can be dangerous to him. I think of *Light in August,* in particular, as worthy of Balzac. The story of Joe Christmas is a triumph of American negation, but Lena Grove, Faulkner's pastoral achievement, like Balzac, speaks to us of the gift of more life. Where biblical parallels disabled late Faulkner in the disaster of *A Fable,* in Lena's saga they enhance and are enhanced. Walt could dare to affirm: "I am large. I contain multitudes." Balzac as persuasively could have said that. James or Faulkner? You would have to (absurdly) mesh them together to get a Balzac or a Whitman, but then giants in the earth are rare phenomena.

From 1867 on, the 1860 *Proto-Leaf* became the first segment of *Starting from Paumanok* and lost something vital in revision:

> Starting from fish-shape Paumanok where I was born,
> Well-begotten, and rais'd by a perfect mother,

After roaming many lands, love of populous pavements,
Dweller in Mannahatta my city, or on southern savannas,
Or a soldier camp'd or carrying my knapsack and gun, or a
    miner in California,
Or rude in my home in Dakota's woods, my diet meat, my
    drink from the spring,
Or withdrawn to muse and meditate in some deep recess,
Far from the clank of crowds intervals passing rapt and
    happy,
Aware of the fresh free giver the flowing Missouri, aware of
    mighty Niagara,
Aware of the buffalo herds grazing the plains, the hirsute
    and strong-breasted bull,
Of earth, rocks, Fifth-month flowers experienced, stars,
    rain, snow, my amaze,
Having studied the mocking-bird's tones and the flight of
    the mountain-hawk,
And heard at dawn the unrivall'd one, the hermit thrush
    from the swamp-cedars,
Solitary, singing in the West, I strike up for a New World.

We wince at "Well-begotten, and rais'd by a perfect mother" and want
returned to us that splendid opening shock:

Free, fresh, savage,
Fluent, luxuriant, self-content, fond of persons and places.

Even in the revised version there is the enormous skill of delayed meaning when at last we reach: "Solitary, singing in the West, I strike up for a
New World." Yet I still miss "self-content," which is Walt's transumption
of "self-reliance." Reading Emerson through Whitman's vista is to see
that this is "*daimon*-reliance," the real Me or Me myself being Emerson's
daimon, who alone knows how poems are done.

Angus Fletcher follows Coleridge in emphasizing that pure energy, free
of morality, is the mark of possession by a daemon. *Proto-Leaf* celebrates
the influx of poetic power and relies upon energetics more Balzacian than
Platonic. Henry James turned to Balzac for a lesson in the daemonic, an

apt choice since the Parisian master invented Vautrin the Death-Dodger, the daemon as criminal. Whitman turned inward, guided by Emerson's dialectics of fate, freedom, and power.

The tragedy of a dialectical eros plays itself out in the forty-five *Calamus* poems of the 1860 *Leaves of Grass*. Whitman learned again that only an intransitive eros could accommodate his daemon, which celebrated contact but could not bear it. I am accustomed to being drubbed on this matter by a self-declared school of homosexual poeticians who generously attribute their achieved gay lives to Walt Whitman. Would it were so, but the great artist of the intransitive verb also avoided objects of his sexual drive; what evidence we have indicates that he carnally embraced himself only, and walked the open road with only the thought of death and the knowledge of death as his close companions. *Calamus* should not be externalized any more than we read Shakespeare's sonnets for veracity.

Shakespeare's sonnets may have been the model for the twelve-poem manuscript *Live Oak, with Moss,* which was the seedbed for *Calamus.*

The great poem of the sequence is the renowned vision of a luxuriant live oak:

> I saw in Louisiana a live-oak growing,
> All alone stood it, and the moss hung down from the
>   branches,
> Without any companion it grew there, glistening out joyous
>   leaves of dark green,
> And its look, rude, unbending, lusty, made me think of
>   myself;
> But I wondered how it could utter joyous leaves, standing
>   alone there without its friend, its lover—For I knew I
>   could not;
> And I plucked a twig with a certain number of leaves upon
>   it, and twined around it a little moss, and brought it
>   away—And I have placed it in sight in my room,
> It is not needed to remind me as of my friends, (for I believe
>   lately I think of little else than of them,)
> Yet it remains to me a curious token—I write these pieces,
>   and name them after it;

For all that, and though the live-oak glistens there in Louisiana,
    solitary in a wide flat space, uttering joyous leaves all its
    life, without a friend, a lover, near—I know very well I
    could not.

The twig is another instance of Whitman's prime emblem of poetic
voice, the "tally." Beautifully paced, this exquisite lyric meditation intimates an erotic self-sufficiency that Walt wants to deny but unpersuasively.
Throughout *Calamus,* Whitman is strongest when he asserts least:

Who is now reading this?

May-be one is now reading this who knows some wrong-doing
    of my past life,
Or may-be a stranger is reading this who has secretly
    loved me,
Or may-be one who meets all my grand assumptions and
    egotisms with derision,
Or may-be one who is puzzled at me.

As if I were not puzzled at myself!
Or as if I never deride myself! (O conscience-struck! O self-
    convicted!)
Or as if I do not secretly love strangers! (O tenderly, a long
    time, and never avow it;)
Or as if I did not see, perfectly well, interior in myself, the
    stuff of wrong-doing,
Or as if it could cease transpiring from me until it must cease.

Such disquietude abounds, whether between the lines or overt:

O love!
O dying—always dying!
O the burials of me, past and present!
O me, while I stride ahead, material, visible, imperious as
    ever!

O me, what I was for years, now dead, (I lament not—I am
    content;)
O to disengage myself from those corpses of me, which I
    turn and look at, where I cast them!
To pass on, (O living! always living!) and leave the corpses
    behind!

My late friend the poet Mark Strand, deeply affected by this, has composed several variations upon it. Allied to such darkness are the fading glimpses that doubt appearances:

That shadow, my likeness, that goes to and fro, seeking a
    livelihood, chattering, chaffering,
How often I find myself standing and looking at it where it
    flits,
How often I question and doubt whether that is really me;
But in these, and among my lovers, and carolling my songs,
O I never doubt whether that is really me.

Indirection, central to Whitman's poetics, attains a triumph in the two final sections of *Calamus:*

Here my last words, and the most baffling,
Here the frailest leaves of me, and yet my strongest-lasting,
Here I shade down and hide my thoughts—I do not expose
    them,
And yet they expose me more than all my other poems.

Full of life, sweet-blooded, compact, visible,
I, forty years old the Eighty-third Year of The States,
To one a century hence, or any number of centuries hence,
To you, yet unborn, these, seeking you.

When you read these, I, that was visible, am become invisible;
Now it is you, compact, visible, realizing my poems,
    seeking me,

Fancying how happy you were, if I could be with you, and
   become your lover;
Be it as if I were with you. Be not too certain but I am now
   with you.

Kenneth Burke enjoyed chanting the four lines of Section 44 to me—
"Here my last words . . ."—as we clambered about the Battery in the autumn of 1976, and he adored equally the envoi to *Calamus.* Both brief
poems dazzle—in the diction of John Ashbery—as shields of a greeting,
protecting what is exposed. That is Whitman's art: to promise absolute
self-revelation and give us fresh gestures of evasion, hesitation, concealment. Better thus, though Walt proclaimed: "I swear I dare not shirk any
part of myself." Stevens learned from Whitman "the intricate evasions of
as." So Walt's last words are the most baffling, his frailest leaves his
strongest-lasting, and his shaded, hidden thoughts expose him more than
all his other poems.

Leaves of Grass 1860 gave no offense with the homoerotic *Calamus* but
was attacked for what became the *Children of Adam* grouping. Emerson
had cautioned Whitman to avoid provocation, doubtless forgetting his
own maxim that what is gained from others is never instruction but only
provocation. Rereading Whitman's celebrations of love for a woman, I
recant my earlier judgment that they are in any way poorer than the *Calamus* hymns to manly love. It is true that the 1860 texts tend to improve in
later revisions, unlike *Calamus.* Whitman agilely assumes the identity of
the American Adam in *To the Garden the World:*

To the garden the world anew ascending,
Potent mates, daughters, sons, preluding,
The love, the life of their bodies, meaning and being,
Curious here behold my resurrection after slumber,
The revolving cycles in their wide sweep having brought me
   again,
Amorous, mature, all beautiful to me, all wondrous,
My limbs and the quivering fire that ever plays through
   them, for reasons, most wondrous,
Existing I peer and penetrate still,

Content with the present, content with the past,
By my side or back of me Eve following,
Or in front, and I following her just the same.

This strong prelude is almost worthy of *As Adam Early in the Morning,* the famous postlude to *Children of Adam:*

As Adam early in the morning,
Walking forth from the bower refresh'd with sleep,
Behold me where I pass, hear my voice, approach,
Touch me, touch the palm of your hand to my body as
    I pass,
Be not afraid of my body.

This compressed epitome of Whitman's aesthetic eminence intimates Walt as Hermetic God-Man, Adam, and American Christ, and makes of us so many doubting Thomases. Subtly cadenced, the major Adamic song goes back to the 1855 *Leaves of Grass,* became *Poem of the Body* in 1856, and took its first line as title from 1867 onward: *I Sing the Body Electric.* A remarkable performance, influential and exuberant, it nevertheless never finds me. I miss Whitman's sublimity whenever I work through its inventories. Far better is *Spontaneous Me,* an ecstatic hymn of self-gratification, perhaps the true scandal of Whitman's work. Kenneth Burke loved reciting the poem, chuckling at its overtness. Though the poem celebrates both heterosexuality and homoeroticism, the only object of the drive is Walt himself:

The young man that wakes deep at night, the hot hand seeking
    to repress what would master him,
The mystic amorous night, the strange half-welcome pangs,
    visions, sweats,
The pulse pounding through palms and trembling encircling
    fingers, the young man all color'd, red, ashamed, angry;
The souse upon me of my lover the sea, as I lie willing and
    naked,
The merriment of the twin babes that crawl over the grass
    in the sun, the mother never turning her vigilant eyes
    from them,

The walnut-trunk, the walnut-husks, and the ripening or
 ripen'd long-round walnuts,
The continence of vegetables, birds, animals,
The consequent meanness of me should I skulk or find
 myself indecent, while birds and animals never once
 skulk or find themselves indecent,
The great chastity of paternity, to match the great chastity
 of maternity,
The oath of procreation I have sworn, my Adamic and fresh
 daughters,
The greed that eats me day and night with hungry gnaw, till
 I saturate what shall produce boys to fill my place when I
 am through,
The wholesome relief, repose, content,
And this bunch pluck'd at random from myself,
It has done its work—I toss it carelessly to fall where it may.

In its first appearance in *Leaves of Grass* 1856, this was called *Bunch Poem,* a more effective title, much admired by Kenneth Burke in our Whitmanian dialogues. He kindled my affection also for the splendid *Facing West from California's Shores* (the first line added in 1867):

Facing west from California's shores,
Inquiring, tireless, seeking what is yet unfound,
I, a child, very old, over waves, towards the house of
 maternity, the land of migrations, look afar,
Look off the shores of my Western sea, the circle almost
 circled;
For starting westward from Hindustan, from the vales of
 Kashmere,
From Asia, from the north, from the God, the sage, and the
 hero,
From the south, from the flowery peninsulas and the spice
 islands,
Long having wandered since, round the earth having
 wander'd,
Now I face home again, very pleas'd and joyous,

(But where is what I started for so long ago?
And why is it yet unfound?)

Indic thought reached Whitman through back channels or by natural affinity. Emerson and Thoreau absorbed it through translations, unlike T. S. Eliot, a profound student of Sanskrit and Pali texts. Cleo Kearns links Eliot's Indic knowledge to Whitman's quest for a gnosis transcending the death of the self. The startling resemblances between *When Lilacs Last in the Dooryard Bloom'd* and *The Waste Land* are in part a matter of repressed influence but also suggest Indic sensibilities shared by the two poets in opening themselves to the thought and knowledge of death.

I leap ahead to the aesthetic puzzle presented to me by Whitman's ambitious poem of 1871, *Passage to India*. Frequent rereadings make me unhappy: It seems unworthy of the poet who composed *Song of Myself, The Sleepers, Crossing Brooklyn Ferry,* and the great threnodies *Out of the Cradle Endlessly Rocking, As I Ebb'd with the Ocean of Life,* and *Lilacs.* And yet I cannot dismiss a poem whose progeny includes *Four Quartets, The Bridge,* D. H. Lawrence's *The Ship of Death,* and E. M. Forster's *A Passage to India.*

Still, what are lovers of Whitman to do with "For what is the present after all but a growth out of the past?" Continuous affirmation wearies the reader and tempts her to long for a few saving touches of negation or of the comic, both of which abound in *Song of Myself,* as does incremental redundancy. After 1865, we receive mostly redundancy unmitigated. There are still a few scattered epiphanies: *The Dalliance of the Eagles, Warble for Lilac-Time, A Noiseless Patient Spider, Night on the Prairies, The Last Invocation, A Clear Midnight.* Yet these are drowned out by banal sentiments and crunching platitudes, as in the *Song of the Universal:*

And thou America,
For the scheme's culmination, its thought and its reality,
For these (not for thyself) thou hast arrived.

Thou too surroundest all,
Embracing carrying welcoming all, thou too by pathways
    broad and new,
To the ideal tendest.

The measur'd faiths of other lands, the grandeurs of the past,
Are not for thee, but grandeurs of thine own,
Deific faiths and amplitudes, absorbing, comprehending all,
All eligible to all.

All, all for immortality,
Love like the light silently wrapping all,
Nature's amelioration blessing all,
The blossoms, fruits of ages, orchards divine and certain,
Forms, objects, growths, humanities, to spiritual images
      ripening.

Give me O God to sing that thought,
Give me, give him or her I love this quenchless faith,
In Thy ensemble, whatever else withheld withhold not
      from us,
Belief in plan of Thee enclosed in Time and Space,
Health, peace, salvation universal.

That is our great poet, perhaps our greatest American, in 1874. At just fifty-five, his extraordinary gift of 1855–65 has abandoned him. Wordsworth provides an illuminating parallel. Almost all his vital poetry emanates from his great decade of 1797–1807. The departure of Wordsworth's daemon remains mysterious, but it seems clear that by 1866 one too many young soldiers had died in Whitman's arms. The cost of absorbing such pain and suffering would have been too high for anyone, even for our nation's ministering angel.

When Lilacs Last in the Dooryard Bloom'd

WHITMAN WAS UNHAPPY WHEN ADMIRERS DECLARED THAT THE MAGNIFicent *Lilacs* elegy for Lincoln was his most distinguished poem. Were it not for *Song of Myself,* I might be tempted to make the same choice, except that *Crossing Brooklyn Ferry* and *As I Ebb'd with the Ocean of Life* are as memorable as *Lilacs. The Sleepers* is more uneven yet even more original.

American dooryards and major American poems continue to be centered upon lilacs: T. S. Eliot and Wallace Stevens incessantly return to Whitman's sprig of lilac, his tally. In 1871, in a wonderful afterthought, Whitman added the glorious phrase "retrievements out of the night" to sum up the transforming tally of the hermit thrush's song, his own answering chant, and the lilacs.

Like so many of the major elegies in poetic tradition, *Lilacs* hymns not only its ostensible subject, President Abraham Lincoln, but also the possible waning of the poet's own imaginative powers. There are scattered splendors by Whitman after 1865 but nothing so vital as *Lilacs*.

I do not know that *Lilacs* could be called the most American of all poems, because *Song of Myself* is the breakthrough. And yet there are nuances in *Lilacs* subtler and more advanced than elsewhere in Whitman. It is as though he stood on the threshold of a more finished art that he failed to attain.

The Wordsworthian equivalent of *Lilacs* is the great *Ode: Intimations of Immortality from Recollections of Early Childhood,* composed between 1802 and 1807. One aspect of this extraordinary poem is that Wordsworth intended to dedicate himself by it to yet higher achievement. Alas, what came was forty-three years of poetic monotony. There are a handful of happy exceptions, as there were in Whitman between 1866 and 1892, but both the major English and principal American poet of the nineteenth century might better have ceased writing. Wordsworth iced over, while Whitman's is an even more mysterious occultation than Wordsworth's decline unless (bearing in mind the pain he must have internalized from the dying soldiers) we literalize his giving up of the tally, the sprig of lilac he throws upon Lincoln's coffin.

Death in Whitman becomes a comprehensive metaphor for the memory we leave beyond us in the affection of others. The influence of this idea can be encountered in Wallace Stevens's majestic elegy for his friend Henry Church, *The Owl in the Sarcophagus.* There is a subtle migration in Stevens from the renewal of the Romantic assertion of the power of the poet's mind over a universe of death, as in *The Idea of Order at Key West,* to a more Whitmanian stance that is receptive to night, death, the mother, and the sea.

Lilacs has no dispute with "sane and sacred death." Its two hundred and six lines are more a hymn to death than a threnody for the unnamed

Lincoln. An Egyptian element in Whitman, going back to his interest in those antiquities in the Brooklyn Museum, may account for the burial-house of Section 11. Yet always the biblical strain surfaces, here as elsewhere in him. The high style of the King James Bible is invoked throughout the elegy.

Under a Venus hovering low in the western sky, Whitman attempts to express his grief but is blocked by a conflict of affects. It may be a hidden guilt that the illness and death of Walter Whitman, Sr., released Walt into the poetic exuberance of 1855, which gave him the first *Leaves of Grass:*

> O powerful western fallen star!
> O shades of night—O moody, tearful night!
> O great star disappear'd—O the black murk that hides the
>   star!
> O cruel hands that hold me powerless—O helpless soul
>   of me!
> O harsh surrounding cloud that will not free my soul.

The cruel hands are Whitman's, and a failed masturbation ensues. From this nadir, *Lilacs* rises into its first sublime:

> In the dooryard fronting an old farm-house near the white-
>   wash'd palings,
> Stands the lilac-bush tall-growing with heart-shaped leaves
>   of rich green,
> With many a pointed blossom rising delicate, with the
>   perfume strong I love,
> With every leaf a miracle—and from this bush in the
>   dooryard,
> With delicate-color'd blossoms and heart-shaped leaves of
>   rich green,
> A sprig with its flower I break.

The uncanny tone of this—direct yet intimating a rich history of elegiac tradition—is a triumph. I think of the ritual lament for Adonis in Alexandrian poetry, which Whitman need not have known. His broken sprig of lilac embodies the same impulse of sacrificial castration.

I have written so much about Whitman's signature image of voice, the tally, that I feel obliged not to repeat what I have already said, which is summed up in my book *The Anatomy of Influence.* In our vernacular, principally in the Southwest, "tally" can mean an illicit eros, whether used as verb or noun. You cut a twig to notch the score of your sexual encounters with your tallymen or tallywomen. Walt, however, is different: Homosexual in desire, he refuses carnal intimacy except with himself. His ecstasies are palpably autoerotic. I puzzle at scholars—of any sexual persuasion—who can read Walt's calibration of self-gratification, here, in *Spontaneous Me,* or elsewhere, as a screen for homoerotic intercourse. How could Walt be clearer? His tally, or solitary image of voice, commences by his making love to himself. Taboo, as Freud knew, is a mode of transference or the making of metaphor. It is fashionable now to regard sadomasochism as an acceptable erotic mode. Walt, devoid of all cruelty, instead breaks the taboo of onanism and goes beyond that, later and in *Lilacs,* by daring to merge himself with the body of the mother.

The Whitmanian quest is for the freedom of voice. My closest friend, John Hollander, recently departed, taught me most about how to read Whitman. John's crucial insight was: "When he announces his expansions, containments, and incorporations, he is frequently enacting a contraction and a withdrawal." John liked it when I remarked how close this was to Gershom Scholem's idea that Whitman was an "intuitive Kabbalist." Without necessarily knowing anything about the Safed Kabbalah of Moses Cordovero and Isaac Luria, the American bard exemplified their theory of creation as the divine *Zimzum,* in which Yahweh makes room for creation by contracting and withdrawing from part of himself.

I relate this to the tally, or image of voice, the breaking of the lilac sprig. Whitman had read *Lycidas* and *Adonais* and other pastoral elegies. To transcend them, he performed an Indic act of self-surrender, akin to Eliot's *The Waste Land,* a revision of *Lilacs.* Eliot takes from Whitman the song of the hermit thrush, the lilacs, the women mourning for Adonis—Lincoln—and the march down the open road with a third being, the thought of death and the knowledge of death.

The death of President Lincoln counts for less in *Lilacs* than does the death of the poet in Whitman, who gives up his image of voice in the hope that an even richer art will follow. Whitman was mistaken, as Wordsworth was, unlike the Milton of *Lycidas.* The tally is double-edged: It counts down as well as up, and breaking it is curiously equivalent to the Lurianic breaking of the vessels.

Whitman breaks the sprig, and the next section, as splendid, parallels this to the hermit thrush's bleeding throat:

> In the swamp in secluded recesses,
> A shy and hidden bird is warbling a song.
>
> Solitary the thrush,
> The hermit withdrawn to himself, avoiding the settlements,
> Sings by himself a song.

After the intensity of the first four sections, the poem opens into grand vistas in Section 5 and centers upon the national mourning, which then narrows to the poet's symbolic act:

> Here, coffin that slowly passes,
> I give you my sprig of lilac.

An extraordinary frenzy of breaking marks the astonishing Section 7:

> (Nor for you, for one alone,
> Blossoms and branches green to coffins all I bring,
> For fresh as the morning, thus would I chant a song for you
>   O sane and sacred death.
>
> All over bouquets of roses,
> O death, I cover you over with roses and early lilies,
> But mostly and now the lilac that blooms the first,
> Copious I break, I break the sprigs from the bushes,
> With loaded arms I come, pouring for you,
> For you and the coffins all of you O death.)

There is a kind of shattering effect in "Copious I break, I break the sprigs from the bushes." It is as though everyone's tally were broken at once, as though there were to be no more images of the voice's freedom.

Whitman shrewdly changes perspective and moves to Venus in the night sky and then to vistas of American landscape and of urban existence. These beautifully measured vistas are prolonged until the sudden epiphany of a personal death march:

> Then with the knowledge of death as walking one side of me,
> And the thought of death close-walking the other side
>   of me,
> And I in the middle as with companions, and as holding the
>   hands of companions,
> I fled forth to the hiding receiving night that talks not,
> Down to the shores of the water, the path by the swamp in
>   the dimness,
> To the solemn shadowy cedars and ghostly pines so still.

The thought of death walks more closely to the poet because it is universal, but the knowledge of death, to one still living, is a difficult and private gnosis. Joining the hermit thrush, the three comrades are rewarded by hearing his carol of death, which restores tallying to the poet:

> *Come lovely and soothing death,*
> *Undulate round the world, serenely arriving, arriving,*
> *In the day, in the night, to all, to each,*
> *Sooner or later delicate death.*
>
> *Prais'd be the fathomless universe,*
> *For life and joy, and for objects and knowledge curious,*
> *And for love, sweet love—but praise! praise! praise!*
> *For the sure-enwinding arms of cool-enfolding death.*
>
> *Dark mother always gliding near with soft feet,*
> *Have none chanted for thee a chant of fullest welcome?*
> *Then I chant it for thee, I glorify thee above all,*
> *I bring thee a song that when thou must indeed come,*
>   *come unfalteringly.*

Whitman's model here is the King James Bible's Song of Songs but with the mother replacing the young woman of that erotic paean. Death the dark mother is a dancer offering total fulfillment, and the erotic merger with her is absolute:

> *Approach strong deliveress,*
> *When it is so, when thou hast taken them I joyously sing*
> *   the dead,*
> *Lost in the loving floating ocean of thee,*
> *Laved in the flood of thy bliss O death.*
>
> *From me to thee glad serenades,*
> *Dances for thee I propose saluting thee, adornments and*
> *   feastings for thee,*
> *And the sights of the open landscape and the high-spread*
> *   sky are fitting,*
> *And life and the fields, and the huge and thoughtful night.*

Night, death, the mother, and the sea comfort Whitman in postcoital tenderness:

> *The night in silence under many a star,*
> *The ocean shore and the husky whispering wave whose*
> *   voice I know,*
> *And the soul turning to thee O vast and well-veil'd death,*
> *And the body gratefully nestling close to thee.*
>
> *Over the tree-tops I float thee a song,*
> *Over the rising and sinking waves, over the myriad fields*
> *   and the prairies wide,*
> *Over the dense-pack'd cities all and the teeming wharves*
> *   and ways,*
> *I float this carol with joy, with joy to thee O death.*

So much wonder and freedom of movement have been packed into *Lilacs'* first fourteen sections that I am always surprised that the two remaining divisions are so freshly inventive. Proclaiming that the hermit thrush's carol constitutes the tally of his soul, Whitman is granted a vision he has earned by his selfless service in the Civil War hospitals:

And I saw askant the armies,
I saw as in noiseless dreams hundreds of battle-flags,
Borne through the smoke of the battles and pierc'd with
    missiles I saw them,
And carried hither and yon through the smoke, and torn
    and bloody,
And at last but a few shreds left on the staffs, (and all in
    silence,)
And the staffs all splinter'd and broken.
I saw battle-corpses, myriads of them,
And the white skeletons of young men, I saw them,
I saw the debris and debris of all the slain soldiers of the
    war,
But I saw they were not as was thought,
They themselves were fully at rest, they suffer'd not,
The living remain'd and suffer'd, the mother suffer'd,
And the wife and the child and the musing comrade suffer'd,
And the armies that remain'd suffer'd.

The image of emasculation introduced by giving up the tally-sprig of lilac is expanded into the sexual apocalypse of battle. Were the elegy to end there, then Whitman's sublime art would have faltered. It does not, as we are given an extraordinary retrievement out of the night and so also out of the mothering sea that is the universe of death:

Passing the visions, passing the night,
Passing, unloosing the hold of my comrades' hands,
Passing the song of the hermit bird and the tallying song of
    my soul,
Victorious song, death's outlet song, yet varying ever-
    altering song,
As low and wailing, yet clear the notes, rising and falling,
    flooding the night,
Sadly sinking and fainting, as warning and warning, and yet
    again bursting with joy,
Covering the earth and filling the spread of the heaven,
As that powerful psalm in the night I heard from recesses,

Passing, I leave thee lilac with heart-shaped leaves,
I leave thee there in the dooryard, blooming, returning
    with spring.

I cease from my song for thee,
From my gaze on thee in the west, fronting the west,
    communing with thee,
O comrade lustrous with silver face in the night.

Yet each to keep and all, retrievements out of the night,
The song, the wondrous chant of the gray-brown bird,
And the tallying chant, the echo arous'd in my soul,
With the lustrous and drooping star with the countenance
    full of woe,
With the holders holding my hand nearing the call of the
    bird,
Comrades mine and I in the midst, and their memory ever
    to keep, for the dead I loved so well,
For the sweetest, wisest soul of all my days and lands—and
    this for his dear sake,
Lilac and star and bird twined with the chant of my soul,
There in the fragrant pines and the cedars dusk and dim.

The metric and rhetoric go back to the King James Bible and to the dissident Quaker services of Elias Hicks in Whitman's childhood. Walt is composing his New Bible for the American Religion but with no impulse to subvert Christianity. Rather, he subsumes it as he does Eastern speculation, Hermeticism (drawn from George Sand), and anything else he desires to include.

The tallying chant is the whole *Lilacs,* and the full-voiced closing pragmatically redefines the tally for us as being at once celebration and lament. The image of Whitman's voice thus fuses freedom and death, a death, though, that is Walt's own invention, indistinguishable from the night and the mothering sea.

HERMAN MELVILLE

Moby-Dick

MOBY-DICK AND LEAVES OF GRASS ALIKE CONFRONT US WITH DEMANDS larger than we initially apprehend. Intricate crosscurrents of Jacksonian democracy are traced in the *Pequod*'s fate and crew by Andrew Delbanco, who shows that Melville in his epic raises American politics to universal destiny. Whitman's aims were parallel, though his personal drama dominates reception when we now immerse ourselves in him. The puzzle for my students, as for me, is how odd it is to think of Walt as the Poet of Democracy. His credo is that each of us is the hero, the divine average, and yet we are not wound dressers, selflessly serving the maimed and the dying.

Shakespeare, worshipped by Melville and ambivalently received by Whitman, is the paradigm of a sublime difficulty that legitimately fascinates us as entertainment. *Moby-Dick,* greatest of sea yarns—to Joseph Conrad's discomfiture—can be read either with or against Ishmael's narrative tonalities; you can either believe what he is saying or not, as you will, since he cannot be trusted. Walt, afloat with his vision, is intoxicated with words. Ishmael, endlessly fascinated by his own narrative, strives to transform a wonder-wounded affect into knowledge.

Cognizance, in Melville's epic, is summed up by Ahab, who concluded Chapter 70, "The Sphynx," with

> O Nature, and O soul of man! how far beyond all utterance are your linked analogies! not the smallest atom stirs or lives in matter, but has its cunning duplicate in mind.

A universe of correspondences, signatures of all things we are there to read, is common to the masters of the nineteenth-century American literary renaissance: Emerson, Poe, Hawthorne, Melville, Whitman, Dickinson, even Henry James. Queequeg's markings trace all personal and historical realities: past, present, future. After Ishmael, Ahab, and the White Whale himself, the book is Queequeg's. As a fourfold, they can be contrasted with Whitman's heroically different quaternity of night, death, the mother, and the sea. It is Ishmael's book of the night; Queequeg's deathly coffin, which saves Ishmael from the vortex; Moby Dick, who, for all his phallic menace, constitutes the epic's only maternal presence; and Ahab's imperial (and imperious) sea.

Angus Fletcher remarked that "The final encounter of Ahab with the White Whale is the apocalyptic vision of the war between two daemonic powers." The daemon crowds out the human in Ahab, when he cries that Moby Dick "heaps me." Herman Melville, like Walt Whitman, makes a heap of all that he can find. We confront a crisis in scale when contemporary works are unable to sustain their ambitions (David Foster Wallace's *Infinite Jest,* Jonathan Franzen's *Freedom*).

After Joyce and Marcel Proust, Franz Kafka and Beckett, trying to write novels in the mode of Dickens, George Eliot, Henry James, and Balzac clearly became unsustainable. I no longer believe in any historicizing, however newfangled. Great literary achievement is personal, and genius is always the enemy of genius. Goethe refused to encourage Heinrich von Kleist and Hölderlin, who implicitly challenged the "happiness and astonishment" upon which his own daemon relied. Baudelaire never resolved his ambivalences toward Victor Hugo, because, unlike most subsequent critics, he knew how much Hugo took up the space of poetry in the French language. Joyce, meeting W. B. Yeats, voiced his regret that the Anglo-Irish "arch-poet" was too old to be influenced by the lyricist of *Chamber Music.*

Did they order these matters differently in nineteenth-century America? Melville dedicated *Moby-Dick* to Hawthorne, whose example enabled the American prose epic to emerge, just as *Leaves of Grass* 1855 needed Emerson as its starting point. Countering the flow, the ebb courses as superbly. Henry James in his book on Hawthorne turns his authentic American precursor into a shadowy form, a kind of Dimmesdale. Much as I love *The Portrait of a Lady* and *The Wings of the Dove,* does either Isabel Archer or Milly Theale match the magnificence of Hester Prynne? On the scale of dreadful American fictive husbands, Osmond is dwarfed by the Satanic Chillingworth.

The young Henry James failed miserably when reviewing *Drum-Taps* in 1865, though as the mature master, he rendered his final verdict on his younger self's tantrum: "that little atrocity." James made copious restitution, to the pathetic extreme of imitating Whitman as a hospital visitor and comforter, a role for which the patrician novelist had little talent. Even in the 1865 dismissal, however, James caught Walt's daemonic spirit as he urged the poet to possess and be possessed by America.

William and Henry James and Edith Wharton were possessed by *Out of the Cradle Endlessly Rocking* and *When Lilacs Last in the Dooryard Bloom'd*. Henry James chanted the poems aloud, an extraordinary resonance with organ-like sonority, as if possessed. Beyond their shared homoeroticism, our greatest poet and novelist were joined through mutual reliance upon their daemons. Shamanistic Walt, charismatic healer, seems more at home in the daemonic cosmos, yet the master James has yet greater zest for daemonic agency. In opposition to Whitman's metaphysical materialism, James is a curiously American Platonist. Sexual passion in James's strongest protagonists is marked by a Platonic daemon's enforcement of authority. Isabel returns to her agon with Osmond; Densher goes away from Kate to the departed Milly; in *The Golden Bowl*, Maggie recovers Amerigo, each in accord with a voice akin to the daemon of Socrates.

Shakespeare entertained a bevy of daemons: Hamlet, Falstaff, Iago, Cleopatra, Macbeth among them. They did not possess him, though Hamlet and Falstaff edged closest. It is a nice question whether daemonic Ahab possessed Melville. The twelve great writers centering this book were all possessed men and a woman so supernally intelligent that she outflanked all those who sought control over her. In spiritual turbulence, Whitman and Melville, Faulkner and Hart Crane appear to exceed Dickinson and Emerson, Hawthorne and James, Stevens and Eliot, Twain and Frost, but that is to mistake rhetorical stance and tone for the inner life. All these were haunted spirits, knowing bearers of hidden traditions.

I HAVE BEEN REREADING *MOBY-DICK* SINCE I FELL IN LOVE WITH THE book in 1940, a boy of ten enthralled with Hart Crane, Whitman, William Blake, Shakespeare. *Moby-Dick* made a fifth with *The Bridge, Song of Myself,* Blake's *The Four Zoas,* and *King Lear,* a visionary company that transformed a changeling child into an exegetical enthusiast adept at appreciation rather than into a poet. A superstitious soul, then and now, I feared being devoured by ravenous daemons if I crossed the line into creation.

Awe of Melville, Shakespeare, Blake, Whitman, Hart Crane continues to augment in my old age. Wounded by wonder, I find their words (below, in order) golden:

No fearless fool now fronts thee. I own thy speechless, placeless power; but to the last gasp of my earthquake life will dispute its unconditional, unintregal mastery in me. In the midst of the personified impersonal, a personality stands here . . .

Be absolute for death . . .

⁕   ⁕   ⁕

Thou hast nor youth nor age,

But as it were an after-dinner's sleep,
Dreaming on both . . .

Tho thou art worship'd by the names Divine of Jesus and Jehovah; thou art still the son of morn in weary night's decline, the lost traveler's dream under the hill.

You will hardly know who I am or what I mean,
But I shall be good health to you nevertheless,
And filter and fibre your blood.

Failing to fetch me at first keep encouraged,
Missing me one place search another,
I stop some where waiting for you.

And so it was I entered the broken world
To trace the visionary company of love, its voice
An instant in the wind (I know not whither hurled)
But not for long to hold each desperate choice.

Ahab confronting the corposants; the enigmatic Vincentio dubiously comforting Claudio in *Measure for Measure;* Blake defying the Accuser, who is the god of this world; Walt eluding us at the close of *Song of My-self;* Hart Crane breaking the vessels of his poethood and life—these are secular Scripture for me. Supreme aesthetic experience sustains me through all loss and augmenting presages of the end.

Matthew Arnold, who expressed exasperation with Whitman, took his own touchstones rather seriously. Mine are marks of pleasure, of delight in reading. I would not change a sentence of *Moby-Dick.* A chapter like 101, "The Decanter," devoted to beef and beer aboard whalers, manifests Ishmael's comic zest:

> The quantity of beer, too, is very large, 10,800 barrels. Now, as those polar fisheries could only be prosecuted in the short summer of that climate, so that the whole cruise of one of these Dutch whalemen, including the short voyage to and from the Spitzbergen sea, did not much exceed three months, say, and reckoning 30 men to each of their fleet of 180 sail, we have 5,400 Low Dutch seamen in all; therefore, I say, we have precisely two barrels of beer per man, for a twelve weeks' allowance, exclusive of his fair proportion of that 550 ankers of gin. Now, whether these gin and beer harpooners, so fuddled as one might fancy them to have been, were the right sort of men to stand up in a boat's head, and take good aim at flying whales; this would seem somewhat improbable. Yet they did aim at them, and hit them too. But this was very far North, be it remembered, where beer agrees well with the constitution; upon the Equator, in our southern fishery, beer would be apt to make the harpooner sleepy at the mast-head and boozy in his boat; and grievous loss might ensue to Nantucket and New Bedford.

Without such ballast, the metaphysics of the hunt might sink *Moby-Dick.* Ahab, daemonic in drive, is not too huge for his book because it contains the cosmos. Walt, benign daemon, is ballasted by the giant cavalcade that *Leaves of Grass* presents; a list alternating epiphanies and commodities transmutes into the story of the American self, glorying Adam early in the morning of a new world.

Are all Americans Ahabs? Some—then and now—surely strive not to be. Jewish, I would prefer to be Ishmael, but forever he is the progenitor of the Arabs. One of my students in a class discussion of *Moby-Dick* declared her choice to be Queequeg, with the White Whale in second place. She read aloud from Chapter 133, "The Chase—First Day":

A gentle joyousness—a mighty mildness of repose in swiftness, invested the gliding whale. Not the white bull Jupiter swimming away with ravished Europa clinging to his graceful horns; his lovely, leering eyes sideways intent upon the maid; with smooth bewitching fleetness, rippling straight for the nuptial bower in Crete; not Jove, not that great majesty Supreme! did surpass the glorified White Whale as he so divinely swam.

On each soft side—coincident with the parted swell, that but once laving him, then flowed so wide away—on each bright side, the whale shed off enticings. No wonder there had been some among the hunters who namelessly transported and allured by all this serenity, had ventured to assail it, but had fatally found that quietude but the vesture of tornadoes. Yet calm, enticing calm, oh, whale! thou glidest on, to all who for the first time eye thee, no matter how many in that same way thou may'st have bejuggled and destroyed before.

This marked erotic intensity fuses delicious Fayaway of *Typee* with the dangerous beauty of innocence in *Billy Budd*. Genders mingle and subdivide in a fluid dissolve of erotic imagination. Snowy androgyne, Moby Dick masks his/her "vesture of tornadoes" enticingly as a gliding calm. Harpooners and lancers are at once phallic and commercial in their fiery hunt.

It can be illuminating to read *Moby-Dick* as Melville's autobiography, just as the 1860 third edition of *Leaves of Grass* is Walt Whitman's. In 1855 and 1856, Whitman's self epiphanies are more like journal entries than a narrative. A crisis, perhaps homoerotic, in the winter of 1859–60, may have sparked Walt's movement toward a fuller story of the self.

Where is Melville the man in *Moby-Dick*? Split at least three ways (Ishmael, Ahab, narrator), he is somewhat parallel to Whitman, who in 1855 also is tripartite (real Me or Me myself, rough Walt as American selfhood, and my Soul). One can venture that Ishmael, who so charms us, has a touch of the Me myself, while Ahab, as unknowable as night, death, the mother, and the sea, is Melville's soul in the Gnostic sense of spark, or *pneuma.* The narrator, scarcely as interesting as "Walt Whitman, one of the roughs, an American," nevertheless shares the metamorphic nature of Walt's elusive self.

The pre-Socratic aphorism—ethos is the daemon—can be translated as "character is fate." In drama, character is action. Shakespeare, too capacious for any formula, leads me to a rival aphorism: Pathos also is the daemon, which could be rendered as "personality is our destiny." In Shakespearean theatricalism, personality is suffering. Action, Wordsworth wrote, is momentary, while suffering is permanent, obscure, dark, and shares the nature of infinity. Against the personified impersonal of the White Whale, Ahab stands as personality, a new Macbeth to be destroyed again by his own proleptic imagination.

I take this as our American modification of Shakespearean heart, mind, consciousness. Whitman and Melville, Emerson and Dickinson, Hawthorne and James, Twain and Frost, Stevens and Eliot, Faulkner and Hart Crane choose theatricalism over drama, suffering over action, personality over character. It is not accidental that our strongest playwrights—Eugene O'Neill, Tennessee Williams, Arthur Miller, Thornton Wilder, Edward Albee, Tony Kushner—do not meet the measure of our greatest poets, novelists, storywriters: Whitman, Hawthorne, Melville, Twain, James, Frost, Dreiser, Cather, Stevens, Eliot, W. C. Williams, Hart Crane, Fitzgerald, Hemingway, Faulkner, Nathanael West, Flannery O'Connor, Thomas Pynchon, Elizabeth Bishop, Ashbery, Ammons, Merrill, Philip Roth, and others.

An intensely theatrical nation—in our politics, spirituality, styles of living and being—how is it that we cannot sustain drama? Let me sharpen the antithesis between character and personality, act and spark, ethos and pathos, unknowing daemon and the daemon who knows how it is done. Ahab vows vengeful action yet only augments suffering: for himself, his cause, their stay-at-home survivors. Walt the wound dresser comforts the suffering at the cost of himself. Dickinson knows transport only by the pain; James at his most eloquent emulates Hawthorne by celebrating (implicitly) his protagonists' renunciations. Eliot's spiritual asceticism provokes Stevens, W. C. Williams, and Hart Crane to reaffirm a Keatsian High Romantic faith in renewed American imaginative vitality, Whitmanian solar intensity.

In the Evening Land, every literary gain ebbs with an ebb of the ocean of life. *Moby-Dick* holds together better than any single volume by Whitman except the 1860 *Leaves of Grass*, where indeed we touch a man by reading his book and we become his poem. Unfortunately, no reprint of the 1860 third edition is now readily available, unlike *Moby-Dick*.

Melville's masterwork was composed in a year and a half by a mariner who had just turned thirty, become a husband and father, and lived on borrowed money from in-laws and relatives. Even the creative wilderness of *Mardi and a Voyage Thither* (1849) could not prepare a reader, then and now, for the magnificence of *Moby-Dick*. Why the corposants electrified Herman Melville into this one absolute sublimity is probably unanswerable. I think of *As I Lay Dying*, McCarthy's *Blood Meridian*, Roth's *Sabbath's Theater*, and—on a smaller scale—West's *Miss Lonelyhearts* and Pynchon's *The Crying of Lot 49* as similar breakthroughs beyond the reach of art. The daemon knows how it is done.

Many readers now exalt the later novella *Billy Budd* to the eminence of *Moby-Dick*, but I regret my inability to agree. Like poor Billy himself, the little book relapses into inarticulateness. *The Confidence-Man*, also now admired, is a botch, though not a disaster like *Pierre*. I have a personal taste for the long poem *Clarel*, but its length is excessive and its metric inadequate. *The Piazza Tales* include the justly renowned "Bartleby, the Scrivener" and "Benito Cereno" and I admire both "The Bell Tower" and *The Encantadas*. What else? Of the poems, *Battle-Pieces* is dwarfed by *Drum-Taps*, but there are a scattering that remain memorable: *After the Pleasure Party*, *The Maldive Shark*, and *Shelley's Vision* among them. *Moby-Dick* rises up from the rest of Herman Melville, a snowy summit and Leviathan surrounded by minnows.

This phenomenon of one singular work scarcely is unique to the United States. Twain has a few hilarious sketches, like "Cannibalism in the Cars" and "Journalism in Tennessee," but only *The Adventures of Huckleberry Finn* has the special status of *Moby-Dick*, *Leaves of Grass* (1860), *Walden*, *The Scarlet Letter*, *The Portrait of a Lady*, *The Great Gatsby*.

I strongly urge readers of *Moby-Dick* to employ the Norton Critical Edition (revised 2002), ably edited by Hershel Parker and Harrison Hayford, so as to provide a reliable text. Shrewdly, Melville divided his immense narrative into one hundred and thirty-five brief chapters. Teaching the great book in three two-hour discussions with a dozen brilliant students, I suggest they think of it as tripartite.

1. 1–49 "Loomings" through "The Hyena"
2. 50–87 "Ahab's Boat and Crew—Fedallah" through "The Grand Armada"
3. 88–135 "Schools and Schoolmasters" through "The Chase—Third Day" and "Epilogue."

Part 1 might be called "Ishmael," Part 2, "Ahab," and Part 3, "Moby Dick." Here I will discuss seven chapters of the first part, seven of the second, a dozen of the third, and the beautiful, Jobean "Epilogue." That is only one-fifth of the text, so this cannot be a total appreciation, but I hope it will suffice.

Few initial chapters haunt me as does "Loomings," with its uncanny onset:

Call me Ishmael. Some years ago—never mind how long precisely—having little or no money in my purse, and nothing particular to interest me on shore, I thought I would sail about a little and see the watery part of the world. It is a way I have of driving off the spleen, and regulating the circulation. Whenever I find myself growing grim about the mouth; whenever it is a damp, drizzly November in my soul; whenever I find myself involuntarily pausing before coffin warehouses, and bringing up the rear of every funeral I meet; and especially whenever my hypos get such an upper hand of me, that it requires a strong moral principle to prevent me from deliberately stepping into the street, and methodically knocking people's hats off—then, I account it high time to get to sea as soon as I can. This is my substitute for pistol and ball. With a philosophical flourish Cato throws himself upon his sword; I quietly take to the ship. There is nothing surprising in this. If they but knew it, almost all men in their degree, some time or other, cherish very nearly the same feelings towards the ocean with me.

I write on a damp, drizzly November day in New Haven (November 13, 2012), at four in the afternoon, when the outside air reminds me (as it does rarely) that our dreary university town actually is a seaport. It startles me how little has changed when Ishmael sketches his playbill:

"Grand Contested Election for the Presidency of the United States"
"WHALING VOYAGE BY ONE ISHMAEL"
"BLOODY BATTLE IN AFFGHANISTAN"

Casual, unhurried, paradoxically driven yet easygoing, Ishmael starts off upon a questless quest not at all his own. His loneliness ends with a New Bedford marriage to the harpooner Queequeg: the single figure in our literature almost as likable as Huck Finn and Nigger Jim. Chapter 110, "Queequeg in His Coffin," is an epitome of the heroic composure of Ishmael's comrade:

> Leaning over in his hammock, Queequeg long regarded the coffin with an attentive eye. He then called for his harpoon, had the wooden stock drawn from it, and then had the iron part placed in the coffin along with one of the paddles of his boat. All by his own request, also, biscuits were then ranged round the sides within: a flask of fresh water was placed at the head, and a small bag of woody earth scraped up in the hold at the foot; and a piece of sailcloth being rolled up for a pillow, Queequeg now entreated to be lifted into his final bed, that he might make trial of its comforts, if any it had. He lay without moving a few minutes, then told one to go to his bag and bring out his little god, Yojo. Then crossing his arms on his breast with Yojo between, he called for the coffin lid (hatch he called it) to be placed over him. The head part turned over with a leather hinge, and there lay Queequeg in his coffin with little but his composed countenance in view. "Rarmai" (it will do; it is easy), he murmured at last, and signed to be replaced in his hammock.

With dignity, yet statelier, the harpooner wills himself to live:

> But now that he had apparently made every preparation for death; now that his coffin was proved a good fit, Queequeg suddenly rallied; soon there seemed no need of the carpenter's box; and thereupon, when some expressed their delighted surprise, he, in substance, said, that the cause of his sudden convalescence was

this;—at a critical moment, he had just recalled a little duty ashore, which he was leaving undone; and therefore had changed his mind about dying: he could not die yet, he averred. They asked him, then, whether to live or die was a matter of his own sovereign will and pleasure. He answered, certainly. In a word, it was Queequeg's conceit, that if a man made up his mind to live, mere sickness could not kill him: nothing but a whale, or a gale, or some violent, ungovernable, unintelligent destroyer of that sort.

Queequeg is not a noble savage but the most civilized man aboard the *Pequod:* gracious, tradition-soaked, loving, spontaneous, responsible, and yet ultimately mysterious. We can read neither the hieroglyphs tattooed upon him nor the living hieroglyph he represents in himself. Why will he not return to reclaim his Maori kingdom, of which he is legitimate successor: "ascending the pure and undefiled throne of thirty pagan Kings before him"? Why does so grand a person adopt Ahab's ferocious quest as his own? Queequeg, unlike Ishmael, has no quarrel (however loving) with existence.

The central mystery of *Moby-Dick* is also its daemonic glory: The reader who is free of cant and creed will also be drawn into Ahab's quest to strike through the mask of a cosmos that fell apart in its own creation. High Romanticism's antithetical religion is a kind of purified Gnosticism. When I teach the book, I ask my students to consider both the contrast and the consonance between the sublime eloquences of Father Mapple and of Captain Ahab. Is Mapple truly more Christian than the Gnostic lord of the *Pequod?* Here is Father Mapple:

He drooped and fell away from himself for a moment; then lifting his face to them again, showed a deep joy in his eyes, as he cried out with a heavenly enthusiasm,—"But oh! shipmates! on the starboard hand of woe, there is a sure delight; and higher the top of that delight, than the bottom of the woe is deep. Is not the main-truck higher than the kelson is low? Delight is to him—a far, far upward, and inward delight—who against the proud gods and commodores of this earth, ever stands forth his own inexorable self. Delight is to him whose strong arms yet support him, when the ship of this base treacherous world has gone down beneath him. Delight is to him, who gives no quarter in the truth, and kills, burns, and destroys all sin though he pluck it out from under the robes of Senators and Judges. Delight,—top-gallant delight is to him, who acknowledges no law or lord, but the Lord his God, and is only a patriot to heaven. Delight is to him, whom all the waves of the billows of the seas of the boisterous mob can never shake from this sure Keel of the Ages. And eternal delight and deliciousness will be his, who coming to lay him down, can say with his final breath—O Father!—chiefly known to me by Thy rod—mortal or immortal, here I die. I have striven to be Thine, more than to be this world's, or mine own. Yet this is nothing; I leave eternity to Thee; for what is man that he should live out the lifetime of his God?"

And here is Ahab:

". . . Thou knowest not how came ye, hence callest thyself unbegotten; certainly knowest not thy beginning, hence callest thyself unbegun. I know that of me, which thou knowest not of thyself, oh, thou omnipotent. There is some unsuffusing thing beyond thee, thou clear spirit, to whom all thy eternity is but time, all thy creativeness mechanical. Through thee, thy flaming self, my scorched eyes do dimly see it. Oh, thou foundling fire, thou hermit immemorial, thou too hast thy incommunicable riddle, thy unparticipated grief. Here again with haughty agony, I read my sire. Leap! leap up, and lick the sky! I leap with thee; I burn with thee; would fain be welded with thee; defyingly I worship thee!'

Father Mapple's colors of rhetoric conceal a Melvillean, un-Christian gnosis: "his own inexorable self." With subtle skepticism—"mortal or immortal, here I die"—Mapple comes to rest upon "for what is man that he should live out the lifetime of his God?" Is not that God also "mortal or immortal"?

Mapple echoes equivocal Job, neither so patient nor so pious a sufferer as orthodoxy wants him to be. Ahab, who shouts, "No! In thunder," to any injunction to submit or yield, is not so much the anti-Job as Job emancipated, set forth to hook and spear him. Moby Dick swims away, while Ahab and all his crew, save Ishmael, are destroyed. Is Ahab vanquished?

No. Like Milton's Satan, what *is* else, provided one is not overcome, except by one's own heart alone.

Melville's heroic protagonists are worthy of the book's dedication to Nathaniel Hawthorne: Ahab, Queequeg, Starbuck, Stubb. Ishmael stands apart: There is no confrontation or exchange between him and Ahab. Instead, he *reads* Ahab, as we are compelled to read Hamlet. The Prince of Denmark's darkness did not commence with the death of his father and his mother's remarriage, and Ahab's sorrow preceded his dismemberment by the White Whale. Ishmael—transcendentalist *and* skeptic (like Emerson himself), his alienation cured by comradeship with Queequeg—intuits Ahab's Gnostic rebellion against the Leviathan, imposed upon us by God through nature, and senses the metaphysics of Ahab's Prometheanism.

As the American Prometheus, Ahab need not steal fire from the gods. Fire is his Zarathustran birthright from far back before the creation and fall. But his right worship of that fire is defiance: "Who's over me?" A man who would strike the sun if it insulted him is beyond good and evil. His paradigm for Melville was Macbeth, a creative choice both brilliant and erring. Macbeth and Ahab share a sense of outrage, metaphysical yet personal. Very subtly, Shakespeare hints at a sexual failing in Macbeth. His enormous passion for Lady Macbeth is afflicted by his powerfully proleptic imagination: He arrives perpetually before the event, as it were. That appears to have been D. H. Lawrence's burden with his wife, Frieda, if we are to believe his disciple John Middleton Murry, though Murry is regarded by Aldous Huxley as a supposed Judas.

Ahab's castration by Moby Dick is rather less than an analogue, but the parallel with Macbeth is suggestive enough. These days we would try to convict Macbeth for crimes against humanity: He is prone to child murder. Ahab has no guilt whatsoever, even though his mad quest suborns and destroys his crew, who yield not only to his authority but to their own huntsman's instinct. If they are not culpable for seeking to spear Yahweh's King Leviathan, why, then, is Ahab? Even as a boy I apprehended, though remotely, that Ahab's drive was ontotheological, like Iago, whose Moby Dick was the war-god Othello, or Edmund, who wanted to coerce the gods into standing up for bastards.

Ahab's cousins are Don Quixote, Hamlet, Milton's Satan, Shelley's Prometheus: antithetical questers almost too large for their negative enterprises. As the American overreacher, Ahab has all the stigmata of a latecomer. Like Milton and Shelley (and Goethe, Ibsen, Joyce, Anton Chekhov, and Beckett), Melville is compelled to rely a little too heavily upon Hamlet, Prince of the Solitary Consciousness. A soliloquy by Ahab can unnerve us:

> There's a sight! There's a sound! The greyheaded woodpecker tapping the hollow tree! Blind and deaf might well be envied now. See! that thing rests on two line-tubs, full of tow-lines. A most malicious wag, that fellow. Rat-tat! So man's seconds tick! Oh! how immaterial are all materials! What things real are there, but imponderable thoughts? Here now's the very dreaded symbol of grim death, by a mere hap, made the expressive sign of the help and hope of most endangered life. A life-buoy of a coffin! Does it go further? Can it be that in some spiritual sense the coffin is, after all, but an immortality-preserver! I'll think of that. But no. So far gone am I in the dark side of earth, that its other side, the theoretic bright one, seems but uncertain twilight to me. Will ye never have done, Carpenter, with that accursed sound? I go below; let me not see that thing here when I return again. Now, then, Pip, we'll talk this over; I do suck most wondrous philosophies from thee! Some unknown conduits from the unknown worlds must empty into thee!

Ahab is Hamlet in the graveyard, with his carpenter playing the gravedigger. Queequeg's coffin, converted to a life buoy, will be Birnam Wood come to Dunsinane, presaging Ahab's doom and providing Ishmael with survival. Earlier, in Chapter 37, a compendium of Shakespearean soliloquies are heard, which I give complete:

> (*The cabin; by the stern windows; Ahab sitting alone, and gazing out.*)
>
>   I leave a white and turbid wake; pale waters, paler cheeks, where'er I sail. The envious billows sidelong swell to whelm my track; let them; but first I pass.
>
>   Yonder, by ever-brimming goblet's rim, the warm waves blush like wine. The gold brow plumbs the blue. The diver sun—slow dived from noon,—goes down; my soul mounts up! she wearies with her endless hill. Is, then, the crown too heavy that I wear? this

Iron Crown of Lombardy. Yet is it bright with many a gem; I the wearer, see not its far flashings; but darkly feel that I wear that, that dazzlingly confounds. 'Tis iron—that I know—not gold. 'Tis split, too—that I feel; the jagged edge galls me so, my brain seems to beat against the solid metal; aye, steel skull, mine; the sort that needs no helmet in the most brain-battering fight!

Dry heat upon my brow? Oh! time was, when as the sunrise nobly spurred me, so the sunset soothed. No more. This lovely light, it lights not me; all loveliness is anguish to me, since I can ne'er enjoy. Gifted with the high perception, I lack the low, enjoying power; damned, most subtly and most malignantly! damned in the midst of Paradise! Good night—good night! *(waving his hand, he moves from the window.)*

'Twas not so hard a task. I thought to find one stubborn, at the least; but my one cogged circle fits into all their various wheels, and they revolve. Or, if you will, like so many ant-hills of powder, they all stand before me; and I their match. Oh, hard! that to fire others, the match itself must needs be wasting! What I've dared, I've willed, and what I've willed, I'll do! They think me mad—Starbuck does; but I'm demoniac, I am madness maddened! That wild madness that's only calm to comprehend itself! The prophecy was that I should be dismembered; and—Aye! I lost this leg. I now prophesy that I will dismember my dismemberer. Now, then, be the prophet and the fulfiller one. That's more than ye, ye great gods, ever were. I laugh and hoot at ye, ye cricket-players, ye pugilists, ye deaf Burkes and blinded Bendigoes! I will not say as schoolboys do to bullies,— Take some one of your own size; don't pommel *me*! No, ye've knocked me down, and I am up again; but *ye* have run and hidden. Come forth from behind your cotton bags! I have no long gun to reach ye. Come, Ahab's compliments to ye; come and see if ye can swerve me. Swerve me? ye cannot swerve me, else ye swerve yourselves! man has ye there. Swerve me? The path to my fixed purpose is laid with iron rails, whereon my soul is grooved to run. Over unsounded gorges, through the rifled hearts of mountains, under torrents' beds, unerringly I rush! Naught's an obstacle, naught's an angle to the iron way!

In Chapter 36, "The Quarter-Deck," Ahab's driving will and rhetoric have seduced the entire crew of his whaler to his dark quest. Knowingly demonic, he harkens back to Elijah's prophecy in Chapter 19, neatly dovetailed with the savage Elijah of First Kings, remorseless enemy of King Ahab, who is slain in battle "and the dogs licked up his blood."

Two daemonic powers, or agents (to adopt Angus Fletcher's term), meet head-on in Moby Dick and Captain Ahab. Daemonic agency *is* the hidden tradition of American literature, an assertion clearer regarding narrative (Poe, Melville, Hawthorne, Twain, James, Faulkner) than wisdom writing (Emerson, Thoreau) or poetry (Whitman, Dickinson, Frost, Stevens, Eliot, Hart Crane). In narrative, the protagonists are possessed by daemons, conquistadores somehow ordering a chaos of unruly other selves. Lyric and essayistic image-making becomes the mode of ordering the autobiographical self in ghostlier demarcations, keener sounds.

Moby-Dick is one major American variant upon the Homeric-Virgilian-Miltonic epic. The other, *Song of Myself,* transumes the mode shared by Wordsworth, Carlyle, Tennyson, and Ruskin (in *Praeterita*): the growth of the poet-sage's mind. Miscalled modernism (Eliot, Pound, Lawrence, Joyce, Woolf) remains in these orbits, though Joyce bursts the vessels of inherited forms as energetically as Whitman and Melville had done.

The art of *Moby-Dick* marvelously balances encyclopedic catalog with a world of diverse personalities. My students find in the *Pequod*'s crew a prophecy of the newer America breaking upon us now, to the perplexity of the wretched theocrats, plutocrats, and aging moralists. Ishmael cheerfully converts from his dried-up Presbyterianism to his comrade Queequeg's South Sea island portable idol, while Ahab is a Quaker turned first to Manichaean Zoroastrian fire worship and then to Melvillean gnosis. Starbuck is a firm Quaker, Stubb and Flask godless New Englanders, while the magnificent Queequeg is joined by three highly disparate fellow harpooners: Tashtego the Native American, Daggoo the African black, and Ahab's daemon, the Parsee Fedallah. And the crew, aside from Fedallah's underlings, comprises a gallery of the nations: from the Azores to the Isle of Man, a "deputation from all the isles of the sea, and all the ends of the earth, accompanying old Ahab in the Pequod to lay the world's grievances before that bar from which not very many of them ever come back."

"The world's grievances" are the Jobean burden of *Moby-Dick,* of so massive a heft that Melville's fighting motto transcends American hyper-bole: "Give me a condor's quill! Give me Vesuvius' crater for an ink-stand! . . . To produce a mighty book, you must choose a mighty theme." That would be Davy Crockett's half horse/half alligator fustian, except that this one time Melville's achievement soars beyond even his astonish-ing ambitions. Whitman overtly intended *Leaves of Grass* to become the New Bible for Americans. Properly regarded, it is, particularly when read in conjunction with Emerson, *Moby-Dick, Huckleberry Finn,* Emily Dickinson, *The Scarlet Letter, Walden, The Portrait of a Lady,* Robert Frost and Wallace Stevens, *As I Lay Dying,* and *The Bridge.* With *Leaves of Grass* 1860, *Moby-Dick* is at the center of this American heretical scripture, our worship of the god within, which pragmatically means of the daemon who knows how it is done.

Is *Moby-Dick* a prophetic book? If we consider its greatest progeny—*Miss Lonelyhearts, Invisible Man, The Crying of Lot 49, Blood Meridian*—we might justify such a placement. Whitman's prodigals—aspects of Stevens, Eliot, W. C. Williams, Ashbery, Ammons, above all Hart Crane (who fuses Walt and *Moby-Dick* together)—are a stronger kind of evi-dence. The hidden strength of Tony Kushner's *Angels in America* is in its own blending of Whitman and Melville; I continue to hope Kushner will return to that heritage, since his later career has yet to match the spiritual and aesthetic splendor of *Perestroika.*

Prophecy in Isaiah, Dante, or Blake has a design upon us. Melville, through deep reading in Shakespeare, turned away from prophecy in *Moby-Dick.* I agree with Roy Harvey Pearce that the prophetic Whitman is not persuasive in preaching the American Union or the erotic democ-racy of comrades. His aesthetic strength is personal, whether he celebrates or laments divisions in the self. And his healing power, his greatest gift, is contrary to prophecy. Prophets do not heal; they exacerbate. I reread and teach *Moby-Dick* to uncover and appreciate the sublimity and the danger of American Promethean heroism. But several prolonged times when close to death, I have recited Whitman to myself as medicine. I hardly recom-mend my personal praxis to students or readers because what works for me may not do much for another. Unable to rise out of bed for months, desperate for self-help, chanting much out of Whitman, particularly *Song of Myself* and the *Sea-Drift* and *Lilacs* elegies, has given me more than the illusion of consolation and recovery. Walt calls this "retrievements out of the night" and persuades me that for once the poet is the man and I have become his poem. Then I recall how often from 1863 through 1867 Whitman labored in the Civil War hospitals, dressing wounds, reading and writing letters, bearing little gifts, holding the maimed and sick as they died in his arms. In itself that was secular sainthood, and Walt was a kind of American Christ. Yet it is at one with the human and aesthetic power of his greatest poems. If finally I value Whitman more than Melville or Emerson, Dickinson or Henry James, Wallace Stevens or Hart Crane, it must be because he has healed me and goes on helping me to get through many sleepless nights of anxiety and pain.

I return to *Moby-Dick*—so vast an epic that discussing it has to be a highly selective process for my daemonic study—and choose first to center upon Chapters 41 and 42, "Moby Dick" and the piercing rhapsody "The Whiteness of the Whale." I give the final paragraph of Chapter 42 and juxtapose it with the trial that ends Chapter 43:

Here, then, was this grey-headed, ungodly old man, chasing with curses a Job's whale round the world, at the head of a crew, too, chiefly made up of mongrel renegades, and castaways, and cannibals—morally enfeebled also, by the incompetence of mere unaided virtue or right-mindedness in Starbuck, the invulnerable jollity of indifference and recklessness in Stubb, and the pervading mediocrity in Flask. Such a crew, so officered, seemed specially picked and packed by some infernal fatality to help him to his monomaniac revenge. How it was that they so aboundingly responded to the old man's ire—by what evil magic their souls were possessed, that at times his hate seemed almost theirs; the White Whale as much their insufferable foe as his; how all this came to be—what the White Whale was to them, or how to their unconscious understandings, also, in some dim, unsuspected way, he might have seemed the gliding great demon of the seas of life,—all this to explain, would be to dive deeper than Ishmael can go. The subterranean miner that works in us all, how can one tell whither leads his shaft by the ever shifting, muffled sound of his pick? Who does not feel the irresistible arm drag? What skiff in tow of a seventy-four can stand still? For one, I gave myself up to the abandonment of the time and the place; but while yet all a-rush to encounter the whale, could see naught in that brute but the deadliest ill.

Though neither knows where lie the nameless things of which the mystic sign gives forth such hints; yet with me, as with the colt, somewhere those things must exist. Though in many of its aspects this visible world seems formed in love, the invisible spheres were formed in fright.

But not yet have we solved the incantation of this whiteness, and learned why it appeals with such power to the soul; and more strange and far more portentous—why, as we have seen, it is at once the most meaning symbol of spiritual things, nay, the very veil of the Christian's Deity; and yet should be as it is, the intensifying agent in things the most appalling to mankind.

Is it that by its indefiniteness it shadows forth the heartless voids and immensities of the universe, and thus stabs us from behind with the thought of annihilation, when beholding the white depths of the milky way? Or is it, that as in essence whiteness is not so much a color as the visible absence of color, and at the same time the concrete of all colors; is it for these reasons that there is such a dumb blankness, full of meaning, in a wide landscape of snows— a colorless, all-color of atheism from which we shrink? And when we consider that other theory of the natural philosophers, that all other earthly hues—every stately or lovely emblazoning—the sweet tinges of sunset skies and woods; yea, and the gilded velvets of but-terflies, and the butterfly cheeks of young girls; all these are but subtle deceits, not actually inherent in substances, but only laid on from without; so that all deified Nature absolutely paints like the harlot, whose allurements cover nothing but the charnel-house within; and when we proceed further, and consider that the mysti-cal cosmetic which produces every one of her hues, the great prin-ciple of light, for ever remains white or colorless in itself, and if operating without medium upon matter, would touch all objects, even tulips and roses, with its own blank tinge—pondering all this, the palsied universe lies before us a leper; and like wilful travelers in Lapland, who refuse to wear colored and coloring glasses upon their eyes, so the wretched infidel gazes himself blind at the monumental white shroud that wraps all the prospect around him. And of all these things the Albino whale was the symbol. Wonder ye then at the fiery hunt?

The intransigent blank begins in English with Shakespeare and Milton. "See better, Lear, and let me still remain," Kent pleads, "the true blank of thine eye," where "blank" means the white center of a target. Milton's very different and more influential blank centers the great invocation to light at the opening of Book III in *Paradise Lost,* where the English Homer laments that nature is to him "a universal blank." This engenders most of the blanks of Anglo-American Romanticism, from Coleridge's *Dejection: An Ode* ("And still I gaze—and with how blank an eye") and Wordsworth's *The Prelude* through Shelley's majestic *Mont Blanc* on to Emerson's "The ruin or blank, that we see when we look at nature, is in our own eye." Emily Dickinson, profuse in the trope, tends to follow the Shakespearean model. For American poetry, the culminations are in Frost's *Design* and in Wallace Stevens's *The Auroras of Autumn,* where the man who is walking turns blankly on the sand and reflects bitterly that "here, being visible is being white."

Ahab's snowy Leviathan oppresses Melville even as "the heft of cathedral tunes" weighed upon Emily Dickinson. "He heaps me," Ahab cries out against the White Whale. "The Whiteness of the Whale" is Ishmael's reverie or meditation, though palpably his views also are Ahab's and Melville's:

Though in many of its aspects this visible world seems formed in love, the invisible spheres were formed in fright.

"Seems" against "were," love against fright, the visible less persuasive than the invisible: The Gnostic religion lurks in this, with its vision of a creation that also was a fall. When Ahab confronts the corposants in Chapter 119, "The Candles," his heretical spiritual stance becomes a subtle, difficult variant in Gnosticism:

Then turning—the last link held fast in his left hand, he put his foot upon the Parsee; and with fixed upward eye, and high-flung right arm, he stood erect before the lofty tri-pointed trinity of flames.

"Oh! thou clear spirit of clear fire, whom on these seas I as Persian once did worship, till in the sacramental act so burned by thee, that to this hour I bear the scar; I now know thee, thou clear spirit, and I now know that thy right worship is defiance. To neither love nor reverence wilt thou be kind; and e'en for hate thou canst but kill; and all are killed. No fearless fool now fronts thee. I own thy speechless, placeless power; but to the last gasp of my earthquake life will dispute its unconditional, unintegral mastery in me. In the midst of the personified impersonal, a personality stands here. Though but a point at best; whencesoe'er I came; wheresoe'er I go; yet while I earthly live, the queenly personality lives in me, and feels her royal rights. But war is pain, and hate is woe. Come in thy lowest form of love, and I will kneel and kiss thee; but at thy highest, come as mere supernal power; and though thou launchest navies of full-freighted worlds, there's that in here that still remains indifferent. Oh, thou clear spirit, of thy fire thou madest me, and like a true child of fire, I breathe it back to thee."

(Sudden, repeated flashes of lightning; the nine flames leap lengthwise to thrice their previous height; Ahab, with the rest, closes his eyes, his right hand pressed hard upon them.)

"I own thy speechless, placeless power; said I not so? Nor was it wrung from me; nor do I now drop these links. Thou canst blind; but I can then grope. Thou canst consume; but I can then be ashes. Take the homage of these poor eyes, and shutter-hands. I would not take it. The lightning flashes through my skull; mine eye-balls ache and ache; my whole beaten brain seems as beheaded, and rolling on some stunning ground. Oh, oh! Yet blindfold, yet will I talk to thee. Light though thou be, thou leapest out of darkness; but I am darkness leaping out of light, leaping out of thee! The javelins cease; open eyes; see, or not? There burn the flames! Oh, thou magnanimous! now I do glory in my genealogy. But thou art but my fiery father; my sweet mother, I know not. Oh, cruel! what hast thou done with her? There lies my puzzle; but thine is greater. Thou knowest not how came ye, hence callest thyself unbegotten; certainly knowest not thy beginning, hence callest thyself unbegun. I know that of me, which thou knowest not of thyself, oh, thou omnipotent. There is some unsuffusing thing beyond thee, thou clear

spirit, to whom all thy eternity is but time, all thy creativeness mechanical. Through thee, thy flaming self, my scorched eyes do dimly
see it. Oh, thou foundling fire, thou hermit immemorial, thou too
hast thy incommunicable riddle, thy unparticipated grief. Here
again with haughty agony, I read my sire. Leap! leap up, and lick the
sky! I leap with thee; I burn with thee; would fain be welded with
thee; defyingly I worship thee!"

Ahab's foot placed upon the Parsee Fedallah signifies his new repudia-
tion of his own earlier Manichaean Zoroastrianism. No longer an adept
of fire worship but still acknowledging fire as his fathering force, he exalts
his unknown mother instead. She would be the abyss, presumably "some
unsuffusing thing beyond," what the Gnostics called the *pleroma* or original fullness of being. Defying the fire, Ahab affirms both independence
and a continued quest to strike through the mask.

The antithetical voice to Ahab's urgent splendors belongs not to
Ishmael but to the narrator of two chapters in particular, each of an un-
equaled beauty: Chapter 87, "The Grand Armada," and Chapter 132,
"The Symphony." The first of these may be *Moby-Dick*'s most surprising
vision:

It had been next to impossible to dart these drugged-harpoons,
were it not that as we advanced into the herd, our whale's way
greatly diminished; moreover, that as we went still further and further from the circumference of commotion, the direful disorders
seemed waning. So that when at last the jerking harpoon drew out,
and the towing whale sideways vanished; then, with the tapering
force of his parting momentum, we glided between two whales into
the innermost heart of the shoal, as if from some mountain torrent
we had slid into a serene valley lake. Here the storms in the roaring
glens between the outermost whales, were heard but not felt. In this
central expanse the sea presented that smooth satin-like surface,
called a sleek, produced by the subtle moisture thrown off by the
whale in his more quiet moods. Yes, we were now in that enchanted
calm which they say lurks at the heart of every commotion. And
still in the distracted distance we beheld the tumults of the outer
concentric circles, and saw successive pods of whales, eight or ten in

each, swiftly going round and round, like multiplied spans of horses in a ring; and so closely shoulder to shoulder, that a Titanic circus-rider might easily have overarched the middle ones, and so have gone round on their backs. Owing to the density of the crowd of reposing whales, more immediately surrounding the embayed axis of the herd, no possible chance of escape was at present afforded us. We must watch for a breach in the living wall that hemmed us in; the wall that had only admitted us in order to shut us up. Keeping at the centre of the lake, we were occasionally visited by small tame cows and calves; the women and children of this routed host.

Now, inclusive of the occasional wide intervals between the revolving outer circles, and inclusive of the spaces between the various pods in any one of those circles, the entire area at this juncture, embraced by the whole multitude, must have contained at least two or three square miles. At any rate—though indeed such a test at such a time might be deceptive—spoutings might be discovered from our low boat that seemed playing up almost from the rim of the horizon. I mention this circumstance, because, as if the cows and calves had been purposely locked up in this innermost fold; and as if the wide extent of the herd had hitherto prevented them from learning the precise cause of its stopping; or, possibly, being so young, unsophisticated, and every way innocent and inexperienced; however it may have been, these smaller whales—now and then visiting our becalmed boat from the margin of the lake—evinced a wondrous fearlessness and confidence, or else a still, becharmed panic which it was impossible not to marvel at. Like household dogs they came snuffling round us, right up to our gunwales, and touching them; till it almost seemed that some spell had suddenly domesticated them. Queequeg patted their foreheads; Starbuck scratched their backs with his lance; but fearful of the consequences, for the time refrained from darting it.

But far beneath this wondrous world upon the surface, another and still stranger world met our eyes as we gazed over the side. For, suspended in those watery vaults, floated the forms of the nursing mothers of the whales, and those that by their enormous girth seemed shortly to become mothers. The lake, as I have hinted, was to a considerable depth exceedingly transparent; and as human infants while suckling will calmly and fixedly gaze away from the breast, as if leading two different lives at the time; and while yet drawing mortal nourishment, be still spiritually feasting upon some unearthly reminiscence;—even so did the young of these whales seem looking up towards us, but not at us, as if we were but a bit of Gulf-weed in their new-born sight. Floating on their sides, the mothers also seemed quietly eyeing us. One of these little infants, that from certain queer tokens seemed hardly a day old, might have measured some fourteen feet in length, and some six feet in girth. He was a little frisky; though as yet his body seemed scarce yet recovered from that irksome position it had so lately occupied in the maternal reticule; where, tail to head, and all ready for the final spring, the unborn whale lies bent like a Tartar's bow. The delicate side-fins, and the palms of his flukes, still freshly retained the plaited crumpled appearance of a baby's ears newly arrived from foreign parts.

"Line! line!" cried Queequeg, looking over the gunwale; "him fast! him fast!—Who line him! Who struck?—Two whale; one big, one little!"

"What ails ye, man?" cried Starbuck.

"Look-e here," said Queequeg, pointing down.

As when the stricken whale, that from the tub has reeled out hundreds of fathoms of rope; as, after deep sounding, he floats up again, and shows the slackened curling line buoyantly rising and spiralling towards the air; so now, Starbuck saw long coils of the umbilical cord of Madame Leviathan, by which the young cub seemed still tethered to its dam. Not seldom in the rapid vicissitudes of the chase, this natural line, with the maternal end loose, becomes entangled with the hempen one, so that the cub is thereby trapped. Some of the subtlest secrets of the seas seemed divulged to us in this enchanted pond. We saw young Leviathan amours in the deep.

Against the defensive ferocity of Ahab's adversary, Melville sets this lovely account of whale mothers and children and of "young Leviathan amours in the deep." After such tenderness, a voice at once Ahab's, Melville's, and Ishmael's, comforts us and itself with a "mute calm" in "the tornadoed Atlantic" of our mutual being.

Chapter 132, "The Symphony," directly precedes the three-day chase of Moby Dick by Ahab and his men of the *Pequod* and constitutes a psychic relief preluding the most violent of American daemonic sublimities. Turning to Starbuck, his perpetually tried and reasonable first mate, Ahab utters his full humanity:

"Oh, Starbuck! it is a mild, mild wind, and a mild looking sky. On such a day—very much such a sweetness as this—I struck my first whale—a boy-harpooneer of eighteen! Forty—forty—forty years ago!—ago! Forty years of continual whaling! forty years of privation, and peril, and storm-time! forty years on the pitiless sea! for forty years has Ahab forsaken the peaceful land, for forty years to make war on the horrors of the deep! Aye and yes, Starbuck, out of those forty years I have not spent three ashore. When I think of this life I have led; the desolation of solitude it has been; the masoned, walled-town of a Captain's exclusiveness, which admits but small entrance to any sympathy from the green country without—oh, weariness! heaviness! Guinea-coast slavery of solitary command!—when I think of all this; only half-suspected, not so keenly known to me before—and how for forty years I have fed upon dry salted fare—fit emblem of the dry nourishment of my soul!—when the poorest landsman has had fresh fruit to his daily hand, and broken the world's fresh bread, to my mouldy crusts—away, whole oceans away, from that young girl-wife I wedded past fifty, and sailed for Cape Horn the next day, leaving but one dent in my marriage pillow—wife? wife?—rather a widow with her husband alive! Aye, I widowed that poor girl when I married her, Starbuck; and then, the madness, the frenzy, the boiling blood and the smoking brow, with which, for a thousand lowerings old Ahab has furiously, foamingly chased his prey—more a demon than a man!—aye, aye! what a forty years' fool—fool—old fool, has old Ahab been! Why this strife of the chase? why weary, and palsy the arm at the oar, and the iron, and the lance? how the richer or better is Ahab now? Behold. Oh, Starbuck! is it not hard, that with this weary load I bear, one poor leg should have been snatched from under me? Here, brush this old hair aside; it blinds me, that I seem to weep. Locks so grey did never grow but from out some ashes! But do I look very old, so very, very old, Starbuck? I feel deadly faint, bowed, and humped, as though I were Adam, staggering beneath the piled centuries since Paradise. God! God! God!—crack my heart!—stave my brain!—mockery! mockery! bitter, biting mockery of grey hairs, have I lived enough joy to wear ye; and seem and feel thus intolerably old? Close! stand close to me, Starbuck; let me look into a human eye; it is better than to gaze into sea or sky, better than to gaze upon God. By the green land; by the bright hearth-stone! this is the magic glass, man; I see my wife and my child in thine eye. No, no; stay on board, on board!—lower not when I do; when branded Ahab gives chase to Moby Dick. That hazard shall not be thine. No, no! not with the far away home I see in that eye!"

Only a firm rhetorical control allows this poignance to not overwhelm us. Ahab, darkest of American Adams, causes us also to stagger beneath the piled centuries since our expulsion from paradise. Though Starbuck makes a final appeal to turn back, Ahab chooses tragedy:

"Oh, my Captain! my Captain! noble soul! grand old heart, after all! why should any one give chase to that hated fish! Away with me! let us fly these deadly waters! let us home! Wife and child, too, are Starbuck's—wife and child of his brotherly, sisterly, play-fellow youth; even as thine, sir, are the wife and child of thy loving, longing, paternal old age! Away! let us away!—this instant let me alter the course! How cheerily, how hilariously, O my Captain, would we bowl on our way to see old Nantucket again! I think, sir, they have some such mild blue days, even as this, in Nantucket."

"They have, they have. I have seen them—some summer days in the morning. About this time—yes, it is his noon nap now—the boy vivaciously wakes; sits up in bed; and his mother tells him of me, of cannibal old me; how I am abroad upon the deep, but will yet come back to dance him again."

"'Tis my Mary, my Mary herself! She promised that my boy, every morning, should be carried to the hill to catch the first glimpse of his father's sail! Yes, yes! no more! it is done! we head for Nantucket! Come, my Captain, study out the course, and let us away! See, see! the boy's face from the window! the boy's hand on the hill!"

But Ahab's glance was averted; like a blighted fruit tree he shook, and cast his last, cindered apple to the soil.

"What is it, what nameless, inscrutable, unearthly thing is it; what cozening, hidden lord and master, and cruel, remorseless emperor commands me; that against all natural lovings and longings, I so keep pushing, and crowding, and jamming myself on all the time; recklessly making me ready to do what in my own proper, natural heart, I durst not so much as dare? Is Ahab, Ahab? Is it I, God, or who, that lifts this arm? But if the great sun move not of himself; but is as an errand-boy in heaven; nor one single star can revolve, but by some invisible power; how then can this one small heart beat; this one small brain think thoughts; unless God does that beating, does that thinking, does that living, and not I. By heaven, man, we are turned round and round in this world, like yonder windlass, and Fate is the handspike. And all the time, lo! that smiling sky, and this unsounded sea! Look! see yon Albicore! who put it into him to chase and fang that flying-fish? Where do murderers go, man! Who's to doom, when the judge himself is dragged to the bar? But it is a mild, mild wind, and a mild looking sky; and the air smells now, as if it blew from a far-away meadow; they have been making hay somewhere under the slopes of the Andes, Starbuck, and the mowers are sleeping among the new-mown hay. Sleeping? Aye, toil we how we may, we all sleep at last on the field. Sleep? Aye, and rust amid greenness; as last year's scythes flung down, and left in the half-cut swaths—Starbuck!"

Abandoning the quest is not possible: "Is Ahab, Ahab?" Identity itself demands the disaster of attempting to draw out Job's Leviathan with a hook. And yet we are given a final grace note in the manner of Sir Thomas Browne: "They have been making hay somewhere under the slopes of the Andes, Starbuck, and the mowers are sleeping among the new-mown hay." But that is not where Ahab, Starbuck, and all the *Pequod*'s crew finally will sleep.

THE CHASE ITSELF is a major literary set piece. On the first day, Moby Dick startlingly appears as a seductive undine:

A gentle joyousness—a mighty mildness of repose in swiftness, invested the gliding whale. Not the white bull Jupiter swimming away with ravished Europa clinging to his graceful horns; his lovely, leering eyes sideways intent upon the maid; with smooth bewitching fleetness, rippling straight for the nuptial bower in Crete; not Jove, not that great majesty Supreme! did surpass the glorified White Whale as he so divinely swam.

On each soft side—coincident with the parted swell, that but once laving him, then flowed so wide away—on each bright side, the whale shed off enticings. No wonder there had been some among the hunters who namelessly transported and allured by all this serenity, had ventured to assail it, but had fatally found that quietude but the vesture of tornadoes. Yet calm, enticing calm, oh, whale! thou glidest on, to all who for the first time eye thee, no matter how many in that same way thou may'st have bejuggled and destroyed before.

And thus, through the serene tranquillities of the tropical sea, among waves whose hand-clappings were suspended by exceeding rapture, Moby Dick moved on, still withholding from sight the full terrors of his submerged trunk, entirely hiding the wrenched hideousness of his jaw. But soon the fore part of him slowly rose from the water; for an instant his whole marbleized body formed a high arch, like Virginia's Natural Bridge, and warningly waving his bannered flukes in the air, the grand god revealed himself, sounded, and went out of sight.

Catastrophe commences on the second day, when Fedallah and his men go down and only Ahab survives the loss of his own whale boat. Increasingly more furious, Moby Dick destroys the *Pequod* itself on the third day.

"I turn my body from the sun. What ho, Tashtego! let me hear thy hammer. Oh! ye three unsurrendered spires of mine; thou uncracked keel; and only god-bullied hull; thou firm deck, and haughty helm, and Pole-pointed prow,—death-glorious ship! must ye then perish, and without me? Am I cut off from the last fond pride of meanest shipwrecked captains? Oh, lonely death on lonely life! Oh, now I feel my topmost greatness lies in my topmost grief. Ho, ho! from all your furthest bounds, pour ye now in, ye bold billows of my whole foregone life, and top this one piled comber of my death! Towards thee I roll, thou all-destroying but unconquering whale; to the last I grapple with thee; from hell's heart I stab at thee; for hate's sake I spit my last breath at thee. Sink all coffins and all hearses to one common pool! and since neither can be mine, let me then tow to pieces, while still chasing thee, though tied to thee, thou damned whale! *Thus,* I give up the spear!"

This, Ahab's final oration, remains desperately heroic. A giant vortex, stirred up by Moby Dick, ends both the *Pequod* and the one surviving battle boat. Yet even at the close, the harpooner Tashtego maintains the eloquent defiance of Ahab and his men:

But as the last whelmings intermixingly poured themselves over the sunken head of the Indian at the mainmast, leaving a few inches of the erect spar yet visible, together with long streaming yards of the flag, which calmly undulated, with ironical coincidings, over the destroying billows they almost touched;—at that instant, a red arm and a hammer hovered backwardly uplifted in the open air, in the act of nailing the flag faster and yet faster to the subsiding spar. A sky-hawk that tauntingly had followed the main-truck downwards from its natural home among the stars, pecking at the flag, and incommoding Tashtego there; this bird now chanced to intercept its broad fluttering wing between the hammer and the wood; and simultaneously feeling that etherial thrill, the submerged savage beneath, in his death-grasp, kept his hammer frozen there; and so the bird of heaven, with archangelic shrieks, and his imperial beak thrust upwards, and his whole captive form folded in the flag of Ahab, went down with his ship, which, like Satan, would not sink to hell till she had dragged a living part of heaven along with her, and helmeted herself with it.

Now small fowls flew screaming over the yet yawning gulf; a sullen white surf beat against its steep sides; then all collapsed, and the great shroud of the sea rolled on as it rolled five thousand years ago.

Noah's flood has returned, though with an American swerve. Melville, glorious as this is, betters it by an "Epilogue":

The drama's done. Why then here does any one step forth?— Because one did survive the wreck.

It so chanced, that after the Parsee's disappearance, I was he whom the Fates ordained to take the place of Ahab's bowsman, when that bowsman assumed the vacant post; the same, who, when on the last day the three men were tossed from out the rocking boat, was dropped astern. So, floating on the margin of the ensuing scene, and in full sight of it, when the half-spent suction of the sunk ship reached me, I was then, but slowly, drawn towards the closing vortex. When I reached it, it had subsided to a creamy pool. Round and round, then, and ever contracting towards the button-like black bubble at the axis of that slowly wheeling circle, like another Ixion I did revolve. Till, gaining that vital centre, the black bubble upward burst; and now, liberated by reason of its cunning spring, and, owing to its great buoyancy, rising with great force, the coffin lifebuoy shot lengthwise from the sea, fell over, and floated by my side. Buoyed up by that coffin, for almost one whole day and night, I floated on a soft and dirge-like main. The unharming sharks, they glided by as if with padlocks on their mouths; the savage sea-hawks sailed with sheathed beaks. On the second day, a sail drew near, nearer, and picked me up at last. It was the devious-cruising Rachel, that in her retracing search after her missing children, only found another orphan.

Ishmael resurrects, saved by Queequeg's coffin, in contrast to Ahab's immolation, where, fulfilling Fedallah's prophecy, the *Pequod* itself serves as its captain's coffin. A haunting final sentence invokes the *Rachel,* still searching for its lost children, finding orphaned Ishmael. Whether he will be a Joseph or a Benjamin, the very different sons of Jacob's beloved wife, we do not know.

II

RALPH WALDO EMERSON
and EMILY DICKINSON

RALPH WALDO EMERSON

Journals

I HAD READ EMERSON'S ESSAYS AND POEMS BEFORE I REACHED A middle-of-the-journey crisis in July 1965. In search of balance, I read through his journals. Almost a half century later, I go on rereading them during sleepless nights.

Emerson's journals go from 1820, when he was sixteen, to 1877, when senility commenced. After 1875 there are no fresh entries but only comments upon former jottings. I have just read them again in the ten-volume set (1909–1914) edited by his son Edward, which I purchased at a book barn for ten dollars in 1965. There is a massive and admirable scholarly edition of the journals, edited by William Gilman and others, and though an inveterate scamp who prefers quoting from memory (for which I am chided), I have checked my citations against Gilman.

The great American books of the nineteenth century certainly include *Moby-Dick, Leaves of Grass* 1855 and 1860, *The Scarlet Letter, The Adventures of Huckleberry Finn,* and two works not then available, the poems of Emily Dickinson and Emerson's journals. Most readers would add *Walden,* the tales of Hawthorne, Poe, and Henry James, and the great sequence of James's novels. Emerson's two series of essays and *The*

Conduct of Life belong there also, but his capacious spirit unfolds fully only in the journals.

There are large modulations of tone throughout fifty-seven years of musing in the journals, yet Emerson seems perpetually in quest to hear his daemon speak to him. He knew the daemonic speculation from many sources: Plutarch on the cessation of oracles, seventeenth-century Cambridge Platonists, Hermetic and neo-Platonic esoterics, and Plato himself. Whitman had encountered the Hermeticists in George Sand, while Melville found them in a wide sweep of Gnostic doctrines. Hart Crane, heir of this American strain, sought to master daemonic lore in the unreadable P. D. Ouspensky, much as Yeats devoted himself to Madame Helena Petrovna Blavatsky's Order of the Golden Dawn and *The Secret Doctrine*.

D. H. Lawrence, studying the classic American writers, named their daemon as America itself. In his strong reading, Melville and Whitman became prophets of the Evening Land, proclaiming the doom of what he called "the white race." Lawrence died at forty-four in 1930 and so never confronted Faulkner or Cormac McCarthy, who might have fit his prophecy more aptly.

In Whitman and Hart Crane, Christopher Columbus is the tragic precursor who first encounters America-as-daemon. Anyone who has sailed the North Atlantic, even in the late 1940s, will recognize the relief of reaching the American shore after many days and nights floating across an abyss of space and time. The Platonic myth of lost Atlantis assimilates readily in Crane's epic *The Bridge* to the lost America of Melville and of Whitman.

Henry James and T. S. Eliot exiled themselves to London, in flight from the daemonic America residing within them. William Faulkner, in the autumn of 1929—the year of the crash that gave him Wallstreet Panic Snopes—worked as night supervisor at the university power plant in Oxford, Mississippi. The labor was minimal and gave him time and solitude to compose his most original novel (I think his masterpiece), *As I Lay Dying*. Mississippi was Faulkner's daemon; here he condenses it into the person of Darl Bundren, schizophrenic and tragic genius and, for many of my students and myself, his own uncanniest representative. Of *As I Lay Dying*'s fifty-nine sections, nineteen are spoken by Darl; it is his book, Faulkner's Book of the Daemon.

Emerson had no effect upon Faulkner, and I doubt the novelist read

him. Most of the Southern literary men and women I have known—
Robert Penn Warren and Allen Tate in particular—had no regard for the
Concord sage, who would have returned their scorn. Warren blamed John
Brown and the American exaltation of violence on Emerson, while Tate
assured me that the author of the essays was the devil.

Isolating daemonization in Emerson's work is not simple: Intensity
varies, though generally it permeates. Condensed in a journal entry on
November 14, 1838, this pervasive spirit is a climax of the essay "Self-
Reliance":

> And now at last the highest truth on this subject remains unsaid;
> probably cannot be said; for all that we say is the far-off remember-
> ing of the intuition. That thought, by what I can now nearest ap-
> proach to say it, is this. When good is near you, when you have life
> in yourself, it is not by any known or accustomed way; you shall not
> discern the footprints of any other; you shall not see the face of
> man; you shall not hear any name; the way, the thought, the good
> shall be wholly strange and new. It shall exclude example and expe-
> rience. You take the way from man, not to man. All persons that
> ever existed are its forgotten ministers. Fear and hope are alike be-
> neath it. There is somewhat low even in hope. In the hour of vision,
> there is nothing that can be called gratitude, nor properly joy. The
> soul raised over passion beholds identity and eternal causation, per-
> ceives the self-existence of Truth and Right, and calms itself with
> knowing that all things go well. Vast spaces of nature, the Atlantic
> Ocean, the South Sea,—long intervals of time, years, centuries,—
> are of no account. This which I think and feel underlay every for-
> mer state of life and circumstances, as it does underlie my present,
> and what is called life, and what is called death.

That precisely is the Voice of the Daemon, of the American Sublime.
Directly we go on to the dialectic of power and height:

> Life only avails, not the having lived. Power ceases in the instant of
> repose; it resides in the moment of transition from a past to a new
> state, in the shooting of the gulf, in the darting to an aim. This one
> fact the world hates, that the soul *becomes;* for that forever de-

grades the past, turns all riches to poverty, all reputation to a shame, confounds the saint with the rogue, shoves Jesus and Judas equally aside. Why then do we prate of self-reliance? Inasmuch as the soul is present, there will be power not confident but agent. To talk of reliance is a poor external way of speaking. Speak rather of that which relies, because it works and is. Who has more obedience than I masters me, though he should not raise his finger. Round him I must revolve by the gravitation of spirits. We fancy it rhetoric when we speak of eminent virtue. We do not yet see that virtue is Height, and that a man or a company of men, plastic and permeable to principles, by the law of nature must overpower and ride all cities, nations, kings, rich men, poets, who are not.

Transition, or coming to be, is potential power. That marks the crucial sentence of "Self-Reliance":

As men's prayers are a disease of the will, so are their creeds a disease of the intellect.

Transition cures us of prayer and creed. As Stevens suggests, this is a cure of the ground and of ourselves in the predicate that there is nothing else. Wallace Stevens uneasily jests with Emerson because too many of his own tropes are derived from the sage of Concord; the Emersonian scholar as a candle and the Stevensian "snow man" shade together in the vivid transparence of "peace" that concludes "Self-Reliance": "Nothing can bring you peace but yourself."

The Central Man or Human Globe is Emerson's figure before it becomes a Stevensian hero in *Asides on the Oboe* and *Notes Toward a Supreme Fiction*. Freedom, power, and fate are the Emersonian triad that reappear in different guises in Whitman, Dickinson, Stevens, and in a neo-orthodox Christian guise in the anti-Emersonian Eliot, fiercer even in his hatred than his disciples Tate and Warren.

I recall a conversation with the wise and wary W. H. Auden in which we avoided his usual disapproval of Shelley, Whitman, and Stevens (all of whom were "flat"!) and instead argued Emerson. Auden rejected my comparisons of the American sage to Montaigne, Nietzsche, Kierkegaard, and Freud. To the English poet and humane wit, Emerson was only a Carlyle.

Resistance to Emerson is a tribute to his strength and perpetual relevance. I quoted Dr. Johnson to Auden—"All censure of a man's self is oblique praise. It is in order to show how much he can spare"—but the poet was no Johnsonian. Where we did agree in that exchange was on my acquaintance and his close friend, the classical scholar Eric Robertson Dodds, whom Auden had known first in Birmingham, England, and from briefer meetings in Oxford and London.

Dodds has been an influence upon me since I first read his *The Greeks and the Irrational* (1951), which I recall purchasing during the autumn of 1951, when I began graduate study at Yale. Angus Fletcher and I discussed the book throughout 1951–52, after which Fletcher departed for Harvard to write his doctoral dissertation under the supervision of I. A. Richards. In time this became *Allegory: The Theory of a Symbolic Mode* (1964), republished in 2012 with a substantial new afterword by the author.

Together with Dodds's book, the best introduction to literary daemonization remains *Allegory*'s first section, "The Daemonic Agent." What I have learned to call the American Sublime is a wholly daemonic phenomenon, but the idea (to call it that) of the daemon is extraordinarily ancient and is as universally prevalent as shamanism. Dodds traced Greek shamanism to the probably mythical Orpheus and to the historical Pythagoras. Ultimately, the philosophical daemonic will end in the preface to Georg Hegel's *Phenomenology of Spirit,* where we must practice a Dionysiac whirl in order to see the ultimate vision the sublime yet may promise. All authentic shamans, like so many dervishes, are devoted to exuberant whirling. The daemon, who divides and distributes, knows through whirling what stasis never brings.

The Orphics, like Pythagoras and Empedocles, brought to Hellas what Dodds called an "occult self . . . older than the body" and outlasting it. Not the psyche or anxious self, this shamanistic spark, or *pneuma,* carries both our divine potential and our titanic guilt at having scattered and devoured Dionysus. Daemon (breath, *pneuma*) and psyche (the ordinary ego) became a radical dualism, prelude to both the Gnostics and Saint Paul.

Emerson, at once monist and dualist, studied the daemon in Ralph Cudworth's *The True Intellectual System of the Universe,* a mad, encyclopedic seventeenth-century Cambridge neo-Platonist confection. Dodds, who startled me in 1977 with the question "Who is your daemon, Harold?," wrote a marvelous autobiography, *Missing Persons*, published that year in Oxford. Its concluding paragraph invoked Dodds's own daemon.

The obscure being I could call Bloom's daemon has known how it is done, and I have not. His true name (has he one?) I cannot discover, but I am grateful to him for teaching the classes, writing the books, enduring the mishaps and illnesses, and nurturing the fictions of continuity that sustain my eighty-fifth year.

Coleridge, deep in daemons, looked to them for his poetic power: They gave him *Kubla Khan, Christabel,* and *The Rime of the Ancient Mariner.* He welcomed his daemon or genius and yet feared it. An orthodox censor, his devotion to the Christian *Logos,* inhibited the freest exercise of his own extraordinary imagination of the poetic sublime. Though he feared it, Coleridge was an authority on daemonization. He felt daemonic urges in his own genius and regarded opium, to which he became addicted, as his career's "avenging Daemon." He came to regard his sexual torments—a bad marriage and unfulfilled desire for Sara Hutchinson—as daemonic: Recall the female and male daemons who cast dice for the Ancient Mariner's soul.

The daemon knows how a poem is written and knows also its own ambivalence, since it runs a scale from divinity to guilt. Being acosmic renders it antithetical to our psyche, self against soul, or nature against poetry. Here I return to Emerson's journals for the American Daemonic:

It is the largest part of a man that is not inventoried. He has many enumerable parts: he is social, professional, political, sectarian, literary, and of this or that set and corporation. But after the most exhausting census has been made, there remains as much more which no tongue can tell. And this remainder is that which interests. This is that which the preacher and the poet and the musician speak to. This is that which the strong genius works upon; the region of destiny, of aspiration, of the unknown. Ah, they have a secret persuasion that as little as they pass for in the world, they are immensely rich in expectancy and power. Nobody has ever yet dispossessed this adhesive self to arrive at any glimpse or guess of the awful Life that lurks under it.

Far the best part, I repeat, of every mind is not that which he knows, but that which hovers in gleams, suggestions, tantalizing unpossessed before him. His firm recorded knowledge soon loses all interest for him. But this dancing chorus of thoughts and hopes is the quarry of his future, is his possibility, and teaches him that his man's life is of a ridiculous brevity and meanness, but that it is his first age and trial only of his young wings, and that vast revolutions, migrations, and gyres on gyres in the celestial societies invite him.

The "remainder," the "awful life," is the daemon, a "dancing chorus" of aspirations. This is Orphic Emerson: shamanistic, anarchic, devoted to self-union, in which majesty is a mirror of the sovereign self, primal and Central Man. The Orphic song chants itself in the "Prospects" chapter of Emerson's *Nature* (1836):

"Man is the dwarf of himself. Once he was permeated and dissolved by spirit. He filled nature with his overflowing currents. Out from him sprang the sun and moon; from man, the sun; from woman, the moon. The laws of his mind, the periods of his actions externized themselves into day and night, into the year and the seasons. But, having made for himself this huge shell, his waters retired; he no longer fills the veins and veinlets; he is shrunk to a drop. He sees that the structure still fits him, but fits him colossally. Say, rather, once it fitted him, now it corresponds to him from far and on high. He adores timidly his own work. Now is man the follower of the sun, the woman the follower of the moon. Yet sometimes he starts in his slumber, and wonders at himself and his house, and muses strangely at the resemblance betwixt him and it. He perceives that if his law is still paramount, if still he have elemental power, if his word is sterling yet in nature, it is not conscious power, it is not inferior but superior to his will. It is instinct."

Hermetic and Kabbalistic, this vision is Americanized by Emerson.

It is scarcely a step from this to *Song of Myself* and on to the sequence in my time of Stevens's *Notes Toward a Supreme Fiction*, Eliot's *The Dry Salvages*, Crane's *The Bridge*, and A. R. Ammons's *Sphere*. Others would add William Carlos Williams's *Paterson*, Book 1, or Ezra Pound's *The Cantos*.

Shamanistic praxis frequently involves metempsychosis, which in

American literary terms manifests as a transformation of precursors into agonistic versions of the authorial self. The American difference that constitutes our sublime breaks from English and Continental models by an *askesis* of the psyche, isolating the daemonic element that exalts seeing at the expense of our awareness of other selves. A profound solipsism ensues, though oddly marked by a more open rhetoric. Whitman is the greatest instance of such a figure of capable imagination, proclaiming as he does his total incorporation of what was, is, or can be, while celebrating a more concealed inwardness than even those of Melville, Hawthorne, Dickinson, Henry James, Stevens, Eliot, Faulkner, or Emerson himself. Hart Crane, tragically the most Orphic of American poets, is the fascinating exception, as his letters and friends testify. Like John Keats, he had a truer sense of other selves than most of us can attain. From the start, Crane knew his doom, in the mode of a Faulknerian hero.

American restlessness, then and now, creates an enormous contrast to the stillness of our strongest writers. They almost never have the relation to natural common life that the great Russian authors have. Whitman aspired to it but remained Hermetic, private, isolated. American daemonization touches the mass of people under the auspices of religion, which provides the only poetry they can apprehend. There are two grand exceptions who were and are welcomed by American readers: Mark Twain and Robert Frost. They offered a deceptive surface to their public while harboring daemonic darknesses available only to deeper readers.

Frost was an absolute Emersonian; Mark Twain had no overwhelming American precursor. Of the other writers discussed here, Faulkner never read Emerson, and Eliot scorned him: "The essays of Emerson are already an encumbrance." Melville read and annotated Emerson and attended his lectures, while manifesting acute ambivalence. Hawthorne was the sage's walking companion in Concord but held out against him, yet Hester Prynne, Ahab, and Ishmael are dark Emersonians. Henry James, linked to Emerson by family traditions, resisted him, though Isabel Archer is wholly a disciple of self-reliance. Walt Whitman, though later he denied it, started from Emerson, just as Wallace Stevens subtly evaded his vast dependence upon Whitman and satirized Emerson while repeating him. Hart Crane, wholly Emersonian, clearly takes his Platonic daemonization both from Concord and from Walter Pater.

The dread of voicelessness afflicts all strong writers and gathers to a greatness in the Americans: Hawthorne, Melville, Whitman, Stevens, Faulkner, and Crane in his closing days. Even Emerson, whose interior oratory flowed constantly, mused in his journal: "The Daemons lurk and are dumb."

Walt Whitman memorably expressed Emerson's personal daemonism:

> I think everybody was fascinated by his personality . . . But his usual manner carried with it something penetrating and sweet beyond mere description. There is in some men an indefinable something which flows out and over you like a flood of light—as if they possessed it illimitably—their whole being suffused with it. Being— in fact that is precisely the word. Emerson's whole attitude shed forth such an impression. . . . Never a face more gifted with power to express, fascinate, maintain.

Waldo's daemon only infrequently composes. When it does, the accent is inescapable:

> The day of days, the great day of the feast of life, is that in which the inward eye opens to the Unity in things, to the omnipresence of law;—sees that what is must be, and ought to be, or is the best. This beatitude dips from on high down on us, and we see. It is not in us so much as we are in it. If the air come to our lungs, we breathe and live; if not, we die. If the light come to our eyes, we see; else not. And if truth come to our mind, we suddenly expand to its dimensions, as if we grew to worlds. We are as lawgivers; we speak for Nature; we prophesy and divine.

The self-begetting is from "Fate" in *The Conduct of Life* (1860) but was written years before, doubtless for a lecture (1851?). Ecstasy is its burden: Hermetic man hovers, to be realized by Walt Whitman in 1855. Away from Emerson, one forgets too readily how wonderfully extreme he can be. His Central Man (an aspiration only) incarnates freedom-as-wildness and power-as-potential, with little reference to moralities.

Thomas Carlyle, a proto-Fascist, made a shibboleth of strength and favored black slavery, judicial murder, and other sadistic joys. Emersonian wildness is not to be mistaken for Carlyle's mania. And yet there is a shaman loose within Emerson that urges us to make all things new through "the terrible freedom."

🌿

THAT FREEDOM FOSTERS THE AMERICAN ORPHIC POET, FROM EMERSON to Hart Crane and some extraordinary poets of our moment, among whom John Ashbery remains paramount. American Orphism is a long tradition, but what was ancient Orphism, which inspired Emerson?

Scholars cannot say precisely *what* Orphism was, though it existed perhaps as early as 600 B.C.E. The historian of classical religion W. K. C. Guthrie speculated that a historical Orphism celebrated the potential divinity of the soul. In his journal for 1849, Emerson participated in the celebration:

Orpheus is no fable: you have only to sing, and the rocks will crystallize; sing, and the plant will organize; sing, and the animal will be born.

But it is in his *Nature* that the Orphic poet is conjured up.

Thus Primal Man is America for Emerson, even as William Blake's Divine Man was Albion (the Britannic name for Great Britain). In Emerson's creation and fall, America still retains an Orphic power that transcends will and approximates a desire manifested as and by eloquence, whose usual emblem is transparency. The most famous passage in *Nature,* and in all Emerson, plays upon this trope:

Standing on the bare ground,—my head bathed by the blithe air, and uplifted into infinite space,—all mean egotism vanishes. I become a transparent eye-ball; I am nothing; I see all; the currents of the Universal Being circulate through me; I am part or particle of God.

The ruin or the blank, that we see when we look at nature, is in our own eye. The axis of vision is not coincident with the axis of things, and so they appear not transparent but opake. The reason why the world lacks unity, and lies broken and in heaps, is, because man is disunited with himself.

That notorious "transparent eye-ball" mocks itself, anticipating other antic turns by anti-Emersonians. It stands here for what should be called "the Native Strain" of American poetry and visionary speculation. About forty years ago I published a book with a Stevensian title, *Figures of Capable Imagination,* which contained several essays on the Native Strain or American Orphism. I refrain from rereading myself but assume that emphasis was given to Emerson's independence from the neo-Platonist traditions that he cites.

In his essay "The Poet"—a strong influence upon Walt Whitman—Emerson lists his precursors as Orpheus, Empedocles, Heraclitus, Plato, Plutarch, Dante, and Emanuel Swedenborg. All these, to him, were Orphics. Could there have been a historical Orpheus? Once I gave outrage by speculating that Yahweh began as an actual person, a Middle Eastern warrior-god. Emerson, like Empedocles, believed there was a historical Orpheus, and the classical scholar Jane Harrison once told me she shared that opinion.

Orphism became a Greek "book religion," oddly akin thus to Judaism, Christianity, and Islam. Its texts, though, are scattered and discontinuous, which was also the fate of Orpheus himself, who suffered a *sparagmos* at the hands and teeth of the Maenads—intoxicated female Dionysiacs. There is an antithetical relationship between Orpheus and Dionysus, who are both allied with and opposed to each other.

We do not have the more or less original Orphic poems but mostly neo-Platonic reconstructions of them, which Emerson read. Much more stirring are the fragments of Empedocles, the great Orphic shaman and daemonic ecstatic.

Ananke, the personification of necessity, haunts poets like the Orphic Empedocles; it is a shadow or avenging daemon, like Shelley's *Alastor,* that trails after all those who would be "liberating gods" (Emerson's term for poets). The three Orphic divinities are Bacchus (Dionysus-Zagreus), Eros, and Ananke, but, alas, the greatest of these is Necessity. Emerson is dangerously blithe about this primacy, as Wallace Stevens will be. Hart Crane, the purest instance of American Orpheus, celebrates Bacchus in *The Wine Menagerie,* Eros in *Repose of Rivers,* and Ananke in *Voyages V,* all with clearly Orphic overtones.

In its seventh and eighth stanzas, *The Wine Menagerie,* by subtle indirection, implies both Dionysian ecstasy and its cost:

New thresholds, new anatomies! Wine talons
Build freedom up about me and distill
This competence—to travel in a tear
Sparkling alone, within another's will.

Until my blood dreams a receptive smile
Wherein new purities are snared; where chimes
Before some flame of gaunt repose a shell
Tolled once, perhaps, by every tongue in hell.
—Anguished, the wit that cries out of me:

The "shell" evokes the lyre of Orpheus, molded by Hermes from a giant tortoise shell and then given to Apollo, who passed it on to Orpheus, his son by Calliope. Crane alludes also to Nietzsche's brilliant conceit that the smiles of Dionysus engendered gods, while his tears gave birth to mortals.

In his extraordinary lyric *Repose of Rivers,* composed in 1926 and added to *White Buildings,* Hart Crane returned to Orpheus and Eurydice in the image of the willow, carried by the questing poet down to the underworld as an offering to Persephone, spouse of Hades. *Voyages VI* travels from Orphic Eros to the fatal Ananke awaiting Orpheus and Crane alike:

O rivers mingling toward the sky
And harbor of the phoenix' breast—
My eyes pressed black against the prow,
—Thy derelict and blinded guest

Waiting, afire, what name, unspoke,
I cannot claim: let thy waves rear
More savage than the death of kings,
Some splintered garland for the seer.

The unspoken name is Orpheus, who in his dismemberment and death by water becomes a prophetic god. Hart Crane stunningly concludes his epic *The Bridge* by boldly reincarnating Walt Whitman's American Orpheus as his own identity also:

Migrations that must needs void memory,
Inventions that cobblestone the heart,—
Unspeakable Thou Bridge to Thee, O Love.
Thy pardon for this history, whitest Flower,
O Answerer of all,—Anemone,—
Now while thy petals spend the suns about us, hold—
(O Thou whose radiance doth inherit me)
Atlantis,—hold thy floating singer late!

So to thine Everpresence, beyond time,
Like spears ensanguined of one tolling star
That bleeds infinity—the orphic strings,
Sidereal phalanxes, leap and converge:
—One Song, one Bridge of Fire! Is it Cathay,
Now pity steeps the grass and rainbows ring
The serpent with the eagle in the leaves . . . ?
Whispers antiphonal in azure swing.

The "floating singer"—Orpheus—and the "orphic strings" converge in the great image of "One Song, one Bridge of Fire," triumphant over Ananke, the fatal god who destroyed Orpheus and Hart Crane. Emerson, grimly blithe, accepted Ananke in his essay "Fate," part of his master-work, *The Conduct of Life* (1860):

Let us build altars to the Beautiful Necessity. If we thought men were free in the sense, that, in a single exception one fantastical will could prevail over the law of things, it were all one as if a child's hand could pull down the sun. If, in the least particular, one could derange the order of nature,—who would accept the gift of life?

Let us build altars to the Beautiful Necessity, which secures that all is made of one piece; that plaintiff and defendant, friend and enemy, animal and planet, food and eater, are of one kind. In astronomy, is vast space, but no foreign system; in geology, vast time, but the same laws as to-day. Why should we be afraid of Nature, which is no other than "philosophy and theology embodied"? Why should we fear to be crushed by savage elements, we who are made up of the same elements? Let us build to the Beautiful Necessity,

which makes man brave in believing that he cannot shun a danger
that is appointed, nor incur one that is not; to the Necessity which
rudely or softly educates him to the perception that there are no contingencies; that Law rules throughout existence, a Law which is not
intelligent but intelligence,—not personal nor impersonal,—it dis-
dains words and passes understanding; it dissolves persons; it vivifies nature; yet solicits the pure in heart to draw on all its omnipotence.

This too is Emersonian Orphism, not in the optative mood but in his
darker side. If "there are no contingencies," then everything that happens
to you is already yourself and inescapable: There are no accidents.

There are a squadron of Emersons, but I take the founder of American
Orphism to be the Central Waldo, father of Walt the American Adam. To
my mind, most scholars of Emerson do not confront our shamanistic
father. The most honorable exception is still Stephen Whicher, whom I
knew all too briefly before his self-inflicted death. Here is Whicher's vision
of the inaugurator of our Native Strain:

> The lesson he would drive home is man's entire independence. The
> aim of this strain in his thought is not virtue, but freedom and mas-
> tery. It is radically anarchic, overthrowing all the authority of the
> past, all compromise or coöperation with others, in the name of the
> Power present and agent in the soul. . . . Yet his true goal was not
> really a Stoic self-mastery, nor Christian holiness, but rather some-
> thing more secular and harder to define—a quality he sometimes
> called *entirety*, or *self-union* . . .
>
> This self-sufficient unity or wholeness, transforming his rela-
> tions with the world about him, is, as I read him, the central objec-
> tive of the egoistic or transcendental Emerson, the prophet of Man
> created in the 1830s by his discovery of the extent of his own proper
> nature. This was what he meant by "sovereignty," or "mastery," or
> the striking phrase, several times repeated, "the erect position."

Power, entirety, self-union, self-sufficiency, "the erect position": These
are not terms of social virtue but Orphic virtue, terms of knowing, not of
being. And what is known is transition—for Emerson, the only dwelling
place of power.

By power however he means potential, more life, something evermore about to be known. Emersonian or American Orphic knowing characterizes our heroines of the will: Hester Prynne, Zenobia of *The Blithedale Romance,* Isabel Archer, Milly Theale, and in actuality Margaret Fuller, Emily Dickinson, Edith Wharton, Willa Cather, Marianne Moore, Elizabeth Bishop.

Emerson, being metamorphic, defies commentary; he departs as soon as you characterize him. To call Emerson a neo-Platonist or an adherent of Eastern religion (Hindu or Buddhist) will work no better than naming him a heretic from Christianity. His American gnosis is his own and abounds in contradictions. Like his disciple Walt Whitman, he keeps changing as he writes. Both men were highly aware of this ebb and flow of consciousness, and to track either of them you need to share their exuberance.

Emerson, a scholar in the broadest sense, formulated what he chose to call "the double consciousness." A seer of unity who yet always beheld doubly and who exalted transition almost for its own sake, he formulates a distinction that he rapidly modified, in accordance with his conviction that "Nothing is secure but life, transition, the energizing spirit."

A good Emersonian, I have to become a bad one to keep going, but he knew and teaches just that. His double consciousness, *for me,* is not mutual awareness of reason and understanding but of Ananke (fate) and Freedom (wildness). When I remarked once to my late friend Paul de Man that I attempted to restore pathos to literary tropes, he protested: "But, Harold, pathos *is* a trope." Yet irony, which Paul considered the condition of all literary languages, is also only another trope. The Nietzschean-Emersonian question, for me, is "How does meaning get started, anyway?" For Nietzsche, in the memory of pain; for Emerson, in the opposition of hope and memory. Where you cannot augment the foundations to increase authority, because the foundations have vanished, you have to embrace the path of power, its potential, including what Emily Dickinson called dwelling in possibility, a fairer house than prose. Her poetics of pain subsumes Emerson's dialectical double consciousness because it takes on the burden of permanent loss.

Anyone in their eighties confronts such loss every week or so. Though Melville and Henry James thought Emerson knew too little of loss, they were mistaken. The three people he loved best died early: his first wife,

Ellen; his brother Charles; his little son Waldo. We all know suffering and evil: Emerson had the wisdom not to let himself be darkened prematurely. Whicher again is the best guide:

> His later thought is characteristically an affirmation of a *second best*. If a perfect freedom was clearly out of reach, man's fate as he found it still turned out to allow him adequate means to free himself. The two chief second-best means of freedom that Emerson found were "obedience to his genius" and "the habit of the observer"—Vocation and Intellect.

My lifelong friend Angus Fletcher, on his eighty-third birthday, remarked to me that Waldo's whim was his word. That is to say, his *Logos* is freedom, as here in "The Poet":

> The poets are thus liberating gods. The ancient British bards had for the title of their order, "Those who are free throughout the world." They are free, and they make free. An imaginative book renders us much more service at first, by stimulating us through its tropes, than afterward when we arrive at the precise sense of the author. I think nothing is of any value in books excepting the transcendental and extraordinary.

The trope, not the truth, makes us free—free for what? "Surprise" is Emerson's answer: That is the goal, the eros of Orphic poets. They quest for power, victory, ecstatic seizure. The American poet is to mount to paradise on the stairway of surprise:

> Great is the art,
> Great be the manners, of the bard.
> He shall not his brain encumber
> With the coil of rhythm and number;
> But, leaving rule and pale forethought,
> He shall aye climb
> For his rhyme.
> "Pass in, pass in," the angels say,
> "In to the upper doors,

Nor count compartments of the floors,
But mount to paradise
By the stairway of surprise."

That is from Emerson's *Merlin,* a poem in which Nemesis, goddess of vengeance, usurps Necessity as the Orphic muse:

And Nemesis,
Who with even matches odd,
Who athwart space redresses
The partial wrong,
Fills the just period,
And finishes the song.

Wallace Stevens, involuntary Emersonian, admonishes the ephebe or would-be young poet in *Notes Toward a Supreme Fiction* that a Whitmanian hobo has to be the *materia poetica* out of which the final elegance is confected: "Not to console / Nor sanctify, but plainly to propound." So *Merlin* avoids consolation and plainly propounds Nemesis. Here we collude again with the double consciousness: How can Nemesis be a surprise if it has fused with Necessity?

In *Letters and Social Aims* (1875), a volume edited by others after Emerson experienced senility, there is a compendium, "Poetry and Imagination," assembled from a few lectures given by the sage in his prime. Nothing else by Emerson has influenced me so deeply as some passages in this chrestomathy:

For the value of a trope is that the hearer is one; and indeed Nature itself is a vast trope, and all particular natures are tropes. As the bird alights on the bough—then plunges into the air again, so the thoughts of God pause but for a moment in any form. All thinking is analogizing, and 'tis the use of life to learn metonymy. The endless passing of one element into new forms, the incessant metamorphosis, explains the rank which the imagination holds in our catalogue of mental powers. The imagination is the reader of these forms. The poet accounts all productions and changes of Nature as the nouns of language, uses them representatively, too well pleased with their ulterior to value much their primary meaning. Every new object so seen gives a shock of agreeable surprise.

All is trope except in the order of play, where the rules are literal. Emerson, who can be blithe, is rarely playful and would never play by the rules, anyway. Analogy is in itself a poetics and becomes an endless chain of contiguities; hence "'tis the use of life to learn metonymy."

In the essay "Illusions," from *The Conduct of Life* (1860), Concord's sage observes the consequences of realizing the use of life as learning tropology. Metonymy, the trope of contiguity, considered inwardly can be an undoing of prior splendors, an emptying out of Primal Man's divinity, of the daemon who goes on knowing. "We cannot write the order of the variable winds. How can we penetrate the law of our shifting moods and susceptibility?"

Emerson may not have invented the American Sublime, yet he took eternal possession of it. You don't take a candle to see the sunrise, he wryly observes. William James, speaking in Concord on the centenary of Emerson's birth, condensed the sage into a brief revelation: "The point of any pen can be an epitome of reality." Twenty years later, one of my idols, D. H. Lawrence (in *Studies in Classic American Literature*), fell into silliness when irritated by Emerson:

> Emerson believes in having the courage to treat all men as equals. It takes some courage *not* to treat them so now.
>
> "Shall I not treat all men as gods?" he cries.
>
> If you like, Waldo, but we've got to pay for it, when you've made them *feel* that they're gods. A hundred million American godlets is rather much for the world to deal with.
>
> The fact of the matter is, all those gorgeous inrushes of exaltation and spiritual energy which made Emerson a great man, now make us sick. They are with us a drug habit.

When he desired to read well, Lawrence was a superb critic. Can we surmise why he could not read Emerson? It may be akin to his weak misreadings of Sigmund Freud, whom Lawrence took as an immoralist! Emerson's double consciousness was mistaken by Lawrence as a simplistic soul-body dualism. Lawrence remained a Puritan, despite his sexual vitalism, while Emerson dived deeper into questions of spontaneity and genius, domain of the daemons. Lawrence ambivalently loved Walt Whitman, who converted his English disciple from composing poems and novels in the mode of Thomas Hardy into the poet of *Look! We Have Come Through* and the novelist of *The Plumed Serpent.*

Under Whitman's influence, the later Lawrence became an American Orphic poet akin to Hart Crane. Daemonization, the trope of the hyperbolic Native Strain of my literature, received its inaugural statement in Angus Fletcher's *Allegory: The Theory of a Symbolic Mode.* I interpret daemonization as the poet's breakthrough into a highly individual counter-sublime, thus preferring possession by an inner drive to a debilitating struggle with the already said. A perilous choice, this is endemic in poets whose ambitions transcend all limits.

Essays

RATHER THAN LEAPFROGGING THROUGH EMERSON'S DAEMONIC INTENsities, I will attempt to ambush him in three of his essays. The crown of his work probably is "Experience," but I judge the most important essay to be "Self-Reliance," the matrix of what I have learned to call "the American Religion." His wildest performance is "Circles," a prose poem chanted by his daemon.

Though published in 1841, "Self-Reliance" began with a sermon he delivered in 1830: "Does anyone fear that a too great reticence in one's self and an obstinate questioning of every practice and institution might beget danger to faith and to virtue? Oh no." It is curious that Emerson quotes from Wordsworth's *Ode: Intimations of Immortality:* "obstinate questionings of sense and outward things," the young child's doomed resistance to the existence of a reality beyond the self.

Here again is the visionary center of "Self-Reliance":

And now at last the highest truth on this subject remains unsaid; probably cannot be said; for all that we say is the far-off remembering of the intuition. That thought, by what I can now nearest approach to say it, is this. When good is near you, when you have life in yourself, it is not by any known or accustomed way; you shall not discern the footprints of any other; you shall not see the face of man; you shall not hear any name; the way, the thought, the good shall be wholly strange and new. It shall exclude example and experience. You take the way from man, not to man. All persons that ever existed are its forgotten ministers. Fear and hope are alike beneath it. There is somewhat low even in hope. In the hour of vision, there is nothing that can be called gratitude, nor properly joy. The soul raised over passion beholds identity and eternal causation, perceives the self-existence of Truth and Right, and calms itself with knowing that all things go well. Vast spaces of nature, the Atlantic Ocean, the South Sea,—long intervals of time, years, centuries,—are of no account. This which I think and feel underlay every former state of life and circumstances, as it does underlie my present, and what is called life, and what is called death.

Life only avails, not the having lived. Power ceases in the instant of repose; it resides in the moment of transition from a past to a new state, in the shooting of the gulf, in the darting to an aim. This one fact the world hates, that the soul *becomes;* for that forever degrades the past, turns all riches to poverty, all reputation to a shame, confounds the saint with the rogue, shoves Jesus and Judas equally aside. Why then do we prate of self-reliance? Inasmuch as the soul is present, there will be power not confident but agent. To talk of reliance is a poor external way of speaking. Speak rather of that which relies, because it works and is. Who has more obedience than I masters me, though he should not raise his finger. Round him I must revolve by the gravitation of spirits. We fancy it rhetoric when we speak of eminent virtue. We do not yet see that virtue is Height, and that a man or a company of men, plastic and permeable to principles, by the law of nature must overpower and ride all cities, nations, kings, rich men, poets, who are not.

"Experience," finding its model in Montaigne, is Emerson's strongest essay. Its long paragraphs are essays in themselves:

It is very unhappy, but too late to be helped, the discovery we have made, that we exist. That discovery is called the Fall of Man. Ever afterwards, we suspect our instruments. We have learned that we do not see directly, but mediately, and that we have no means of correcting these coloured and distorting lenses which we are, or of computing the amount of their errors. Perhaps these subject-lenses have a creative power; perhaps there are no objects. Once we lived in what we saw; now, the rapaciousness of this new power, which threatens to absorb all things, engages us. Nature, art, persons, letters, religions,—objects, successively tumble in, and God is but one of its ideas. Nature and literature are subjective phenomena; every evil and every good thing is a shadow which we cast. The street is full of humiliations to the proud. As the fop contrived to dress his bailiffs in his livery, and make them wait on his guests at table, so the chagrins which the bad heart gives off as bubbles, at once take form as ladies and gentlemen in the street, shopmen or bar-keepers in hotels, and threaten or insult whatever is threatenable and insultable in us. 'Tis the same with our idolatries. People forget that it is the eye which makes the horizon, and the rounding mind's eye which makes this or that man a type or representative of humanity with the name of hero or saint. Jesus, the "providential man," is a good man on whom many people are agreed that these optical laws shall take effect. By love on one part, and by forbearance to press objection on the other part, it is for a time settled, that we will look at him in the centre of the horizon, and ascribe to him the properties that will attach to any man so seen. But the longest love or aversion has a speedy term. The great and crescive self, rooted in absolute nature, supplants all relative existence, and ruins the kingdom of mortal friendship and love. Marriage (in what is called the spiritual world) is impossible, because of the inequality between every subject and every object. The subject is the receiver of Godhead, and at every comparison must feel his being enhanced by that cryptic might. Though not in energy, yet by presence, this magazine of substance cannot be otherwise than felt: nor can any force of intellect attribute to the object the proper deity which sleeps or wakes for ever in every subject. Never can love make consciousness and ascription equal in force. There will be the same gulf between every me and thee, as between the original and the picture. The universe is the bride of the soul. All private sympathy is partial. Two human beings are like globes, which can touch only in a point, and, whilst they remain in contact, all other points of each of the spheres are inert; their turn must also come, and the longer a particular union lasts, the more energy of appetency the parts not in union acquire.

It may be the essence of Emersonianism to remark ironically that common sense is the basis of genius. Pondered, that has a touch of outrageousness: Daemonic surprise would thus be a mode of every morning light. The question of genius might then be an everyday commonplace and not the voice of the god within us. But power is Emerson's central concern, and his "God" is power in the particular sense of *potentia,* something evermore about to be, "vital force."

Emerson's wisdom, like that of Geoffrey Chaucer and of Shakespeare, is to tell us that we are always keeping appointments we never made. Chaucer's response is to say we should bear ourselves with equanimity, while Shakespeare advises that we bear us "like the time." The Concord sage, precursor of Nietzsche, instead codifies what Chaucer and Shakespeare embody in their grandest creations. The Wife of Bath and Falstaff are *meaning that gets started.*

For Nietzsche, meaning is produced by painful memories, a formula that darkly inverts Emerson's reading of the poets. Like Chaucer and Shakespeare, Emerson pragmatically knows that you cannot augment the foundations because they never existed; so much for the Roman concept of *authority.* In Emerson, and in Nietzsche following him, authority is merely a matter of authorship, which always is a question. The answer to that question is that the originals are not original: Everything may be quotation. Yet we choose what we quote and how to rephrase it.

Homer and Plato, Dante and Chaucer, Shakespeare and Cervantes are primary creators. Odysseus and Socrates, Dante the Pilgrim and Chaucer the Pilgrim, Hamlet and Don Quixote start meanings. Their work inspires the primary interpreters: Montaigne, Emerson, Nietzsche, Kierkegaard, who define limits and possibilities for transmitting meanings and then transmitting them into wisdoms.

Where shall wisdom be found? The poets, harboring great unwisdoms, comfort and console even when they do not enlighten. Nietzsche may have thought they kept us from perishing of the truth, Hamlet's truth of annihilation. On that account, poetry lies against time and time's definitive "it was." Emerson, speaking for American hope, urged otherwise, exalting the newness.

Whitman, more Emersonian than Emerson himself, proclaims two Supreme Fictions in *Song of Myself:* "Walt Whitman" and "America." These remain our greatest poems, but only in the perfect self-reliance that begins Canto 3 of *Song of Myself:*

> I have heard what the talkers were talking, the talk of the
>   beginning and the end,
> But I do not talk of the beginning or the end.
>
> There was never any more inception than there is now,
> Nor any more youth or age than there is now,
> And will never be any more perfection than there is now,
> Nor any more heaven or hell than there is now.

At eighty-four, in the American spring of 2015, can I believe that? That was one hundred and fifty-nine years ago, in the summer of 1855, when Walt was thirty-six. Reading *Song of Myself,* I believe him. How can I not, when near the close he challenges me: "Will you speak before I am gone? Will you prove already too late?" In a noble response, John Ashbery heartens me: "All that we know is that we are a little early."

"Walt Whitman, an American, one of the roughs," is another fiction that gets meaning started, in the mode of Sir John Falstaff and Alice, the Wife of Bath. The soul of Whitman, a retrievement out of the night, sleep, death, the mother, and the sea, is a very different fiction, with affinities to Hamlet. Daemonic and unstable, Whitman's third fiction, real Me or Me myself, directly alludes to Shakespeare's Edgar of *King Lear,* in *Crossing Brooklyn Ferry,* the "Sun-Down Poem" of 1856.

In his *On Poetry and Poets,* T. S. Eliot named poetic possession as the work of the demon and urged poets to overcome this force in order to achieve individual voice. In time, the daemon (as I prefer to name it), *contra* Eliot, can be recognized as the god within who generates poetic power. Eliot was perfectly consistent in his fear of the daemonic and fully cognizant that his own poetic strength was the gift of his daemon. I doubt he ever read "Experience"; what could he have made of it?

Emerson's is not the Christian fall of man but a daemonic and

Hermetic fall of the divine man—into the sleep of love and death, in which self-reliance is abrogated. Opposed to this failure in self-recognition is the daemon or genius proper, "the great and crescive self," in Emerson's words, which is forever expanding.

It is striking that Emerson, happily married first to Ellen, who died young, and then to his superb Lidian, totally dismisses marriage for the higher self. I think of Henry James in *The Sacred Fount,* but might also reflect upon misogynists like Eliot and Faulkner, or even Melville and Frost in certain moods. Hawthorne, in his life and his writings, is a refreshing contrast to all of these.

I want to conclude my account of our American prophet by contrasting him with his rueful disciple Nietzsche, who loved Emerson while never quite grasping him. Just seventeen, Nietzsche read a German translation of *The Conduct of Life* and was converted by it and by later readings in Emerson to the religion of self-reliance. Eventually he came to fear that the sage of Concord had read too much German philosophy, but the fear was mistaken: Emerson looked into Kant and Hegel, but they failed to touch him. David Hume was altogether a different story. Hume troubled him, though Emerson could not accept the Scottish philosopher.

I am one of several Emersonians who have fused him with Nietzsche. Since I also mix Walter Pater into the brew, the consequences might not have pleased Emerson, but my allegiance is to the poets, and I follow Wallace Stevens and Hart Crane in this regard. Two departed close friends, Richard Rorty and Richard Poirier, told me they found such eclecticism acceptable, but other lovers of Emerson protest my ways.

Nietzsche learned from Emerson how to impart wisdom by provocation, not instruction. I am neither philosopher nor sage but a schoolteacher, and I keep trying to learn from Emerson how not to teach. Here in America we should be blessedly free of authority: There are no foundations for us to augment.

Nietzsche, thinking about Emerson, learned to think about Nietzsche. For me, Emerson is the fountain of the American will to know the self and its drive for sublimity. The American poets who (to me) matter most are all Emersonians of one kind or another: Walt Whitman, Emily Dickinson, Edwin Arlington Robinson, Robert Frost, Wallace Stevens, Hart Crane, John Ashbery, A. R. Ammons, Elizabeth Bishop, May Swenson, Henri Cole. Our greatest creators of prose fiction were not Emersonians, yet the protagonists of Hawthorne, Melville, and Henry James frequently are beyond our understanding if we do not see Hester Prynne, Captain Ahab, and Isabel Archer as self-reliant questers.

The American Eve and American Adam are Emerson early in the morning, prelapsarian though always free to fall forward and inward, not downward and outward. Our experience of God, if you travel to the realms of American Religionists, as I did when younger, has little to do with European theology and instead renews ancient shamanisms, Gnostic heresies, and assorted Enthusiasms, Emersonian Orphism included. I have listened to Pentecostals, Independent Baptists, and wild churches of the unchurched, and I heard again and again that these women and men were uncreated and so could not perish. I was told that many in solitude had talked and walked with the resurrected Jesus. In their highest moments, these women and men *were* a vision. Face-to-face I experienced no skepticism but was overwhelmed by immediacy. I do not think these people would have recognized the names of Emerson and Whitman, but they seemed closer to those American prophets than I could ever be.

EMERSON'S MOST DAEMONIC ESSAY IS THE WHIRLIGIG HE CALLED "CIRCLES," a kind of cosmology of the spirit. Daemons divide up divine power and are in perpetual movement from their supernal heights to us. They bring down messages, each day's news of the metamorphic meanings of the division between our mundane shell and the upper world.

In a discussion of "Circles," Angus Fletcher and I began to wonder if Lidian had spiced up Waldo's late-morning meat pie with psychedelic mushrooms first harvested in the Concord woods by Amerindian shamans! The opening paragraph wildly commences by tossing us into the midst of a speculative energetics:

> The eye is the first circle; the horizon which it forms is the second; and throughout nature this primary figure is repeated without end. It is the highest emblem in the cipher of the world. St. Augustine described the nature of God as a circle whose centre was everywhere, and its circumference nowhere. We are all our lifetime reading the copious sense of this first of forms. One moral we have

already deduced in considering the circular or compensatory character of every human action. Another analogy we shall now trace; that every action admits of being outdone. Our life is an apprenticeship to the truth, that around every circle another can be drawn; that there is no end in nature, but every end is a beginning; that there is always another dawn risen on midnoon, and under every deep a lower deep opens.

Slyly, Emerson attributes a Hermetic notion to Saint Augustine. Nicholas of Cusa, in the fifteenth century, had absorbed this from Alexandrian gnosis. An intense reader of English neo-Platonists—Henry More, Ralph Cudworth, John Norris—the author of "Circles" found this heretical formula in Norris and exfoliated it gorgeously. Milton's Satan enters with "under every deep a lower deep opens," and Emerson cheerfully explores those deeps:

> Step by step we scale this mysterious ladder: the steps are actions; the new prospect is power. Every several result is threatened and judged by that which follows. Every one seems to be contradicted by the new; it is only limited by the new. The new statement is always hated by the old, and, to those dwelling in the old, comes like an abyss of scepticism. But the eye soon gets wonted to it, for the eye and it are effects of one cause; then its innocency and benefit appear, and presently, all its energy spent, it pales and dwindles before the revelation of the new hour.
>
> Fear not the new generalization. Does the fact look crass and material, threatening to degrade thy theory of spirit? Resist it not; it goes to refine and raise thy theory of matter just as much.
>
> There are no fixtures to men, if we appeal to consciousness. Every man supposes himself not to be fully understood; and if there is any truth in him, if he rests at last on the divine soul, I see not how it can be otherwise. The last chamber, the last closet, he must feel, was never opened; there is always a residuum unknown, unanalyzable. That is, every man believes that he has a greater possibility.
>
> Our moods do not believe in each other. To-day I am full of thoughts, and can write what I please. I see no reason why I should not have the same thought, the same power of expression to-

morrow. What I write, whilst I write it, seems the most natural thing
in the world: but yesterday I saw a dreary vacuity in this direction in
which now I see so much; and a month hence, I doubt not, I shall
wonder who he was that wrote so many continuous pages. Alas for
this infirm faith, this will not strenuous, this vast ebb of a vast flow!
I am God in nature; I am a weed by the wall.

From a Jacob's ladder ascending to power, we fall through our moods
or whims into a prophecy of Walt Whitman's most poignant poem, *As I
Ebb'd with the Ocean of Life* (1860), and go from godhood into the very
Whitmanian "I am a weed by the wall." Yet the only escape from moody
decline is poetry and the poet:

> Therefore, we value the poet. All the argument and all the wisdom
> is not in the encyclopaedia, or the treatise on metaphysics, or the
> Body of Divinity, but in the sonnet or the play. In my daily work I
> incline to repeat my old steps, and do not believe in remedial force,
> in the power of change and reform. But some Petrarch or Ariosto,
> filled with the new wine of his imagination, writes me an ode or a
> brisk romance, full of daring thought and action. He smites and
> arouses me with his shrill tones, breaks up my whole chain of hab-
> its, and I open my eye on my own possibilities. He claps wings to
> the sides of all the solid old lumber of the world, and I am capable
> once more of choosing a straight path in theory and practice.

This inspiring force culminates in a startling movement, first to a
Hermetic self-recognition and then to a savage irony directed at an Idiot
Questioner (Blake's fine term):

> It is the highest power of divine moments that they abolish our con-
> tritions also. I accuse myself of sloth and unprofitableness day by
> day; but when these waves of God flow into me, I no longer reckon
> lost time. I no longer poorly compute my possible achievement by
> what remains to me of the month or the year; for these moments
> confer a sort of omnipresence and omnipotence, which asks noth-
> ing of duration, but sees that the energy of the mind is commensu-
> rate with the work to be done, without time.

And thus, O circular philosopher, I hear some reader exclaim, you have arrived at a fine Pyrrhonism, at an equivalence and indifferency of all actions, and would fain teach us that, *if we are true,* forsooth, our crimes may be lively stones out of which we shall construct the temple of the true God.

I am not careful to justify myself. I own I am gladdened by seeing the predominance of the saccharine principle throughout vegetable nature, and not less by beholding in morals that unrestrained inundation of the principle of good into every chink and hole that selfishness has left open, yea, into selfishness and sin itself; so that no evil is pure, nor hell itself without its extreme satisfactions. But lest I should mislead any when I have my own head and obey my whims, let me remind the reader that I am only an experimenter. Do not set the least value on what I do, or the least discredit on what I do not, as if I pretended to settle anything as true or false. I unsettle all things. No facts are to me sacred; none are profane; I simply experiment, an endless seeker, with no Past at my back.

The subtle first paragraph is a universal experience: I repeat it to myself on torpid days when I weary of my own sloth. Since that leads to a new sense that *somehow* I have been at work, it abolishes utterly the morality we falsely attach to labor. When the Idiot Questioner denounces the defender of circles as a rock-bottom skeptic, Emerson replies in the mode of Montaigne, who made of psychic experience a new kind of humanism.

Is whirl then king, having displaced Zeus? Emerson rises to new thresholds of eloquence in response:

Thus there is no sleep, no pause, no preservation, but all things renew, germinate, and spring. Why should we import rags and relics into the new hour? Nature abhors the old, and old age seems the only disease: all others run into this one. We call it by many names,—fever, intemperance, insanity, stupidity, and crime: they are all forms of old age; they are rest, conservatism, appropriation, inertia, not newness, not the way onward. We grizzle every day. I see no need of it. Whilst we converse with what is above us, we do not grow old, but grow young. Infancy, youth, receptive, aspiring, with religious eye looking upward, counts itself nothing, and abandons itself to the instruction flowing from all sides. But the man and woman of seventy assume to know all, they have outlived their hope, they renounce aspiration, accept the actual for the necessary, and talk down to the young. Let them, then, become organs of the Holy Ghost; let them be lovers; let them behold truth; and their eyes are uplifted, their wrinkles smoothed, they are perfumed again with hope and power. This old age ought not to creep on a human mind. In nature every moment is new; the past is always swallowed and forgotten; the coming only is sacred. Nothing is secure but life, transition, the energizing spirit. No love can be bound by oath or covenant to secure it against a higher love. No truth so sublime but it may be trivial to-morrow in the light of new thoughts. People wish to be settled: only as far as they are unsettled is there any hope for them.

Life is a series of surprises. We do not guess to-day the mood, the pleasure, the power of to-morrow, when we are building up our being. Of lower states,—of acts of routine and sense,—we can tell somewhat; but the masterpieces of God, the total growths and universal movements of the soul, he hideth; they are incalculable. I can know that truth is divine and helpful, but how it shall help me I can have no guess, for, *so to be* is the sole inlet of *so to know.* The new position of the advancing man has all the powers of the old, yet has them all new. It carries in its bosom all the energies of the past, yet is itself an exhalation of the morning. I cast away in this new moment all my once hoarded knowledge, as vacant and vain. Now, for the first time, seem I to know anything rightly. The simplest words,—we do not know what they mean, except when we love and aspire.

At eighty-four, I hardly know whether to grimace or be strengthened by this. Emerson tells me to become young again by conversing with my daemon, by unsettling my exhausted accommodation with the days going on, by accepting surprise. Yes and no, no and yes, I have to reply, until he sweeps me away with his magnificent concluding paragraph:

The one thing which we seek with insatiable desire is to forget ourselves, to be surprised out of our propriety, to lose our sempiternal memory, and to do something without knowing how or why; in short, to draw a new circle. Nothing great was ever achieved without enthusiasm. The way of life is wonderful; it is by abandonment. The great moments of history are the facilities of performance through the strength of ideas, as the works of genius and religion. "A man," said Oliver Cromwell, "never rises so high as when he knows not whither he is going." Dreams and drunkenness, the use of opium and alcohol, are the semblance and counterfeit of this oracular genius, and hence their dangerous attraction for men. For the like reason, they ask the aid of wild passions, as in gaming and war, to ape in some manner these flames and generosities of the heart.

Drawing a new daemonic circle, at any age, risks self-destruction, and abandonment courts the abyss. It is odd to hear Emerson quoting Cromwell, a hero to Thomas Carlyle but not, I would have thought, to the sane and sacred American oracle. Everything depends upon how you define "these flames and generosities of the heart" that are parodied by addiction, gambling, the organized murder of warfare. We are left to perform the definition for ourselves.

Emerson is not the only national sage who relies upon daemonic influx: I think of Montaigne, Goethe, Carlyle, and even Freud, a Romantic rationalist who was fascinated by the uncanny. We ransack Shakespeare, largest of all consciousnesses, but he will never reveal himself.

Nietzsche, Emerson's disciple, lost himself to the daemon and went down into madness. As I have mentioned, before his descent he cautioned us that origin and end for the sake of life had to be kept apart. The prestige of origins did not matter to Emerson, for whom more life meant the incessant renewal of surprise.

EMILY DICKINSON

THERE IS NO MOMENT OF BREAKTHROUGH IN WHICH WE BEHOLD AND
hear the emergence of Emily Dickinson's authentic tone, stance, voice.
Poem 21, in 1858, fascinated Hart Crane:

21

The Gentian weaves her fringes—
The Maple's loom is red—
My departing blossoms
Obviate parade.

I myself find her first in 1860; thirty years old, she astonishes:

178

To learn the Transport by the Pain—
As Blind Men learn the sun!
To die of thirst—suspecting
That Brooks in Meadows run!

To stay the homesick—homesick feet
Opon a foreign shore—
Haunted by native lands, the while—
And blue—beloved Air!

This is the sovereign Anguish!
This—the signal wo!
These are the patient "Laureates"
Whose voices—trained—below—

Ascend in ceaseless Carol—
Inaudible, indeed,
To us—the duller scholars
Of the Mysterious Bard!

I read this as a tribute to Shakespeare: "sovreign Anguish!" and "Mysterious Bard!" Is that arbitrary? Her truest precursor, Shakespeare taught her how to think—through images, tropes, poems. A year later the "Empress of Calvary" achieves a first triumph:

> 243
>
> That after Horror—that 'twas *us*—
> That passed the mouldering Pier—
> Just as the Granite crumb let go—
> Our Savior, by a Hair—
>
> A second more, had dropped too deep
> For Fisherman to plumb—
> The very profile of the Thought
> Puts Recollection numb—
>
> The possibility—to pass
> Without a moment's Bell—
> Into Conjecture's presence
> Is like a Face of Steel—
> That suddenly looks into our's
> With a metallic grin—
> The Cordiality of Death—
> Who drills his Welcome in—

Difficult? But this only begins her ardent wayfaring at evading meanings, mastered by 1862:

> 320
>
> There's a certain Slant of light,
> Winter Afternoons—
> That oppresses, like the Heft
> Of Cathedral Tunes—
>
> Heavenly Hurt, it gives us—
> We can find no scar,

But internal difference—
Where the Meanings, are—

None may teach it—Any—
'Tis the Seal Despair—
An imperial affliction
Sent us of the Air—

When it comes, the Landscape listens—
Shadows—hold their breath—
When it goes, 'tis like the Distance
On the look of Death—

She lived another quarter century, composing several scores of poems as strong but none stronger, as this is lyric perfection. I am now old and get around too poorly to teach her as once I did, walking with my class through Yale's splendid Phelps Gateway on the way to our seminar room in the university's original building, Connecticut Hall. One December Thursday some years back, I had the occult experience of emerging from there with my discussion group at three-thirty on a dark afternoon, directly after they and I had worked through this poem. Waiting for us precisely was that "certain Slant of light."

A young woman, now an admirable and recognized poet, led us in startled and uneasy laughter at this Wildean instance of nature imitating high art. If I had possessed the show-womanship of the wonderful Anne Carson, I would have urged us to a group encore reciting the poem. But I was transported in the Dickinsonian sense, dazzled and forlorn.

"Certain"—both particular and assured—"Slant"—angled and circuitously truthful: The winter light is perpendicular weight pressing down upon us. Keatsian oxymorons—"Heavenly Hurt" and "imperial affliction"—convey a seal purely Dickinsonian, not one of the seven of Saint John's Revelation. Despair hurts us without a mark, except for an internal disordering of "meanings."

For my students, the enigmatic line was and is "None may teach it—Any." Is the light unwilling or incapable of absorbing instruction? Or are we not able to interpret the slant so as to transform ocular experience into teaching?

The listening landscape and breathless shadows share our apprehension at the light's downward slant: Yet its withdrawal is scariest, the departure suggesting the estrangement from all of us of our beloved dead, when last we gaze upon them.

In just seventy-two words, roughly equal to an octave of a Shakespearean sonnet, Dickinson has forged a monument to what her best critic, Sharon Cameron, called "lyric time." Any poem necessarily is a fiction of duration. Cameron—like Angus Fletcher, an authority on thinking in imaginative literature—heightened my awareness of tensions in Dickinson's subtle mastery of playing language games with tense. All of the "Slant of light" lyric is present tense yet somehow can seem past perfect. I think a Shakespearean trick is involved in such illusion, but that needs a touch of adumbration.

Despite inferential foregroundings, Shakespeare dramatizes presence, fullness of being *now*. Of all lyric poets in the language, Dickinson is closest to him. Pathos is the daemon, and personality creates itself through theatricality. I have experimented by teaching discussion groups in which Shakespeare's sonnets alternate with Dickinson's lyrics, setting them for and against each other, "Desire is death" juxtaposing with "Death is the supple Suitor."

My late friend and drinking companion Anthony Burgess, who consumed Fundador with vivacity akin to his ingesting Joyce and Shakespeare, always insisted the Dark Lady of the Sonnets was Lucy Negro, Elizabethan England's dominant East Indian sex worker. Urging him to consider Dickinson as Shakespeare's poetic inheritor, I persuaded him of the lineage but had difficulties with his lapsed Catholicism, which, like Joyce's, colored sex and death with delicious remorses and Augustinian nostalgias. A lapsed Amherst Congregationalist confused Anthony, who had little patience for Dickinson's "agile disbelievings." Lust in the Dark Lady sonnets is the furnace come up at last. In Dickinson, heated desire prevails, masked in decorum, though the mode of desire is so severely self-questioned as to become something else. That too is Shakespearean.

From Shakespeare, Dickinson learned to slow her reader down. Elliptical gnomes awaken our function of being wonder-wounded hearers. Hamlet's speed of mind is matched only by that of the seer of Amherst. Her relation to Shakespeare is crucial to her work and its importance yet is difficult to define. Why was *Othello* so central to her? After the Moor's tragedy, her particular favorites included *Antony and Cleopatra, Hamlet, Macbeth, Romeo and Juliet, King Lear, As You Like It, The Tempest,* and *The Merchant of Venice.* She sometimes seems to share in Shakespeare's apparent bisexuality, but her letters are prose poems and no more reliable guides to her eros than her lyrics are. Whatever her attachment to her volatile sister-in-law Sue, it seems dwarfed by the mutual flame of her passion with Judge Otis Lord. This is somewhat akin to the contrast between Shakespeare's sonnets addressed to the Fair Youth and the cauldron of those directed to the Dark Lady. It is a good irony that Shakespeare's enigmatic personal reserve is matched by Dickinson's.

A useful study, Páraic Finnerty's *Emily Dickinson's Shakespeare* (2006), examines her "circulation of the Bard"—her allusive reliance upon him for life as for work. Anthony Hecht, in a letter accompanying his gift to me of *Obbligati: Essays in Criticism* (1986), spoke of wanting to write a second Dickinson essay centering on her relation to Shakespeare, to emphasize her defenses against too many overt invocations of him. I think the essay remained unwritten and in honor of my late friend I gesture at it here.

As a preternaturally strong poet, Dickinson was wary lest she drown in Shakespeare. Parody was one resource, particularly in her letters. Deftly, she cultivated a mode of allusion self-curtailed enough to qualify any Shakespearean borrowings, whether in letters or lyrics. I return here to one of her grandest poems, *The Tint I Cannot Take Is Best* (1863):

696

The Tint I cannot take—is best—
The Color too remote
That I could show it in Bazaar—
A Guinea at a sight—

The fine—impalpable Array—
That swaggers on the eye
Like Cleopatra's Company—
Repeated—in the sky—

The Moments of Dominion
That happen on the Soul

And leave it with a Discontent
Too exquisite—to tell—

The eager look—on Landscapes—
As if they just repressed
Some secret—that was pushing
Like Chariots—in the Vest—

The Pleading of the Summer—
That other Prank—of Snow—
That Cushions Mystery with Tulle,
For fear the Squirrels—know.

Their Graspless manners—mock us—
Until the Cheated Eye
Shuts arrogantly—in the Grave—
Another way—to see—

I stand by my commentary on this in *The Western Canon* (1994), though I somewhat slighted the allusion to "Cleopatra's Company." Like Shakespeare's Cleopatra, Dickinson throughout her poems and letters sets out to beguile everyone; men of power, and women who test that power through seduction. Though Dickinson evidently refrained from meeting her brother's mistress and second wife, Millicent Todd Bingham, her letters to Sue's rival and displacer manifest a rhetoric similar to her correspondence with Susan Gilbert Dickinson. Millicent replaces Sue as decisively with Emily as she did with Austin Dickinson. Scholars disagree as to whether the poet casts herself as Cleopatra or Antony, but clearly she fuses the two personages even as she compounds Sue and Millicent. One comes to feel that Emily Dickinson might have enjoyed playing the role of the serpent of Amherst.

My former student Camille Paglia hinted that the poet was the Sade of Amherst, but that seems a strong misreading. Emily Dickinson does not merely flirt with us, her future readers. She catches us in her strong toil of grace, rendering each of us another Antony. This is akin to her use of *Epipsychidion*, Shelley's rapturous hymn to free love, where she identifies with his "Emily" (Emilia Viviani), particularly in the splendidly brazen quatrain 1636:

1636

Circumference thou Bride of Awe
Possessing thou shalt be
Possessed by every hallowed Knight
That dares—to Covet thee

She is "Circumference," Judge Lord is "Awe," and after his demise she awaits further prospects, with "possessing" and "possessed" echoing Shelley's vision of Emilia and himself. Shelley and Keats, like Wordsworth, she appropriated without anxiety. Shakespeare was different, as her puzzling relation to *Othello* may show.

You would not know from its effect upon Emily Dickinson that Othello's tragedy is Iago's play or that the noble Moor is a heroic protagonist. Still, her empathy for him increases with time, though carefully avoiding identification. Instead, she fuses him with Antony and more completely associates Desdemona with both Cleopatra and Ophelia. Her personal theater of mind appears to have approached the being more than the role of Hamlet.

776

Drama's Vitallest Expression is the Common Day
That arise and set about Us—
Other Tragedy

Perish in the Recitation—
This—the best enact
When the Audience is scattered
And the Boxes shut—

"Hamlet" to Himself were Hamlet—
Had not Shakespeare wrote—
Though the "Romeo" left no Record
Of his Juliet,

It were infinite enacted
In the Human Heart—
Only Theatre recorded
Owner cannot shut—

This is a critical observation rather than a poem. For Dickinson it is a throwaway, but it augments thinking about Shakespeare in Emerson's mode: "He wrote the text of modern life." The demarcation between Shakespeare and life fades. Hazlitt observed: "It is we who are Hamlet." Who among the poets thinks through every question so probingly as Dickinson does?:

817
This Consciousness that is aware
Of Neighbors and the Sun
Will be the one aware of Death
And that itself alone

Is traversing the interval
Experience between
And most profound experiment
Appointed unto Men—

How adequate unto itself
It's properties shall be
Itself unto itself and None
Shall make discovery—

Adventure most unto itself
The Soul condemned to be—
Attended by a single Hound
It's own identity.

I am pleased to comment upon this masterly lyric on December 10, 2012, the poet's one hundred and eighty-second birthday. Born a century after her, I have spent a chilly wet afternoon alternately exercising and meditating upon Dickinson. Consciousness ("conscience" in *Hamlet*) is her resource and her sublime agon with the limits of existence. She will not say with Hamlet: "Let be" or "Let it be." Poem 817 marches with a radical Protestant beat in rhythm of thought, proudly asserting her un-sponsored freedom to be in the difficulty of what it is to be. No solipsist, "aware / Of Neighbors and the Sun," her consciousness proudly calls out its autonomy. "Itself alone," "adequate unto itself," "Itself unto itself," "most unto itself" constitute a rugged litany of spiritual independence.

Death her death is an awareness, a most profound experiment, discovery, adventure, condemnation. The poem's surprise is its marvelous close: a shamanistic single Hound, the image of a doubled identity. Antony, bungling even his suicide, has not heard the music of his god or daemon Heracles abandoning him. Dickinson's daemon will attend her in the final experiment and implicitly marks the poet's shamanistic capacity for shape-shifting survival.

The Walt Whitman of *Song of Myself* declares his role and function as healing shaman. Close reading reveals Dickinson to be as uncanny:

355

It was not Death, for I stood up,
And all the Dead, lie down—
It was not Night, for all the Bells
Put out their Tongues, for Noon.

It was not Frost, for on my Flesh
I felt Siroccos—crawl—
Nor Fire—for just my marble feet
Could keep a Chancel, cool—

And yet, it tasted, like them all,
The Figures I have seen
Set orderly, for Burial,
Reminded me, of mine—

As if my life were shaven,
And fitted to a frame,
And could not breathe without a key,
And 'twas like Midnight, some—

When everything that ticked—has stopped—
And spare stares—all around—
Or Grisly frosts—first Autumn morns,
Repeal the Beating Ground—

But, most, like Chaos—Stopless—cool—
Without a Chance, or spar—
Or even a Report of Land—
To justify—Despair.

Beneath the spooky clarity of this vision darker speculations cluster. In teaching Dickinson I find that students emphasize their fascination with where in relation to what she depicts is the lyric's speaker *now?* The classical critic on this enigma remains Sharon Cameron in her *Lyric Time* where Kant is the ultimate model: The realities of space and of time are modes of perception rather than objects, and yet appearances in time have something permanent in them.

Still, archaic ecstasies and shamanistic dislocations are closer to the daemonic Dickinson, who dodges death while knowing the necessities of dying. Her temporal displacements exceed whatever norms lyric tradition manifests. Bells ring for high noon, and Dickinson *tastes* oxymoronic cold-and-heat and beholds herself as a standing cadaver:

As if my life were shaven,
And fitted to a frame,
And could not breathe without a key . . .

Time stops, space stares. The final quatrain challenges limits of poetic difficulty:

But, most, like Chaos—Stopless—cool—
Without a Chance, or spar—
Or even a Report of Land—
To justify—Despair.

"Justify" itself is tropological—despair does not convey the affect of this poem. "Chaos" is formless ocean; the poet's power of mind over that universe of death is firm enough to achieve Kant's sense of "something permanent," of images cohering into a fiction of duration. One of my students, answering her own query, regarded Dickinson's *now* as Emersonian Newness, opening into disclosures of the poem's own potential for survival.

Tone or stance is Dickinson's strength, as it is Whitman's, yet Walt—an American, one of the roughs—centers his poems upon himself, as the Amherst visionary would not. Always she is there: self-assertive, self-reliant, self-radiant. And yet Whitmanian advertisements-for-myself are antithetical to her experiment in renunciation. Like her only American poetic rival, she is joined to what Yeats in *Per Amica Silentia Lunae* called "the place of the daemon," but she enters it through another gate.

Shamans are not prophets, and Whitman composed poorly when he proclaimed futurity. The pathos of annihilation, Dickinson's truest conviction, is shared by her with Hamlet. Whitman at his darkest incarnates this truth. Dickinson, dark and light, teaches it incessantly, but she is masked by her diction, and most readers get this wrong. Immortality in Whitman is our survival in the memory of others. In Dickinson it is merely a metaphor, the duenna or chaperone who accompanies Death and the Maiden on their buggy ride.

Is there a more radical nihilist in American literature than Miss Dickinson of Amherst? Hamlet-like again, she thinks not too much but much too well and thinks her way to the truth. She possesses her art lest she perish of the truth, and her truth is annihilation: The rest is silence.

EMERSON REMARKED THAT THERE WERE SEVERAL STEPS BUT ONLY TWO facts: "I and the Abyss." Disenchanted even with Shakespeare, he kept calling for a poetry never to be written. Whitman sent *Leaves of Grass* 1855 to Emerson, who saw immediately what it was. If only Dickinson, who had met the sage of Concord, had turned to him as her reader, then her reception would have begun in her own lifetime. She chose instead the heroic and obtuse Thomas Wentworth Higginson, who was incapable of comprehending her work. Higginson, a fighting Abolitionist who raised and led into battle his own black regiment, denounced Walt Whitman for not joining the firing line, ignoring Walt's age and disparaging the magnificence of the wound dresser who sacrificed his health and genius in nursing the maimed and dying of both sides. But then Higginson capped his career by excoriating the young Oscar Wilde, who wrote and lectured sublimely when he should have been dying for the cause of Irish independence.

Like Melville and Hawthorne, Dickinson found her daemon in Shakespeare. Whitman insisted otherwise, yet his debt also was substantial. Still, of the twelve writers centering this book he was the least Shakespearean. Henry James wrote brilliantly on *The Tempest,* while Wallace Stevens was haunted by *A Midsummer Night's Dream* and *Hamlet.* T. S. Eliot, who asserted a preference for *Coriolanus* over *Hamlet,* nevertheless was deeply contaminated by both prince and play. Faulkner seems steeped more in the King James Bible than in Shakespeare, but this may be illusory. *The Tempest* is prevalent throughout Hart Crane's poetry, and so are *Hamlet, Macbeth,* and other plays.

Melville and Dickinson (strange coupling) are the most Shakespearean of our classic American writers. Shakespeare's capacious heart (in Hamlet's sense of mind) provided room enough for two great imaginations so diverse that they touch at no point. Even their disputes with power (under the name of God) have little affinity. They link only in their apprehensions of Shakespeare's tragedies.

Jay Leyda, who logged both novelist and poet, remarked to me that Melville had a cinematic sense of Shakespeare, while Dickinson comprehended him lyrically. There are a thousand Shakespeares and we make of him what we can. If you are Emily Dickinson or Herman Melville, then a cognitive music emanating from him will inform a lifetime's "loved Philology" or *Moby-Dick.* In their wake, I quest to discern what they found that renewed life's fountains and enlarged its vistas. Melville sings no songs of himself, unless you take *Moby-Dick* as a vast Homeric song of the sea. James Joyce, yearning beyond *Finnegans Wake,* longed to go on to his own epic of ocean but died too soon. Proust, supreme rival, barely had time to revise the final volume of his human comedy, recapturing past time.

Of my twelve Americans, it may be just to observe that eleven lived to write themselves out. Whitman declines after 1865; Emerson edges into senility; Melville has a late epiphany in *Billy Budd;* Dickinson goes on to the end, though becoming sparser. Hawthorne's heights are *The Scarlet Letter* and the tales; James's majesty would not have been augmented by finishing *The Ivory Tower*. Twain never again attains the splendor of *Huckleberry Finn*, while Frost went from strength to strength until his final surge in *In the Clearing*. Eliot subsides after *Four Quartets*, while Stevens develops superbly in his death poems. Even Faulkner's most fervent admirers are embarrassed by *A Fable*. Only Hart Crane, drowning himself at thirty-two, deprives us of a magnificence that could have surpassed *The Bridge* and *The Broken Tower*.

Their greatest precursor, to my perpetual wonder, wrote nothing in the last three years of his life while residing in Stratford-upon-Avon as an esteemed but scarcely renowned local citizen. After composing Acts I and V of *The Two Noble Kinsmen* (the humdrum II–IV are John Fletcher's), Shakespeare chose the rest of silence. No remotely comparable figure—Dante, Petrarch, Cervantes, Montaigne, Spenser, Molière, Goethe, Tolstoy, Dickens, Balzac, and onward—gives up so completely. Why does Shakespeare abruptly cease?

External evidence is scanty and dubious. One notion is that lingering syphilis terminated the work three years before ending the man at fifty-one. There is palpable outrage at the male sexual drive continuing into some men's eighties in Shakespeare's last play, yet it is overmatched by a horror of violence, however organized.

Only the plays matter, and their sequence suggests a strategic retreat from the terrifying affect of the high tragedies—*Othello, King Lear, Macbeth*—into what I have come to regard as glorious tragicomedies—*Antony and Cleopatra, The Winter's Tale, The Tempest,* all of which should be played as comedies, though I despair of that being done.

Shakespeare's daemons (he possessed a multitude) did not abandon him after *Macbeth*, but he spared himself by evading and diverting them. Hamlet and *Hamlet* had cost him too much, a human price fearfully augmented by Iago and Othello, Lear and Edgar, and perhaps most intimately by Macbeth, who dies offstage because the proleptic element in Shakespeare's imagination dies with him.

Dickinson and Whitman, of all Americans, most engaged death and dying as adventures in consciousness. Eliot joins this engagement from the early *Death of Saint Narcissus* onward and achieves final splendor in *The Dry Salvages* of *Four Quartets,* where the dark wisdom of Whitman and Mark Twain, enhanced by Hart Crane, merges with Indic traditions, of which the creator of *The Waste Land* was an erudite scholar.

Eliot, with deep knowledge of the original, was immersed in the *Bhagavad-Gita,* as Emerson and Thoreau were. Whitman was not (if we are to believe him), though Thoreau and Emerson wondered otherwise. I am haunted by the shade of the great Gershom Scholem, who urged me to associate Walt with Kabbalah, of which the poet had no knowledge. Capacious Whitman intuitively contains traditions he never overtly studied.

The seer of *Passage to India* connected his daemon or real Me to the cosmos. Illuminated from the start, he did not need to quest for release. Emersonian idealism was rejected by Whitman in favor of Lucretian materialism, itself not compatible with Indian speculations. And yet Walt, unlike a consistent Epicurean, sings loss in and to the self. Without having read the *Gita,* Whitman discovered its discipline in himself. The activity of mourning in his elegies moves away from dark inertia to enlightened renunciation of any fruit of sorrow except the poem itself. Immortality departs from literal survival to being joined together with the memory of other selves, with the hope of being included in their memories.

The *Gita* is a severe poem, once compared to Dante by Eliot. Possessing no Sanskrit, I rely most on the spirited version by Barbara Stoler Miller (1986). Certainly it seems far more Eliotic than Whitmanian, since *Song of Myself* and the *Calamus* poems move toward merging Walt and the cosmos by and through sexual exuberance. And yet Eliot discerned that Whitman more profoundly quested for the tally, an image of voice conferred only by a daemonic surrender to a larger sense of death, whose outlet song emerges from the mockingbird in *Out of the Cradle Endlessly Rocking* and the hermit thrush in *When Lilacs Last in the Dooryard Bloom'd.* *The Waste Land* owes its hermit thrush to Whitman, as Eliot was slow to acknowledge, for the good reason that its debts are so great as to jeopardize the originality of the Eliotic masterwork. Walt is the daemon of *The Waste Land,* the corpse planted in its forsaken garden.

Eliot's elegiac tonalities are his peculiar strength and account for much of the beauty of his cadences. His long palaver as to his supposed precursors embraced Dante, Baudelaire, Jules Laforgue, Tristan Corbière, Pound, various metaphysicals and Jacobeans, anyone but Shelley, Tennyson, and Whitman, the actual forerunners. Daemonic possession by the poetic voices of Shelley, Whitman, and Tennyson was an endless danger for Eliot, early and late. Vulnerable to the poetics of loss, he recognized masters of regret in Whitman and in Tennyson. "My heart is a handful of dust" is

Tennyson's trope in *Maud,* and the corpse planted last year in the garden was buried first in Walt Whitman's *This Compost.*

Eliot's Arthur Henry Hallam, a young critic dead at twenty-one whom Tennyson loved, was Jean Verdenal: his version of Whitman's Winter Comrade of the *Calamus* poems, another "awful daring of a moment's surrender, / Which an age of prudence can never retract." That frankly dubious observation makes sense to me only in that Tennyson, Whitman, and Eliot all had androgynous imaginations. The greatest instance of that fecund faculty is William Shakespeare. Tiresias, the Oedipal seer who suffered sexual experience both as woman and as man, is appropriate as a figure for poets and poetry in Tennyson and in Eliot.

W. B. Yeats enriched the idea of the daemon by identifying it with his muse, Maud Gonne. In the Paterian treatise *Per Amica Silentia Lunae* (1917), he condenses his fruitful lifetime of frustration by Maud into a superb sentence that has haunted me since first I read it seventy years ago:

> I shall find the dark grow luminous, the void fruitful when I understand I have nothing, that the ringers in the tower have appointed for the hymen of the soul a passing bell.

Several of Hart Crane's friends—Walker Evans, Malcolm Cowley, Kenneth Burke, Allen Tate—told me the poet quoted this to them more than once and I hear it in the intricate slain numbers of *The Broken Tower.*

In *Per Amica Silentia Lunae,* Yeats boldly (if a little foolishly) first assimilated sexual love to "the warfare of man and Daemon":

> When I think of life as a struggle with the Daemon who would ever set us to the hardest work among those not impossible, I understand why there is a deep enmity between a man and his destiny, and why a man loves nothing but his destiny. In an Anglo-Saxon poem a certain man is called, as though to call him something that summed up all heroism, "Doom eager." I am persuaded that the Daemon delivers and deceives us, and that he wove that netting from the stars and threw the net from his shoulder. Then my imagination runs from Daemon to sweetheart, and I divine an analogy that evades the intellect. I remember that Greek antiquity has bid us look for the principal stars, that govern enemy and sweetheart alike,

among those that are about to set, in the Seventh House as the as-
trologers say; and that it may be "sexual love," which is "founded
upon spiritual hate," is an image of the warfare of man and Daemon; and I even wonder if there may not be some secret communion, some whispering in the dark between Daemon and sweetheart.
I remember how often women when in their love grow superstitious,
and believe that they can bring their lovers good luck; and I remember an old Irish story of three young men who went seeking for help
in battle into the house of the gods at Slieve-na-mon. "You must
first be married," some god told them, "because a man's good or
evil luck comes to him through a woman."

In the original published text of *A Vision* (1925), the beloved muse and
the Daimon emerge:

Man's *Daimon* has therefore her energy and bias, in man's *Mask*,
and her constructive power in man's fate, and man and *Daimon*
face each other in a perpetual conflict or embrace. This relation (the
Daimon being of the opposite sex to that of man) may create a passion like that of sexual love. The relation of man and woman, in so
far as it is passionate, reproduces the relation of man and *Daimon*,
and becomes an element where man and *Daimon* sport, pursue one
another, and do one another good or evil. This does not mean, however, that the men and women of opposite phases love one another,
for a man generally chooses a woman whose *Mask* falls between his
Mask and his *Body of Fate*, or just outside one or other; but that
every man is, in the right of his sex, a wheel, or group of *Four Facul-
ties*, and that every woman is, in the right of her sex, a wheel which
reverses the masculine wheel. In so far as man and woman are
swayed by their sex they interact as man and *Daimon* interact,
though at other moments their phases may be side by side. The
Daimon carries on her conflict, or friendship with a man, not only
through the events of life, but in the mind itself, for she is in possession of the entire dark of the mind.

I doubt that Eliot devoted much study to either version of *A Vision*,
and his own meetings with the Irish arch-poet, under Pound's manage-

ment, seemed to annoy him. Surprisingly, Yeats surfaces in *Four Quartets* as a late precursor, powerfully informing Eliot's final poetic achievement.

The incorporation of Yeats's voice is accomplished by a strange fusion with the figure of Dante, whose tonalities are filtered through Shelley, particularly his unfinished death poem, *The Triumph of Life*. Shelley's Italian surpassed Eliot's, and there is a curious rightness in this late assimilation, since all that Yeats and Eliot share is the paradox of Shelley's influence—primary and affirmed by Yeats, and mysteriously prevalent though denied by Eliot, much in the same way that he dismissed Walt Whitman. Such departures-by-fiat are unworkable. Eliot's *What the Thunder Said* is said initially by the *Lilacs* elegy, and the Whitmanian shore ode returns with vigor in *The Dry Salvages*.

Eliot is shrewdly eclectic in echoes and allusions in *Four Quartets*, including in his scope his friend Conrad Aiken's *Preludes* and Hart Crane's *The River* from *The Bridge*. He recognized both Crane's agon with him and Crane's complex debt by printing *The Tunnel* section of *The Bridge* in *The Criterion*. In old age I enter upon a kind of peace in my own lifelong struggle against Eliot's criticism and regret some harshness indulged through the decades. These things have served their purpose; let them be. I employed Northrop Frye and Kenneth Burke against Eliot, but by my own dialectic he was my antithetical precursor.

A Yiddish-speaking Bronx proletarian, arriving at Yale as a twenty-one-year-old enthusiast of Blake, Shelley, Hart Crane, Stevens, Yeats, Hardy, Pater, Ruskin, Whitman, Spenser, and Milton, was not made welcome by an English faculty dominated by neo-Christian New Critics of the Eliotic persuasion: Cleanth Brooks and Robert Penn Warren, Maynard Mack and Louis Martz, William Wimsatt and René Wellek and their ephebes and camp followers. Rough, shaggy, parenthetical, self-conscious, and amiably polemical, I alienated most of them and would not have survived past a year but for the encouragement and kindness of two distinguished scholars, Dean William Clyde DeVane and Professor Frederick Albert Pottle. Sixty-three years later I remain at Yale, trying to do for my students what Pottle and DeVane did for me.

In that long-vanished context, the criticism and cultural stance, the genteel anti-Semitism, of T. S. Eliot were not acceptable to me. I enjoyed quoting from *After Strange Gods: A Primer of Modern Heresy*, both in my student essays and class discussions. Eliot himself had dismissed his book as "sick," but it was and is perfectly representative of his stance as a human being and a literary intellectual. For a long time it blinded me to the indubitable achievement of his best poetry, though beneath my scorn I kept hearing its cadences, since I had and have nearly all of it by heart.

From January 1973 until his death in 1989, the poet-novelist Robert Penn Warren and I became close friends, lunching together every week, corresponding about his poetry, and mutually setting aside our prior disagreements, particularly on Eliot. Our relationship began because he purchased a small book by me, *The Anxiety of Influence,* on its publication day; he read it immediately and sent me a postcard in its praise, inviting me to lunch. From 1966 on his poetry had swerved away from Eliot's into his own idiom, and he felt my new book was parallel to his own work. A quarter century older and wiser than I was, he became a fatherly counselor. Since then I have become close to his daughter, herself a poet, and taught her nephew, Warren's grandson, also a poet. I bring in the poet-novelist here because his effect upon me has been permanent. A kind of secular Augustinian, Warren thirsted to know the true nature of time. Even in exhausted old age, that is not my own quest. For a Gnostic, time is the great enemy and blocking agent to whatever freedom remains. The world is a catastrophe-creation and time is the Demiurge's tyranny.

I learned from "Red" Warren as I have from only a few others— Gershom Scholem, M. H. Abrams, Frederick Pottle—a distrust of my own daemon, or, rather, the necessity of standing apart from it without repudiating the energies upon which I relied. We learn face-to-face, kindled by immediacy. Reading Dickinson yields a similar gnosis.

IN 1863, DICKINSON COMPOSED A SINGULAR GNOME:

579

The Soul unto itself
Is an imperial friend—
Or the most agonizing Spy—
An Enemy—could send—

Secure against it's own—
No treason it can fear—
Itself—it's Sovreign—Of itself
The Soul should stand in Awe—

These thirty-seven words are deceptively packed with antithetical meanings. "The Soul unto itself" is the germ of the famous "single Hound" lyric of a year later, which I repeat below:

817

This Consciousness that is aware
Of Neighbors and the Sun
Will be the one aware of Death
And that itself alone

Is traversing the interval
Experience between
And most profound experiment
Appointed unto Men—

How adequate unto itself
It's properties shall be
Itself unto itself and None
Shall make discovery—

Adventure most unto itself
The Soul condemned to be—
Attended by a single Hound
It's own identity.

Shamanism, as in the daemonic Walt, is prevalent in Dickinson's ventures. Whitman might have taken alarm at "The Soul unto itself / Is an imperial friend—." In *Song of Myself* the unknowable soul swims apart from Walt's rough self and can experience only mutual abasement with his real Me, the Me myself. The Whitmanian soul in *The Sleepers* begins its long venture into a fourfold manifestation: night, death, the mother, and the sea. But Dickinson's "Sovreign" soul dwells close at hand, ambivalently imperial friend and agonizing spy, always in awe of itself.

In a kind of triumphal post-Protestant march, the later *This Consciousness That Is Aware* equates soul with her Shakespearean consciousness; no solipsist, she is "aware / Of Neighbors and the Sun." "Itself" is repeated five times in sixty-seven words across four quatrains and becomes a refrain.

The poet's pride, invested by Dickinson in her brevity, is also a stylistic ideal. The abruptness is cognitive. She seeks identity through self-identification, which for her, as for Emerson and Whitman, perpetually is discovery and adventure.

An internal alliteration (to call it that) marks poem 817: "Neighbors," "aware," "traversing," "interval," "Experience," "experiment," "properties," "discovery," "Adventure." Those ninefold words roll a litany of "r"s for the death of consciousness, rather like Macbeth's "tomorrow and tomorrow and tomorrow." Awareness links Shakespeare and Dickinson, heightened consciousness both cognitive and uncanny. Her Shakespearean speed of mind works to slow the reader down. In both, gnomic ellipses awaken our function to make us wonder-wounded hearers.

The long experience of teaching Dickinson has been sublimely exhausting: She is the most rewardingly difficult of American poets. My late mentor William K. Wimsatt delightedly would scoff at me whenever we had coffee together after my Dickinson class. I invariably complained of a headache. That, he assured me, was because I was a Longinian critic and not an Aristotelian like himself. I remember Bill, ruefully, each time I teach Dickinson; her cognitive originality daunts me as much now as when first I attempted an introduction of her poetry to others almost sixty years ago.

Here is an eight-line gnome of 1865:

1012

Best Things dwell out of Sight
The Pearl—the Just—Our Thought—
Most shun the Public Air
Legitimate, and Rare—

The Capsule of the Wind
The Capsule of the Mind

Exhibit here, as doth a Burr—
Germ's Germ be where?

Can this be unpacked? We catch the drift, but how shall we decipher the connections?

Dickinson's work, like Shakespeare's, has no design upon us, no dark allegory we are summoned to search for pure power. Though prompted by Emerson, she subtly qualifies his emphases and plays similarly against Wordsworth (called "the Stranger" by her) and even Keats, whose oxymoronic rhetoric persuades her. Shakespeare and the Bible, her main resources, nevertheless provoke her to selective merriment when her stance demands it:

776

Drama's Vitallest Expression is the Common Day
That arise and set about Us—
Other Tragedy

Perish in the Recitation—
This—the best enact
When the Audience is scattered
And the Boxes shut—

"Hamlet" to Himself were Hamlet—
Had not Shakespeare wrote—
Though the "Romeo" left no Record
Of his Juliet,

It were infinite enacted
In the Human Heart—
Only Theatre recorded
Owner cannot shut—

Is that a critique or another ellipsis? And how shall we read this uncanny parable concerning King Lear and the Fool?

1356

A little Madness in the Spring
Is wholesome even for the King,
But God be with the Clown—
Who ponders this tremendous scene—
This whole Experiment of Green—
As if it were his own!

In 1862, Dickinson composed a poem endless to meditation:

479

Because I could not stop for Death—
He kindly stopped for me—
The Carriage held but just Ourselves—
And Immortality.

We slowly drove—He knew no haste
And I had put away
My labor and my leisure too,
For His Civility—

We passed the School, where Children strove
At Recess—in the Ring—
We passed the Fields of Gazing Grain—
We passed the Setting Sun—

Or rather—He passed Us—
The Dews drew quivering and Chill—
For only Gossamer, my Gown—
My Tippet—only Tulle—

We paused before a House that seemed
A Swelling of the Ground—
The Roof was scarcely visible—
The Cornice—in the Ground—

Since then—'tis Centuries—and yet
Feels shorter than the Day
I first surmised the Horses' Heads
Were toward Eternity—

The Lady and Death, Demon Lover or Daemon, behave exquisitely as upper-class citizens of Civil War Amherst performing a strict courtship ritual; this is necessary since, as she said in a letter to Thomas Wentworth Higginson, "I do not cross my Father's ground to any house or town."

The duenna Immortality counts for little when Death is the driver. Time, modulating away from surprise toward calm acceptance, here as so often is part of Dickinson's secret mastery. By convention, an afternoon's courtship prolongs "toward Eternity," and civility yields to abduction. Yet the poet's voice betrays no affect in response: We might be hearing an account of simply the way things were or how it was done on an afternoon in Amherst.

With her interest in ballad forms, from which she swerved into her own modes, Dickinson may have known some version of the Scottish song "The Demon Lover." I think of the parallel in Elizabeth Bowen's 1945 short story of that title in which a London woman of fashion is on her way to an event in a cab until she discovers that the driver, who is not obeying her directions, is a defunct jilted suitor. Unable to get out, she is taken to some dark location where doubtless a vengeful ravishment will be enacted.

Dickinson's abduction is uncannier, at once more commonplace, and even more unexpected. It is a daemonic version of a quest-romance and compares fruitfully with another of her poems of 1862:

453
Our journey had advanced—
Our feet were almost come
To that odd Fork in Being's Road—
Eternity—by Term—

Our pace took sudden awe—
Our feet—reluctant—led—

Before—were Cities—but Between—
The Forest of the Dead—

Retreat—was out of Hope—
Behind—a Sealed Route—
Eternity's White Flag—Before—
And God—at every Gate—

John Bunyan's *Pilgrim's Progress* may be part of the foreground; some have suggested Dante, but he seems less relevant. The "Cities" may be those of Destruction and Salvation; the "Forest of the Dead" seems more familiar than it proves to be. What dominates the poem is impasse; you cannot go on and cannot go back. This is one of several instances of the prolepsis of Samuel Beckett in Dickinson.

What "Eternity" signifies in *Because I Could Not Stop for Death* is uncertain; here it bewilders. The wordplay "Eternity—by Term" is wit raised to sublimity; "Term" is word, period of a sentencing, terminus. And what is "Eternity's White Flag": truce, surrender, banner of purity?

Eve and Adam, expelled from Eden, have their way back to it blocked by a cherub at the gate, waving a flaming sword. Is that like "God—at every Gate"? Dickinson implies no answers. She is not at all an allegorist and cannot be one since all her daemonic agency is her own.

"Our journey had advanced" does not say one thing and mean another, yet her enigmatic art is so elliptical as to leave us uncertain of what she says or what it might mean. Originality, her strongest attribute, exacts its costs of confirmation. Paul Celan, whose translations of Dickinson are alive beyond belief, rightly found in her a negative poetics anticipating his own.

Like Walt Whitman, Emily Dickinson is a dangerous influence. Between them, they can threaten to take up all the space for an American poetry of blinding originality. Robert Frost, Wallace Stevens, T. S. Eliot, and Hart Crane, our strongest since, have complex relations to her; Frost least, though he shares their sources in Emerson. Whitman—as I keep observing—haunts Stevens, Eliot, and Crane, who includes Dickinson and Melville (and Eliot) in his American ancestry.

The first principle for confronting and reading Dickinson is akin to what Whitman forces us to accept about his poetry: self-conscious, self-affirmative aggressivity against Western literary tradition. Dickinson conceals her furious vitalism beneath a mask of elegant good manners and modesty, but that clearly belies her actual stance of energetic self-reliance. I would argue that she goes beyond Whitman in her aggressive assertion of her own poetic authority and accomplishment. She is almost as sweet as Emerson, accurately compared by my late friend Bart Giamatti to barbed wire.

Another of her triumphs is *Essential Oils Are Wrung,* a poem of 1863:

772

Essential Oils—are wrung—
The Attar from the Rose
Be not expressed by Suns—alone—
It is the gift of Screws—

The General Rose—decay—
But this—in Lady's Drawer
Make Summer—When the Lady lie
In Ceaseless Rosemary—

There is a helpful reading of this by Vernon Shetley (*Genre,* 45–1, Spring 2012), which is my starting point. He turns aside from feminist contextualizations of this poem that place it within the nineteenth-century culture of a woman's domestic role. Instead, he sees "Essential Oils—are wrung" as a negation of the Petrarchan tradition of celebrating (and exploiting) a lady's beauty. Its bloom soon will be gone, and she will be only the fruit thereof unless her beauty be immortalized in a timeless sonnet, yet that depends upon her yielding in time to the lustful poet.

Powerfully condensed, Dickinson's lyric contrasts the natural "General Rose" with "Attar," the distilled rose oil that may represent poetry itself. "The gift of Screws" reminds us of how attar results from the oil press operated by screws. Dickinson stored her poems in a drawer, knowing they would be taken up after her death. She is her own Petrarch or Shakespeare and requires no other.

The elliptical mode in her poetry recalls late Shakespeare but is more extreme. A daemonic drive to negate precursors while maintaining their standards of excellence distinguishes her from some recent poetical ideologues of the feminist persuasion, whether in verse or prose. They claim Dickinson as ancestor, yet they do her wrong, she being so majestical, to offer her the show of violence.

Few great poets have dared Dickinson's boastfulness:

381

I cannot dance opon my Toes—
No Man instructed me—
But oftentimes, among my mind,
A Glee possesseth me,

That had I Ballet Knowledge—
Would put itself abroad
In Pirouette to blanch a Troupe—
Or lay a Prima, mad,

And though I had no Gown of Gauze—
No Ringlet, to my Hair,
Nor hopped for Audiences—like Birds—
One Claw upon the air—

Nor tossed my shape in Eider Balls,
Nor rolled on wheels of snow
Till I was out of sight, in sound,
The House encore me so—

Nor any know I know the Art
I mention—easy—Here—
Nor any Placard boast me—
It's full as Opera—

Glee, audacious merriment, is one of her signatures, as in this boister-ous vaunt of 1862. The denial in "No Man instructed me" is absolute: Emerson, Keats, Wordsworth, Shakespeare, the Bible. Her fullness of "Opera" is unknown to them. Vaingloriously outrageous, this would court absurdity if the poem failed to exemplify and to justify such pugna-cious audacity.

Dickinson's agonistic stance is so vehemently consistent that I wonder how critics can mistake her daemonic Romanticism for a throwback to seventeenth-century metaphysical and meditative poetry. Her affinities are with Emerson, Whitman, Thoreau, and Melville, though she read Emerson as combatively as she did Wordsworth and Keats, Shelley and Shakespeare, and, above all, the King James Bible. She cast glances at the Brontës and Mrs. Browning, but her consciousness of her womanhood was just as fiercely independent as Emily Brontë's. Nietzsche's maxim that every free spirit must unfold itself in fighting applies to her as it does to Emerson and Melville. She surpasses even the strongest of her American contemporaries in self-reliance.

DICKINSON RESISTED CONGREGATIONALIST ANCESTRAL TRADITION: HER idiosyncratic Jesus was the exemplary sufferer but not a resurrected savior of anyone, himself included:

> 1485
> Spurn the temerity—
> Rashness of Calvary—
> Gay were Gethsemane
> Knew we of thee—

That is her sisterly warning to Jesus. Her spiritual stance was summed up brilliantly by Hart Crane in a sonnet, *To Emily Dickinson,* composed sometime after he started to read her incessantly in 1926:

> You who desired so much—in vain to ask—
> Yet fed your hunger like an endless task,
> Dared dignify the labor, bless the quest—
> Achieved that stillness ultimately best,
>
> Being, of all, least sought for: Emily, hear!
> O sweet, dead Silencer, most suddenly clear
> When singing that Eternity possessed
> And plundered momently in every breast;

—Truly no flower yet withers in your hand.
The harvest you descried and understand
Needs more than wit to gather, love to bind.
Some reconcilement of remotest mind—

Leaves Ormus rubyless, and Ophir chill.
Else tears heap all within one clay-cold hill.

Dickinson's final harvest—hundreds of enduring poems—does not
yield to wit and love alone and requires also a very difficult "reconcilement
of remotest mind," that undiscovered country from which no traveler returns: death our death. Immortality, in Whitman, is our survival in the
love of others. What is it for Dickinson?

Certainly not Christian salvation and translation to a higher sphere.
Stale ideas of a hereafter are dismissed by Dickinson as worn-out
images:

1684

The immortality she gave
We borrowed at her Grave—
For just one Plaudit famishing,
The Might of Human Love—

Love is stronger than death in the Song of Songs; Dickinson is more
wistful. She does not entertain anything like Henry James's fascination
with ghostly phenomena, and she shares Emerson's rejection: "Other
world! there is no other world. Here or nowhere is the whole fact."

Though she died in her mid-fifties, never knowing old age, Dickinson's
clarity, her power of mind, would not have altered had she lived another
three decades:

1223

Immortal is an ample word
When what we need is by
But when it leaves us for a time
'Tis a necessity.

Of Heaven above the firmest proof
We fundamental know
Except for it's marauding Hand
It had been Heaven below—

Only a word, "Immortal," is here and now. The longer you read
Dickinson, the clearer it becomes that immortality is a trope for the love
she has known and lost or gained only as aspiration. The sorrow of old
age, for everyone I know, is that we wake up many mornings to the discovery that another lifetime friend has departed.

As losses accumulate, I return often to Dickinson, not for consolation
but plainly to propound the costs that confirm aesthetic contemplation.
When my students ask me to select a single poem by Dickinson as my
personal favorite, I always choose what I believe to be her farewell to her
love, Judge Otis Lord, perhaps as he lay dying in 1884. I am aware that
R. W. Franklin's dating of this poem as 1874 renders my surmise unlikely,
and yet Dickinson had proleptic abilities:

1314
Because that you are going
And never coming back
And I, however absolute
May overlook your Track—

Because that Death is final,
However first it be
This instant be suspended
Above Mortality.

Significance that each has lived
The other to detect
Discovery not God himself
Could now annihilate

Eternity, Presumption
The instant I perceive

That you, who were Existence
Yourself forgot to live—

The "Life that is" will then have been
A Thing I never knew—
As Paradise fictitious
Until the Realm of you—

The "Life that is to be," to me,
A Residence too plain
Unless in my Redeemer's Face
I recognize your own.

Of Immortality who doubts
He may exchange with me
Curtailed by your obscuring Face
Of Everything but He—

Of Heaven and Hell I also yield
The Right to reprehend
To whoso would commute this Face
For his less priceless Friend.

If "God is Love" as he admits
We think that he must be
Because he is a "jealous God"
He tells us certainly

If "All is possible with" him
As he besides concedes
He will refund us finally
Our confiscated Gods—

Even if the dying male muse here is purely imaginary, these ten quatrains have an urgent power of force unusual even for Emily Dickinson. They march to a displaced Protestant militancy of the self found frequently in her poetry but with a noteworthy degree of aggressive self-assertion. Sharon Cameron called it "the dialectic of rage," in which the function of "rage" is to prevent "the convergence of death and sexuality." Or as Shakespeare pronounced in a *Dark Lady* sonnet: "Desire is death."

Dickinson's formidable persuasive redefinitions of terms and transvaluation of values pass now into a rage to order words so that they suggest a wholly culpable God, almost a Gnostic Demiurge, like Philip Pullman's Metatron. "Because that Death is final" redefines "Immortality" as the "obscuring Face" of the lost lover curtailing "Everything but He."

God annihilates the life-exchanging discovery of love and then reluctantly concedes his supposed role as love while dogmatically proclaiming his possessive jealousy. Recalcitrance commences again with his possible power to wake the dead. Scorching scorn ignites the final lines:

> He will refund us finally
> Our confiscated Gods—

"Refund" and "confiscated" touch one limit of outrage; a larger one extends by naming our late beloved as "Gods." Despite my high regard for scholars of Dickinson who see her as alternating, in her own words, "agile belief and disbelief," she has faith only in poetry and herself.

I recall a James Thurber cartoon I enjoyed decades ago, in which two women observed a third one, tending flowers. The caption, spoken by one woman to the other, was "She has the true Emily Dickinson spirit except that she gets fed up occasionally." The poet I read is outraged and outrageous, with her high art working concealment of her drive against anteriority. Her life was conventional only on the surface—a furnace comes up at last in her poetry:

> 1742
> In Winter in my Room
> I came upon a Worm
> Pink lank and warm
> But as he was a worm
> And worms presume

Not quite with him at home
Secured him by a string
To something neighboring
And went along—

A Trifle afterward
A thing occurred
I'd not believe it if I heard
But state with creeping blood
A snake with mottles rare
Surveyed my chamber floor
In feature as the worm before
But ringed with power
The very string with which
I tied him—too
When he was mean and new
That string was there—

I shrank—"How fair you are"!
Propitiation's Claw—
"Afraid he hissed
Of me"?
"No Cordiality"—
He fathomed me—
Then to a Rhythm *Slim*
Secreted in his Form
As Patterns swim
Projected him.

That time I flew
Both eyes his way
Lest he pursue
Nor ever ceased to run
Till in a distant Town
Towns on from mine
I set me down
This was a dream—

Nobody's favorite dream, but was Miss Dickinson of Amherst more amused than scared? Or is "bemused" a better word? We scarcely think of her as a comic poet, but her "glee" gives us

> 1150
>
> These are the Nights that Beetles love—
> From Eminence remote
> Drives ponderous perpendicular
> His figure intimate—
> The terror of the Children
> The merriment of men
> Depositing his Thunder
> He hoists abroad again—
> A Bomb opon the Ceiling
> Is an improving thing—
> It keeps the nerves progressive
> Conjecture flourishing—
> Too dear the Summer evening
> Without discreet alarm—
> Supplied by Entomology
> With it's remaining charm—

How to define the precise humor of: "A Bomb opon the Ceiling / Is an improving thing—"? Or of the presuming worm secured by a string who powers himself into a snake, or this:

> 1766
>
> The waters chased him as he fled,
> Not daring look behind;
> A billow whispered in his Ear,
> "Come home with me, my friend;
> My parlor is of shriven glass,
> My pantry has a fish
> For every palate in the Year,"—
> To this revolting bliss
> The object floating at his side
> Made no distinct reply.

"This revolting bliss" deliciously contrasts with the grotesque "object floating at his side," residium of the man fleeing the waters. If there could be such an affect as "daemonic insouciance," then Dickinson is its master.

Of the major American poets, Dickinson is the least tendentious. Like Shakespeare, she has no design upon her readers. Walt Whitman sought to be the national poet and desired to write a new Bible for Americans, thus following Emerson's rejection of history. The most eminent of our twentieth-century makers—Robert Frost, Wallace Stevens, Hart Crane— seek only the purposes of the pure poet. T. S. Eliot, whether in prose or verse, was a Christian ideologue, who in a few poems transcended that extra-poetic drive to convert himself and others.

Dickinson's freedom from the past is still underestimated. Haunted by the English Bible and Shakespeare, and by the High Romantics, she nevertheless was inspired and troubled most by her older contemporary, the fountain of the American will, Emerson. That agon is at her center, and to it I now return.

THOUGH SHE MET EMERSON, DICKINSON DISTANCED HERSELF FROM THE sage as best she could, fearing over-influence, as an Emersonian should. He recognized himself in *Leaves of Grass* (1855) and would have seen many of his aspirations for America had he read her poetry. Self-reliance, his faithless faith, found two of its prime exemplars in Whitman and Dickinson:

Man is timid and apologetic; he is no longer upright; he dares not say "I think," "I am," but quotes some saint or sage. He is ashamed before the blade of grass or the blowing rose. These roses under my window make no reference to former roses or to better ones; they are for what they are; they exist with God to-day. There is no time to them. There is simply the rose; it is perfect in every moment of its existence. Before a leaf-bud has burst, its whole life acts; in the full-blown flower there is no more; in the leafless root there is no less. Its nature is satisfied, and it satisfies nature, in all moments alike. But man postpones, or remembers; he does not live in the present, but with a reverted eye laments the past, or, heedless of the riches that surround him, stands on tiptoe to foresee the future. He cannot be happy and strong until he too lives with nature in the present, above time.

That is a starting point, yet not unique to poets. Emerson's essay "The Poet" directly animated Dickinson and Whitman:

It is a secret which every intellectual man quickly learns, that, beyond the energy of his possessed and conscious intellect, he is capable of a new energy (as of an intellect doubled on itself), by abandonment to the nature of things; that, beside his privacy of power as an individual man, there is a great public power, on which he can draw, by unlocking, at all risks, his human doors, and suffering the ethereal tides to roll and circulate through him: then he is caught up into the life of the Universe, his speech is thunder, his thought is law, and his words are universally intelligible as the plants and animals. The poet knows that he speaks adequately, then only when he speaks somewhat wildly, or, "with the flower of the mind;" not with the intellect, used as an organ, but with the intellect released from all service, and suffered to take its direction from its celestial life; or, as the ancients were wont to express themselves, not with intellect alone, but with the intellect inebriated by nectar. As the traveller who has lost his way, throws his reins on his horse's neck, and trusts to the instinct of the animal to find his road, so must we do with the divine animal who carries us through this world. For if in any manner we can stimulate this instinct, new passages are opened for us into the nature, the mind flows into and through things hardest and highest, and the metamorphosis is possible.

Emersonianism proclaims daemonic influx as both the question of genius and its answer. We can locate that influx of the daemon into Walt Whitman in the summer of 1854. Dickinson's advent is more mysteriously indeterminate. In 1850 she read Emerson's *Poems* (published in 1847), but only after eight years are her own poems an authentic response. I hear her individuation first in *I Never Lost as Much but Twice:*

39

I never lost as much but twice—
And that was in the sod.
Twice have I stood a beggar
Before the door of God!

Angels—twice descending
Reimbursed my store—
Burglar! Banker—Father!
I am poor once more!

At twenty-seven, she refreshingly addresses her God as "Burglar! Banker—Father!," a verbal audacity beyond Emerson's, but then Dickinson had (and has) the helpful singularity of being the greatest of all women poets in Western tradition.

In the *Phaedrus,* Plato ironically informs us that "the man who is his own master knocks in vain at the doors of poetry." Emerson more positively added this as epigraph to his ecstatic chant *Bacchus,* which is the Latin name for the god Dionysus. The poem was composed in 1846 and read by Dickinson in 1847 or thereabouts. In his journal of 1843, Emerson set down:

I take many stimulants and often make an art of my inebriation. I read Proclus for my opium; it excites my imagination to let sail before me the pleasing and grand figures of gods, daemons and demoniacal men.

Neo-Platonic intoxication whirls Emerson, in *Bacchus,* below, into a state that inspired Dickinson to a sly mischief:

We buy ashes for bread;
We buy diluted wine;
Give me of the true,—
Whose ample leaves and tendrils curled
Among the silver hills of heaven,
Draw everlasting dew;
Wine of wine,

Blood of the world,
Form of forms, and mould of statures,
That I intoxicated,
And by the draught assimilated,
May float at pleasure through all natures.

207

I taste a liquor never brewed—
From Tankards scooped in Pearl—
Not all the Frankfort Berries
Yield such an Alcohol!

Inebriate of air—am I—
And Debauchee of Dew—
Reeling—thro' endless summer days—
From inns of molten Blue—

When "Landlords" turn the drunken Bee
Out of the Foxglove's door—
When Butterflies—renounce their "drams"—
I shall but drink the more!

Till Seraphs swing their snowy Hats—
And Saints—to windows run—
To see the little Tippler
Leaning against the—Sun!

We read Emerson on "The Poet" and hear passages of Whitman, Stevens, and Hart Crane, rather than of Dickinson. Yet when I read Emerson's "Circles," I cannot stop thinking about the poet of circumferences:

There is no outside, no enclosing wall, no circumference to us. The man finishes his story,—how good! how final! how it puts a new face on all things! He fills the sky. Lo! on the other side rises also a man, and draws a circle around the circle we had just pronounced the outline of the sphere. Then already is our first speaker not man, but only a first speaker. His only redress is forthwith to draw a circle outside of his antagonist. And so men do by themselves. The result of to-day, which haunts the mind and cannot be escaped, will presently be abridged into a word, and the principle that seemed to explain nature, will itself be included as one example of a bolder generalization. In the thought of to-morrow there is a power to upheave all thy creed, all the creeds, all the literatures, of the nations, and marshal thee to a Heaven which no epic dream has yet depicted. Every man is not so much a workman in the world, as he is a suggestion of that he should be. Men walk as prophecies of the next age.

I have quoted the continuation of this excerpt on pp. 176–77; yet "Circumference" has so many meanings in and for Dickinson that they defy cataloging and can seem to signify everything and nothing. Once I regarded Circumference not only as her daemon or genius, but as a metaphor for her own poetry, though she used it to refer to her own genius, not to her poems.

"There is . . . no circumference to us," Emerson proclaimed; "My Business is Circumference," Dickinson declared, while dismissing the Bible as dealing with the center and not with the circumference. Her reference may be to the tradition that God is a circle whose center is everywhere and circumference nowhere, ascribed by Emerson to Saint Augustine but actually starting in the Hermetic Corpus, from which it passed to Nicholas of Cusa and then to the Cambridge Platonists—Cudworth, More, Norris—whom Emerson read so avidly.

Subverting this tradition, as she did most others, Dickinson ascribed vitality to circumference and stasis to the center. She went out upon circumference, trusting to her daemonic autonomy. This self-trust was imaginatively prodigal for her poetry and deep suffering, in her days and ours. Ethos (character) is the daemon (destiny or fate) for the pre-Socratics and for Emerson, Nietzsche, and Frost but not for Plato and Dickinson, for whom Eros was the mightiest of the daemons. "Sumptuous destitution," in her marvelous phrase, ensued.

Her art of crisis mounts the stairway of surprise in progressive daemonization:

485

The Whole of it came not at once—
'Twas Murder by degrees—
A Thrust—and then for Life a chance—
The Bliss to cauterize—

The Cat reprieves the mouse
She eases from her teeth
Just long enough for Hope to teaze—
Then mashes it to death—

'Tis Life's award—to die—
Contenteder if once—
Than dying half—then rallying
For consciouser Eclipse—

My students and I find this disturbing and unforgettable. Camille Paglia always read Dickinson as nurturing sadomasochistic impulses. I remember disputing with Camille concerning that chapter in a dissertation that developed into her strong book *Sexual Personae*. The dispute centered partly on how to interpret poem 833:

833

Pain—expands the Time—
Ages coil within
The minute Circumference
Of a single Brain—

Pain contracts—the Time—
Occupied with Shot
Gammuts of Eternities
Are as they were not—

Dickinson's reality itself was elliptical: Geometrically, an ellipse has two centers, left and right, joined together in an oval shape. In Dickinson, they shift gradually back and forth as points of departure for her thinking in poetry. "Pain—expands the Time—" handles us as though we were moving about on a cosmic egg. The strangeness of pain is that it can either expand or contract the time in which we suffer.

Dickinson is at home—unlike most lyric poets—in shifting two or even more centers of consciousness, in a wild revel or Bacchic whirl. In this she is Emersonian and is unlike Arthur Schopenhauer and his disciple Ludwig Wittgenstein, who forged a memorable apothegm:

> Love is not a feeling. Love, unlike pain, is put to the test. One does not say: "That was not a true pain because it passed away so quickly."

Dickinson's perspectivism, like Nietzsche's, puts pain to the test of fostering memorability: Her losses never pass away. She exemplifies what could be called Nietzsche's poetics of pain, and I find no erotic element in this aspect of either great consciousness. She had never heard of Nietzsche; their similarities stem from Emerson's enormous influence, which they share.

There is no formula that can encompass Dickinson: After Shakespeare's, hers is one of the most capacious poet's consciousnesses in the language. It becomes arbitrary to choose among her several hundred fully achieved lyrics in order to illustrate her "saliences," as my late friend A. R. Ammons would have phrased it. For her the burden of existence is the loss to death of those we love. That of course is universal.

I complete this chapter at dawn on an August morning just after being informed of the death of a very close friend of sixty years. Opening Dickinson at random, I found this:

951
Unable are the Loved to die
For Love is Immortality,
Nay, it is Deity—

Unable they that love—to die
For Love reforms Vitality
Into Divinity.

NATHANIEL HAWTHORNE
and HENRY JAMES

NATHANIEL HAWTHORNE

Tales and Sketches

R EREADING THE TALES AND SKETCHES OF HAWTHORNE CAN GIVE the impression of a bewildering plenitude. Some never leave my memory: "The Wives of the Dead," "Wakefield," and "Feathertop" are three of the finest stories in the language. Others waver when I recollect them yet are wonderfully fresh to re-experience: "The Artist of the Beautiful," "Ethan Brand," "My Kinsman, Major Molineux," "Dr. Heidegger's Experiment." Perusing this "experiment" at eighty-four disconcerts: A parable of the Fountain of Youth, "Dr. Heidegger's Experiment" is charmingly grim. Three aged rascals and their onetime doxy participate in the experiment and momentarily cavort at having recovered youth, then rapidly lose it again. Something severely cruel in Hawthorne is exposed:

> They all gathered round her. One caught both her hands in his passionate grasp—another threw his arm about her waist—the third buried his hand among the glossy curls that clustered beneath the widow's cap. Blushing, panting, struggling, chiding, laughing, her warm breath fanning each of their faces by turns, she strove to dis-

engage herself, yet still remained in their triple embrace. Never was there a livelier picture of youthful rivalship, with bewitching beauty for the prize. Yet, by a strange deception, owing to the duskiness of the chamber, and the antique dresses which they still wore, the tall mirror is said to have reflected the figures of the three old, gray, withered grand-sires, ridiculously contending for the skinny ugliness of a shriveled grand-dam.

The dance of lust yields to one of death. "Ethan Brand" is darker yet, being a parable of the quester who wanders eighteen years in search of the Unpardonable Sin that simply is the pride of his own heart. All of Hawthorne's sketches move toward negative epiphanies, whether it be the tar-and-feathering of Major Molineux or the complex self-deception of Owen Warland in "The Artist of the Beautiful":

> With a wavering movement, and emitting a tremulous radiance, the butterfly struggled, as it were, towards the infant, and was about to alight upon his finger. But, while it still hovered in the air, the little Child of Strength, with his grand-sire's sharp and shrewd expression in his face, made a snatch at the marvellous insect, and compressed it in his hand. Annie screamed! Old Peter Hovendon burst into a cold and scornful laugh. The blacksmith, by main force, unclosed the infant's hand, and found within the palm a small heap of glittering fragments, whence the Mystery of Beauty had fled for ever. And as for Owen Warland, he looked placidly at what seemed the ruin of his life's labor, and which was yet no ruin. He had caught a far other butterfly than this. When the artist rose high enough to achieve the Beautiful, the symbol by which he made it perceptible to mortal senses became of little value in his eyes, while his spirit possessed itself in the enjoyment of the Reality.

At their strongest, Hawthorne's stories open up that other realm. Kafka accomplishes the same a century later. Hawthorne's "Wakefield," which Borges called his favorite tale, sustains being read side by side with Melville's "Bartleby, the Scrivener." A mere cipher of a man, at best, Wakefield absents himself twenty years from wife and home, dwelling a

London block away. Why? There is no cause, motive, meaning in this blank act, Wakefield himself being a perfect blank or "crafty nincompoop." His "long whim-wham" ends when he hovers near his house (a frequent event) and is soaked by a sudden London shower.

What is "Wakefield"? It is not a story: Nothing happens. Hardly even an anecdote, it cannot be termed a parable. But I read it perpetually, ransack it to find what is not there. Hawthorne's daemon, his genius, knows how it is done. I scramble to ambush it, since the tale yields nothing to analysis, as the second paragraph concedes:

> But the incident, though of the purest originality, unexampled, and probably never to be repeated, is one, I think, which appeals to the general sympathies of mankind. We know, each for himself, that none of us would perpetrate such a folly, yet feel as if some other might. To my own contemplations, at least, it has often recurred, always exciting wonder, but with a sense that the story must be true, and a conception of its hero's character. Whenever any subject so forcibly affects the mind, time is well spent in thinking of it. If the reader choose, let him do his own meditation; or if he prefer to ramble with me through the twenty years of Wakefield's vagary, I bid him welcome; trusting that there will be a pervading spirit and a moral, even should we fail to find them, done up neatly, and condensed into the final sentence. Thought has always its efficacy, and every striking incident its moral.

"Vagary" indeed, "moral" none. The final paragraph subtly misleads us:

> This happy event—supposing it to be such—could only have occurred at an unpremeditated moment. We will not follow our friend across the threshold. He has left us much food for thought, a portion of which shall lend its wisdom to a moral; and be shaped into a figure. Amid the seeming confusion of our mysterious world, individuals are so nicely adjusted to a system, and systems to one another, and to a whole, that, by stepping aside for a moment, a man exposes himself to a fearful risk of losing his place forever. Like Wakefield, he may become, as it were, the Outcast of the Universe.

Wakefield is no Wandering Jew or Ancient Mariner. It reverberates hollowly to call this nonexistent person "the Outcast of the Universe." Why does Hawthorne's odd sketch achieve so troubling a permanence? I sit here at 5:00 on a cold, wet, ordinary December evening in New Haven, on the first floor of the house I have shared with my wife for more than half a century. A red notebook is on the writing table in front of me. Never having learned to type, let alone master a computer, because of a tremor I possessed even when a baby, I write these pages with a ballpoint pen, as I have throughout my life, sustained by continuity yet chagrined by augmented tremors.

"Wakefield" frightens me because wife and home constitute my reality in old age. Several students came to see me here today, and a close friend who is a trainer came by to supervise my exercise. Otherwise, I have been alone when my wife went forth on errands or to meet a friend. Hawthorne had perhaps the happiest marriage of any major American writer, if not indeed of the great writers of all ages and nations. He met Sophia Peabody in 1837, when he was thirty-three, and married her five years later. Until he died—sadly, at fifty-nine—they had twenty-seven years of unbroken harmony together. "Wakefield" and its nincompoop protagonist are absolutely antithetical to Hawthorne's superb married existence. Is that a pathway to meaning here?

"Wakefield" is an allegorical fiction only in Angus Fletcher's sense of a compulsive syndrome. Wretched Wakefield, then, would be a kind of daemon for whom there is no freedom of choice. Obsessed by the idea of living a block away, Wakefield is out of control, a possessed nonentity. Weirdly, he has no goal except staying not too far from home. He is the polar opposite of the artist-thinkers in Hawthorne's stories "The Artist of the Beautiful," "The Prophetic Pictures," "Drowne's Wooden Image," "Chippings with a Chisel." They, however brokenly, are purposeful without purpose, but Wakefield does not exist in the realm of purpose.

Why is this tale so powerful? Its reverberation is out of proportion with its slight, offhand tonality. None of us would wish to lunch with the Wakefields; we do not even care to speculate how Mrs. Wakefield received him after his two-decade jape. I think we are troubled because so few among us can be so perfectly married as Hawthorne and his Sophia. Haunted each by her or his own daemon, how can we know that a compulsion will not suddenly detach us from home and companion?

There is another deep opening beneath that one. Women and men in their eighties are not given to unexpected passions or violent elopements. Only a master of the grotesque—Carson McCullers or Flannery O'Connor—would seek such images. Dying and death have more to do with the effect of "Wakefield" upon all of us and on aged readers in particular. Mrs. Wakefield lives as a widow after her husband's daemonic withdrawal, and her presumed two-decade bereavement seems unlikely to be redressed by his rain-drenched reentry. Each time I reread and teach "Wakefield," I limp through our large New England shingle house (late nineteenth century) and try to envision it occupied only by my wife. I stare at the innumerable bookcases and murmur the Stevensian tag from *The Auroras of Autumn:* "The house will crumble and the books will burn."

For reasons I cannot comprehend, "Rappaccini's Daughter," a tale that gives me nightmares, haunts my days also. I take no pleasure from rereading it, yet even Hawthorne is rarely this powerful. It is as though his unmediated daemon composed this allegory of the heart in Shakespeare's sense of "heart": total consciousness of Hamlet's sort.

Image generates action in Hawthorne: The power of an icon determines event and character. He sees and then points, and we follow as though we are fixed, divided, and determined by a cosmic vision not our own. Each time I turn to this erotic tale, I am enthralled by Beatrice and appalled by her father, her lover, and the envious Baglioni, whose remedy actually murders her. What was Hawthorne trying to do for himself, as man and romancer, by writing "Rappaccini's Daughter"? Once, when Kenneth Burke and I gave a joint lecture, we discussed this, with Kenneth observing that he emphasized the personal side of the question while I wanted to talk about the tale and not its teller. Kenneth is gone, to my lasting sorrow, but if we could make a joint appearance again, I now would agree with the primacy of the person over the artist.

Of the twelve writers discussed in this book only Hawthorne and Emerson sustained lifelong happy marriages. (Though, as I have noted, Emerson's beloved first wife, Ellen, died of tuberculosis before she was nineteen. His formidable second wife, Lidian, and the sage enjoyed a lifetime of harmony together but it was not the perfect vision that Hawthorne achieved with Sophia Peabody.)

Hawthorne's major heroines—Hester Prynne in *The Scarlet Letter,* Zenobia in *The Blithedale Romance,* Miriam in *The Marble Faun*—

manifest a sexual splendor far more persuasive than the Dark Ladies of Henry James—Madame Merle in *The Portrait of a Lady,* Charlotte Stant in *The Golden Bowl,* Kate Croy in *The Wings of the Dove.* One would have to turn to D. H. Lawrence's major phase—*The Rainbow* in particular—to find a near equivalent, yet the honors still would go to Hawthorne. That is one of his aesthetic glories and yet remains a puzzle to me.

With the exceptions of Nina Baym and a few more recent scholars, most criticism of Hawthorne seems to me wrong. He is an American High Romantic, akin to Emerson, Melville, and Whitman, and not at all a neo-orthodox ancestor of T. S. Eliot. He celebrates the sexual vitality of women as a potentially saving force, tragically curtailed by male inadequacy and societal restraint. "Rappaccini's Daughter" is a frightening parable of a paternal will converting that vitality into poison. Dr. Rappaccini's madness is a daemonization of the male dread of female sexual power and expresses Hawthorne's subtle despair at the prolongation of patriarchal society. Of all Hawthorne, this story is closest to William Blake, whom the author of *The Scarlet Letter* could not have read.

"Feathertop," his final tale, is my favorite. Hawthorne's concern with witchcraft attained a first perfect expression in "Young Goodman Brown" and ended with what he called "a moralized legend." In this deceptively light story, a formidable New England witch, Mother Rigby, plays at being the Creator and transforms an old broomstick into what she initially intends to be a scarecrow. She is in a benign mood, having slept well and been soothed by her incessantly lit pipe, which is kept going with mysterious coals by Dickon, her familiar spirit.

Charmed by her own creation, Mother Rigby decides that her New Adam, whom she names Feathertop, is too splendid to be a scarecrow. A proud mother, she inspirits her creature by placing her pipe in his mouth:

> "Puff away, my pet! Puff away, pretty one!" Mother Rigby kept repeating, with her pleasantest smile. "It is the breath of life to ye; and that you may take my word for!"
>
> Beyond all question, the pipe was bewitched. There must have been a spell, either in the tobacco, or in the fiercely glowing coal that

so mysteriously burned on top of it, or in the pungently aromatic smoke, which exhaled from the kindled weed. The figure, after a few doubtful attempts, at length blew forth a volley of smoke, extending all the way from the obscure corner into the bar of sunshine. There it eddied and melted away among the motes of dust. It seemed a convulsive effort; for the two or three next whiffs were fainter, although the coal still glowed, and threw a gleam over the scarecrow's visage. The old witch clapt her skinny palms together, and smiled encouragingly upon her handiwork. She saw that the charm worked well. The shrivelled, yellow face, which heretofore had been no face at all, had already a thin, fantastic haze, as it were, of human likeness, shifting to-and-fro across it; sometimes vanishing entirely, but growing more perceptible than ever, with the next whiff from the pipe. The whole figure, in like manner, assumed a show of life, such as we impart to ill-defined shapes among the clouds, and half-deceive ourselves with the pastime of our own fancy.

She smiles her work to see, and the reader joins her. Feathertop proves amiable, an endearing creature who is sent forth to woo the comely Polly Gookin, daughter of the wealthy Master Gookin, secret adherent of Mother Rigby:

By and by, Feathertop paused, and throwing himself into an imposing attitude, seemed to summon the fair girl to survey his figure, and resist him longer, if she could. His star, his embroidery, his buckles, glowed, at that instant, with unutterable splendor; the picturesque hues of his attire took a richer depth of coloring; there was a gleam and polish over his whole presence, betokening the perfect witchery of well-ordered manners. The maiden raised her eyes, and suffered them to linger upon her companion with a bashful and admiring gaze. Then, as if desirous of judging what value her own simple comeliness might have, side by side with so much brilliancy, she cast a glance towards the full-length looking-glass, in front of which they happened to be standing. It was one of the truest plates in the world, and incapable of flattery. No sooner did the images, therein reflected, meet Polly's eye, than she shrieked, shrank from the stranger's side, gazed at him, for a moment, in the wildest dismay, and sank insensible upon the floor. Feathertop, likewise, had looked towards the mirror, and there beheld, not the glittering mockery of his outside show, but a picture of the sordid patchwork of his real composition, stript of all witchcraft.

After this debacle, wretched Feathertop returns to his mother and to suicide:

"What has gone wrong?" demanded the witch. "Did yonder snuffling hypocrite thrust my darling from his door? The villain! I'll set twenty fiends to torment him, till he offer thee his daughter on his bended knees!"

"No, mother," said Feathertop despondingly, "it was not that!"

"Did the girl scorn my precious one?" asked Mother Rigby, her fierce eyes glowing like two coals of Tophet. "I'll cover her face with pimples! Her nose shall be as red as the coal in thy pipe! Her front teeth shall drop out! In a week hence, she shall not be worth thy having!"

"Let her alone, mother!" answered poor Feathertop. "The girl was half-won; and methinks a kiss from her sweet lips might have made me altogether human! But," he added, after a brief pause, and then a howl of self-contempt, "I've seen myself, mother!—I've seen myself for the wretched, ragged, empty thing I am! I'll exist no longer!"

Snatching the pipe from his mouth, he flung it with all his might against the chimney, and, at the same instant, sank upon the floor, a medley of straw and tattered garments, with some sticks protruding from the heap; and a shriveled pumpkin in the midst. The eyeholes were now lustreless; but the rudely-carved gap, that just before had been a mouth, still seemed to twist itself into a despairing grin, and was so far human.

What remains is for Mother Rigby to moralize the legend:

While thus muttering, the witch had filled a fresh pipe of tobacco, and held the stem between her fingers, as doubtful whether to thrust it into her own mouth or Feathertop's.

"Poor Feathertop!" she continued. "I could easily give him another chance, and send him forth again to-morrow. But, no! his feelings are too tender; his sensibilities too deep. He seems to have too
much heart to bustle for his own advantage, in such an empty and
heartless world. Well, well! I'll make a scarecrow of him, after all.
'Tis an innocent and a useful vocation, and will suit my darling
well; and if each of his human brethren had as fit a one, 'twould be
the better for mankind; and as for this pipe of tobacco, I need it
more than he!"

So saying, Mother Rigby put the stem between her lips. "Dickon!"
cried she, in her high, sharp tone, "another coal for my pipe!"

A strangely joyous tale to conclude a great storyteller's lifelong romance with the marvelous! Poor Feathertop from one perspective is Emerson's American Adam, without foundations, with no past at his back. He
parodies also Hawthorne's own male protagonists: Dimmesdale, Holgrave, Coverdale, Kenyon. His catastrophe, like their avoidances of what
could have broken them, testifies to a fused sojourn in weakness and residual decency.

The tale's honors go, however, to Mother Rigby, with her vitalizing "I
need it more than he!" Rigby is right: We need her more than we need
Feathertop, who already is too deeply embedded in your nature, whoever
you are.

"Feathertop" is my threshold for crossing over to Hawthorne's four
major romances: *The Scarlet Letter* (1850), *The House of the Seven
Gables* (1851), *The Blithedale Romance* (1852), and *The Marble Faun*
(1860). Hawthorne's place in American literature approximates and is related to Emerson's: They are our central writers. A bad critical tradition
founded by T. S. Eliot and his followers has now largely passed. It held
that Hawthorne opposed Emerson and returned to Puritan strictures
founded upon original sin. No more a Christian than were Emerson,
Thoreau, Whitman, and Melville, Hawthorne actually matched even
Whitman and William Blake as an exalter of female sexuality. His most
memorable creations are the magnificent Hester Prynne of *The Scarlet
Letter,* Zenobia in *The Blithedale Romance,* and Miriam in *The Marble
Faun,* and their salient quality is their heroic erotic vitality.

Emerson, Hawthorne's walking companion, did not know what to make of him, and did not care for prose fiction anyway. After Hawthorne's death, Emerson sorrowed that true friendship never was established between them, because of the romancer's silence. Yet Hawthorne was listening and learning, and he read deeply in Emerson, who became a major influence upon him.

That influx was subtly diverted by Hawthorne from a doctrine of the soul to an apotheosis of the erotic drive. Though akin to Whitman's eroticizing of Emersonianism, Hawthorne's swerve was very different. Whitman was an Epicurean materialist, while Hawthorne remained a low transcendentalist in some aspects, including Emerson's American Religion of self-reliance. Hester Prynne exemplifies one version of that faithless faith, and Henry James's Isabel Archer will attain another. Both heroines secularize what might be called the American Will, which Hester manifests by remaining in New England rather than joining her daughter, Pearl, in Europe:

But there was a more real life for Hester Prynne, here, in New England, than in that unknown region where Pearl had found a home. Here had been her sin; here, her sorrow; and here was yet to be her penitence. She had returned, therefore, and resumed,—of her own free will, for not the sternest magistrate of that iron period would have imposed it,—resumed the symbol of which we have related so dark a tale. Never afterwards did it quit her bosom. But, in the lapse of the toilsome, thoughtful, and self-devoted years that made up Hester's life, the scarlet letter ceased to be a stigma which attracted the world's scorn and bitterness, and became a type of something to be sorrowed over, and looked upon with awe, yet with reverence too. And, as Hester Prynne had no selfish ends, nor lived in any measure for her own profit and enjoyment, people brought all their sorrows and perplexities, and besought her counsel, as one who had herself gone through a mighty trouble. Women, more especially,—in the continually recurring trials of wounded, wasted, wronged, misplaced, or erring and sinful passion,—or with the dreary burden of a heart unyielded, because unvalued and unsought,—came to Hester's cottage, demanding why they were so wretched, and what the remedy! Hester comforted and counselled them, as best she might. She assured them, too, of her firm belief, that, at some brighter period, when the world should have grown ripe for it, in Heaven's own time, a new truth would be revealed, in order to establish the whole relation between man and woman on a surer ground of mutual happiness. Earlier in life, Hester had vainly imagined that she herself might be the destined prophetess, but had long since recognized the impossibility that any mission of divine and mysterious truth should be confided to a woman stained with sin, bowed down with shame, or even burdened with a life-long sorrow. The angel and apostle of the coming revelation must be a woman, indeed, but lofty, pure, and beautiful; and wise, moreover, not through dusky grief, but the ethereal medium of joy; and showing how sacred love should make us happy, by the truest test of a life successful to such an end!

The reader murmurs: Where indeed in American fiction could there be a woman loftier, purer, as beautiful, and as wise as Hester Prynne? Isabel Archer is the only likely candidate, though she experienced the great unwisdom of having chosen the odious Osmond. Her return to him is founded upon the precedent of Hester's staying in New England, as if to do a kind of penance only for the great unwisdom of initially taking the Satanic Chillingworth. That Henry James was aware of this influence of Hawthorne is palpable but will be featured more fully in my discussion of *The Portrait of a Lady.*

Hawthorne's daemon was his own; it could be argued that he is the most possessed of all our strongest writers, at least until Faulkner and Hart Crane. And yet the effect of Emerson upon him was to enhance his self-daemonization, in a response at once sympathetic and antithetical.

The daemon wanes in the progression of Hawthorne's four major romances, until it becomes all but mute in the closing cadences of *The Marble Faun,* a noble failure yet a disappointment nevertheless. Hilda has been quite justly characterized as a "vapid" American girl, who reduces Kenyon from a promising sculptor to another mere copyist like herself. Poor Miriam and Donatello deserve a better book, but the ebbing Hawthorne could not create it for them. The rest of his career is silence, as each fresh romance venture proves abortive. Hawthorne's decline mystifies me, and I propose to understand it better by revisiting each of the four narratives in turn.

The Scarlet Letter

OF ALL THE PRINCIPAL FEMALE CHARACTERS IN OUR NATIONAL LITERATURE, Hester Prynne is clearly the central figure. Except for Hawthorne and James, American male novelists have not been able to represent American women with the force and vivacity that have marked the English tradition, from Samuel Richardson's Clarissa Harlowe through E. M. Forster's Schlegel sisters in *Howards End.* In our century, the women portrayed by Faulkner, Hemingway, and Fitzgerald are generally less vivid than the men, with a few significant exceptions. James's heroines, from Isabel Archer on, have a clear family resemblance to aspects of Hawthorne's Hester. If we have a national heroine of our version of the Protestant will in America, then it must be Hester Prynne; yet Hester, though Hawthorne's triumph, yields only grudgingly to our criticism. She is larger than her book, admirable as *The Scarlet Letter* certainly is, because she incarnates more paradoxes and even contradictions than does Dimmesdale, let alone Chillingworth or the visionary Pearl. Hopelessly old-fashioned critic that I am, I do not regard achieved literary characters as so many marks upon the page or as metaphors for racial, gender, and class differences. The extraordinary Hawthornean imagination, wandering between mimetic realism and High Romance, has given us an overwhelming personality and puzzling moral character in the sensual and tragic Hester, who is at once the ideal object of Hawthorne's desire and a troubled projection of Hawthorne's authorial subjectivity, cast out from him but never definitively. Strong writers of romance are both subject and object of their own quests, and there is a profound sense in which Hester is as much a representation of Hawthorne's deep inwardness as Clarissa is Richardson's vision of his inmost self.

As many critics tell us, Hester Prynne is primarily a sexual being, a truth about her that scarcely can be overemphasized. As a truth, it possesses terrible pathos, for her heroic sexuality has yielded her two impossible men: her Satanic husband, Chillingworth, and her inadequate lover, Dimmesdale, each of them admirably named. Hester has Pearl, a few poor memories of Dimmesdale, and mostly her own pride to sustain her. Her sexuality has been balked, yet it constitutes the core of her resistance to her Puritan persecutors. It constitutes also a considerable part of her strong appeal to Hawthorne and to his readers. What matters most about Hester is the vital intensity of her being, her frustrated promise of more life, which is the Hebraic sense of the Blessing. There are a number of valid ways of explaining Hester's charismatic quality, both in and out of the pages of *The Scarlet Letter,* but the most accurate, I am convinced, is to see her charisma as implicit sexual power.

Critics have found both Puritan and Emersonian strands in Hester, and her uneasy religion indeed is a highly contradictory blend of Calvinism and Emerson's American Religion of self-reliance. Her daughter, Pearl, is something wilder, but then Pearl belongs almost wholly to the representational order of High Romance. Hester's inconsistencies have exercised critics, but the wonder is that there are not more of them in someone so tormented by an insanely, even obscenely moralistic society, which is to make a judgment that Hawthorne the novelist might have repudiated. It would be fairer to say that the strains in Hester uncover some of the strains in Hawthorne, whose creative drive ensues from a temperament more dialectical even than that of his grudging and involuntary heir, Henry James. Hawthorne has something of the same relationship to Calvinism as his truest precursor, Edmund Spenser, who harmonized antithetical elements with a freedom not available to American romance. It is a kind of aesthetic miracle that *The Scarlet Letter* could have been written at all in a cultural situation as belated as Hawthorne's, one that enabled *The Marble Faun* and *The House of the Seven Gables* far more readily than it did Hawthorne's higher achievement in *The Scarlet Letter* and the best of the tales.

We sense the movement of sexual power into an antinomian context, but Hawthorne partly evades such a movement in Hester. He will not let her prophesy and will not quite prophesy for her. This makes the book spiritually irritating to some readers, particularly at the present time, but undoubtedly helps create its aesthetic strength, since the reader becomes convinced that there is more to Hester than the storyteller is willing to unfold. We want her to say more, to do more, and yet we understand the appropriateness of the way the book both arouses such desires and refuses to gratify them. Hester does not run away from her story, but she runs off with it. We are left not caring much about Dimmesdale, Chillingworth, and Pearl, because they are not adequate to Hester's greatness—nor are we. Critics who chide Hester for her self-deceptions and her moral inconsistencies always sound as silly to me as the endless heaps of scholars who denounce Shakespeare's Falstaff. Hester does not contain us as Falstaff and Rosalind, Hamlet and Cleopatra contain us, but Hester always precedes us as the most representative fictive portrait of an American woman. She cannot hold together her incompatible impulses, yet she survives an outrageously dreadful societal and erotic context that ought to have driven her either to madness or to suicide. It is absurd for any reader not to learn from her, while speculating again as to the sources of her extraordinary strength of being.

Hester sends us back to Hawthorne, despite his subtlest efforts to evade an identity with her—efforts that profoundly influenced James's similar evasions in regard to Isabel Archer. Isabel's recoil from Goodwood's aggressive sexuality has no parallel in Hester, who would have enveloped Goodwood had he been available to her and if he could have been endowed by his author with a few touches of what after all is massively present in poor Dimmesdale: spiritual awareness. There was an overt separation in Hawthorne's consciousness between sexual power and the quest of the Protestant will for its own autonomy and dignity, and that separation is painfully repeated in Hester's mind. But the great artist in Hawthorne knew more, and we receive a sense throughout the novel that Hester is working not toward an impossible integration but toward a stance prophetic of something evermore about to be, the possible sublimity of a changed relationship between men and women. Since that relationship would require a coherent social sanction, it could not achieve the full autonomy of the American Religion of self-reliance, but then even the theologian of our religion, Emerson himself, refrained from extending his vision into the sexual domain, except in certain poems.

Hester, as critics acknowledge, is herself an artist, and her embroidery has its own affinities to Hawthorne's mixed mode of novel and romance, as well as to the outward show of Puritan Boston in *The Scarlet Letter*. But I think she fails her art, which may be part of the cost of Hawthorne not failing his, and it may be that Hester's compromised condition at the book's close is the consequence of being sacrificed by the author as a substitute for himself. Even as Hester devotes herself to the sufferings of other women, she has yielded to Puritan society's initial judgment upon her. In doing so, she certainly has abandoned much of value in her own passional stance, and we can be tempted into an admiring anger against Hawthorne for having diminished her. And yet the "Conclusion" is not the book—

though how else Hawthorne could have concluded, one scarcely knows. Hester does not break, and we can believe Hawthorne's affirmation that her own free will prevails, but it becomes a very negative will indeed. The alternative presumably would have been for Hawthorne to convert the book from romance to tragedy, but that he would not do. Hester was not to be a female version of Melville's Ahab, dying in Promethean and Gnostic defiance of a tyrannical universe, darting a final harpoon into the sanctified flesh of a merely demiurgical creation. Instead, Hester submits, but only in part, and with sublime trust in the coming revelation of a woman yet to be.

What if Hawthorne had made of Hester not an embroiderer but a romancer, a writer of narrative, whose "rich, voluptuous, Oriental" nature had ensued in twice-told tales? Since Hawthorne grants Hester extraordinary vitality but inadequate articulation, it might seem as though my question is inappropriate to what is, after all, Hawthorne's Hester. Still, Hester is always telling herself, and Pearl, fictions about her situation, and her refusal in the "Conclusion" to forsake her role is a stubborn extension of her will to power over her own story. Chillingworth and Pearl are well content to be figures of romance, and Dimmesdale finally falls back into the marvelous also, though in the saddest way. Hester forces Hawthorne out of romance and into the psychological novel, which is a mark of her relative freedom and of her author's curious bondage, his inability to make his strongest character conform to his moral expectations. Hester deceives others and for a time herself, but she does not allow Hawthorne to deceive himself. He might have preferred to see her as a dark woman of romance, but in her he did not create either another masochist, as he did with Dimmesdale, or another sadist, as with Chillingworth. We ought never to forget that Dimmesdale fails Hester yet once more, at the novel's conclusion, when, at his insistence, she goes up to the scaffold to join him but goes very reluctantly and against her true will. Inadequate as Dimmesdale is to her, she still wants him, and until he dies, her impulses remain totally healthy. She does not deny her vitalism; Hawthorne defrauds her, for the sake of his art.

No one who lived in Hawthorne's Puritan Boston could hope to defeat it, and Hawthorne thought better than to allow Hester to try so impossible a project. Yet he lavishes upon Hester all his innermost resources of vital apprehension, while denying her the preternatural strength that would have turned his novel into the Promethean mode he rejected. I begin to doubt that any American novelist, female or male, is going to create a character who transcends Hester Prynne as a representation of the irreconcilable demands placed upon an American woman, even in an age supposedly no longer Puritan. Feminism, in its latest phase, struggles with the lasting residuum of Puritan values while remaining deeply contaminated by them. It may even be that current literary feminism is destined to become our new or newest Puritanism, imposing uniform ideals upon intellectual women, by again refusing any alliance between their sexuality and their potential antinomianism. Hester will then abide as the image condensed into the most powerful single sentence of Hawthorne's book: "The scarlet letter had not done its office." No societal emblem will perform a definitive judgment upon Hester, nor will she be contained by any program, however belatedly it would do justice to her. Richardson's Clarissa achieved her formidable strength, too strong even for the demonic Lovelace, by her unmediated relationship to the Protestant God, who purified her will until only dying to this life was possible for her. Hawthorne celebrates his version of the Protestant will in Hester, but he has no way open to the Puritan God and would not wish one, even if it were available to him or to Hester. Dimmesdale finds the way back to God but hardly out of strength, as Clarissa did. Hester is very strong, certainly too strong for Dimmesdale, and finally too strong even for Hawthorne. It is a very dialectical moment when Hawthorne condenses into a single sentence both Hester's stance toward life and her grand effect upon his own art: "It was only the darkened house that could contain her."

The House of the Seven Gables

PUBLISHED A YEAR AFTER *THE SCARLET LETTER*, *THE HOUSE OF THE SEVEN Gables* (1851) now seems to me the best of Hawthorne's novels after his unchallenged masterwork. I once would have given that rank to *The Marble Faun* (1860), but rereading both, side by side, persuades me that *House* is much the better book, because it is shapely, stays within its limits, and engrosses me throughout. I strongly want *The Marble Faun* to cohere, but, alas, it does not. Hilda has archetypal force as the American girl, idealistic and socialized, a good copyist but no painter. She resembles Mark

Twain's wife, Livy, designated and evaluated by him as societal censor, rather more than the mature heroines of Henry James, who are daughters of Hester Prynne. Hilda, perhaps dreading her own sexuality, quests invariably for an ideal portrait of the Virgin to copy.

Why Hawthorne, rather ambivalently, exalted Hilda and Kenyon, the failed sculptor who seeks her, while rejecting the darkly vital Miriam and Donatello, has not been clear enough to critics, and the fault has to be the author's. Nina Baym, one of Hawthorne's best readers, rightly observes that his gloomiest work is *The Marble Faun*. In contrast, *The House of the Seven Gables* strives for humor, though its deeper strata constitute considerable darkness and desperation. If you want comedy, you don't turn to Nathaniel Hawthorne, except perhaps for his charming final tale, "Feathertop."

Unlike the fourfold of Hester, Pearl, Chillingworth, and Dimmesdale, no single personage in *House* is sketched by Hawthorne with intense vividness, presumably by design. The most energetic is Holgrave, the last of the Maules, whose ancestral founder was executed by Salem as a wizard at the instigation of the first Judge Pyncheon, in a landgrab.

Holgrave is an artist, carpenter, gardener, a kind of version of Thoreau, whom Hawthorne knew well. He is also, like Hawthorne, a storyteller, who reads aloud to Phoebe Pyncheon (whom he later marries) his tale of "Alice Pyncheon" (Chapter XIII). The Matthew Maule of the story, Holgrave's surrogate, is the grandson of the martyred and defrauded wizard, whose dying curse haunts all Pyncheons: "God will give him blood to drink!"

The beautiful, fictive Alice Pyncheon is erotically mesmerized by the charismatic Maule, who treats her with a peculiar sadism, reminding us that Hawthorne created the tormenter Chillingworth:

But alas, for the beautiful, the gentle, yet too haughty Alice! A power, that she little dreamed of, had laid its grasp upon her maiden soul. A will, most unlike her own, constrained her to do its grotesque and fantastic bidding. Her father, as it proved, had martyred his poor child to an inordinate desire for measuring his land by miles, instead of acres. And, therefore, while Alice Pyncheon lived, she was Maule's slave, in a bonding more humiliating, a thousand-fold, than that which binds its chain around the body. Seated by his humble fireside, Maule had but to wave his hand; and, wherever the proud lady chanced to be—whether in her chamber, or entertaining her father's stately guests, or worshipping at church—whatever her place or occupation, her spirit passed from beneath her own control, and bowed itself to Maule. "Alice, laugh!"—the carpenter, beside his hearth, would say; or perhaps intensely will it, without a spoken word. And, even were it prayer-time, or at a funeral, Alice must break into wild laughter. "Alice, be sad!"—and, at the instant, down would come her tears, quenching all the mirth of those around her, like sudden rain upon a bonfire. "Alice, dance!"—and dance she would, not in such court-like measures as she had learned abroad, but some high-paced jig, or hop-skip rigadoon, befitting the brisk lasses at a rustic merry-making. It seemed to be Maule's impulse, not to ruin Alice, nor to visit her with any black or gigantic mischief, which would have crowned her sorrow with the grace of tragedy, but to wreak a low, ungenerous scorn upon her. Thus all the dignity of life was lost. She felt herself too much abased, and longed to change natures with some worm!

Phoebe, who emulates the fictive Alice in erotic response to Holgrave, is saved from similar degradation by his actual decency in sexual matters. And yet Holgrave's love for her is a return to his Maule heritage and a movement away from social radicalism. Holgrave Maule all but becomes the last Pyncheon while entering into a happy marriage founded upon the model union of Sophia Peabody and Nathaniel Hawthorne.

Henry James, anxiously evading his precursor, dismissed Hawthorne's romances as adhering "to the fairy-tale period of taste." Certainly *House* ends in that mode and so falls away from the darker eroticism of *The Scarlet Letter*, where sexual love is quite as dialectical as it is in *The Bostonians* or *The Golden Bowl*.

The House of the Seven Gables survives partly by and through the charm of its fable and characters and partly by its energizing and quite gentle comedy. Hawthorne's daemon composes only the tale of "Alice Pyncheon" and then subsides elsewhere in the romance.

House falls short of Hawthorne's sublimity in *The Scarlet Letter* and the best of the tales, such as "Wakefield" and "Feathertop." We need not judge it in that way: Its values are elsewhere, particularly in the presence of Phoebe:

As to Phoebe's not being a lady, or whether she were a lady or no, it was a point perhaps difficult to decide, but which could hardly have come up for judgement at all in any fair and healthy mind. Out of New England, it would be impossible to meet with a person, combining so many ladylike attributes with so many others, that form no necessary, if compatible, part of the character. She shocked no canon of taste; she was admirably in keeping with herself, and never jarred against surrounding circumstances. Her figure, to be sure—so small as to be almost childlike, and so elastic that motion seemed as easy, or easier to it than rest—would hardly have suited one's idea of a countess. Neither did her face—with the brown ringlets on either side, and the slightly piquant nose, and the wholesome bloom, and the clear shade of tan, and the half-a-dozen freckles, friendly remembrancers of the April sun and breeze—precisely give us a right to call her beautiful. But there was both lustre and depth, in her eyes. She was very pretty; as graceful as a bird, and graceful much in the same way; as pleasant, about the house, as a gleam of sunshine falling on the floor through a shadow of twinkling leaves, or as a ray of firelight that dances on the wall, while evening is drawing nigh. Instead of discussing her claim to rank among ladies, it would be preferable to regard Phoebe as the example of feminine grace and availability combined, in a state of society, if there were any such, where ladies did not exist. There, it should be woman's office to move in the midst of practical affairs, and to gild them all—the very homeliest, were it even the scouring of pots and kettles—with an atmosphere of loveliness and joy.

The daemonic splendor of Hester Prynne has been replaced by this humane atmosphere. It takes considerable literary art to present wholesomeness of this order and persuade us of the aesthetic interest and spiritual value. Hawthorne relaxes from the stress of creating Hester and Pearl, Chillingworth and Dimmesdale, and subdues his daemon for most of the book. In the sphere of Phoebe, it works and gives us rather more than

Henry James would concede. In contrast, T. S. Eliot once pronounced that *The House of the Seven Gables* was the best of all American novels, a judgment difficult to sustain.

The Blithedale Romance

THE BLITHEDALE ROMANCE OPENS SPLENDIDLY AND GOES WELL FOR A while, but then becomes a downhill race of the daemon against forgetting how it was done.

Though Hawthorne writes with consummate artistry, his four protagonists do not sustain our initial interest. Zenobia, the most vivid, is a failed feminist, perhaps suggested to Hawthorne by Margaret Fuller, whom he ardently disliked. Hawthorne is persuasive in representing Zenobia's sexual aura:

> While this passed, and while she spoke to my companions, I was taking note of Zenobia's aspect; and it impressed itself on me so distinctly, that I can now summon her up like a ghost, a little wanner than the life, but otherwise identical with it. She was dressed as simply as possible, in an American print, (I think the dry-goods people call it so,) but with a silken kerchief, between which and her gown there was one glimpse of a white shoulder. It struck me as a great piece of good-fortune that there should be just that glimpse. Her hair—which was dark, glossy, and of singular abundance—was put up rather soberly and primly, without curls, or other ornament, except a single flower. It was an exotic, of rare beauty, and as fresh as if the hot-house gardener had just clipt it from the stem. That flower has struck deep root into my memory. I can both see it and smell it, at this moment. So brilliant, so rare, so costly as it must have been, and yet enduring only for a day, it was more indicative of the pride and pomp, which had a luxuriant growth in Zenobia's character, than if a great diamond had sparkled among her hair.
>
> Her hand, though very soft, was larger than most women would like to have—or than they could afford to have—though not a whit

too large in proportion with the spacious plan of Zenobia's entire development. It did one good to see a fine intellect (as hers really was, although its natural tendency lay in another direction than towards literature) so fitly cased. She was, indeed, an admirable figure of a woman, just on the hither verge of her richest maturity, with a combination of features which it is safe to call remarkably beautiful, even if some fastidious persons might pronounce them a little deficient in softness and delicacy. But we find enough of those attributes, everywhere. Preferable—by way of variety, at least—was Zenobia's bloom, health, and vigor, which she possessed in such overflow that a man might well have fallen in love with her for their sake only. In her quiet moods, she seemed rather indolent; but when really in earnest, particularly if there were a spice of bitter feeling, she grew all alive, to her fingertips.

The male reader may not fall in love with Zenobia as he should with Hester Prynne, yet like Hawthorne he will be aroused by her. Reflecting upon the twelve authors studied in this book, I find it palpable that Hawthorne was most at home with what might be called a normative heterosexuality. Fulfilled by a harmonious marriage to Sophia Peabody, he was free to appreciate the sexual vitality in which women tend to surpass men.

Zenobia, unfulfilled, drowns herself for love of the ungrateful Hollingsworth, an intemperate moralist and failed reformer. The narrator Coverdale is a failed poet and bachelor evader of life, who decides to abandon the muse as *The Blithedale Romance* comes to an end. Priscilla, the enigma among the four, almost saves the book. Virtually indescribable, she challenges interpretation, since she is both a naturalistic portrait of a rather needy young woman and a daemonic agent touching upon allegory. With Hollingsworth, self-punished for his guilt, she will drive Zenobia to suicide.

Unaware sisters, Priscilla and Zenobia are antithetical to each other. Fading away at the transcendentalist commune Blithedale, Priscilla acquires a dangerous vitality when the book moves to Boston (Chapters 17 to 20). Unlike Zenobia, a creature of the past and the future, Priscilla is both the victim of the present age (it is intimated she had been what some now call a "sex worker") and finally its legatee. Rebuffed by Zenobia, she turns to the odious Hollingsworth, who is only a relic after Zenobia drowns herself.

Priscilla's epiphany commences in Chapter 20:

> But, for my part, it was Priscilla's beauty, not Zenobia's, of which I was thinking, at that moment. She was a person who could be quite obliterated, so far as beauty went, by anything unsuitable in her attire; her charm was not positive and material enough to bear up against a mistaken choice of color, for instance, or fashion. It was safest, in her case, to attempt no art of dress; for it demanded the most perfect taste, or else the happiest accident in the world, to give her precisely the adornment which she needed. She was now dressed in pure white, set off with some kind of a gauzy fabric, which—as I bring up her figure in my memory, with a faint gleam on her shadowy hair, and her dark eyes bent shyly on mine, through all the vanished years—seems to be floating about her like a mist. I wondered what Zenobia meant by evolving so much loveliness out of this poor girl. It was what few women could afford to do; for, as I looked from one to the other, the sheen and splendor of Zenobia's presence took nothing from Priscilla's softer spell, if it might not rather be thought to add to it.

This equivocal purity transforms itself into passive charlatanry when she is exhibited to an audience by a showman as the Veiled Lady:

> "You see before you the Veiled Lady," said the bearded Professor, advancing to the verge of the platform. "By the agency of which I have just spoken, she is, at this moment, in communion with the spiritual world. That silvery veil is, in one sense, an enchantment, having been dipt, as it were, and essentially imbued, through the potency of my art, with the fluid medium of spirits. Slight and ethereal as it seems, the limitations of time and space have no existence within its folds. This hall—these hundreds of faces, encompassing her within so narrow an amphitheatre—are of thinner substance, in her view, than the airiest vapor that the clouds are made of. She beholds the Absolute!"

As preliminary to other, and far more wonderful psychological experiments, the exhibitor suggested that some of his auditors should endeavor to make the Veiled Lady sensible of their presence by such methods—provided, only, no touch were laid upon her person—as they might deem best adapted to that end. Accordingly, several deep-lunged country-fellows, who looked as if they might have blown the apparition away with a breath, ascended the platform. Mutually encouraging one another, they shouted so close to her ear, that the veil stirred like a wreath of vanishing mist; they smote upon the floor with bludgeons; they perpetrated so hideous a clamor, that methought it might have reached, at least a little way, into the eternal sphere. Finally, with the assent of the Professor, they laid hold of the great chair, and were startled, apparently, to find it soar upward, as if lighter than the air through which it rose. But the Veiled Lady remained seated and motionless, with a composure that was hardly less than awful, because implying so immeasurable a distance betwixt her and these rude persecutors.

"These efforts are wholly without avail," observed the Professor, who had been looking on with an aspect of serene indifference. "The roar of a battery of cannon would be inaudible to the Veiled Lady. And yet, were I to will it, sitting in this very hall, she could hear the desert-wind sweeping over the sands, as far off as Arabia; the ice-bergs grinding one against the other, in the polar seas; the rustle of a leaf in an East Indian forest; the lowest whispered breath of the bashfullest maiden in the world, uttering the first confession of her love! Nor does there exist the moral inducement, apart from my own behest, that could persuade her to lift the silvery veil, or arise out of that chair!"

Greatly to the Professor's discomposure, however, just as he spoke these words, the Veiled Lady arose. There was a mysterious tremor that shook the magic veil. The spectators, it may be, imagined that she was about to take flight into that invisible sphere, and to the society of those purely spiritual beings, with whom they reckoned her so near akin. Hollingsworth, a moment ago, had mounted the platform, and now stood gazing at the figure, with a sad intentness that brought the whole power of his great, stern, yet tender soul, into his glance.

"Come!" said he, waving his hand towards her. "You are safe!"

She threw off the veil, and stood before that multitude of people, pale, tremulous, shrinking, as if only then had she discovered that a thousand eyes were gazing at her. Poor maiden! How strangely had she been betrayed! Blazoned abroad as a wonder of the world, and performing what were adjudged as miracles—in the faith of many, a seeress and a prophetess—in the harsher judgment of others, a mountebank—she had kept, as I religiously believe, her virgin reserve and sanctity of soul, throughout it all. Within that encircling veil, though an evil hand had flung it over her, there was as deep a seclusion as if this forsaken girl had, all the while, been sitting under the shadow of Eliot's pulpit, in the Blithedale woods, at the feet of him who now summoned her to the shelter of his arms. And the true heart-throb of a woman's affection was too powerful for the jugglery that had hitherto environed her. She uttered a shriek and fled to Hollingsworth, like one escaping from her deadliest enemy, and was safe forever!

This is a long passage to bring forward, but it seems to me the visionary center of *The Blithedale Romance*. It possesses a mythic complexity worthy of William Blake (whom Hawthorne never read) and is strikingly similar to the conclusion of Blake's *The Book of Thel*. At the close of that fragile but lovely epyllion, the virgin Thel utters a shriek and flees back to the realm of Innocence, after a brief venture out into the harsh world of Generation or Experience. Priscilla, an American Thel, flees to the stifling moralism of Hollingsworth. Her fate, after his collapse, will be to serve as Hollingsworth's nursemaid and solace.

Coverdale, in Chapter 28, encounters the now-pathetic Hollingsworth and the protective Priscilla:

But, Hollingsworth! After all the evil that he did, are we to leave him thus, blest with the entire devotion of this one true heart, and with wealth at his disposal, to execute the long contemplated project that had led him so far astray? What retribution is there here? My mind being vexed with precisely this query, I made a journey, some years since, for the sole purpose of catching a last glimpse at

Hollingsworth, and judging for myself whether he were a happy man or no. I learned that he inhabited a small cottage, that his way of life was exceedingly retired, and that my only chance of encountering him or Priscilla was, to meet them in a secluded lane, where, in the latter part of the afternoon, they were accustomed to walk. I did meet them, accordingly. As they approached me, I observed in Hollingsworth's face a depressed and melancholy look, that seemed habitual; the powerfully built man showed a self-distrustful weakness, and a childlike, or childish, tendency to press close, and closer still, to the side of the slender woman whose arm was within his. In Priscilla's manner, there was a protective and watchful quality, as if she felt herself the guardian of her companion, but, likewise, a deep, submissive, unquestioning reverence, and also a veiled happiness in her fair and quiet countenance.

Drawing nearer, Priscilla recognized me, and gave me a kind and friendly smile, but with a slight gesture which I could not help interpreting as an entreaty not to make myself known to Hollingsworth. Nevertheless, an impulse took possession of me, and compelled me to address him.

"I have come, Hollingsworth," said I, "to view your grand edifice for the reformation of criminals. Is it finished yet?"

"No—nor begun!" answered he, without raising his eyes. "A very small one answers all my purposes."

Priscilla threw me an upbraiding glance. But I spoke again, with a bitter and revengeful emotion, as if flinging a poisoned arrow at Hollingsworth's heart.

"Up to this moment," I inquired, "how many criminals have you reformed?"

"Not one!" said Hollingsworth, with his eyes still fixed on the ground. "Ever since we parted, I have been busy with a single murderer!"

There is power in this pathos, but Priscilla is possessed in a mode that discomforts me; yet that is Hawthorne's deliberate artistry. Her clinging weakness provokes eros in Hollingsworth and perhaps even in Coverdale, as he finally confesses. It brings revulsion toward her in Zenobia, whom

Priscilla desires far more than she wishes attachment to any man. A somehow still-virginal former prostitute, she seems almost to be Fyodor Dostoyevsky's creation.

We never do get to know Priscilla. Hawthorne gives her almost nothing memorable to say. This is daemonic design: An inarticulate muse who lacks a will of her own, Priscilla with her animated power drives out Zenobia and flees within Hollingsworth. More vitally, she stimulates readers into a better grasp of Hawthorne's deep allegiance to his genre of romance. Take away awareness of romance conventions and you arrive at the strong misreadings of Hawthorne by Henry James, who owed his precursor rather too much and chided him for lack of realism.

Hawthorne's downward path to wisdom diminished his art. The greater tales and *The Scarlet Letter* are absolute achievements, while *The House of the Seven Gables* is a lesser one. Alas, *The Blithedale Romance* charms and fails. In a final attempt, Hawthorne went on to the flawed greatness of *The Marble Faun*, thus ending his art.

The Marble Faun

HAWTHORNE IS PALPABLY THE MOST NEW ENGLAND IN SPIRIT OF OUR great writers. Emerson, New England's prophet to the world, was not an artist of place and time. Born in Salem, Hawthorne lived there, and in Emerson's Concord, the Berkshires, and again in Concord. From 1853 through 1857 he was American consul in Liverpool and then lived in Italy from 1858 to 1859. He began *The Marble Faun* (1860) in Italy and completed it in England. After that he accomplished nothing, though he was only fifty-six when *The Marble Faun* was published. His final four years of life were marked by the inability to finish another romance. The daemon had abandoned him.

Unlike the genius of Henry James, Hawthorne's daemon could not flourish in England or on the Continent. For eight months in 1841, the master of American romance lived as a member of Brook Farm, the transcendentalist commune that is the model for Blithedale, but the romance is not much illuminated by that biographical fact. *The Marble Faun* is different: Its Roman setting is crucial and I think at last a lessening of what ought to be the book's splendor. Too much of the romance is a clumsy guidebook to the history, art, and architecture of a city profoundly alien to Hawthorne and to his American protagonists Hilda and Kenyon.

Henry James was thirty-six when he published his little book on Hawthorne in London. It has mixed critical value and does not accurately reflect his literary indebtedness to his prime American precursor, though it is not the disaster of his review of Walt Whitman's *Drum-Taps* (1865). Still, the Whitman review is so bad that its self-revelation is of considerable value. Even so, *Hawthorne* tells us more about James than it does concerning its ostensible subject. Here James sums up *The Marble Faun* (using its English title, *Transformation*):

Like all of Hawthorne's things, it contains a great many light threads of symbolism, which shimmer in the texture of the tale, but which are apt to break and remain in our fingers if we attempt to handle them. These things are part of Hawthorne's very manner— almost, as one might say, of his vocabulary; they belong much more to the surface of his work than to its stronger interest. The fault of *Transformation* is that the element of the unreal is pushed too far, and that the book is neither positively of one category nor of another. His "moonshiny romance," he calls it in a letter; and, in truth, the lunar element is a little too pervasive. The action wavers between the streets of Rome, whose literal features the author perpetually sketches, and a vague realm of fancy, in which quite a different verisimilitude prevails. This is the trouble with Donatello himself. His companions are intended to be real—if they fail to be so, it is not for want of intention; whereas he is intended to be real or not, as you please. He is of a different substance from them; it is as if a painter, in composing a picture, should try to give you an impression of one of his figures by a strain of music. The idea of the modern faun was a charming one; but I think it a pity that the author should not have made him more definitely modern, without reverting so much to his mythological properties and antecedents, which are very gracefully touched upon, but which belong to the region of picturesque conceits, much more than to that of real psychology. Among the young Italians of to-day there are still plenty of models for such an image as Hawthorne appears to have wished to present in the easy and natural Donatello. And since I am speaking critically, I may go on to say that the art of narration, in *Transfor-mation,* seems to me more at fault than in the author's other novels. The story straggles and wanders, is dropped and taken up again, and towards the close lapses into an almost fatal vagueness.

This is acute and yet a touch too Jamesian. Hawthorne indeed falters between romance and realism, yet that does not much distress good read-ers. Donatello, the Italian faun, like his lover—the dark and mysteriously Jewish Miriam—and also like his friend—the American sculptor Kenyon—falls victim to the Puritan moralism of Hilda, the *Alastor* or avenging daemon of the romance. Still, Hawthorne loves Hilda and can-not condemn her or even see clearly that her dogmatism makes her deadly, to all others who are her friends or lovers and at last to Hawthorne him-self as an artist. Hilda believes she worships art but sacrifices it upon the altar of societal respectability. She transforms herself into another mere copyist of the Old Masters, accepts Kenyon as a potential husband at the cost of his ceasing to be an authentic sculptor, and betrays Miriam and Donatello to the police. Hilda is the pure American girl as daemon of destruction. Though Hawthorne creates her, he seems not to recognize just what he has wrought.

Hilda enhances *The Marble Faun* and mars it; she is the muse of much in American tradition that deprives high art of its audience. What she does to Hawthorne can be seen (in part) by her last conversation with Kenyon in the romance:

"Here comes my perplexity," continued Kenyon. "Sin has educated Donatello, and elevated him. Is Sin, then—which we deem such a dreadful blackness in the Universe—is it, like Sorrow, merely an ele-ment of human education, through which we struggle to a higher and purer state than we could otherwise have attained? Did Adam fall, that we might ultimately rise to a far loftier Paradise than his?"

"Oh, hush!" cried Hilda, shrinking from him with an expression of horror which wounded the poor, speculative sculptor to the soul. "This is terrible; and I could weep for you, if you indeed believe it. Do not you perceive what a mockery your creed makes, not only of all religious sentiment, but of moral law, and how it annuls and obliterates whatever precepts of Heaven are written deepest within us? You have shocked me beyond words!"

"Forgive me, Hilda!" exclaimed the sculptor, startled by her agitation; "I never did believe it! But the mind wanders wild and wide; and, so lonely as I live and work, I have neither pole-star above, nor light of cottage-windows here below, to bring me home. Were you my guide, my counsellor, my inmost friend, with that white wisdom which clothes you as with a celestial garment, all would go well. Oh, Hilda, guide me home!"

"We are both lonely; both far from home!" said Hilda, her eyes filling with tears. "I am a poor, weak girl, and have no such wisdom as you fancy in me."

A peculiar badness of style and sentiment like this makes the reader wince: Is this worthy of Hawthorne? I hear no detachment on his part; does he, like Kenyon, apprehend Hilda as sustaining wisdom while clothing her as with a celestial garment? The self-described "poor, weak girl" employs her passivity and chastity as weapons against human dignity and the best interests of art. A supposed Christian who knows nothing of mercy, she would not have survived in Hawthorne's esteem when he wrote *The Scarlet Letter*. Hilda is as much an aesthetic and moral disaster as the magnificent Hester Prynne is a sublime triumph.

The daemon knows how it is done and also undone.

HENRY JAMES

THE ACKNOWLEDGED MASTER OF AMERICAN PROSE FICTION COMPOSED his critical essays and reviews intrepidly but perhaps not always wisely. His book *Hawthorne* (1879) reveals something about Henry James while displaying little insight into his prime American precursor. At thirty-six, the superbly intelligent James could be expected to have done better, yet a repressed influence-anxiety was at work.

James's two low points as a reviewer were his self-described "little atrocity" on Walt Whitman's *Drum-Taps* in 1865 and an incredible reaction to *Our Mutual Friend*, Charles Dickens's last completed novel, in that same year. Maturity made the master no kinder to Dickens or to Tolstoy, who was guilty of separating "method from manner."

Tolstoy was remote; Dickens had and kept the readership James desired and rarely achieved. Still, I am grateful for the badness of James on *Our Mutual Friend*:

> *Our Mutual Friend* is, to our perception, the poorest of Mr. Dickens's works. And it is poor with the poverty not of momentary embarrassment, but of permanent exhaustion. It is wanting in inspiration. For the last ten years it has seemed to us that Mr. Dickens has been unmistakably forcing himself. *Bleak House* was forced; *Little Dorrit* was labored; the present work is dug out as with a spade and pickaxe. Of course—to anticipate the usual argument— who but Dickens could have written it? Who, indeed? Who else would have established a lady in business in a novel on the admirably solid basis of her always putting on gloves and tying a handkerchief round her head in moments of grief, and of her habitually addressing her family with "Peace! hold!" It is needless to say that Mrs. Reginald Wilfer is first and last the occasion of considerable true humor. When, after conducting her daughter to Mrs. Boffin's carriage, in sight of all the envious neighbors, she is described as enjoying her triumph during the next quarter of an hour by airing herself on the door-step "in a kind of splendidly serene trance," we

laugh with as uncritical a laugh as could be desired of us. We pay the same tribute to her assertions, as she narrates the glories of the society she enjoyed at her father's table, that she has known as many as three copper-plate engravers exchanging the most exquisite sallies and retorts there at one time. But when to these we have added a dozen more happy examples of the humor which was exhaled from every line of Mr. Dickens's earlier writings, we shall have closed the list of the merits of the work before us.

To say that the conduct of the story, with all its complications, betrays a long-practised hand, is to pay no compliment worthy the author. If this were, indeed, a compliment, we should be inclined to carry it further, and congratulate him on his success in what we should call the manufacture of fiction; for in so doing we should express a feeling that has attended us throughout the book. Seldom, we reflected, had we read a book so intensely *written,* so little seen, known, or felt.

This sent me back to yet one more rereading of Dickens's sublimely dark hymn to the River Thames and to a fetid London washed filthier by it. *Our Mutual Friend* is a nightmare, deserving to be called an apocalypse of Britain, in the mode of William Blake's prophecies. Doubtless the master, even in his early seventies, sent *Our Mutual Friend* and *Bleak House* to join the company of "loose, baggy monsters" such as *War and Peace* and *The Brothers Karamazov.* The wonder is James's love for Balzac, whose affinities are with Dickens, Tolstoy, Dostoyevsky, rather than with the author of *The Golden Bowl.*

My own love for the novels of Henry James—*The Bostonians, The Portrait of a Lady, The Wings of the Dove* in particular—does not blind me to the still-greater literary power of Dickens, Balzac, Tolstoy. Nothing is got for nothing, and James sacrificed some of his own exuberance of being upon the altar of form. Yet, like those contemporaries who surpassed him in aesthetic force, James too was a heroic vitalist, though in him it manifests by and through a subtle mode of apparent renunciation. This *askesis* excluded him from the ultimate American literary achievement dwelled in by *The Scarlet Letter, Leaves of Grass, Moby-Dick, The Adventures of Huckleberry Finn,* and a few companions.

And yet James's art of sublimation remained a brilliant ruse that enabled his daemon to create a dozen major novels and scores of admirable shorter narratives. What he meant by renunciation is as difficult to describe as Goethe's art of renunciation, in which so little actually is forsaken.

Renouncing the literary past is not an object for the strong novelist. James Joyce, wrestling only with the mightiest of the everliving precursors, parodies Homer, Dante, Shakespeare, and wins his own central place in their triumphal pageant. Henry James engages in a different agon of consciousness against consciousness. Too wary to engage Dante and Shakespeare, James substitutes Hawthorne as his daemon. Herman Melville, who accurately valued Hawthorne as the best we had in his time, would have understood, though the titanic seer of *Moby-Dick* confronted the Bible and Shakespeare.

An odd parallel can be sketched between Shakespeare's relation to Christopher Marlowe and Henry James's venture into subsuming Hawthorne. Shakespeare owed to Marlowe's *Tamburlaine the Great* the pragmatic instruction of how to capture an audience through "pathetical persuasion"—the heightened rhetorical eloquence of the roaring player, in Marlowe's case Edward Alleyn and in Shakespeare's, Richard Burbage. James learned from Hawthorne the lesson of daemonic agency, by which Verena Tarrant in *The Bostonians* can chant her spellbinding protofeminist performances in emulation of Priscilla's mesmeric utterances as the Veiled Lady in *The Blithedale Romance*.

There are parodistic elements in Shakespeare's utilization of Marlovian rhetoric in the farcical *Titus Andronicus* and in *Richard III*, but they are less interesting than the upending of Doctor Faustus in *The Tempest* and of *The Jew of Malta* by *The Merchant of Venice*. James does not parody Hawthorne so much as raise him to an apotheosis in *The Portrait of a Lady*, which renews *The Scarlet Letter*, and *The Wings of the Dove*, which in turn corrects and transcends *The Marble Faun*. It cannot be asserted that Isabel Archer has the inward strength of Hester Prynne, though she repeats her forerunner's refusal to abandon an Emersonian self-reliance. Her elliptical motives in rejecting Goodwood and returning to Rome and a duel of wills with Osmond can be illuminated by Hester's deliberate return to Boston rather than joining her daughter, Pearl, in England.

Henry James preferred *The Tempest* among Shakespeare's plays, but his introduction (1907) to it does not explain why. Generally, James has been overpraised as a literary critic; he flames forth only in his "The Lesson of Balzac." Mannerism, which rarely impedes his fiction, is so heightened in the criticism that he is more self-conscious than most readers can absorb.

In her *Meaning in Henry James* (1991), Millicent Bell usefully describes an "ellipsis of beginning" prevalent in James's longer fictions. The art of ellipsis was learned by James partly from Hawthorne, partly from Shakespeare. His way of leaving things out became a highly individual absence of Shakespearean and Hawthornean foregrounding. Isabel Archer, with whom he identified, seems freest of a circumstantial past. I wonder if this radical Emersonianism is not deeply flowing in all the James clan, part of the legacy of the senior Henry James, Emerson's uneasy disciple. William and Henry, sons of this inheritance, manifest the Native Strain in allied though differing modes.

Emerson insisted he had no past at his back, a startling declaration from the disciple of Plato, Plotinus, Plutarch, Montaigne, Shakespeare, Wordsworth, and Coleridge (among others). Walt Whitman carried Emerson's stance to apotheosis: The past and present wilted, and "an American bard at last" proceeded to fill his next fold of the future.

So copious was Henry James that any choices among his major novels and tales must have some arbitrary elements. Guided mostly by aesthetic pleasure, I confine myself here to *The Portrait of a Lady* (1881), *The Bostonians* (1886), *The Wings of the Dove* (1902), and the tale "The Jolly Corner" (1908). That omits perhaps his subtlest triumph, *The Golden Bowl* (1904), and many earlier splendors. James's tales are an endless richness, but "The Jolly Corner" haunts me, and something crucial in the master is neglected if we turn away from the ghostly aspect of his work.

The Portrait of a Lady

LIKE MANY SOCIALLY AWKWARD SMALL BOYS OF THE 1930S, MY FIRST love affairs were with the heroines of novels, in my instance with Thomas Hardy's young women—Marty South and Eustacia Vye in particular—and with D. H. Lawrence's Ursula and Gudrun Brangwen. As a nine-year-old, I wept when Marty South cut off her long hair, and I experienced exultance when Hardy celebrated Eustacia Vye as his Queen of Night.

Falling in love with Isabel Archer a few years later, in adolescence, was very different, since unlike Marty, Eustacia, and the Brangwen sisters, James's wonderful heroine seemed outside the sphere of sexual desire. Scholars with the patience to read the earlier *Portrait of a Lady* (1880–81) closely against its revision in the 1908 New York Edition have demonstrated the master's new emphasis upon Isabel Archer's aversion to the erotic drive. Implicit in 1881, it became overt twenty-seven years later:

> His kiss was like white lightning, a flash that spread, and spread again, and stayed; and it was extraordinarily as if, while she took it, she felt each thing in his hard manhood that had least pleased her, each aggressive fact of his face, his figure, his presence, justified of its intense identity and made one with this act of possession. So had she heard of those wrecked and under water following a train of images before they sink. But when darkness returned she was free.

Anthony Mazzella deftly observes that Isabel learns again from Goodwood's desperate kiss that her self-reliance depends upon what Sigmund Freud was to term the freeing of thought from its sexual past. Had Henry James himself accomplished that act of liberation?

With his beautiful evasiveness he renders the question unanswerable, and yet he regarded Isabel Archer with what seems a particular fondness, frequently ascribed to his love for his Albany cousin Mary Temple. "Minny," as Mary was called, was a "shining apparition" who died very young, unlike Isabel but resembling in this Milly Theale, the tragic heroine-dove of *The Wings of the Dove*. Certainly Minny Temple haunted James throughout his long life. His affectionate memory of her is an instance of his singular power of appreciation, in Walter Pater's sense: to liberate even the deepest sorrows of his experience into the freedom of art.

Not, alas, that he frees Isabel Archer from the dreadful consequences of her choice of the odious Osmond (a character so loathsome that I am comforted by lifting that repeated modifier from Saki). For years I resented James's sly genius for making Osmond the ultimate fate of the magnificent Isabel, but in old age I have come to accept the Shakespearean rightness of Isabel's great error about life. In turning down the amiable Warburton, she says that she cannot escape unhappiness, but the mystery is why her implausible choice of Osmond should invite her plunge into the abyss of everything most alien to her free and open nature. Why must the heiress of all the ages settle for so fourth-rate a *poseur*?

So close is James to her that I suspect self-punishment, though that observation seems odd. Aside from his likely homoeroticism, James had both a passion against marriage and a contrary tendency to exalt it. Henry James, Sr., scarcely had been other than an eccentric husband and father, repeatedly hauling wife, sons, and daughter back and forth across the Atlantic, unsafe and uncomfortable argosies. The elder Henry James, disciple both of Emerson and of Swedenborg, was a rather curious religious writer—something of an acquired taste, I reflect, each time I attempt to read him. Compared to the achievement of William James and the younger Henry, the life's work of their father dwindles to nothingness.

Prompted by Nina Baym's challenging essay on revision and thematic change in *Portrait*, I have just reread the 1881 version for the first time in a half century. Baym's central contention is forceful: James sacrificed rather too much social context in shifting the emphasis to Isabel's transcendental consciousness of her nature and destiny. Her "emotional responsiveness" vanishes in favor of her intellectual self-awareness.

My direct experience, having just now read the 1881 and 1908 versions in sequence, heads to a different conclusion, though I am grateful to Baym for her investigations into revisionary gain and loss. The Emersonianism of Isabel seems to me a constant in both versions: her aspiration to fully realize her own potential spiritual independence.

Where Baym might have troubled James is in her augmented awareness that a subtler new Isabel seems less likely to have fallen into the trap set by Madame Merle and Osmond, especially because their few likable qualities diminish in the 1908 reworking. But James, I think, wanted the enigma of Isabel's blundering choice to be even more shocking.

In *Antony and Cleopatra*, the Herculean Antony is heroic but in decline: His guardian daemon, or genius, wanes in the presence of Octavius. James's daemons, like Shakespeare's, are messengers, or envoys, and become negations in regard to Isabel Archer, whom they abandon in her initial encounters with Osmond. The high cost of absolute transcendental yearnings manifests as a social blindness, a failure to see through the mask. Here Isabel joins her strongest precursor, Hester Prynne, whose amazingly dreadful choice of Chillingworth dwarfs the mistake concerning the pseudo-aesthete Osmond. Granted that Isabel is no Hester, who is a triumph of a woman's sexual vitality, and yet Hester is an Emersonian before the fact, even as Isabel is a latecomer transcendentalist.

James's adroit prefaces disguise or evade the daemonic drives that animate his primordial visions of his grandest personae: Isabel Archer, Lambert Strether, Kate Croy, Milly Theale, Charlotte Stant, Maggie Verver. None of these ultimately retain any simpler continuities with their initial self-presentations. They are not endless to meditation: Henry James is not Shakespeare or Dante, Cervantes or Joyce. Falstaff and Hamlet, Iago and Cleopatra, Dante the Pilgrim and Don Quixote, Sancho Panza and Poldy Bloom exist both within and without their dramas and sages. James's Dark Ladies—Madame Merle, Kate Croy, Charlotte Stant—possess an intensity singular enough to call for more development, but James's artistry would not countenance it. As I have noted, his mastery of ellipsis was stirred by the example of Shakespeare: We are not to be told at all precisely why Isabel blunders into accepting Osmond's proposal of marriage.

Madame Merle murders her own soul. Why? Densher is as inadequate to Kate Croy as he would have been to Milly Theale: How can they see in him what is not there? Charlotte Stant *and* Maggie Verver each are worth a score of Prince Amerigos: James slyly sees it, but they do not. Again, why would James compose parables in which marvelous women must descend to mate?

I cannot think of a woman in Shakespeare who does not marry down. What choices did James give Isabel? Goodwood and Warburton do not much appeal to my women students, while the superb Ralph Touchett is mortally ill:

> She was full of the sense that he was beyond the reach of pain; he seemed already so little of this world. But even if she had not had it she would still have spoken, for nothing mattered now but the only knowledge that was not pure anguish—the knowledge that they were looking at the truth together. "He married me for my money," she said.
>
> She wished to say everything; she was afraid he might die before she had done so.
>
> He gazed at her a little, and for the first time his fixed eyes lowered their lids. But he raised them in a moment, and then—"He was greatly in love with you," he answered.

"Yes, he was in love with me. But he would not have married me if I had been poor. I don't hurt you in saying that. How can I? I only want you to understand. I always tried to keep you from understanding; but that's all over."

"I always understood," said Ralph.

"I thought you did, and I didn't like it. But now I like it."

"You don't hurt me—you make me very happy." And as Ralph said this there was an extraordinary gladness in his voice. She bent her head again, and pressed her lips to the back of his hand. "I always understood," he continued, "though it was so strange—so pitiful. You wanted to look at life for yourself—but you were not allowed; you were punished for your wish. You were ground in the very mill of the conventional!"

"Oh yes, I've been punished," Isabel sobbed.

He listened to her a little, and then continued: "Was he very bad about your coming?"

"He made it very hard for me. But I don't care."

"It is all over then between you?"

"Oh no; I don't think anything's over."

"Are you going back to him?" Ralph gasped.

"I don't know—I can't tell. I shall stay here as long as I may. I don't want to think—I needn't think. I don't care for anything but you, and that's enough for the present. It will last a little yet. Here on my knees, with you dying in my arms, I'm happier than I have been for a long time. And I want you to be happy—not to think of anything sad; only to feel that I'm near you and I love you. Why should there be pain? In such hours as this what have we to do with pain? That's not the deepest thing; there's something deeper."

Ralph evidently found from moment to moment greater difficulty in speaking; he had to wait longer to collect himself. At first he appeared to make no response to these last words; he let a long time elapse. Then he murmured simply: "You must stay here."

"I should like to stay—as long as seems right."

"As seems right—as seems right?" He repeated her words. "Yes, you think a great deal about that."

"Of course one must. You're very tired," said Isabel.

"I'm very tired. You said just now that pain's not the deepest thing. No—no. But it's very deep. If I could stay—"

"For me you'll always be here," she softly interrupted. It was easy to interrupt him.

But he went on, after a moment: "It passes, after all; it's passing now. But love remains. I don't know why we should suffer so much. Perhaps I shall find out. There are many things in life. You're very young."

"I feel very old," said Isabel.

"You'll grow young again. That's how I see you. I don't believe— I don't believe—" But he stopped again; his strength failed him.

She begged him to be quiet now. "We needn't speak to understand each other," she said.

"I don't believe that such a generous mistake as yours can hurt you for more than a little."

"Oh Ralph, I'm very happy now," she cried through her tears.

"And remember this," he continued, "that if you've been hated you've also been loved. Ah but, Isabel—*adored*!" he just audibly and lingeringly breathed.

"Oh my brother!" she cried with a movement of still deeper prostration.

I have quoted all of this because it is the great set piece of the novel and a Jamesian triumph of pace, proportion, diction, and profound compassion. The perfect rightness of the mutual tact that is a mode of love is exquisitely rendered. Here, at least, Isabel's story touches tragic dignity. Ralph has been kept alive by his desire to see Isabel work through her destiny, but even that can no longer sustain him.

Henry James, elliptical throughout *The Portrait of a Lady,* does not allow any closure to Isabel's story. Her return to Osmond has a touch in it of Hamlet's return to Elsinore from the sea. Nobody except Horatio (and the outsider Fortinbras) survives that return, and it is unlikely that Osmond's "beautiful mind" will be at all serene in the embattled reunion and afterward. To Madame Merle, Isabel is direct: "I think I should like never to see you again." James spares us the long-drawn-out warfare to come with Osmond yet rewards us with a brilliant, harrowing presage:

Isabel stood a moment looking at the latter missive; then, thrusting it into her pocket, she went straight to the door of her husband's study. Here she again paused an instant, after which she opened the door and went in. Osmond was seated at the table near the window with a folio volume before him, propped against a pile of books. This volume was open at a page of small coloured plates, and Isabel presently saw that he had been copying from it the drawing of an antique coin. A box of water-colours and fine brushes lay before him, and he had already transferred to a sheet of immaculate paper the delicate, finely-tinted disk. His back was turned toward the door, but he recognised his wife without looking round.

"Excuse me for disturbing you," she said.

"When I come to your room I always knock," he answered, going on with his work.

"I forgot; I had something else to think of. My cousin's dying."

"Ah, I don't believe that," said Osmond, looking at his drawing through a magnifying glass. "He was dying when we married; he'll outlive us all."

Isabel gave herself no time, no thought, to appreciate the careful cynicism of this declaration; she simply went on quickly, full of her own intention: "My aunt has telegraphed for me; I must go to Gardencourt."

"Why must you go to Gardencourt?" Osmond asked in the tone of impartial curiosity.

"To see Ralph before he dies."

To this, for some time, he made no rejoinder; he continued to give his chief attention to his work, which was of a sort that would brook no negligence. "I don't see the need of it," he said at last. "He came to see you here. I didn't like that; I thought his being in Rome a great mistake. But I tolerated it because it was to be the last time you should see him. Now you tell me it's not to have been the last. Ah, you're not grateful!"

"What am I to be grateful for?"

Gilbert Osmond laid down his little implements, blew a speck of dust from his drawing, slowly got up, and for the first time looked at his wife. "For my not having interfered while he was here."

This begins a marital death march that proceeds downward and outward to the truth:

"Oh yes, I am. I remember perfectly how distinctly you let me know you didn't like it. I was very glad when he went away."

"Leave him alone then. Don't run after him."

Isabel turned her eyes away from him; they rested upon his little drawing. "I must go to England," she said, with a full consciousness that her tone might strike an irritable man of taste as stupidly obstinate.

"I shall not like it if you do," Osmond remarked.

"Why should I mind that? You won't like it if I don't. You like nothing I do or don't do. You pretend to think I lie."

Osmond turned slightly pale; he gave a cold smile. "That's why you must go then? Not to see your cousin, but to take a revenge on me."

"I know nothing about revenge."

"I do," said Osmond. "Don't give me an occasion."

"You're only too eager to take one. You wish immensely that I would commit some folly."

"I should be gratified in that case if you disobeyed me."

"If I disobeyed you?" said Isabel in a low tone which had the effect of mildness.

"Let it be clear. If you leave Rome to-day it will be a piece of the most deliberate, the most calculated, opposition."

"How can you call it calculated? I received my aunt's telegram but three minutes ago."

"You calculate rapidly; it's a great accomplishment. I don't see why we should prolong our discussion; you know my wish." And he stood there as if he expected to see her withdraw.

But she never moved; she couldn't move, strange as it may seem; she still wished to justify herself; he had the power, in an extraordinary degree, of making her feel this need. There was something in her imagination he could always appeal to against her judgement. "You've no reason for such a wish," said Isabel, "and I've every reason for going. I can't tell you how unjust you seem to me. But I think you know. It's your own opposition that's calculated. It's malignant."

"Malignant" is exact for Osmond. What follows is an epitome of his hatred for Isabel:

If she must renounce, however, she would let him know she was a victim rather than a dupe. "I know you're a master of the art of mockery," she said. "How can you speak of an indissoluble union— how can you speak of your being contented? Where's our union when you accuse me of falsity? Where's your contentment when you have nothing but hideous suspicion in your heart?"

"It is in our living decently together, in spite of such drawbacks."

"We don't live decently together!" cried Isabel.

"Indeed we don't if you go to England."

"That's very little; that's nothing. I might do much more."

He raised his eyebrows and even his shoulders a little: he had lived long enough in Italy to catch this trick. "Ah, if you've come to threaten me I prefer my drawing." And he walked back to his table, where he took up the sheet of paper on which he had been working and stood studying it.

"I suppose that if I go you'll not expect me to come back," said Isabel.

He turned quickly round, and she could see this movement at least was not designed. He looked at her a little, and then, "Are you out of your mind?" he enquired.

"How can it be anything but a rupture?" she went on; "especially if all you say is true?" She was unable to see how it could be anything but a rupture; she sincerely wished to know what else it might be.

He sat down before his table. "I really can't argue with you on the hypothesis of your defying me," he said. And he took up one of his little brushes again.

With every common reader, I wince and wonder again just why Isabel does not proceed to a final rupture of this travesty-marriage. James will not do the work for us. Recoiling from Goodwood's kiss, Isabel has a final epiphany that reveals little:

She had not known where to turn; but she knew now. There was a very straight path.

And yet that straight path will take her back into the labyrinthine struggle with Osmond. Each of us is freed by James to imagine how brief or long that fiction of duration will prove to be. Those who love Isabel—as James did—will believe that she will win her way back to independence long before any destined end.

The Bostonians

MY STUDENTS DURING THE LAST DECADE AGREE ON FINDING *THE Bostonians* (1886) the most readable of James's novels, a preference I tend to share. Taking up again the example of Hawthorne's *The Blithedale Romance*, James fuses the lesson of Balzac into his narrative, though his aspiring young man from the provinces, Basil Ransom of Mississippi, is no Rastignac and the Balzacian energetics of the daemonic Vautrin are wisely evaded. It is the supreme artistry of Henry James to know and keep within his limitations: The heroic vitalists of Chaucer, Shakespeare, Balzac, and Dickens are beyond his range and ambitions.

That conceded, *The Bostonians* is an achievement almost endlessly in-exhaustible: Olive Chancellor, Verena Tarrant, and Basil Ransom leap off the page with force and vivacity equal to Isabel Archer, Kate Croy, and to James himself in his autobiographical writings.

Though what is now termed "feminism" is handled justly in *The Bostonians,* James himself is dispassionate toward it and toward Ransom's unreconstructed Thomas Carlyle–like stance against both black and female emancipation. Essentially, *The Bostonians* is a comic novel with tragicomic overtones, though its ambiguities are more labyrinthine than that suggests. Verena may inherit her gentle daemonism from Priscilla in *The Blithedale Romance,* but Verena Tarrant is an intensely Emersonian spirit, open to influx from powers above and beyond her. They are indif-ferent to her personal welfare and do not protect her from enslavement by Basil Ransom in a marriage through which he will assert masculine domi-nation. At least, though, he is no Osmond, and to that degree she fares better than Isabel Archer, whose consciousness and ardent sense of self is far beyond hers.

I will discuss rather fully the three protagonists: Olive Chancellor, Basil Ransom, and Verena Tarrant in that order. Though all three are successfully rendered by James, Olive seems to me his triumph in *The Bostonians*. Her complexities and divisions are poignant and intricate, somewhat Shakespearean in their range and intensity.

Olive's obsessive passion for Verena is lesbian, however repressed, just as Miles Coverdale's weakly expressed love for Priscilla screened his homoerotic desire for Hollingsworth. One needs to start by considering how radically James diverges in his presentation of Olive from the tradition of the heroines of the Protestant will in Samuel Richardson and his descendants: Jane Austen, Fanny Burney, Charlotte Brontë, George Eliot. The cavalcade of Clarissa Harlowe, Elizabeth, Emma, Anne, Fanny, Evelina, Jane Eyre, Dorothea, and Gwendolyn—none is alienated from the marriage bond, as Olive so fiercely is. She has no true precedent in British fiction or in Hawthorne, and this originality makes her startlingly prophetic of Virginia Woolf and much that comes after.

Sexual orientation doubtless is a central component in Olive's difference, but it may distract the reader from her singularity as a characterization. Here she is first, as filtered through the wary consciousness of her kinsman Basil Ransom:

> This, however, was in the future; what Basil Ransom actually perceived was that Miss Chancellor was a signal old maid. That was her quality, her destiny; nothing could be more distinctly written. There are women who are unmarried by accident, and others who are unmarried by option; but Olive Chancellor was unmarried by every implication of her being. She was a spinster as Shelley was a lyric poet, or as the month of August is sultry. She was so essentially a celibate that Ransom found himself thinking of her as old, though when he came to look at her (as he said to himself) it was apparent that her years were fewer than his own. He did not dislike her, she had been so friendly; but, little by little, she gave him an uneasy feeling—the sense that you could never be safe with a person who took things so hard. It came over him that it was because she took things hard she had sought his acquaintance; it had been because she was strenuous, not because she was genial; she had had in her eye—and what an extraordinary eye it was!—not a pleasure, but a duty. She would expect him to be strenuous in return; but he couldn't—in private life, he couldn't; privacy for Basil Ransom con-

sisted entirely in what he called 'laying off.' She was not so plain on further acquaintance as she had seemed to him at first; even the young Mississippian had culture enough to see that she was refined. Her white skin had a singular look of being drawn tightly across her face; but her features, though sharp and irregular, were delicate in a fashion that suggested good breeding. Their line was perverse, but it was not poor. The curious tint of her eyes was a living colour; when she turned it upon you, you thought vaguely of the glitter of green ice. She had absolutely no figure, and presented a certain appearance of feeling cold. With all this, there was something very modern and highly developed in her aspect; she had the advantages as well as the drawbacks of a nervous organisation. She smiled constantly at her guest, but from the beginning to the end of dinner, though he made several remarks that he thought might prove amusing, she never once laughed. Later, he saw that she was a woman without laughter; exhilaration, if it ever visited her, was dumb. Once only, in the course of his subsequent acquaintance with her, did it find a voice; and then the sound remained in Ransom's ear as one of the strangest he had heard.

"She was a spinster as Shelley was a lyric poet" and "a woman without laughter" are crucial observations of Ransom's and imply more than as yet he could know. His daemonic quality is prolepsis: a kind of Macbeth-like power of foretelling. Olive's converse sort of daemonic influx is anticipatory dread, awakened in her early by Ransom's presence, even before both of them first encounter Verena on the same occasion. Fierce throwback to an archaic masculine chauvinism, he too falls in love with Verena at first sight and so from the start implicitly becomes Olive's destroyer.

There are antipathetic elements in all three protagonists: Olive is near-hysterical, Ransom's Mississippi masculine chivalry is pragmatically brutal, and the genial, loving Verena can be empty-headed. Nevertheless, James dispassionately creates them fit to stand though free to fall, and all of them do fall, though Basil Ransom believes he emerges triumphant. Verena is going to suffer a kind of enslavement as his wife, yet her own daemonic proclivity to feminist visions and voices cannot depart, and in time Ransom will pay a high cost of confirmation for his post-Carlylean American repressiveness.

I return to Olive, the book's exemplary sufferer, who gains much more sympathy as the novel flows on to her defeat by Ransom. James achieves extraordinary poignance by the contrast between the (at times) grotesque Boston feminist and the charming Mississippi monster. Even Thomas Carlyle's *Shooting Niagara: And After?*, a polemic informing Ransom, is not so extreme as to sexual inequality compared to democracy, which excites equal scorn in the savage Scotsman and the chivalric Southerner.

Olive's agony achieves expressive apotheosis in Chapter XXXIX when, on Cape Cod, Verena has gone boating with Ransom:

> Did Verena's strange aberration, on this particular day, suggest to Olive that it was no use striving, that the world was all a great trap or trick, of which women were ever the punctual dupes, so that it was the worst of the curse that rested upon them that they must most humiliate those who had most their cause at heart? Did she say to herself that their weakness was not only lamentable but hideous—hideous their predestined subjection to man's larger and grosser insistence? Did she ask herself why she should give up her life to save a sex which, after all, didn't wish to be saved, and which rejected the truth even after it had bathed them with its auroral light and they had pretended to be fed and fortified? These are mysteries into which I shall not attempt to enter, speculations with which I have no concern; it is sufficient for us to know that all human effort had never seemed to her so barren and thankless as on that fatal afternoon. Her eyes rested on the boats she saw in the distance, and she wondered if in one of them Verena were floating to her fate; but so far from straining forward to beckon her home she almost wished that she might glide away for ever, that *she* might never see her again, never undergo the horrible details of a more deliberate separation. Olive lived over, in her miserable musings, her life for the last two years; she knew, again, how noble and beautiful her scheme had been, but how it had all rested on an illusion of which the very thought made her feel faint and sick. What was before her now was the reality, with the beautiful, indifferent sky pouring down its complacent rays upon it. The reality was simply that Verena had been more to her than she ever was to Verena, and that, with her exquisite natural art, the girl had cared for their cause

only because, for the time, no interest, no fascination, was greater. Her talent, the talent which was to achieve such wonders, was nothing to her; it was too easy, she could leave it alone, as she might close her piano, for months; it was only to Olive that it was everything. Verena had submitted, she had responded, she had lent herself to Olive's incitement and exhortation, because she was sympathetic and young and abundant and fanciful; but it had been a kind of hothouse loyalty, the mere contagion of example, and a sentiment springing up from within had easily breathed a chill upon it. Did Olive ask herself whether, for so many months, her companion had been only the most unconscious and most successful of humbugs? Here again I must plead a certain incompetence to give an answer. Positive it is that she spared herself none of the inductions of a reverie that seemed to dry up the mists and ambiguities of life. These hours of backward clearness come to all men and women, once at least, when they read the past in the light of the present, with the reasons of things, like unobserved finger-posts, protruding where they never saw them before. The journey behind them is mapped out and figured, with its false steps, its wrong observations, all its infatuated, deluded geography. They understand as Olive understood, but it is probable that they rarely suffer as she suffered. The sense of regret for her baffled calculations burned within her like a fire, and the splendour of the vision over which the curtain of mourning now was dropped brought to her eyes slow, still tears, tears that came one by one, neither easing her nerves nor lightening her load of pain. She thought of her innumerable talks with Verena, of the pledges they had exchanged, of their earnest studies, their faithful work, their certain reward, the winter-nights under the lamp, when they thrilled with previsions as just and a passion as high as had ever found shelter in a pair of human hearts. The pity of it, the misery of such a fall after such a flight, could express itself only, as the poor girl prolonged the vague pauses of her unnoticed ramble, in a low, inarticulate murmur of anguish.

What pains most here is the emptiness of Olive's enterprise, both in the relationship with Verena and as an ideology with no pragmatic program for political organization and reform. Olive's aura is martyrdom, but has she earned it? Like Ransom, Olive is in love with Verena, yet there is no design to such love. What can Verena do with it? Ransom offers her the excitement of victimization, a suspect satisfaction that will lead to tears, but all Olive can give, since her lesbianism is so dreadfully repressed, is a kind of Shelleyan sense of being "pinnacled dim in the intense inane": spinsterism as poetic lyric.

Backward clarity and murmuring anguish blend in Olive's beach reverie. Though the narrator avoids judgment, Olive's lament is the consequence of the only communication between the three protagonists, daemon-to-daemon ghostliness, a discourse we overhear. Though lovers who will marry, Verena and Ransom rarely listen to each other, while Olive and Verena's evaded passion is both one-sided and inchoate.

What was Henry James attempting to do for himself as a novelist in composing *The Bostonians*? He evidently hoped to fuse Hawthorne with Alphonse Daudet and Balzac, thus opening the American romance form to a kind of purged naturalism, while exposing the weak premises of a fictive mode that excluded transcendental aspirations. American daemonism is very much more extreme than the energetics even of Balzac. In a curious way, Basil Ransom is as dangerously driven as Vautrin, who will ascend to the highest place in the hierarchy of the Parisian secret police after first reigning as Death-Dodger, Prince of the Underworld.

Were the American Confederacy to rise again, some actual Basil Ransom would make an admirable president. Essentially the Mississippean would be glad to reinstitute black slavery, to disenfranchise women and return them to a role as adored but brutalized household items. A degree of charm masks this in Ransom, yet he truly is bad news:

'Oh, I suppose you want to destroy us by neglect, by silence!' Verena exclaimed, with the same brightness.

'No, I don't want to destroy you, any more than I want to save you. There has been far too much talk about you, and I want to leave you alone altogether. My interest is in my own sex; yours evidently can look after itself. That's what I want to save.'

Verena saw that he was more serious now than he had been before, that he was not piling it up satirically, but saying really and a trifle wearily, as if suddenly he were tired of much talk, what he meant. 'To save it from what?' she asked.

'From the most damnable feminisation! I am so far from thinking, as you set forth the other night, that there is not enough woman
in our general life, that it has long been pressed home to me that
there is a great deal too much. The whole generation is womanised;
the masculine tone is passing out of the world; it's a feminine, a
nervous, hysterical, chattering, canting age, an age of hollow
phrases and false delicacy and exaggerated solicitudes and coddled
sensibilities, which, if we don't soon look out, will usher in the
reign of mediocrity, of the feeblest and flattest and the most preten-
tious that has ever been. The masculine character, the ability to dare
and endure, to know and yet not fear reality, to look the world in the
face and take it for what it is—a very queer and partly very base
mixture—that is what I want to preserve, or rather, as I may say, to
recover; and I must tell you that I don't in the least care what becomes of you ladies while I make the attempt!'

The poor fellow delivered himself of these narrow notions (the
rejection of which by leading periodicals was certainly not a matter
for surprise), with low, soft earnestness, bending towards her so as
to give out his whole idea, yet apparently forgetting for the moment
how offensive it must be to her now that it was articulated in that
calm, severe way, in which no allowance was to be made for hyper-
bole. Verena did not remind herself of this; she was too much im-
pressed by his manner and by the novelty of a man taking that sort
of religious tone about such a cause. It told her on the spot, from
one minute to the other and once for all, that the man who could
give her that impression would never come round. She felt cold,
slightly sick, though she replied that now he summed up his creed
in such a distinct, lucid way, it was much more comfortable—one
knew with what one was dealing; a declaration much at variance
with the fact, for Verena had never felt less gratified in her life. The
ugliness of her companion's profession of faith made her shiver; it
would have been difficult to her to imagine anything more crudely
profane. She was determined, however, not to betray any shudder
that could suggest weakness, and the best way she could think of to
disguise her emotion was to remark in a tone which, although not
assumed for that purpose, was really the most effective revenge, inasmuch as it always produced on Ransom's part (it was not pecu-

liar, among women, to Verena), an angry helplessness—'Mr. Ransom, I assure you this is an age of conscience.'

'That's a part of your cant. It's an age of unspeakable shams, as Carlyle says.'

'Well,' returned Verena, 'it's all very comfortable for you to say that you wish to leave us alone. But you can't leave us alone. We are here, and we have got to be disposed of. You have got to put us somewhere. It's a remarkable social system that has no place for *us!*' the girl went on, with her most charming laugh.

'No place in public. My plan is to keep you at home and have a better time with you there than ever.'

Though outrageous, Ransom's rant against cant and sham is perpetually valid. As an aged academic, I long have seen the triumph all around me of cant as the prime signature of university life in the era of Title IX. Basil Ransom would be laughed out of the academy now or suffer expulsion. That allows him to gain not sympathy, perhaps, but a touch of refreshing pathos.

James is at his strongest again in Chapter XXXVII, when Olive's crucifixion becomes most harrowing:

These remarks were uttered by Verena after Basil Ransom had been three days at Marmion, and when she reached this point her companion interrupted her with the inquiry, 'Is that what he proposes to support you with—his pen?'

'Oh yes; of course he admits we should be terribly poor.'

'And this vision of a literary career is based entirely upon an article that hasn't yet seen the light? I don't see how a man of any refinement can approach a woman with so beggarly an account of his position in life.'

'He says he wouldn't—he would have been ashamed—three months ago; that was why, when we were in New York, and he felt, even then—well (so he says) all he feels now, he made up his mind not to persist, to let me go. But just lately a change has taken place; his state of mind altered completely, in the course of a week, in consequence of the letter that editor wrote him about his contribution, and his paying for it right off. It was a remarkably flattering letter.

He says he believes in his future now; he has before him a vision of distinction, of influence, and of fortune, not great, perhaps, but sufficient to make life tolerable. He doesn't think life is very delightful, in the nature of things; but one of the best things a man can do with it is to get hold of some woman (of course, she must please him very much, to make it worth while), whom he may draw close to him.'

'And couldn't he get hold of any one but you—among all the exposed millions of our sex?' poor Olive groaned. 'Why must he pick you out, when everything he knew about you showed you to be, exactly, the very last?'

'That's just what I have asked him, and he only remarks that there is no reasoning about such things. He fell in love with me that first evening, at Miss Birdseye's. So you see there was some ground for that mystic apprehension of yours. It seems as if I pleased him more than any one.'

Olive flung herself over on the couch, burying her face in the cushions, which she tumbled in her despair, and moaning out that he didn't love Verena, he had never loved her, it was only his hatred of their cause that made him pretend it; he wanted to do that an injury, to do it the worst he could think of. He didn't love her, he hated her, he only wanted to smother her, to crush her, to kill her—as she would infallibly see that he would if she listened to him. It was because he knew that her voice had magic in it, and from the moment he caught its first note he had determined to destroy it. It was not tenderness that moved him—it was devilish malignity; tenderness would be incapable of requiring the horrible sacrifice that he was not ashamed to ask, of requiring her to commit perjury and blasphemy, to desert a work, an interest, with which her very heartstrings were interlaced, to give the lie to her whole young past, to her purest, holiest ambitions. Olive put forward no claim of her own, breathed, at first, at least, not a word of remonstrance in the name of her personal loss, of their blighted union; she only dwelt upon the unspeakable tragedy of a defection from their standard, of a failure on Verena's part to carry out what she had undertaken, of the horror of seeing her bright career blotted out with darkness and tears, of the joy and elation that would fill the breast of all their adversaries at this illustrious, consummate proof of the fickleness, the futility, the predestined servility, of women. A man had only to whistle for her, and she who had pretended most was delighted to come and kneel at his feet. Olive's most passionate protest was summed up in her saying that if Verena were to forsake them it would put back the emancipation of women a hundred years. She did not, during these dreadful days, talk continuously; she had long periods of pale, intensely anxious, watchful silence, interrupted by outbreaks of passionate argument, entreaty, invocation.

The nadir in Olive's life is her moaning litany that Ransom "didn't love her, he hated her, he only wanted to smother her, to crush her, to kill her . . . It was because he knew that her voice had magic in it, and from the moment he caught its first note he had determined to destroy it." All dignity has departed, and the proud Miss Chancellor has been reduced to the hysteria of childhood.

Verena soars above both her lovers in this storm of stress:

It was Verena who talked incessantly, Verena who was in a state entirely new to her, and, as any one could see, in an attitude entirely unnatural and overdone. If she was deceiving herself, as Olive said, there was something very affecting in her effort, her ingenuity. If she tried to appear to Olive impartial, coldly judicious, in her attitude with regard to Basil Ransom, and only anxious to see, for the moral satisfaction of the thing, how good a case, as a lover, he might make out for himself and how much he might touch her susceptibilities, she endeavoured, still more earnestly, to practise this fraud upon her own imagination. She abounded in every proof that she should be in despair if she should be overborne, and she thought of arguments even more convincing, if possible, than Olive's, why she should hold on to her old faith, why she should resist even at the cost of acute temporary suffering. She was voluble, fluent, feverish; she was perpetually bringing up the subject, as if to encourage her friend, to show how she kept possession of her judgment, how independent she remained.

No stranger situation can be imagined than that of these extraordinary young women at this juncture; it was so singular on Verena's part, in particular, that I despair of presenting it to the reader with the air of reality. To understand it, one must bear in mind her peculiar frankness, natural and acquired, her habit of discussing questions, sentiments, moralities, her education, in the atmosphere of lecture-rooms, of *séances,* her familiarity with the vocabulary of emotion, the mysteries of 'the spiritual life.' She had learned to breathe and move in a rarefied air, as she would have learned to speak Chinese if her success in life had depended upon it; but this dazzling trick, and all her artlessly artful facilities, were not a part of her essence, an expression of her innermost preferences. What *was* a part of her essence was the extraordinary generosity with which she could expose herself, give herself away, turn herself inside out, for the satisfaction of a person who made demands of her. Olive, as we know, had made the reflection that no one was naturally less preoccupied with the idea of her dignity, and though Verena put it forward as an excuse for remaining where they were, it must be admitted that in reality she was very deficient in the desire to be consistent with herself.

Though the Jamesian narrator despairs of representing Verena's new state, he nevertheless conveys it with a rare pungency. At once infinitely open to the wishes of others, generous at giving herself away, Verena also now possesses a spiritual recalcitrance to return to earlier modes of compliant being. Briefly, she has fallen into the abyss of love so utterly as to have burned through all of her lifetime convictions.

Where does James station us—his readers—as *The Bostonians* closes? In the place of the daemon, and not in the social world of Boston with the later nineteenth century moving toward uncertainty. When I have been away from *The Bostonians* for a few years, I recall only Verena and her rival lovers, Olive and Ransom. Their confrontations and despairs are what endure, though none of them incarnate human value as Isabel Archer does. Olive Chancellor is too grotesque to move us for long, despite her integrity, while Ransom can be accepted only as the archetypal Young Man from the Provinces, and he becomes absurd when we contemplate his narrow views.

Verena remains the challenge. She is open to daemonic influx, to an eloquence not her own, and only the daemon knows how and why it is done. Ransom cannot surmise that marriage will become as difficult for him as for her, no matter how strongly he subdues Verena's will to his own daemonic drive. What has been thwarted in her, though with her consent, will rise up again, however meaningless its bleak transcendence.

The Wings of the Dove

THE WINGS OF THE DOVE TAKES ITS BEAUTIFUL TITLE FROM PSALM 68:13, perhaps by way of Walter Pater, who in the fourth edition of *The Renaissance* added the first line as epigraph:

> Though ye have lien among the pots, yet shall ye be as the
> wings of a dove
> covered with silver, and her feathers with yellow gold.

I place *The Portrait of a Lady* first among James's novels, yet this later masterwork seems to me his most beautiful performance, outdoing even *The Golden Bowl*. *Wings* (as I will call it for brevity) is even more fabulistic than its companions of 1902–04, *The Ambassadors* and *The Golden Bowl*. Walter Pater's positive influence on *Wings* remains underesteemed, perhaps because Jamesian scholars do not know and appreciate the sublime Walter, one of my critical heroes. Odious Osmond is a mock-Paterian; Henry James was a true aesthetic novelist and critic, no more ironic toward the aesthetic vision than Pater himself was.

Most literary modernism stemmed from Pater: Yeats, Joyce, Eliot, Pound, Woolf, Stevens, and Hart Crane, among others—and Henry James and Conrad as much as anyone else. What Pater called the privileged moment became the secularized epiphany of the modernists, sudden bursts of illumination against the gathering darkness. As a mode of narrative, that suits poetry and drama, prophecy and wisdom-writing, better than the Balzacian novel that Henry James affirmed he deserved to attain. Balzac's friends nicknamed him Vautrin, who was his daemon, and the furiously energetic seer of *The Human Comedy* indeed achieved an all-but-Shakespearean "complete representation" in prose fiction. That was part of the lesson of Balzac for Henry James, who shrewdly observed the Parisian master's command of the "conditions" that inform each and all of us. *Wings*, though, is not a very Balzacian performance—unlike *The*

Bostonians—and the question of just who Milly Theale, Kate Croy, and Merton Densher *are* is not fully resolved. Since *Wings* ultimately is a fable, that may be an aesthetic advantage.

Milly is the transcendent being of the fable, the true daemon of love and loss, except that Kate and Densher also love and lose each other. Since Densher loves Milly only posthumously, as it were, his loss is doubled. I confess to finding him plainly inadequate to both his superb young women and always wonder at his all-but-universal appeal to everyone in the book. James loves Milly and Kate and seems oddly charmed by Densher, something I will examine as I turn now to the three protagonists.

When I have been away from *Wings* for a year or two, I think first about Kate Croy, because it is her book just as much as *The Portrait of a Lady* is Isabel Archer's. Milly Theale, famously founded on James's cousin Minny Temple, who also died tragically young, somehow does not quite inhabit the book. She surrounds it like an aura no matter how firmly James delineates her conditions and circumstances. Orphaned, wealthy, doomed, marked for victimization, she nevertheless triumphs over what ought to have obliterated her acute consciousness.

I recall amiable arguments with my late friend Dorothea Krook back in mid-1950s Cambridge, when she was developing her lectures that became *The Ordeal of Consciousness in Henry James* (1962). Her Milly was nothing but a victim and guilty also of spiritual pride, judgments I still find unacceptable. Like James's other American heroines, Milly is an Emersonian, a believer in self-reliance, aspiration, and the soul's sufficiency unto itself, as in a lyric by Emily Dickinson. A High Transcendentalist, Milly is too grand a figure to be categorized as anyone's victim. Kate and Densher ultimately realize this, and Kate states it beyond argument:

> Kate waited as for how to say it. "It's worthy of her. It's what she was herself—if you remember what we once said *that* was."
>
> He hesitated—as if there had been many things. But he remembered one of them. "Stupendous?"
>
> "Stupendous." A faint smile for it—ever so small—had flickered in her face, but had vanished before the omen of tears, a little less uncertain, had shown themselves in his own. His eyes filled—but that made her continue. She continued gently. "I think that what it really is must be that you're afraid. I mean," she explained, "that

you're afraid of *all* the truth. If you're in love with her without it, what indeed can you be more? And you're afraid—it's wonderful!—to be in love with her."

"I never was in love with her," said Densher.

She took it, but after a little she met it. "I believe that now—for the time she lived. I believe it at least for the time you were there. But your change came—as it might well—the day you last saw her; she died for you then that you might understand her. From that hour you *did*." With which Kate slowly rose. "And I do now. She did it *for* us." Densher rose to face her, and she went on with her thought. "I used to call her, in my stupidity—for want of anything better—a dove. Well she stretched out her wings, and it was to *that* they reached. They cover us."

"They cover us," Densher said.

"That's what I give you," Kate gravely wound up. "That's what I've done for you."

His look at her had a slow strangeness that had dried, on the moment, his tears. "Do I understand then—?"

"That I do consent?" She gravely shook her head. "No—for I see. You'll marry me without the money; you won't marry me with it. If I don't consent *you* don't."

"You lose me?" He showed, though naming it frankly, a sort of awe of her high grasp. "Well, you lose nothing else. I make over to you every penny."

Prompt was his own clearness, but she had no smile this time to spare. "Precisely—so that I must choose."

"You must choose."

Strange it was for him then that she stood in his own rooms doing it, while, with an intensity now beyond any that had ever made his breath come slow, he waited for her act. "There's but one thing that can save you from my choice."

"From your choice of my surrender to you?"

"Yes"—and she gave a nod at the long envelope on the table—"your surrender of that."

"What is it then?"

"Your word of honour that you're not in love with her memory."

"Oh—her memory!"

"Ah"—she made a high gesture—"don't speak of it as if you couldn't be. *I* could in your place; and you're one for whom it will do. Her memory's your love. You *want* no other."

He heard her out in stillness, watching her face but not moving. Then he only said: "I'll marry you, mind you, in an hour."

"As we were?"

"As we were."

But she turned to the door, and her headshake was now the end. "We shall never be again as we were!"

What could surpass "Well she stretched out her wings, and it was to *that* they reached. They cover us"? The artistry of this conclusion to *Wings* is the summit of Henry James's American Sublime.

It is not that I have found in growing older any one marked or momentous line in the life of the mind or in the play and the freedom of the imagination to be stepped over; but that a process takes place which I can only describe as the accumulation of the very treasure itself of consciousness. I won't say that "the world," as we commonly refer to it, grows more attaching, but will say that the universe increasingly does, and that this makes us present at the enormous multiplication of our possible relations with it; relations still vague, no doubt, as undefined as they are uplifting, as they are inspiring, to think of, and on a scale beyond our actual use or application, yet filling us (through the "law" in question, the law that consciousness gives us immensities and imaginabilities wherever we direct it) with the unlimited vision of being. This mere fact that so small a part of one's visionary and speculative and emotional activity has even a traceably indirect bearing on one's doings or purposes or particular desires contributes strangely to the luxury—which is the magnificent waste—of thought, and strongly reminds one that even should one cease to be in love with life it would be difficult, on such terms, not to be in love with living.

That is Henry James in his late (1910) essay "Is There a Life after Death?" It speaks also for Milly Theale and her love of living. Of all James's heroines she is presented the most obliquely, and I want to ask why. Richard Blackmur, with whom my literary relations were rather vexed, remarked to me once that I failed to see Milly's moral beauty. I think I murmured as rejoinder that her transcendence took her forgiveness of Kate and Densher beyond mere morality, but Blackmur seemed to confound both Milly Theale and Maggie Verver with Dante's Beatrice, not a very Jamesian identity. The sufferings of Jamesian heroines, while doubtless spiritual, are secular enough.

Where shall we find contexts in antecedent high literature for late James? Shakespeare is more relevant than Dante; *The Tempest* haunts *Wings* and *The Golden Bowl*. Ellipsis, the art of leaving things out, transmits from late Shakespeare to the final James. We know Milly far less overtly than we do Kate Croy, and yet intimations that kindle wonder radiate from the doomed American heiress, whereas Kate deepens perpetually without surprising us. The plotlessness of *The Tempest,* where almost nothing happens while everything is implied, is a model for the meaningful absences of Milly, down through the farewell audience and forgiveness she grants Densher, which we do not see represented.

James divides *Wings* into ten books: It is instructive to read them as the absence or presence of Milly Theale. She is nowhere mentioned in the first two, which concern only Densher and Kate. The third book briefly foregrounds Milly and then shows her European arrival with Susan Stringham, a popular lady novelist of the Boston variety. Book Four brings them to England and to the world of Kate's officious aunt Maud.

In Book Five, Milly becomes London's social lioness and manifests a rare radiance and joy. That is her apogee, since Kate's plot using Densher to court the ailing girl is launched in the sixth book, in the shrewd expectation he will inherit enough of the Theale wealth to make possible his marriage to Kate.

In Book Seven we move to Venice, where at last Milly is realized for us, though from then onward we see only what Milton's Adam calls "A long day's dying to augment our pain." Book Eight features her last social gathering, as she fetes her admirers, and then James allows us to see her just once more, conversing with Densher. That marvelous declaration of her poignant desire for life and love is her legacy to us. Only darknesses follow: The frustrated fortune hunter Lord Mark divulges the truth of Kate and Densher to her, but neither this nor her final meeting with Densher reaches us except by report.

A plot summary generally is tedious, but I give it here to instance James's skill at ellipsis. Milly is an absence in the final movement as at the start, yet her atmosphere envelops Kate, Densher, and the reader. As it is Iago's play but Othello's tragedy, so this is Milly's passion yet Kate's novel. Of Jamesian Dark Ladies, incarnations of the will to live, Kate Croy far surpasses even Charlotte Stant and Madame Merle in imaginative splendor. A heroine-villain of the Protestant will, she seems to me near to Isabel Archer as James's grandest invention of personality. Before meditating upon her in full, I return first to Milly and then to Densher.

The Shakespearean element in Milly renders her more akin to a figure like Perdita in *The Winter's Tale* than to any heroine in Balzac or George Eliot. This makes it peculiarly fitting that James identifies her appearance with the portrait of a sixteenth-century noblewoman by Shakespeare's older contemporary, the Venetian Agnolo Bronzino, in the Uffizi Gallery, Florence. This portrait centers the fifth book, Chapter II:

> Once more things melted together—the beauty and the history and the facility and the splendid midsummer glow: it was a sort of magnificent maximum, the pink dawn of an apotheosis coming so curiously soon. What in fact befell was that, as she afterwards made out, it was Lord Mark who said nothing in particular—it was she herself who said all. She couldn't help that—it came; and the reason it came was that she found herself, for the first moment, looking at the mysterious portrait through tears. Perhaps it was her tears that made it just then so strange and fair—as wonderful as he had said: the face of a young woman, all splendidly drawn, down to the hands, and splendidly dressed; a face almost livid in hue, yet handsome in sadness and crowned with a mass of hair, rolled back and high, that must, before fading with time, have had a family resemblance to her own. The lady in question, at all events, with her slightly Michaelangelesque squareness, her eyes of other days, her full lips, her long neck, her recorded jewels, her brocaded and wasted reds, was a very great personage—only unaccompanied by a joy. And she was dead, dead, dead. Milly recognized her exactly in words that had nothing to do with her. "I shall never be better than this."

> He smiled for her at the portrait. "Than she? You'd scarce need

to be better, for surely that's well enough. But you *are,* one feels, as it happens, better; because, splendid as she is, one doubts if she was good."

He hadn't understood. She was before the picture, but she had turned to him, and she didn't care if for the minute he noticed her tears. It was probably as good a moment as she should ever have with him. It was perhaps as good a moment as she should have with any one, or have in any connexion whatever. "I mean that everything this afternoon has been too beautiful, and that perhaps everything together will never be so right again. I'm very glad therefore you've been a part of it."

As prophecy, neglecting only the brief glory of Densher's false romance, this alas is accurate. Describing beautifully ruined Venice in his *Italian Hours,* James spoke of "the poetry of misfortune," apt enough though Milly's doom is darker. Densher calls her "embodied poetry," which would do as well for Perdita. "Disconcerting poetry," the duplicitous Densher also calls it, and this proves to be what partially saves his spirit and to some degree mitigates his guilt.

Densher and even his implacably lucid Kate ultimately prove less strong than Milly, perhaps because she belongs to fable, fairy tale, the sublime, and they to a less strenuous order of representation: naturalist, pragmatist, realist, Balzac without the Vautrinian daemonism. James—as we would expect—precedes and betters all of us in this. The preface to the New York Edition (1909) kindles to a critical glory:

With the clearness I have just noted, accordingly, the last thing in the world it proposed to itself was to be the record predominantly of a collapse. I don't mean to say that my offered victim was not present to my imagination, constantly, as dragged by a greater force than any she herself could exert; she had been given me from far back as contesting every inch of the road, as catching at every object the grasp of which might make for delay, as clutching these things to the last moment of her strength. Such an attitude and such movements, the passion they expressed and the success they in fact represented, what were they in truth but the soul of drama?—which is the portrayal, as we know, of a catastrophe determined in spite of oppositions. My young woman would *herself* be the opposition—to the catastrophe announced by the associated Fates, powers conspiring to a sinister end and, with their command of means, finally achieving it, yet in such straits really to *stifle* the sacred spark that, obviously, a creature so animated, an adversary so subtle, couldn't but be felt worthy, under whatever weaknesses, of the foreground and the limelight. She would meanwhile wish, moreover, all along, to live for particular things, she would found her struggle on particular human interests, which would inevitably determine, in respect to her, the attitude of other persons, persons affected in such a manner as to make them part of the action. If her impulse to wrest from her shrinking hour still as much of the fruit of life as possible, if this longing can take effect only by the aid of others, their participation (appealed to, entangled and coerced as they find themselves) becomes their drama too—that of their promoting her illusion, under her importunity, for reasons, for interests and advantages, from motives and points of view, of their own. Some of these promptings, evidently, would be of the highest order—others doubtless mightn't; but they would make up together, for her, contributively, her sum of experience, represent to her somehow, in good faith or in bad, what she should have *known*. Somehow, too, at such a rate, one would see the persons subject to them drawn in as by some pool of a Lorelei—see them terrified and tempted and charmed; bribed away, it may even be, from more prescribed and natural orbits, inheriting from their connexion with her strange difficulties and still stranger opportunities, confronted with rare questions and called upon for new discriminations. Thus the scheme of her situation would, in a comprehensive way, see itself constituted; the rest of the interest would be in the number and nature of the particulars. Strong among these, naturally, the need that life should, apart from her infirmity, present itself to our young woman as quite dazzlingly liveable, and that if the great pang for her is in what she must give up we shall appreciate it the more from the sight of all she has . . .

What one had discerned, at all events, from an early stage, was that a young person so devoted and exposed, a creature with her security hanging so by a hair, couldn't but fall somehow into some abysmal trap—this being, dramatically speaking, what such a situation most naturally implied and imposed. Didn't the truth and a great part of the interest also reside in the appearance that she would constitute for others (given her passionate yearning to live while she might) a complication as great as any they might constitute for herself?—which is what I mean when I speak of such matters as "natural." They would be as natural, these tragic, pathetic, ironic, these indeed for the most part sinister, liabilities, to her living associates, as they could be to herself as prime subject. If her story was to consist, as it could so little help doing, of her being let in, as we say, for this, that and the other irreducible anxiety, how could she not have put a premium on the acquisition, by any close sharer of her life, of a consciousness similarly embarrassed? I have named the Rhine-maiden, but our young friend's existence would create rather, all round her, very much that whirlpool movement of the waters produced by the sinking of a big vessel or the failure of a great business; when we figure to ourselves the strong narrowing eddies, the immense force of suction, the general engulfment that, for any neighbouring object, makes immersion inevitable. I need scarce say, however, that in spite of these communities of doom I saw the main dramatic complication much more prepared *for* my vessel of sensibility than by her—the work of other hands (though with her own imbrued too, after all, in the measure of their never not being, in some direction, generous and extravagant, and thereby provoking).

Milly in James's vision is a maelstrom of daemonic force, like Moby Dick's vortex that drowns Ahab, the *Pequod,* and all its crew save Ishmael, as well as a Lorelei or Ondine, whose enchanted melodies also capsize voyagers. Initially startling, this testifies to the Jamesian accomplishment in the extraordinarily mixed genre of *Wings.* In herself totally benign, Milly is a touchstone exposing imaginative flaws in all drawn to her; above all, she illuminates everything in them curtailing the blessing of more life. Paradoxically, though she is stricken (presumably by cancer or tuberculosis), she bears the blessing, even her wealth betokening a Ruskinian aspect: "The only wealth is life."

In Kate Croy, only the will is daemonic, the true Balzacian element in her makeup. My students more often than not are charmed by her, as I always am. A superb adventure in Jamesian characterization, she also, I assume, charmed the master of American prose fiction. He could look upon his work in her and pronounce it more than good, aesthetically rather than ethically. And yet in the otherwise supremely astute and helpful New York Edition preface, he is marvelous both on the Kate-Densher eros and on Densher himself but curiously reserved in regard to Kate. I think she may have surprised him in her relative exuberance and moral pragmatism, her desperate ability to accept the consequences that a Balzacian complexity of conditions and circumstance imposed upon someone who *needed* affluence as the only context in which her gifts could flourish.

In the preface, James calls Kate Croy's sexual surrender (for an hour only) to Densher in Venice her heroic payment—a startling touch, at least to me. In that regard, Kate has little in her of the fierce lust Charlotte Stant manifests toward the pliant Prince Amerigo. What does she find in Densher; what can she want from him? But then James himself seems uncertain as to how admirably he has created her. Is Kate's drive only toward family and redemption, or is hers potentially a free spirit that only a strong will can liberate? I do not believe that readers can agree upon the strength and value of Kate Croy. Is that a blemish of James's art?

Clearly, James's affectionate regard for her is considerable. What is it that Densher loves in her? He praises her "lucidity," which appears to mean her will's drive to accomplish all it plots. As *Wings* approaches its conclusion in Chapter V of Book Ten, Densher offers her his final, unopened letter from the departed Milly:

He waited again a moment. "I love you. It's because I love you that I'm here. It's because I love you that I've brought you this." And he drew from behind him the letter that had remained in his hand.

But her eyes only—though he held it out—met the offer. "Why you've not broken the seal!"

"If I had broken the seal—exactly—I should know what's within. It's for *you* to break the seal that I bring it."

She looked—still not touching the thing—inordinately grave. "To break the seal of something to you from *her*?"

"Ah precisely because it's from her. I'll abide by whatever you think of it."

"I don't understand," said Kate. "What do you yourself think?" And then as he didn't answer: "It seems to me *I* think you know. You have your instinct. You don't need to read. It's the proof."

Densher faced her words as if they had been an accusation, an accusation for which he was prepared and which there was but one way to face. "I have indeed my instinct. It came to me, while I worried it out, last night. It came to me as an effect of the hour." He held up his letter and seemed now to insist more than to confess. "This thing had been timed."

"For Christmas Eve?"

"For Christmas Eve."

Kate had suddenly a strange smile. "The season of gifts!" After which, as he said nothing, she went on: "And had been written, you mean, while she could write, and kept to *be* so timed?"

Only meeting her eyes while he thought, he again didn't reply. "What do *you* mean by the proof?"

"Why of the beauty with which you've been loved. But I won't," she said, "break your seal."

"You positively decline?"

"Positively. Never." To which she added oddly: "I know without."

He had another pause. "And what is it you know?"

"That she announces to you she had made you rich."

His pause this time was longer. "Left me her fortune?"

"Not all of it, no doubt, for it's immense. But money to a large amount. I don't care," Kate went on, "to know how much." And her strange smile recurred. "I trust her."

"Did she tell you?" Densher asked.

"Never!" Kate visibly flushed at the thought. "That wouldn't, on my part, have been playing fair with her. And I did," she added, "play fair."

Densher, who had believed her—he couldn't help it—continued, holding his letter, to face her. He was much quieter now, as if his torment had somehow passed. "You played fair with me, Kate; and that's why—since we talk of proofs—I want to give *you* one. I've wanted to let you see—and in preference even to myself—something I feel as sacred."

She frowned a little. "I don't understand."

"I've asked myself for a tribute, for a sacrifice by which I can peculiarly recognise—"

"Peculiarly recognise what?" she demanded as he dropped.

"The admirable nature of your own sacrifice. You were capable in Venice of an act of splendid generosity."

"And the privilege you offer me with that document is my reward?"

He made a movement. "It's all I can do as a symbol of my attitude."

She looked at him long. "Your attitude, my dear, is that you're afraid of yourself. You've had to take yourself in hand. You've had to do yourself violence."

"So it is then you meet me?"

She bent her eyes hard a moment to the letter, from which her hand still stayed itself. "You absolutely *desire* me to take it?"

"I absolutely desire you to take it."

"To do what I like with it?"

"Short of course of making known its terms. It must remain—pardon my making the point—between you and me."

She had a last hesitation, but she presently broke it. "Trust me." Taking from him the sacred script she held it a little while her eyes again rested on those fine characters of Milly's that they had shortly before discussed. "To hold it," she brought out, "is to know."

"Oh I *know*!" said Merton Densher.

"Well then if we both do—!" She had already turned to the fire, nearer to which she had moved, and with a quick gesture had jerked the thing into the flame. He started—but only half—as to undo her action: his arrest was as prompt as the latter had been decisive. He only watched, with her, the paper burn; after which their eyes again met. "You'll have it all," Kate said, "from New York."

This lengthy passage vindicates James's art, while continuing to give the reader the burden of understanding and judging Kate, Densher, and their mutual love. In the 1909 New York Edition preface, James perfectly calls Densher "a bland Hermes," which leaves not much of the hapless journalist whose attractiveness to the incarnate Female Will (Blake's term) that is Kate and to the vortex that is Milly is not easily understood.

What is cruel about the passage is that both Densher and Kate abuse Milly's trusting, final letter to the bland Hermes, who abandons it, seal unbroken, to Kate, who burns it. Aside from such barbarism, is there any saving grace emanating from this dialogue of lovers? Kate insists that she "played fair" with Milly. That astonishes, considering her plot—now successful—to finance her own eros by consigning Densher to suborn the dying girl's affections. Guilt, remorse, conscience have no part in her. James, like Shakespeare, is complicit, disinterested, above and beyond mere judgment, and so should we be.

Yet does Kate not deceive herself, thus belying her beautiful lucidity? And how should we take Densher's notion that her one-hour sexual surrender to him in Venice was "an act of splendid generosity," indeed a "sacrifice"? Is that the language of a mutual passion?

I do not want to import irrelevant moral distaste into any reader's reaction to the Kate-Densher commercial transaction. Something is aesthetically amiss here, and I wish Walter Pater, who died in Oxford on July 30, 1894, had lived to appreciate *Wings*. In Pater's seminal essay "Style," in his *Appreciations* (1889), the Oxford apostle of Gustave Flaubert, "style's martyr," murmurs sadly against the grain that the burden of the common life makes us finally choose Victor Hugo over Flaubert. Greatness depends on the matter and not style alone, and so Hugo joins Dante, Milton, and the King James Bible in a sublime beyond Flaubert.

By that test, *Wings* touches its limits, or does it? The Kate-Densher aspect of the novel, for all James's brilliance, is common-all-too-common, saved from a sordid kind of hypocrisy by the master's dazzlement of development. Milly's fairy-tale saga is richer and darker, and her imaginative greatness is beyond denial. *Wings* at last is the Milly Theale Passion, another scripture of Emerson's American Religion, akin to *Song of Myself, Moby-Dick, Walden, The Scarlet Letter,* the poems of Emily Dickinson. *Wings* also raises the burden of our common life to a daemonic sublimity.

"The Jolly Corner"

AS EPILOGUE TO HENRY JAMES, I CHOOSE HIS GRAND LATE TALE "THE
Jolly Corner" (1909). Though I would hesitate to call this the best of "the
ghostly tales"—they are almost all superb—it has become part of my consciousness to the extent that I dream about encountering my own daemon, as James's Spencer Brydon confronts his dark double near the story's
end.

The Americanist Millicent Bell suggests that the image Brydon looks
upon—"rigid and conscious, spectral yet human"—may have been alluding to John Singer Sargent's splendid portrait of Henry Lee Higginson,
which James had seen at the Harvard Union in 1904. A cousin of the aggressive soldier-Abolitionist Thomas Wentworth Higginson, the less-fiery
Higginson was also a Civil War hero, having fought in the Union Cavalry
against Jeb Stuart's Confederates and been severely wounded in battle.
After the war, he became a prominent Boston businessman-philanthropist,
founder of the Boston Symphony Orchestra and a major Harvard bene-
factor.

Brydon's specter has a mutilated hand with two missing fingers, but
there the resemblance to Sargent's painting ends. Few tales even by James
are so acutely integrated as "The Jolly Corner," yet the absent fingers are
not explained. Perhaps they augment the daemonic otherness of the apparition, except that, of the two forms—as I will argue—Spencer Brydon
is himself more *daemon* and therefore the scarier and more potent being.

"The Jolly Corner," unlike "The Beast in the Jungle" and other works
of James, is not a parable of the unlived but of the alternate life. Henry
James, himself never more daemonic, designs a shuttle in which Brydon
and the black stranger or dark double stalk each other but with the protagonist more remorseless. His reward is multiform: self-acceptance, reconcilement with past time, above all an exalting and enduring exchange of
love with a woman perfect for him, an instance all but unique in James's
fiction.

In other writers, a ghostly tale that flowers into a love story might be
commonplace; in Henry James it is a wonder. Since Brydon at moments
seems perilously close to a surrogate for the self-exiled master, the wistful

aura that emanates from Alice Staverton may testify to a longing for the ideal (still safely homoerotic) marriage to an intelligently loving woman, never of course to be attained, save in "The Jolly Corner."

Though small in scale, the representation of Alice Staverton is a triumph of tact. She is introduced as Brydon's "old friend":

His old friend lived with one maid and herself dusted her relics and trimmed her lamps and polished her silver; she stood off, in the awful modern crush, when she could, but she sallied forth and did battle when the challenge was really to "spirit," the spirit she after all confessed to, proudly and a little shyly, as to that of the better time, that of *their* common, their quite far-away and antediluvian social period and order. She made use of the street-cars when need be, the terrible things that people scrambled for as the panic-stricken at sea scramble for the boats; she affronted, inscrutably, under stress, all the public concussions and ordeals; and yet, with that slim mystifying grace of her appearance, which defied you to say if she were a fair young woman who looked older through trouble, or a fine smooth older one who looked young through successful indifference; with her precious reference, above all, to memories and histories into which he could enter, she was as exquisite for him as some pale pressed flower (a rarity to begin with), and, failing other sweetnesses, she was a sufficient reward of his effort. They had communities of knowledge, "their" knowledge (this discriminating possessive was always on her lips) of presences of the other age, presences all overlaid, in his case, by the experience of a man and the freedom of a wanderer, overlaid by pleasure, by infidelity, by passages of life that were strange and dim to her, just by "Europe" in short, but still unobscured, still exposed and cherished, under that pious visitation of the spirit from which she had never been diverted.

She had come with him one day to see how his "apartment-house" was rising; he had helped her over gaps and explained to her plans, and while they were there had happened to have, before her, a brief but lively discussion with the man in charge, the representative of the building-firm that had undertaken his work. He had found himself quite "standing-up" to this personage over a failure

on the latter's part to observe some detail of one of their noted
conditions, and had so lucidly argued his case that, besides ever so
prettily flushing, at the time, for sympathy in his triumph, she had
afterwards said to him (though to a slightly greater effect of irony)
that he had clearly for too many years neglected a real gift. If he had
but stayed at home he would have anticipated the inventor of the
sky-scraper. If he had but stayed at home he would have discovered
his genius in time really to start some new variety of awful architec-
tural hare and run it till it burrowed in a gold-mine. He was to remember these words, while the weeks elapsed, for the small silver
ring they had sounded over the queerest and deepest of his own
lately most disguised and most muffled vibrations.

Having waited a third of a century for Brydon's return, Alice Staverton
at first seems like a prolepsis of T. S. Eliot's Emily Hale, who doubtless
goes on waiting for him in the netherworld. Fortunately, the preternaturally patient Alice and Brydon conclude happily by inheriting each other,
after he passes through the ordeal of confronting and routing his alternate
self.

The gradations of the trial by ordeal are wrought by James with a deft-
ness itself daemonic, manifested first as speculation: "very much as he
might have been met by some strange figure, some unexpected occupant,
at a turn of one of the dim passages of an empty house." A richer speculation ensues:

> He found all things come back to the question of what he person-
> ally might have been, how he might have led his life and "turned
> out," if he had not so, at the outset, given it up. And confessing
> for the first time to the intensity within him of this absurd
> speculation—which but proved also, no doubt, the habit of too
> selfishly thinking—he affirmed the impotence there of any other
> source of interest, any other native appeal. "What would it have
> made of me, what would it have made of me? I keep for ever won-
> dering, all idiotically; as if I could possibly know! I see what it has
> made of dozens of others, those I meet, and it positively aches
> within me, to the point of exasperation, that it would have made
> something of me as well. Only I can't make out *what,* and the

worry of it, the small rage of curiosity never to be satisfied, brings back what I remember to have felt, once or twice, after judging best, for reasons, to burn some important letter unopened. I've been sorry, I've hated it—I've never known what was in the letter.

Brydon's own exegesis a third of a century earlier, when he went abroad at twenty-three, is "that I had then a strange *alter ego* deep down somewhere within me," compared to a flower in the bud that blighted in foreign climes. Alice identifies this as a loss of power while making clear that her love for Brydon moves beyond gain or loss:

"You'd have liked me that way?" he asked.

She barely hung fire. "How should I not have liked you?"

"I see. You'd have liked me, have preferred me, a billionaire!"

"How should I not have liked you?" she simply again asked.

He stood before her still—her question kept him motionless. He took it in, so much there was of it; and indeed his not otherwise meeting it testified to that. "I know at least what I am," he simply went on; "the other side of the medal's clear enough. I've not been edifying—I believe I'm thought in a hundred quarters, to have been barely decent. I've followed strange paths and worshipped strange gods; it must have come to you again and again—in fact, you've admitted to me as much—that I was leading, at any time these thirty years, a selfish frivolous scandalous life. And you see what it has made of me."

She just waited, smiling at him. "You see what it has made of *me*."

"Oh you're a person whom nothing can have altered. You were born to be what you are, anywhere, anyway: you've the perfection nothing else could have blighted. And don't you see how, without my exile, I shouldn't have been waiting till now—?" But he pulled up for the strange pang.

"The great thing to see," she presently said, "seems to me to be that it has spoiled nothing. It hasn't spoiled your being here at last. It hasn't spoiled this. It hasn't spoiled your speaking—" She also however faltered.

He wondered at everything her controlled emotion might mean.

"Do you believe then—too dreadfully!—that I *am* as good as I might ever have been?"

"Oh no! Far from it!" With which she got up from her chair and was nearer to him. "But I don't care," she smiled.

"You mean I'm good enough?"

She considered a little. "Will you believe it if I say so? I mean will you let that settle your question for you?" And then as if making out in his face that he drew back from this, that he had some idea which, however absurd, he couldn't yet bargain away: "Oh you don't care either—but very differently: you don't care for anything but yourself."

Spencer Brydon recognised it—it was in fact what he had absolutely professed. Yet he importantly qualified. "*He* isn't myself. He's the just so totally other person. But I do want to see him," he added. "And I can. And I shall."

She is a perfection unblighted by his neglect, but then this passage hesitates on the threshold of mutual recognition that their affinity is daemonic and permanent. Alice's preternatural patience does not belong to the realm of naturalistic representation. More than Brydon yet sees and says, she has found her own way to the end of their story. She divines him more rapidly than we can, since she is his ideal reader and accurate interpreter:

What she said however was unexpected. "Well, *I've* seen him."

"You—?"

"I've seen him in a dream."

"Oh a 'dream'—!" It let him down.

"But twice over," she continued. "I saw him as I see you now."

"You've dreamed the same dream—?"

"Twice over," she repeated. "The very same."

This did somehow a little speak to him, as it also gratified him. "You dream about me at that rate?"

"Ah about *him*!" she smiled.

His eyes again sounded her. "Then you know all about him." And as she said nothing more: "What's the wretch like?"

She hesitated, and it was as if he were pressing her so hard that, resisting for reasons of her own, she had to turn away. "I'll tell you some other time!"

She *knows* yet realizes he must learn it for and by himself. Brydon's quest for his daemon occupies Part II of "The Jolly Corner." He keeps night vigils in his empty ancestral house while he and his "alter ego" roam about, just missing each other. Until at last the confrontation takes place:

> Rigid and conscious, spectral yet human, a man of his own substance and stature waited there to measure himself with his power to dismay. This only could it be—this only till he recognised, with his advance, that what made the face dim was the pair of raised hands that covered it and in which, so far from being offered in defiance, it was buried as for dark deprecation. So Brydon, before him, took him in; with every fact of him now, in the higher light, hard and acute—his planted stillness, his vivid truth, his grizzled bent head and white masking hands, his queer actuality of evening-dress, of dangling double eye-glass, of gleaming silk lappet and white linen, of pearl button and gold watch-guard and polished shoe. No portrait by a great modern master could have presented him with more intensity, thrust him out of his frame with more art, as if there had been "treatment," of the consummate sort, in his every shade and salience. The revulsion, for our friend, had become, before he knew it, immense—this drop, in the act of apprehension, to the sense of his adversary's inscrutable manoeuvre. That meaning at least, while he gaped, it offered him; for he could but gape at his other self in this other anguish, gape as a proof that *he,* standing there for the achieved, the enjoyed, the triumphant life, couldn't be faced in his triumph. Wasn't the proof in the splendid covering hands, strong and completely spread?—so spread and so intentional that, in spite of a special verity that surpassed every other, the fact that one of these hands had lost two fingers, which were reduced to stumps, as if accidentally shot away, the face was effectually guarded and saved.
>   "Saved," though, *would* it be?—Brydon breathed his wonder till the very impunity of his attitude and the very insistence of his eyes produced, as he felt, a sudden stir which showed the next instant as

a deeper portent, while the head raised itself, the betrayal of a braver purpose. The hands, as he looked, began to move, to open; then, as if deciding in a flash, dropped from the face and left it uncovered and presented. Horror, with the sight, had leaped into Brydon's throat, gasping there in a sound he couldn't utter; for the bared identity was too hideous as *his,* and his glare was the passion of his protest. The face, *that* face, Spencer Brydon's?—he searched it still, but looking away from it in dismay and denial, falling straight from his height of sublimity. It was unknown, inconceivable, awful, disconnected from any possibility—! He had been "sold," he inwardly moaned, stalking such game as this: the presence before him was a presence, the horror within him a horror, but the waste of his nights had been only grotesque and the success of his adventure an irony. Such an identity fitted his at *no* point, made its alternative monstrous. A thousand times yes, as it came upon him nearer now—the face was the face of a stranger. It came upon him nearer now, quite as one of those expanding fantastic images projected by the magic lantern of childhood; for the stranger, whoever he might be, evil, odious, blatant, vulgar, had advanced as for aggression, and he knew himself give ground. Then harder pressed still, sick with the force of his shock, and falling back as under the hot breath and the roused passion of a life larger than his own, a rage of personality before which his own collapsed, he felt the whole vision turn to darkness and his very feet give way. His head went round; he was going; he had gone.

Is this self-revulsion as to what he could have become or yet might be? Either way, Brydon faints and is revived by Alice, in more than one sense of revival:

"It must have been that I *was.*" He made it out as she held him. "Yes—I can only have died. You brought me literally to life. Only," he wondered, his eyes rising to her, "only, in the name of all the benedictions, how?"

It took her but an instant to bend her face and kiss him, and something in the manner of it, and in the way her hands clasped and locked his head while he felt the cool charity and virtue of her lips, something in all this beatitude somehow answered everything. "And now I keep you," she said.

"Oh keep me, keep me!" he pleaded while her face still hung over him: in response to which it dropped again and stayed close, clingingly close. It was the seal of their situation—of which he tasted the impress for a long blissful moment in silence. But he came back. "Yet how did you know—?"

"I was uneasy. You were to have come, you remember—and you had sent no word."

"Yes, I remember—I was to have gone to you at one to-day." It caught on to their "old" life and relation—which were so near and so far. "I was still out there in my strange darkness—where was it, what was it? I must have stayed there so long." He could but wonder at the depth and the duration of his swoon.

"Keep" is the mutual word of their love, so long delayed for this fulfillment. The black stranger or dusky daemon, like and unlike, is also taken into her keeping:

It brought Spencer Brydon to his feet. "You 'like' that horror—?"

"I *could* have liked him. And to me," she said, "he was no horror. I had accepted him."

"'Accepted'—?" Brydon oddly sounded.

"Before, for the interest of his difference—yes. And as *I* didn't disown him, as *I* knew him—which you at last, confronted with him in his difference, so cruelly didn't, my dear—well, he must have been, you see, less dreadful to me. And it may have pleased him that I pitied him."

She was beside him on her feet, but still holding his hand—still with her arm supporting him. But though it all brought for him thus a dim light, "You 'pitied' him?" he grudgingly, resentfully asked.

"He has been unhappy, he has been ravaged," she said.

"And haven't I been unhappy? Am not I—you've only to look at me!—ravaged?"

"Ah I don't say I like him *better*," she granted after a thought. "But he's grim, he's worn—and things have happened to him. He doesn't make shift, for sight, with your charming monocle."

"No"—it struck Brydon; "I couldn't have sported mine 'downtown.' They'd have guyed me there."

"His great convex pince-nez—I saw it, I recognised the kind—is for his poor ruined sight. And his poor right hand—!"

"Ah!" Brydon winced—whether for his proved identity or for his lost fingers. Then, "He has a million a year," he lucidly added. "But he hasn't you."

"And he isn't—no, he isn't—*you*!" she murmured as he drew her to his breast.

One wonders if ever Henry James was more the master than here? Brydon's "lucidity" at the close echoes Kate Croy's in *The Wings of the Dove*. But his fate is finer than hers: Alice, unlike Milly a survivor, has stretched out her wings, and it is to Brydon that they reach. They cover him.

IV.

MARK TWAIN
and ROBERT FROST

MARK TWAIN

The Adventures of Huckleberry Finn

O F THE DOZEN AUTHORS STUDIED IN THIS BOOK, ONLY TWAIN and Frost join the earlier Emerson and Hawthorne as national writers acknowledged in their own time. The reputations of Whitman, Melville, Dickinson, and Henry James were still being established during my opening years as a university teacher (1955–60), and much the same was true of Stevens, Faulkner, and Hart Crane. Eliot was celebrated from the 1920s on but only by an elite audience. Emerson, who had an original relation to the universe, all but began as the national sage, since the initial resistance to him soon crumbled. Hawthorne, much more than Henry Wadsworth Longfellow and the other Fireside Poets, was widely seen during all of the nineteenth century as our prime imaginative writer.

From about 1876 on, Mark Twain made a second luminary, alongside Hawthorne. Except for Longfellow, we had no national poet until the emergence of Robert Frost in 1915 (with books first published in England in 1913–14). Frost's American triumphs with a burgeoning readership surged on from 1915 to 1963 with *In the Clearing,* his final book.

When I began composing *The Daemon Knows,* I did not plan to include Twain and Frost, though I had considered doing so. What was decisive was the realization that they were our closest analogues to the French, German, Italian, Russian, and British national writers of the nineteenth and twentieth centuries: Hugo, Balzac, Émile Zola, Goethe, Thomas Mann, Alessandro Manzoni, Tolstoy, Alexandr Pushkin, Dostoyevsky, Ivan Turgenev, Dickens, George Eliot, Tennyson, Yeats. I set aside here such daemonic luminaries as Ibsen, Joyce, Proust, Kafka, Beckett, Valéry, even T. S. Eliot, as these spoke to an elite, as did Whitman, Melville, Henry James, Stevens, Hart Crane, and the sublime Faulkner of *As I Lay Dying* and *Light in August*.

Twain and Frost wrote on several levels, some apparently populist yet deeply darkened with the human truths of annihilation. Frost, a classical ironist, had few overt affinities with Twain, a Swiftian parodist more savage than his descendants Nathanael West and Philip Roth. Their only common element was the common reader, who found in them what could suffice.

After finishing *The Adventures of Huckleberry Finn*, Twain wrote his *Pierre* (as it were) with *A Connecticut Yankee in King Arthur's Court*. *Pierre* is unreadable, but *A Connecticut Yankee* is offensive, a rather nasty work: sadistic, in the manner of a bad joke attempting to rescue itself by increasing brutalities. I recall seeing a film version many years ago with Bing Crosby playing Hank Morgan, in a genial softening of Twain. Bad as the movie was, I would rather endure it again than reread the novel, as I just have after many years.

My late friend Robert Penn Warren, who loathed Emerson and was indifferent to Whitman, considered nineteenth-century American imaginative literature to have achieved an apotheosis in Mark Twain, with Melville and John Greenleaf Whittier also admitted to admiration. Something of Warren's ferocity toward the protagonists of his own fiction caught its zeal from Twain's ambivalence toward most of his adult creations.

In our weekly luncheons, before Warren went off to research at the Yale library and I stumbled out to teach, he discoursed eagerly upon our national literature. A quarter century his junior, I mostly listened and learned, dissenting only upon Emerson, whom at last we agreed never to discuss again.

Warren saw Mark Twain as the ultimate American nihilist, but that was a bad eminence he also granted to the abhorred Emerson, champion of the murderous John Brown. A secular Augustinian, Warren would not agree with my seeing Twain as a secular American Gnostic, damning Yahweh as the God of this hellish world.

I first met my late friend James Cox in the summer of 1969, when he kindly gave me a copy of his splendid *Mark Twain: The Fate of Humor* (1966). It remains for me the most illuminating of Twain studies, because it argues that this parodistic humor subverts and unmasks all of the demands made upon us by the censorious superego. Parody could not save Mark Twain from himself, yet it opened his daemon to the great achievement of *The Adventures of Huckleberry Finn* (1885), a work of the stature of *The Scarlet Letter, Moby-Dick,* and *Leaves of Grass.* If our literature has produced a single work of universal appeal, popular *and* elitist, it must be the story of Huck Finn. There are only a few dissenters: Jane Smiley, who insists she prefers *Uncle Tom's Cabin,* and a phalanx of ecocritics who shrug Twain and Huck away as mere materialists who entertained equivocal stances toward nature. I do not adhere to this school but agree in a limited way: Huck's longed-for "freedom" is not natural. Freedom for both Mark Twain and his daemon Huck Finn is the freedom of the storyteller, partly alienated from society and from nature.

I turn now to freshly reread *The Adventures of Huckleberry Finn,* centering upon Huck himself, whose character and personality reflect the lifelong act of renaming by which Samuel Langhorne Clemens became Mark Twain, at once scathing critic yet also embodiment of the Gilded Age, which he named. As a financial speculator, he came to resemble Jay Gould rather more than Huck Finn.

The great dragon guarding *The Adventures of Huckleberry Finn* cannot be slain: black slavery and all its consequences for the spirit of the fourteen-year-old Huck, who need never grow up. Toni Morrison, in an essay included in the Norton Critical Edition, has had what could be the last word here:

Pleasant as this relationship is, suffused as it is by a lightness they both enjoy and a burden of responsibility both assume, it cannot continue. Knowing the relationship is discontinuous, doomed to separation, is (or used to be) typical of the experience of white/ black childhood friendships (mine included), and the cry of inevitable rupture is all the more anguished by being mute. Every reader knows that Jim will be dismissed without explanation at some point; that no enduring adult fraternity will emerge. Anticipating this loss may have led Twain to the over-the-top minstrelization of Jim.

This perhaps is founded on the assumption that *The Adventures of Huckleberry Finn* is a Balzacian novel or a Woolfian-Faulknerian blend, like the best earlier narratives of Morrison. However, Twain's masterpiece is Cervantine and belongs to the Quixotic order of play. Huck is as evasive as Walt Whitman: The goal of the book and its protagonist is a freedom whose single aim is storytelling pleasure.

T. S. Eliot, in an essay that magnified the Mississippi River into Huck's god, nevertheless observed usefully the high quality of Huck's awareness. The boy sees everything and everyone and avoids all judging. He decidedly is not a critic. Always interested, he nevertheless is remarkably disinterested. For a fourteen-year-old, Huck is uncanny in certain aspects of maturity and knowledge. But then he is not just Mark Twain's daemon; the storytelling genius of America is incarnate in him, and its principles are: evade, escape, keep lying against time.

Huck's father is murderous, alcoholic, hateful. You have to flee from him; otherwise, you have to slay him before he kills you, and Huck has no interest in hurting anyone. Unlike in *The Adventures of Tom Sawyer,* the violence of Huck's book is incessant. With a Shakespearean detachment, Huck records much of what he sees and hears while saying little in response. But we learn over and again the pragmatic goodness of the boy. Nigger Jim says it best: "Dah you goes, de ole true Huck; de on'y white genlman dat ever kep' his promise to ole Jim."

Defining Huck's character is difficult, in part because he is not a quester striving to attain a goal. Cox sensibly emphasizes that Huck's journey is "a flight *from* tyranny, not a flight toward freedom." A survivor, virtually a refugee, the boy has become expert in the arts of evasion and dissimulation.

My students do not consider *The Adventures of Huckleberry Finn* to be a tale "about" cruelty. Initially that surprised me; gradually I have joined their party. I recall arguing with James Cox his strong contention, following Sigmund Freud, that the cruelty ensues from conscience, the censorious superego that wallops us, shouting, "Do not be so aggressive!" and then hits us harder the more we surrender aggressivity. That is Freud's grimly humorous Punch-and-Judy show but not Mark Twain's, whose humor is parodistic and sidles away even from the pleasure principle.

Cox has the virtue of bravely attempting to explain why Mark Twain could not maintain the glory of Huck Finn's book during the quarter century remaining to him: The culprit is conscience.

Why am I not persuaded? Mark Twain and Sigmund Freud were contemporaries and shared dark views of mankind. Huck declines that sharing, though he knows more than enough to have justified it. Here I agree with another much-missed friend, Red Warren:

> Huck is, in short, an antinomian of an educable "consciousness," not of the absolute "conscience." As an antinomian, he is much closer to the naturalist William James than to the idealist Emerson; he would recognize, even in the moment when he violates "conscience" and follows the dictates of "consciousness," putting his soul in jeopardy of hellfire, that a crucial decision is always a gamble (the awareness that there is no absolute standard by which a choice is to be judged). Furthermore, if the consciousness has been educated to the freedom of choice, the process has also been an education in humility—not only humility but charity—and this aspect of Huck's development comes into focus (there are many other aspects of it) when he learns to recognize and accept the love of a creature for whom he had had only the white man's contempt, however amiable, and whose company he had originally accepted only because of an animal loneliness. And here we may recall that if Jim comes to Huck originally in the moment of loneliness, it is significant that when Huck goes to seek Jim after his reported capture, the description of the Phelps plantation is centered on the impression of loneliness: ". . . then I knowed for certain I wished I was dead—for that the distant wail and hum of a spinning wheel is the lonesomest sound in the whole world."

The freedom of consciousness enables the storyteller's liberty, and Huck gives us more than the narrative of his isolated self. Who else in Western prose fiction is as free of malice as Huck Finn? There are Cer-

vantes's Mournful Knight and Sancho, Dickens's Samuel Pickwick, and
Joyce's Poldy Bloom. Pap Finn calls him the Angel of Death when he attempts to butcher Huck, but that is an inversion of actuality.

Twain's one full-length masterwork is a comedy only because it concludes insouciantly. Of no genre, Twain's book of the daemon has been
creatively misread by Sherwood Anderson and Hemingway, Fitzgerald
and J. D. Salinger. To different degrees, they interpreted it as a parable of
their own inception and as nostalgia for a lost American dream. Their
Huck is not a shape-shifter. Twain's Huck *wants* to stay the same, yet his
need to keep moving means he must change. It is as though his creator,
Twain, wants him to emulate Benjamin Franklin and Henry Thoreau but
cannot keep Huck away from Emersonianism. *Contra* Eliot, the river,
though a refuge, is not Huck's god. There is a god within us, Emerson tells
us. This god speaks when it will. Genius, daemon, god—they were the
same to Huck, who used none of these names, and to Emerson, who did.
The aesthetic wonder of Huck's book centers upon not the river but the
life it makes possible for Jim and Huck:

> Two or three days and nights went by; I reckon I might say they
> swum by, they slid along so quiet and smooth and lovely. Here is the
> way we put in the time. It was a monstrous big river down there—
> sometimes a mile and a half wide; we run nights, and laid up and
> hid daytimes; soon as night was most gone, we stopped navigating
> and tied up—nearly always in the dead water under a towhead; and
> then cut young cotton-woods and willows and hid the raft with
> them. Then we set out the lines. Next we slid into the river and had
> a swim, so as to freshen up and cool off; then we set down on the
> sandy bottom where the water was about knee deep, and watched
> the daylight come. Not a sound, anywheres—perfectly still—just
> like the whole world was asleep, only sometimes the bull-frogs a-
> cluttering, maybe. The first thing to see, looking away over the
> water, was a kind of dull line—that was the woods on t'other side—
> you couldn't make nothing else out; then a pale place in the sky;
> then more paleness, spreading around; then the river softened up,
> away off, and warn't black any more, but gray; you could see little
> dark spots drifting along, ever so far away—trading scows, and
> such things; and long black streaks—rafts; sometimes you could

hear a sweep screaking; or jumbled up voices, it was so still, and sounds come so far; and by and by you could see a streak on the water which you know by the look of the streak that there's a snag there in a swift current which breaks on it and makes that streak look that way; and you see the mist curl up off of the water, and the east reddens up, and the river, and you make out a log cabin in the edge of the woods, away on the bank on t'other side of the river, being a wood-yard, likely, and piled by them cheats so you can throw a dog through it anywheres; then the nice breeze springs up, and comes fanning you from over there, so cool and fresh, and sweet to smell, on account of the woods and the flowers; but sometimes not that way, because they've left dead fish laying around, gars, and such, and they do get pretty rank; and next you've got the full day, and everything smiling in the sun, and the songbirds just going it!

There is no creator-god in the cosmos of Huck, Jim, and Mark Twain. Just two paragraphs on in the chapter, Jim initially argues for such a god, but Huck chooses otherwise:

Sometimes we'd have that whole river all to ourselves for the longest time. Yonder was the banks and the islands, across the water; and maybe a spark—which was a candle in a cabin window—and sometimes on the water you could see a spark or two—on a raft or a scow, you know; and maybe you could hear a fiddle or a song coming over from one of them crafts. It's lovely to live on a raft. We had the sky, up there, all speckled with stars, and we used to lay on our backs and look up at them, and discuss about whether they was made, or only just happened—Jim he allowed they was made, but I allowed they happened; I judged it would have took too long to *make* so many. Jim said the moon could a *laid* them; well, that looked kind of reasonable, so I didn't say nothing against it, because I've seen a frog lay most as many, so of course it could be done. We used to watch the stars that fell, too, and see them streak down. Jim allowed they'd got spoiled and was hove out of the nest.

Accident is king, having replaced Yahweh. Except for Eliot, my daemonic authors in this book were not Christians, and Twain shows a particular vehemence against normative faith. Unlike Huck's, though, Twain's skepticism is not cheerful.

Pudd'nhead Wilson

MELVILLE, HAVING TRIUMPHED IN *MOBY-DICK*, PROCEEDED TO FOUNDER in *Pierre*, which I continue to find unreadable after several attempts, including a recent setback. Clemens, four years after *The Adventures of Huckleberry Finn*, published *A Connecticut Yankee in King Arthur's Court* (1889), readable but awkwardly unworthy of him. The most balanced judgment is that of James Cox:

> Thus, in much the same way that its motive turns within it from creation toward destruction, the book stands as a turning point in Twain's career. The work is not a destructive act however; rather it is an incomplete creative gesture, leaving an opening—a ligature— between the form and creative personality of the artist. As such a gesture, *A Connecticut Yankee* is what we may call Mark Twain's treaty with his Genius, for Hank Morgan in the last analysis is the unmasked demon—the practical joker and compulsive showman— so much a part of Mark Twain's humor. Seen in such a way the book is a great comedian's nightmare vision of himself, grotesquely exposing the secret manipulator behind the mechanism of the comic performance. The terms of the treaty may not be as favorable as we would wish, but they were the best that Twain could make with the fatalities of his art. Revealing as it does the inexorable logic of a creative life, the book stands as a channel marker which Mark Twain left behind him in his precarious voyage downstream.

I wish something could be salvaged from the book, but it is too sadistic to be funny, rather like a Quentin Tarantino film. Twain evidently had been reading Thomas Carlyle's *The French Revolution* and *Sartor Resartus*, two of my favorite works, but he weakly misinterpreted the Scottish sage's demolition of democracy while also distorting the Hartford mechanic into a Carlylean hero. Hank Morgan, who proudly becomes "the Boss" of Britain, is just as much a spurious showman as his enemy Merlin,

and technology makes him finally a genocidal mass murderer. It is difficult
to see and know how aware Twain is of this development. His authorial
intention certainly was to exalt Hank Morgan; Clemens himself was
gadget-mad and worshipped Andrew Carnegie with the same fervor he
devoted to Ulysses Grant.

After Twain's Mississippi writings—including *Tom Sawyer* and
Huckleberry Finn—*Pudd'nhead Wilson* now seems his major work. It was
published five years after *A Connecticut Yankee*, in 1894, to mixed reviews. I scarcely was aware of it until the autumn of 1955, when I first met
the genial Leslie Fiedler and he urged me to read it. At first it puzzled me,
yet through the years I came to appreciate its daemonic ironies.

A large critical literature now surrounds *Pudd'nhead Wilson*, commencing with Leslie Fiedler and the British moralist F. R. Leavis, continuing through to such major interpreters of Twain as Henry Nash Smith and
James Cox, and on to a regiment of historicists, gender enthusiasts, and
other ideologues. A dozen of these cluster in the Norton Critical Edition
of *Pudd'nhead Wilson*. I have read them as well as various other "war-
whoops" (the word is Twain's) and am instructed. None of them ask: Is
the book a pleasure to read and what, if any, is its aesthetic achievement?

My own students do not take to it, partly because a person of twenty
finds the notion of a one-thirty-second touch of the tarbrush to be not
very stirring. The South's version of the Nazi Nuremberg Laws is now too
quaint to outrage a generation where every group will marry into every
other. I doubt Faulkner ever read *Pudd'nhead Wilson* yet it presages *Light
in August,* one of his strongest narratives, and *Absalom, Absalom!,* widely
praised but toward which I harbor some reservations. The prolepsis is
only thematic, since Twain and Faulkner have little in common except the
latter's even more intense apprehension of Southern miscegenation.

Pudd'nhead Wilson is rather less than a fully achieved work of fictional
art, a view I recall arguing with Leslie Fiedler, who regarded it as amazingly good. Only after Leslie's death in 2003 did I read his essay on what
he called "a nightmare worthy of America."

For him the book was *Huckleberry Finn*'s even darker side:

Perhaps the best way to understand *Pudd'nhead* is to read it as a
complement to *Huckleberry Finn*, a dark mirror image of a world
evoked in the earlier work. Nearly ten years come between the two

books, ten years in which guilt and terror had passed from the periphery of Twain's life and imagination to their center. *Huckleberry Finn* is also steeped in horror, to be sure; but it is easier to know this than to feel it. Though the main fable of the earlier book begins with a boy standing off with a rifle, his father gone berserk with the D.T.'s, and ends with the revelation of that father's death in a seedy and flooded room scrawled with obscenities, it has so poetic a texture, so genuine though unmotivated a tone of joy—that one finds himself eternally doubting his own sense of its terrible import. In *Pudd'nhead*, however, the lyricism and the euphoria are gone; we have fallen to a world of prose, and there are no triumphs of Twain's rhetoric to preserve us from the revealed failures of our own humanity.

The tone of *Pudd'nhead Wilson* is original, even for Twain, a parodistic irony unlike anything else in our literature before Nathanael West's *A Cool Million,* where Shagpoke Whipple (a version of Calvin Coolidge and prophecy of Ronald Reagan) speaks to the Davy Crockett boys (in coonskin caps and bearing loaded muskets) at Madison Square Garden, culminating in an American version of a Hitler Youth jamboree. West's subject is Lemuel Pitkin, the book's hapless and dismantled protagonist, who becomes an involuntary Horst Wessel, an early Nazi martyr.

Of what is it that he [Lemuel Pitkin] speaks? Of the right of every American boy to go into the world and there receive fair play and a chance to make his fortune by industry or probity without being laughed at or conspired against by sophisticated aliens.

Twain is not that outrageous (except in my favorites among his sketches, "Cannibalism in the Cars" and "Journalism in Tennessee"), but there are curious tonalities throughout *Pudd'nhead Wilson.* To appreciate them, the peculiar contours of the sadly mechanical plot need rehearsal. Twain had begun a farcical tale, *Those Extraordinary Twins,* about "a human creature that had two heads, two necks, four arms, and one body, with a single pair of legs attached." They are the Counts Luigi and Angelo Cappello. Eventually one is lynched; the other survives. This unpromising parable was sensibly amputated from what became *Pudd'nhead Wilson,* though traces of it linger.

Only one character in the finished novel engages the reader—the slave Roxana (Roxy). She is regarded by everyone, including herself, as a "nigger," though she is only one-sixteenth black and is "white" in appearance. Henry Nash Smith, a critic of authentic discernment, finds in Roxy a "subversive threat to the dominant culture." One wants her to be such a threat but alas she isn't, for the slavers have imprinted their racism upon her. Otherwise she is exuberant, vital, dangerous, and prideful in most things. Roxy is not only unique in Mark Twain, there is no one else in American literature who resembles her.

But who and what is she?

From Roxy's manner of speech, a stranger would have expected her to be black, but she was not. Only one-sixteenth of her was black, and that sixteenth did not show. She was of majestic form and stature, her attitudes were imposing and statuesque, and her gestures and movements distinguished by a noble and stately grace. Her complexion was very fair, with the rosy glow of vigorous health in the cheeks, her face was full of character and expression, her eyes were brown and liquid, and she had a heavy suit of fine soft hair which was also brown, but the fact was not apparent because her head was bound about with a checkered handkerchief and the hair was concealed under it. Her face was shapely, intelligent, and comely—even beautiful. She had an easy, independent carriage—when she was among her own caste—and a high and "sassy" way, withal; but of course she was meek and humble enough where white people were.

To all intents and purposes Roxy was as white as anybody, but the one-sixteenth of her which was black out-voted the other fifteen parts and made her a negro. She was a slave, and salable as such.

The implicit ferocity of tone here is controlled by a master hand. I cannot recall any other woman in Twain who is presented as being so attractive. Circumspect as to his own desires, except sometimes in letters to his wife or in private jottings, Twain nearly is released from his censors—societal and personal—in regard to Roxy.

She is not idealized: Roxy is a petty thief, yet Twain defends her massively:

Was she bad? Was she worse than the general run of her race? No. They had an unfair show in the battle of life, and they held it no sin to take military advantage of the enemy—in a small way; in a small way, but not in a large one. They would smouch provisions from the pantry whenever they got a chance; or a brass thimble, or a cake of wax, or an emery-bag, or a paper of needles, or a silver spoon, or a dollar bill, or small articles of clothing, or any other property of light value; and so far were they from considering such reprisals sinful, that they would go to church and shout and pray their loudest and sincerest with their plunder in their pockets. A farm smokehouse had to be kept heavily padlocked, for even the colored deacon himself could not resist a ham when Providence showed him in a dream, or otherwise, where such a thing hung lonesome and longed for someone to love. But with a hundred hanging before him the deacon would not take two—that is, on the same night. On frosty nights the humane negro prowler would warm the end of a plank and put it up under the cold claws of chickens roosting in a tree; a drowsy hen would step onto the comfortable board, softly clucking her gratitude, and the prowler would dump her into his bag, and later into his stomach, perfectly sure that in taking this trifle from the man who daily robbed him of an inestimable treasure—his liberty—he was not committing any sin that God would remember against him in the Last Great Day.

This has the fine relish of Twain greatly enjoying what he writes. It is then overmatched when Percy Northumberland Driscoll, Missouri slaveholder and proud grandee of Old Virginia First Families vintage, discovers that three of his four servants (Roxy being the other) have pilfered a few of his dollars. He threatens them with sale down the river, where the lash awaits them, and they confess:

"Very good," said the master, putting up his watch, "I will sell you *here,* though you don't deserve it. You ought to be sold down the river."

The culprits flung themselves prone, in an ecstasy of gratitude, and kissed his feet, declaring that they would never forget his goodness and never cease to pray for him as long as they lived. They were sincere, for like a god he had stretched forth his mighty hand and closed the gates of hell against them. He knew, himself, that he had done a noble and gracious thing, and he was privately well pleased with his magnanimity; and that night he set the incident down in his diary, so that his son might read it in after years and be thereby moved to deeds of gentleness and humanity himself.

The irony here is proleptic, since his son, Thomas à Becket Driscoll, will lose his identity and name to Roxy's son, born on the same day, with the slave name of Valet de Chambre, known as "Chambers":

She stepped over and glanced at the other infant; she flung a glance back at her own; then one more at the heir of the house. Now a strange light dawned in her eyes, and in a moment she was lost in thought. She seemed in a trance; when she came out of it she muttered, "When I 'uz a-washin' 'em in de tub, yistiddy, his own pappy asked me which of 'em was his'n."

She began to move about like one in a dream. She undressed Thomas à Becket, stripping him of everything, and put the tow-linen shirt on him. She put his coral necklace on her own child's neck. Then she placed the children side by side, and after earnest inspection she muttered—

"Now who would b'lieve clo'es could do de like o' dat? Dog my cats if it ain't all *I* kin do to tell t'other fum which, let alone his pappy."

She put her cub in Tommy's elegant cradle and said—

"You's young Marse *Tom* fum dis out, en I got to practice and git used to 'memberin' to call you dat, honey, or I's gwyne to make a mistake some time en git us bofe into trouble. Dah—now you lay still en don't fret no mo', Marse Tom—oh, thank de good Lord in heaven, you's saved, you's saved!—dey ain't no man kin ever sell mammy's po' little honey down de river now!"

Alas, Roxy's child, the false Tom Driscoll, will grow up a petulant and selfish wastrel, while the actual Driscoll heir becomes a stalwart if docile slave. Poor Roxy's duplicity is rewarded by vicious treatment from her own child. After Percy Driscoll's death, Roxy, set free by his will, goes off to a better life as a chambermaid on a Cincinnati–to–New Orleans excursion boat on the Mississippi. But she returns after becoming ill and then losing her savings, hoping that her miscreant son (who does not know she is his mother) will have softened toward her.

The brat, however, is now a monster and provokes her into revealing the truth of his identity. Nothing redeems the insufferable Tom; indeed, he worsens at the revelation:

> Every now and then, after Tom went to bed, he had sudden wakings out of his sleep, and his first thought was, "O, joy, it was all a dream!" Then he laid himself heavily down again, with a groan and the muttered words, "A nigger!—I am a nigger!—oh, I wish I was dead!"
>
> He woke at dawn with one more repetition of this horror, and then he resolved to meddle no more with that treacherous sleep. He began to think. Sufficiently bitter thinkings they were. They wandered along something after this fashion:
>
> "Why were niggers *and* whites made? What crime did the uncreated first nigger commit that the curse of birth was decreed for him? And why is this awful difference made between white and black? . . . How hard the nigger's fate seems, this morning!—yet until last night such a thought never entered my head."

With adroitly labyrinthine turnings, Twain traces Tom Driscoll's out-and-down self-destruction. After selling his own mother down the river, he culminates by murdering his supposed uncle and guardian, is sentenced to life imprisonment, and is released to be sold down the river as a slave. Poor Roxy finds whatever consolation she can in the black church, but even her indomitable spirit at last breaks.

After *Huckleberry Finn, Tom Sawyer,* and *Life on the Mississippi, Pudd'nhead Wilson* is Twain's most enduring work, but what are its aesthetic merits? Wilson himself is a cipher; Tom Driscoll also has no personality. Roxana is the only strength of the book, aside from Twain's daemonic ingenuity at freshly depicting the outrage of slavery. Somewhere in his journal Twain remarked: "The skin of every human being contains a slave."

Aside from the character of Roxana, the book comes alive in the frequent savagery of Twain's tone. In effect, his narrative voice intimates that God or the gods sell all of us down the river, there to be lashed like so many slaves, whether we are black or pinko-gray (E. M. Forster's exquisite term for "white").

That my study of Mark Twain in this book should be less extensive than my accounts of the other eleven authors is not an indication of lower critical esteem. Essentially he is magnificent only in *The Adventures of Huckleberry Finn,* though *Tom Sawyer* and *Life on the Mississippi* retain their freshness, as do the best of the stories and sketches. Yet the later writings disappoint me when I reread them, including *The Mysterious Stranger* and the *Autobiography.* The daemon abandoned him. Why? We can surmise that his vein of Swiftian irony cost him too much, as it did Jonathan Swift himself.

Still, how many books by an American stand upon the heights with *Huckleberry Finn?* Rivals are few: *The Scarlet Letter, Leaves of Grass, Moby-Dick.* In that exalted company, works as vital as *Walden, The Portrait of a Lady,* and *As I Lay Dying* do not quite find unquestioning assent.

There is no American Shakespeare or Chaucer, though Whitman comes closest and Dickinson, Frost, Stevens, and Hart Crane approach Walt's splendor. The scope of Henry James's writing—fiction, travel, criticism, memoir—astonishes, and invariably his work is superb, yet Tolstoy, Dickens, and Balzac have a Shakespearean immediacy that James lacks. Anna Karenina and Pierre, Uriah Heep and Fagin, Vautrin and Goriot, convey an illusion of actual existence so richly textured that even Isabel Archer seems insubstantial in their company.

Mark Twain's triumph in his one great book places him in the company of Dickens and Balzac, though not of Shakespeare and Tolstoy. Huck himself is joined by Nigger Jim, the scary Pap Finn, those wonderful scamps the Duke and the Dauphin, and others in a carnival of personalities turbulent and supple in act and stance. To have created one book so crammed with life is enough and more than enough to live forever.

ROBERT FROST

I LIKE TO BEGIN TEACHING FROST BY ASKING STUDENTS TO READ AND DISCUSS Emerson's *Uriel,* judged by Frost as "the greatest Western poem yet." (I take "Western" there to mean "American.") *Uriel* is a very good poem but hardly superior to *Song of Myself,* Dickinson's crisis lyrics, *Notes Toward a Supreme Fiction, The Waste Land, The Bridge,* or Frost at his frequent best.

In a brief speech, "On Emerson" (October 8, 1958), Frost listed the four Americans he most admired: Washington, Jefferson, Lincoln, and Emerson—three presidents and a poet-essayist. Freedom in the Emersonian sense, which to Frost is the reason for his discipleship, is another name for "the Wildness," or daemonic possession.

Robert Frost manifested extraordinary cunning as person and as poet. I met him twice, in 1960 or so, when I lectured at Bread Loaf, and recall awe and some uneasiness at his presence, though his conversation was not unkind. But he was two generations older than I was, and all we had in common was a shared love of Emerson.

To my surprise, Frost praised Hart Crane for making his poetry "imply everything." On reflection my surprise waned, since Frost's "logic of metaphor" (Crane's phrase) was another subtle modulation of power, as Emerson says, "in the moment of transition from a past to a new state, in the shooting of the gulf, in the darting to an aim." Wallace Stevens's intricate "evasions of as" seemed a more roundabout mode of implication, Frost also remarked. He and Stevens spent time together in Key West and felt mutual esteem. Whitman, always nearby in Stevens and in Crane, hardly touched Frost. I remember his saying that Edwin Arlington Robinson, an admirable poet who prefigured Frost, cared more for Whitman than he could.

Of the principal twentieth-century American poets, only Frost, Marianne Moore, Robert Penn Warren, Elizabeth Bishop, and James Merrill had little feeling for Whitman, even at his most astonishing. Whatever their pronouncements, Whitman pervades Eliot, Pound, W. C. Williams, and Theodore Roethke. In Wallace Stevens, Hart Crane, A. R.

Ammons, and John Ashbery, he scarcely requires invocation, though he is called on overtly.

Frost had affinities with Wordsworth, as Emerson did. In his youth he had listed Keats's *Hyperion,* Shelley's *Prometheus Unbound,* Browning's *Saul,* and Tennyson's *Morte d'Arthur* as favorite poems, but his poetry resembles none of these so much as it does the poems of Horace. His authentic precursors were Wordsworth and Emerson, but the agon was always with Wordsworth. I venture that Frost implicitly grasped that Wordsworth had kept Emerson from poetic strength and caused the Concord sage to go into the other harmony, of prose. Throughout Frost's career he battled with Wordsworth, determined not to be defeated as Emerson had been.

A direct struggle with Wordsworth is unwise for any belated poet: Wordsworth is too strong to be overcome upon his own ground. Matthew Arnold is one instance of that failure; George Meredith, another. Both are admirable poets but so contaminated by Wordsworth that the reader of *Empedocles on Etna* or *The Woods of Westermain* can be made uncomfortable. Arnold rarely achieves his own voice: Wordsworth and Keats crowd him out except in a few lyrics like *Palladium* (a rather Frostian poem, as David Bromwich notes). Meredith does come into his own tonalities in *Modern Love* and *Love in the Valley,* where Wordsworth is negated. Frost is not the American Wordsworth, but he holds up as only a few other modern American poets can: Stevens, Hart Crane, Moore, Williams, Eliot, Bishop, Ammons, Ashbery, Merrill. Others would add Ezra Pound, but I at last weary of his sprawl and squalor.

Frost was shy of too openly challenging Wordsworth, and ambushed him where possible. In the book *Mountain Interval* (1916), Frost has an odd poem, *The Gum-Gatherer,* which parodies *Resolution and Independence.*

Though his myriad gifts included parody, Frost finishes a poor third behind Lewis Carroll's *The White Knight's Ballad* and Edward Lear's *Incidents in the Life of My Uncle Arly,* both of which targeted Wordsworth's ancient leech-gatherer. Frost's gum-gatherer is so remote from Wordsworth that he becomes a self-parody:

> I told him this is a pleasant life
> To set your breast to the bark of trees

That all your days are dim beneath,
And reaching up with a little knife,
To loose the resin and take it down
And bring it to market when you please.

A relationship too uneasy for parody was established by David Bromwich. *Two Tramps in Mud Time,* one of Frost's strongest poems, manifests a surprising anxiety in regard to *Resolution and Independence.* Bromwich subtly establishes the link:

It may help at first to think of Frost's poem as a kind of riddle. At some level he knew all along that he was occupied with another version of Wordsworth's poem, but part of his "fooling" with the reader was to withhold his definitive clue until the middle of the poem, when many other pieces had fallen into place. It comes in the fourth stanza, with the unexpected appearance of a bluebird:

A bluebird comes tenderly up to alight
And turns to the wind to unruffle a plume,
His song so pitched as not to excite
A single flower as yet to bloom.

To the question, Why this, in a poem about tramps?—the answer is that the bird, along with the topic it introduces, is entirely within its rights by authority of the jay, the magpie, the hare, and the "plashy earth" of the misted sunny moor that occupy the opening stanzas of "Resolution and Independence." It is of the essence of both poems that they should work hard to separate landscape from the scene of labor proper: the pleasures of landscape will belong to the poet alone, and be felt at the intervals of his self-questioning; to the figure who confronts the poet, on the other hand, landscape hardly exists; it thus works its way through the poem as a double counterpoint, always present, but vividly present only to the poet, and much of the time not even to him.

A poem of America in 1934, still caught in the aftermath of the economic Depression, *Two Tramps in Mud Time* always arouses ambivalence in me, even as its nine superb octaves stun me with admiration. Some days I hobble around on my cane and keep chanting it to myself, without at first recalling what it is. Bordering constantly on the proverbial, it seems as though it has always been there:

> Good blocks of oak it was I split,
> As large around as the chopping block;
> And every piece I squarely hit
> Fell splinterless as a cloven rock.
> The blows that a life of self-control
> Spares to strike for the common good
> That day, giving a loose to my soul,
> I spent on the unimportant wood.

What Frost considered "the common good" is difficult to ascertain, but there seems a certain disproportion throughout the poem between the example and the precept, palpably in the three final stanzas:

> Out of the woods two hulking tramps
> (From sleeping God knows where last night,
> But not long since in the lumber camps).
> They thought all chopping was theirs of
>   right.
> Men of the woods and lumberjacks,
> They judged me by their appropriate
>   tool.
> Except as a fellow handled an ax,
> They had no way of knowing a fool.

> Nothing on either side was said.
> They knew they had but to stay their stay
> And all their logic would fill my head:
> As that I had no right to play
> With what was another man's work for gain.
> My right might be love but theirs was need.
> And where the two exist in twain
> Theirs was the better right—agreed.

But yield who will to their separation,
My object in living is to unite
My avocation and my vocation
As my two eyes make one in sight.
Only where love and need are one,
And the work is play for mortal stakes,
Is the deed ever really done
For Heaven and the future's sakes.

Wonderful in itself, that final octave is so comprehensive that one wonders how the tramps provoke it. It could be anyone's credo, from school teaching to soldiering. Wordsworth in his great crisis poems ascends from the particular to the universal effortlessly, or so he makes it seem. Frost, haunted by Wordsworth, never worked out a pact with him. Frost does give us figures like the old Cumberland beggar or the even more ancient leech-gatherer, but, as Bromwich phrases this, "never in a poem where the poet also appears as himself." Is it that Frost, a monstrous egoist, did not take enough pride in being a major poet?

"The originals are not original," Emerson remarked, with good cheer. After a conversation with the prince of source-hunters, John Livingston Lowes, Frost reduced poetic influence to a joke:

Lowes took the obvious position
That all of art is recognition
And I agreed. But the perfection
Of recognition is detection
That's why Lowes reads detective stories
And why in scholarship he glories
A poet need make no apology
Because his works are one anthology
Of other poets' best creations
Let him be nothing but quotations
(That's not as cynic as it sounds)
The game is one like Hare and Hounds
To entertain the critic pack
The poet has to leave a track
Of torn up scraps of prior poets.

Wordsworth proved to be rather more than Frost could subsume. Emerson, at his most daemonic in *The Conduct of Life,* was the congenial precursor, guiding his professed disciple to the heights of self-reliance. In 1959 Frost remarked, "I owe more to Emerson than anyone else for troubled thoughts about freedom," after which he added, "freedom is nothing but departure." Transition, the desire to be elsewhere, became Frost's legacy from Emerson.

In a 1960 interview with Richard Poirier, Frost agrees with his questioner on double meanings throughout his poetry, as managed by varied tonalities in voicing: "Talk by contraries." That understates Frost's stance, which is reliant on the passage in Mark's gospel that he employs in his final major poem, *Directive*:

> And he said unto them, Unto you it is given to know the mystery of the kingdom of God: but unto them that are without, all these things are done in parables:
>
> That seeing they may see, and not perceive; and hearing they may hear, and not understand; lest at any time they should be converted, and their sins should be forgiven them.

Inside readers, deep in Frost's poetry, are expected to apprehend his ironies, while his large public audience is to misunderstand. By design, this is strikingly akin to Mark Twain: Most of us are not to see how deep a work he brought forth in *Huckleberry Finn.*

Frost's daemon is a trickster and mischief-maker, to the aesthetic benefit of the poetry. I admire what so endlessly disconcerts me. If at times I become queasy, it is because Frost can be cruel, ambiguous toward women, and thoroughly morbid, but a great poet can afford all that and more. There is something bleak about Emerson's American Religion of self-reliance, and perhaps only Frost captures that blank whiteness in terms homelier than does Emerson himself, or Melville in Ishmael and Wallace Stevens in perpetual solitude. Herbert Marks, an authentic authority on the Bible, observes tellingly that Frost found in the Christian myth of the fall a rationale for his deep drive toward poetic concealment. He found also, Marks notes, a personal myth in which the American Eve was unfallen or in some ways still a male idealization of the female.

Frost's long marriage to Elinor White (from 1895 until her death in

1938) cannot easily be characterized. He survived her for a quarter century and never remarried, though he proposed to Kathleen Morrison, who refused him but then sustained his remaining years as secretary and companion. I distrust the account of the Frosts' marriage by his resentful biographer Lawrance Thompson but can offer only surmise. Like Frost, Elinor White had a strong personality and a stoic tenacity. From the start, his passion for her was consuming, Frost being just seventeen and Elinor two years older. Gifted as a painter and poet, she initially resisted but yielded when his behavior became suicidal. Two children died very early; four held on but three of them had troubled lives, one ending in a mental hospital and another self-slain. Despite all this, or because of it, Frost and Elinor lived on in relative harmony.

It may be that the poet-in-a-poet, or daemon, cannot marry, and by that test the long but difficult lives together of the Frosts, or of Wallace and Elsie Stevens, or of Herman Melville and his wife, are more or less the norm. All this is worth observing in regard to Frost because of four extraordinary poems in *A Witness Tree* (1942): *The Silken Tent, The Most of It, The Subverted Flower,* and what is a kind of elegy for Elinor, *Never Again Would Birds' Song Be the Same.*

The Silken Tent, a superb Shakespearean sonnet in one sentence, is a love poem addressed to Elinor:

> She is as in a field a silken tent
> At midday when a sunny summer breeze
> Has dried the dew and all its ropes relent,
> So that in guys it gently sways at ease,
> And its supporting central cedar pole,
> That is its pinnacle to heavenward
> And signifies the sureness of the soul,
> Seems to owe naught to any single cord,
> But strictly held by none, is loosely bound
> By countless silken ties of love and thought
> To everything on earth the compass round,
> And only by one's going slightly taut
> In the capriciousness of summer air
> Is of the slightest bondage made aware.

Critics always note the exquisite balance here between feminine and masculine and the masterly skill at blending sound and sense. So delicate is Frost's touch that you need to be very alert to hints that the woman experiences loss as well as gain: "its ropes relent," "loosely bound," "capriciousness," "the slightest bondage."

The phallic element is too palpable for commentary, since the poem's perspective does not include the woman's consciousness, which hardly is an aesthetic blemish. Marks notes the subversion in Second Corinthians of Saint Paul, whose "earthly tent" will be devoured by a "heavenly dwelling," made irrelevant by Frost's "pinnacle to heavenward."

Frost's principal legacies from Emerson were the double consciousness and the incessant struggle between freedom and fate. For both Emerson and Frost, the pre-Socratic formula held: Ethos is the daemon, character is fate, so everything that happens to you is what you always were and are. Freud secretly shared this view, as did his precursor Nietzsche: There are no accidents; love your fate, because there is little alternative, if any. Richard Poirier, faithful both to Frost and to Emerson—his two favorites among American authors—argued with me that my preference for Stevens and Whitman showed a refusal to take choice as being overdetermined. There is always evasion, nuance, swerve, misprision, the necessity of misreading, I would reply to no avail.

Poirier applied his convictions quite directly to Frost's most famous prose statement, "The Figure a Poem Makes," the preface to *Collected Poems* (1939):

It should be of the pleasure of a poem itself to tell how it can. The figure a poem makes. It begins in delight and ends in wisdom. The figure is the same as for love. No one can really hold that the ecstasy should be static and stand still in one place. It begins in delight, it inclines to the impulse, it assumes direction with the first line laid down, it runs a course of lucky events, and ends in a clarification of life—not necessarily a great clarification, such as sects and cults are founded on, but in a momentary stay against confusion. It has denouement. It has an outcome that though unforeseen was predestined from the first image of the original mood—and indeed from the very mood. It is but a trick poem and no poem at all if the best of it was thought of first and saved for the last. It finds its own name as it goes and discovers the best waiting for it in some final phrase at once wise and sad—the happy-sad blend of the drinking song.

For Poirier, this is akin to "ongoing sexual activity," an odd judgment since making love is frequently far from "a momentary stay against confusion," or any stay at all. Still, it is enlightening when Poirier finds the affinity between Frost and D. H. Lawrence. We tend not to think of Frost in the company of heroic vitalists, where Lawrence joins Blake and Shelley, Browning and Balzac, but Frost too endorses (in his poetry) a similar energetics.

A Witness Tree

IN *NEW HAMPSHIRE* (1923), FROST COMPOSED HIS SINGLE ELEGY, *TO E.T.*, for his closest friend and "only brother," the wonderful English poet Edward Thomas, killed in battle during World War I. Alas, the poem is clumsy and unworthy of both men yet poignant because Frost was not an elegiac poet, unlike his few peers among the greatest American poets: Whitman, Dickinson, Stevens, Eliot, Hart Crane. Uneasiness at elegy is another quality Frost shares with Emerson. Both distrusted mourning for reasons both temperamental and imaginative, related to their shared faith in the double consciousness and in their Ananke, or *amor fati*.

Frost's first volume, *A Boy's Will*, was published in England in 1913. Though it contains *Mowing* and *The Tuft of Flowers*, the poem in it I care most for is *The Trial by Existence*. A century after publication, it remains intensely alive:

> Even the bravest that are slain
>   Shall not dissemble their surprise
> On waking to find valor reign,
>   Even as on earth, in paradise;
> And where they sought without the sword
>   Wide fields of asphodel fore'er,
> To find that the utmost reward
>   Of daring should be still to dare.

The light of heaven falls whole and white
　　And is not shattered into dyes,
The light for ever is morning light;
　　The hills are verdured pasture-wise;
The angel hosts with freshness go,
　　And seek with laughter what to
　　　　brave;—
And binding all is the hushed snow
　　Of the far-distant breaking wave.

And from a cliff-top is proclaimed
　　The gathering of the souls for birth,
The trial by existence named,
　　The obscuration upon earth.
And the slant spirits trooping by
　　In streams and cross- and counter-streams
Can but give ear to that sweet cry
　　For its suggestion of what dreams!

And the more loitering are turned
　　To view once more the sacrifice
Of those who for some good discerned
　　Will gladly give up paradise.
And a white shimmering concourse rolls
　　Toward the throne to witness there
The speeding of devoted souls
　　Which God makes his especial care.

And none are taken but who will,
　　Having first heard the life read out
That opens earthward, good and ill,
　　Beyond the shadow of a doubt;
And very beautifully God limns,
　　And tenderly, life's little dream,
But naught extenuates or dims,
　　Setting the thing that is supreme.

Nor is there wanting in the press
   Some spirit to stand simply forth,
Heroic in its nakedness,
   Against the uttermost of earth.
The tale of earth's unhonored things
   Sounds nobler there than 'neath
      the sun;
And the mind whirls and the heart sings,
   And a shout greets the daring one.

But always God speaks at the end:
   "One thought in agony of strife
The bravest would have by for friend,
   The memory that he chose the life;
But the pure fate to which you go
   Admits no memory of choice,
Or the woe were not earthly woe
   To which you give the assenting voice."

And so the choice must be again,
   But the last choice is still the same;
And the awe passes wonder then,
   And a hush falls for all acclaim.
And God has taken a flower of gold
   And broken it, and used therefrom
The mystic link to bind and hold
   Spirit to matter till death come.

'Tis of the essence of life here,
   Though we choose greatly, still to lack
The lasting memory at all clear,
   That life has for us on the wrack
Nothing but what we somehow chose;
   Thus are we wholly stripped of pride
In the pain that has but one close,
   Bearing it crushed and mystified.

I give this entire because most of Frost's readers neglect the poem, perhaps because it resembles nothing else by him. When I first read it, seventy years back, I assumed it was by Edwin Arlington Robinson, an admirable poet who exchanged letters and mutual esteem with Frost. Robinson's *Eros Turannos* and *Luke Havergal* in particular share shape and stance with *The Trial by Existence*. Like Frost, Robinson was an Emersonian, devoted to the dark later essays of *The Conduct of Life*.

Plato's *Republic* concludes with the story of a mythic hero, Er, bravest of soldiers, who dies in battle and is resurrected after twelve days. In between, Er has beheld the final things. The dead are judged and either ascend or go down beneath the ground. After a thousand years of bliss or purgation, they must choose their next incarnations; then they experience forgetfulness and are born again.

That is not quite Plato and resembles in some ways Yeats's occult story in *A Vision*. Frost's scheme of heroic trial turns upon choice, though I wonder if that is the right word. "The obscuration upon earth" results from a singular God who blots out memory, but what is glory without remembrance?

Where necessity governs all, what can choice mean? Like Emerson, Frost seems to revel in a freedom that is merely fate and a fate that somehow is freedom. There is a dissonance in *The Trial by Existence* between its tonal exuberance and mystified import. Style goes in one direction, substance another. Starting with *North of Boston* (1914), Frost achieves mastery, and the fascinating weakness of *The Trial by Existence* dwindles away.

I return first, though, to *A Witness Tree* and its three postludes to *The Silken Tent*, commencing with *The Most of It*:

> He thought he kept the universe alone;
> For all the voice in answer he could wake
> Was but the mocking echo of his own
> From some tree-hidden cliff across the lake.
> Some morning from the boulder-broken beach
> He would cry out on life, that what it wants
> Is not its own love back in copy speech,
> But counter-love, original response.

And nothing ever came of what he cried
Unless it was the embodiment that crashed
In the cliff's talus on the other side,
And then in the far distant water splashed,
But after a time allowed for it to swim,
Instead of proving human when it neared
And someone else additional to him,
As a great buck it powerfully appeared,
Pushing the crumpled water up ahead,
And landed pouring like a waterfall,
And stumbled through the rocks with horny
    tread,
And forced the underbrush—and that was all.

Is this the American Adam as Robert Frost? On one level it responds to Wordsworth's boy of Winander in *The Prelude*. There, the boy (Wordsworth) engages in a dialogue of calls with answering owls, until a pause of deep silence causes him to listen while a "shock of mild surprise has carried far into his heart the voice / Of mountain torrents."

Frost, as titanic a solipsist as Wordsworth, cries out for counter-love but receives only his own daemon in the shape of a great buck, emblem of masculine force—hardly the Eve for whom he longed. And yet this "embodiment" has majesty as well as male desire.

The Subverted Flower is a poem much admired by Richard Poirier and others, including Herbert Marks, who provided a brilliant reading. As I tell my students, we ought to be capable of saying "This is a work of astonishing skill, but I dislike it with my whole being." I recall arguing this with Poirier, who held, with Frost, that its subject was "frigidity in women." Whether it refers to a nightmare of the seventeen-year-old poet or an actual incident between him and the nineteen-year-old Elinor White is ambiguous: Either way, both man and woman behave badly.

Richard Poirier contended that my reaction was merely moral, yet to me the matter was and is one of aesthetic response. Case histories—whether this one, or in Robert Lowell, Frank Bidart, Allen Ginsberg, Anne Sexton, Sylvia Plath, and others—court the hazards of the confessional. Clinical details defeat the distance that needs to separate the reader from the poet. Walt Whitman understood this: His intransitive eros relies for expression upon intransitive verbs. It may be that disputing this matter finally resolves itself in the vagaries of personal taste.   .

Frost, almost never confessional, is altogether formidable in *The Subverted Flower*. The embarrassment is mine, not his. Still, teaching the poem has not worked for me, since I do not love it, yet many of my students admire its candor. Whether its recalcitrance should be called candid I cannot know, but the concluding lines have the quality of inevitability:

> A girl could only see
> That a flower had marred a man,
> But what she could not see
> Was that the flower might be
> Other than base and fetid:
> That the flower had done but part,
> And what the flower began
> Her own too meager heart
> Had terribly completed.
> She looked and saw the worst.
> And the dog or what it was,
> Obeying bestial laws,
> A coward save at night,
> Turned from the place and ran.
> She heard him stumble first
> And use his hands in flight.
> She heard him bark outright.
> And oh, for one so young
> The bitter words she spit
> Like some tenacious bit
> That will not leave the tongue.
> She plucked her lips for it,
> And still the horror clung.
> Her mother wiped the foam
> From her chin, picked up her comb
> And drew her backward home.

When worried about my reaction to *The Subverted Flower,* I recite out loud to myself Frost's surpassingly beautiful sonnet *Putting In the Seed* from *Mountain Interval* (1916):

You come to fetch me from my work tonight
When supper's on the table, and we'll see
If I can leave off burying the white
Soft petals fallen from the apple tree
(Soft petals, yes, but not so barren quite,
Mingled with these, smooth bean and wrinkled pea;)
And go along with you ere you lose sight
Of what you came for and become like me,
Slave to a springtime passion for the earth.
How Love burns through the Putting in the Seed
On through the watching for that early birth
When, just as the soil tarnishes with weed,
The sturdy seedling with arched body comes
Shouldering its way and shedding the earth crumbs.

Can this be surpassed as a poem of married love? I have intoned it a hundred times and cannot exhaust the sonnet's burnished splendor. Placing it directly after *The Subverted Flower* (I wish Frost had done so) reconciles me to the latter. A fit Emersonian goes from surprise to surprise, and Frost never ceases to surprise.

No phrase, no word is wasted by *Putting In the Seed,* a poem of springtime passion for the earth and of reciprocal passion between wife and husband. The harmonies of the two loves are intricately balanced until they mingle and merge: Frost's reluctance to go to supper and leave off planting and Elinor's possibility of losing sight of the purpose of fetching him. Difficult to overpraise, the marvelous transition from the ninth to the tenth line, "slave to a springtime passion" on to Love burning "through the Putting in the Seed" is matched by the seedling's birth, implicitly akin to a baby's advent "shouldering its way."

The culmination of what may be called "the marriage group" in Frost is *A Witness Tree*'s famous sonnet *Never Again Would Birds' Song Be the Same,* the closest he would come to elegizing Elinor:

He would declare and could himself believe
That the birds there in all the garden round
From having heard the daylong voice of Eve
Had added to their own an oversound,

Her tone of meaning but without the words.
Admittedly an eloquence so soft
Could only have had an influence on birds
When call or laughter carried it aloft.
Be that as may be, she was in their song.
Moreover her voice upon their voices crossed
Had now persisted in the woods so long
That probably it would never be lost.
Never again would birds' song be the same.
And to do that to birds was why she came.

The qualifiers fascinate me: "could himself believe," "admittedly," "be that as may be," "moreover," "probably": This is an ambivalent American Adam, not Walt early in the morning or Waldo with no past at his back. "Crossed" is a further ambiguity. Frost is bereaved but accepts again what happens as the working out of character into event, of choice fated and loved as such, without regrets.

Frost's largeness is not so much in the enigma of his reservations as in his full acceptance of contingencies so far within us as to hedge any drive toward freeing choice. His strongest poem, to me and many others, is *Directive*, in *Steeple Bush* (1947), which was published when he was seventy-three. Again, Poirier, Frost's central critic, dissented, since he told me he preferred many others among the poems and that overemphasizing *Directive* distorted its poet. I do not think so: It is Frost's poem-of-poems, a summa of his life and his work. As we would expect from him, it is a summa twisted askew and a poem so manifold that no two readings of it can agree.

To fully appreciate *Directive*, you need to hold many of Frost's poems together in your mind, too many to discuss here. Before I discuss it, I want to visit a few: *After Apple-Picking; The Oven Bird; For Once, Then, Something; Sitting by a Bush in Broad Sunlight; Desert Places;* and *Design.* Those six, with the poems already glanced at, all prepare for *Directive* and its tonal and visionary perplexities.

North of Boston

AFTER APPLE-PICKING FROM NORTH OF BOSTON IS TOO FLAWLESSLY CON-
trived not to quote entire:

My long two-pointed ladder's sticking through a tree
Toward heaven still,
And there's a barrel that I didn't fill
Beside it, and there may be two or three
Apples I didn't pick upon some bough.
But I am done with apple-picking now.
Essence of winter sleep is on the night,
The scent of apples: I am drowsing off.
I cannot rub the strangeness from my sight
I got from looking through a pane of glass
I skimmed this morning from the drinking trough
And held against the world of hoary grass.
It melted, and I let it fall and break.
But I was well
Upon my way to sleep before it fell,
And I could tell
What form my dreaming was about to take.
Magnified apples appear and disappear,
Stem end and blossom end,
And every fleck of russet showing clear.
My instep arch not only keeps the ache,
It keeps the pressure of a ladder-round.
I feel the ladder sway as the boughs bend.
And I keep hearing from the cellar bin
The rumbling sound
Of load on load of apples coming in.
For I have had too much
Of apple-picking: I am overtired
Of the great harvest I myself desired.
There were ten thousand thousand fruit to touch,
Cherish in hand, lift down, and not let fall.

For all
That struck the earth,
No matter if not bruised or spiked with stubble,
Went surely to the cider-apple heap
As of no worth.
One can see what will trouble
This sleep of mine, whatever sleep it is.
Were he not gone,
The woodchuck could say whether it's like his
Long sleep, as I describe its coming on,
Or just some human sleep.

An early-twentieth-century American John Keats might have composed this: I hear an undersong of his *To Autumn*. That ode is Shakespearean; Frost's has a touch of the lyric Milton, appropriate to that second fall we name the fall. Like the harvest girl in Keats's ode, Frost is falling asleep, drowsed with the scent of apples. There the parallel ends, and the elliptical individuality of Frost commands the poem. Surpassingly beautiful in its textured surface, *After Apple-Picking* implies a strangeness we cannot entirely apprehend:

I cannot rub the strangeness from my sight
I got from looking through a pane of glass
I skimmed this morning from the drinking trough
And held against the world of hoary grass.
It melted, and I let it fall and break.

That melting pane of ice keys the poem's optics, a visionary slide into hibernation for the questing spirit: "I am overtired / Of the great harvest I myself desired." Frost's rugged and recalcitrant personality becomes very winning in this mode that touches the universal. When you talked to him, as I did twice at Bread Loaf, it was difficult not to experience a sense of awe: You saw why Vermont named a mountain after him. Frost was eighty-six, I was thirty, when we met, and I recognized in him the poet of *Directive* but not of *After Apple-Picking* or *The Silken Tent*.

There are several Frosts, including the least interesting—the homespun version, which attracted and held a substantial national readership. The most interesting, at least to me, adds Frost's own Lucretian *clinamen* (swerve) to the American literary trope of whiteness. The trope is crucial in *After Apple-Picking* though the word is absent; here "strangeness" tropes for "whiteness." A "pane of glass," translucent thin ice skimmed from the water trough, constitutes a speculum through which an uncanny whiteness shines. Frost is no Kabbalist, yet his genius approximates a great Zoharic metaphor, almost as though his wintry sleep coming on will gain him access to a female radiance he both desires and shuns.

The marriage of two people whose surnames are White and Frost engendered in one of the strongest of American poets both awareness and wariness of the trope of blank whiteness he encountered in Emerson, Melville, Dickinson, and his Key West crony Wallace Stevens. I have written so much about this metaphor that it partly suffices if I refer any interested reader to a little book I published in 1982, *The Breaking of the Vessels*.

As I have mentioned earlier, the trope begins in Shakespeare, where the banished Kent pleads with Lear to let him still remain "the true blank of thine eye," where "blank" refers to the center of a target. In later poets this fuses with Milton, in his blindness lamenting that nature to him is "a universal blank." In Coleridge's *Dejection: An Ode,* this informs "And still I gaze—and with how blank an eye!" Wordsworth and Shelley beholding Mont Blanc transmit the trope to American poets.

Emerson memorably speaks of the "ruin or blank" that we see in nature as being in our own eye. Ishmael's great meditation on the whiteness of the whale is matched by Emily Dickinson's blanks, emblems of the loss of loved ones to abandonment and death. Frost's true rival in his own generation, Stevens (just five years younger), is obsessed by the trope of blank whiteness throughout his poetry, where it culminates in his masterwork *The Auroras of Autumn*. The aged poet walking the beach at twilight, appalled by the Northern Lights, turns "blankly" on the sand. By the glare of the auroras he intones the eloquent litany that here everything visible is being white, is being of the solid of white, the accomplishment of an extremist in the exercise of a daemonic imagination.

Frost's wry sonnet *The Oven Bird*, from *Mountain Interval*, avoids images of whiteness while conveying a bleak poetics:

> There is a singer everyone has heard,
> Loud, a mid-summer and a mid-wood bird,

Who makes the solid tree trunks sound again.
He says that leaves are old and that for flowers
Mid-summer is to spring as one to ten.
He says the early petal-fall is past
When pear and cherry bloom went down in showers
On sunny days a moment overcast;
And comes that other fall we name the fall.
He says the highway dust is over all.
The bird would cease and be as other birds
But that he knows in singing not to sing.
The question that he frames in all but words
Is what to make of a diminished thing.

The American ovenbird is known for its hammering song: *teacher-teacher-teacher*. I have listened to it in Vermont and New Hampshire with some annoyance, but I am not Robert Frost. Emerson said, "Ask the fact for the form," and that is what Frost does here. This sonnet is properly irregular: The highway dust has settled over it; Frost too knows when in singing not to sing. If to make is to interpret the diminished thing rather than to create from it, the poem is perfect in itself. I take it that the ovenbird is darkly a critic and not a poet.

I turn to Frost at his full greatness in *For Once, Then, Something*, from *New Hampshire*:

Others taunt me with having knelt at well-curbs
Always wrong to the light, so never seeing
Deeper down in the well than where the water
Gives me back in a shining surface picture
Me myself in the summer heaven godlike
Looking out of a wreath of fern and cloud puffs.
Once, when trying with chin against a well-curb,
I discerned, as I thought, beyond the picture,
Through the picture, a something white, uncertain,
Something more of the depths—and then I lost it.
Water came to rebuke the too clear water.
One drop fell from a fern, and lo, a ripple
Shook whatever it was lay there at bottom,

Blurred it, blotted it out. What was that whiteness?
Truth? A pebble of quartz? For once, then, something.

This evidently began as a deft exercise in a meter of Catullus, the Roman lyric poet who was one of Frost's favorites. In his useful *The Art of Robert Frost* (2012), Tim Kendall notes the poem's use of Democritus—"truth lies at the bottom of a well"—and also its mastery of perspective.

The others taunting Frost evidently are a necessary fiction to get the poem started. His supposed angle of vision is "always wrong to the light," as though believing Christians mocked him. I cannot recall anyone writing that Frost was narcissistic—he is too harsh for that. Kneeling at a well-curb replaces any church's porch and altar, but the poet's self-image in the water's surface yields to the godlike vision as befits an Emersonian self-reliance.

What fascinates me is that "*Once*" in the poem, when Frost perhaps beheld "a something white, uncertain," until a drop of water ended it. "What was that whiteness?" "Truth" would be disquieting in the American tradition of whiteness, with all its implications, yet a pebble of quartz is too reductive to be interesting. The title returns at the close: "For once, then, something." How should we interpret it? If the "something" was truth momentarily glimpsed, are we to say that the truth as well as Frost is in itself uncertain? Kendall sensitively reads it that way, but I demur. If the whiteness has the aura of an American Counter-Sublime—as in Emerson, Dickinson, Melville, Stevens—then the truth is certain though rather indefinite. Title and closing phrase have a tone of defiance or insistence that does not suggest uncertainty.

Juxtapose this enigmatic poem with the strongly asserted *Sitting by a Bush in Broad Sunlight* from *West-Running Brook:*

When I spread out my hand here today,
I catch no more than a ray
To feel of between thumb and fingers;
No lasting effect of it lingers.

There was one time and only the one
When dust really took in the sun;

And from that one intake of fire
All creatures still warmly suspire.

And if men have watched a long time
And never seen sun-smitten slime
Again come to life and crawl off,
We must not be too ready to scoff.

God once declared he was true
And then took the veil and withdrew,
And remember how final a hush
Then descended of old on the bush.

God once spoke to people by name.
The sun once imparted its flame.
One impulse persists as our breath;
The other persists as our faith.

Popular debasements, whether of Darwin or of God, receive their qui-
etus. For me this poem anticipates *For Once, Then, Something*, except
that Frost here is firmly skeptical toward all stories masking as truth. Light
and heat are momentary, but "We must not be too ready to scoff." "Once"
and "true" collide; the bush no longer speaks or burns. What persists are
impulses: breath and faith, and clearly breath takes priority.

A greater poem, one of Frost's scariest, is *Desert Places* in *A Further
Range,* which returns us to "a blanker whiteness":

Snow falling and night falling fast, oh, fast
In a field I looked into going past,
And the ground almost covered smooth in snow,
But a few weeds and stubble showing last.

The woods around it have it—it is theirs.
All animals are smothered in their lairs.
I am too absent-spirited to count;
The loneliness includes me unawares.

And lonely as it is that loneliness
Will be more lonely ere it will be less—
A blanker whiteness of benighted snow
With no expression, nothing to express.

They cannot scare me with their empty spaces
Between stars—on stars where no human race is.
I have it in me so much nearer home
To scare myself with my own desert places.

One could say that this subverts Pascal's wager, which chooses faith because otherwise the silence of infinite space becomes a terror. Frost stays with the terror. Robert Penn Warren and I sometimes argued the interpretation of *Desert Places*. Though Warren was a thoroughgoing secularist and skeptic, he saw Frost here as hinting at the need for piety. Frost, though, is writing his analogy to Stevens's *The Snow Man*, and, like that poem, *Desert Places* excludes the imputation of human life or any pathos to the object world: "With no expression, nothing to express."

Yet I dissent also from Tim Kendall, who accurately dismisses the argument for faith but also asserts that *Desert Places* repudiates self-trust and Emersonian self-reliance. The daemon dwells in Frost's desert places and composes the poem for him; Frost knows, with Emerson, that the ruin or blank we see when we look upon nature is in our own eyes. I take it that is consonant with Frost's meaning: "To scare myself with my own desert places." The *genius loci* of *Desert Places* lurks in that "nothing," so the poem's motto well could be Emerson's iron law of compensation, or Lear's "Nothing will come of nothing."

This is the mode of the powerful *Design* in *A Further Range*:

I found a dimpled spider, fat and white,
On a white heal-all, holding up a moth
Like a white piece of rigid satin cloth—
Assorted characters of death and blight
Mixed ready to begin the morning right,
Like the ingredients of a witches' broth—
A snow-drop spider, a flower like a froth,
And dead wings carried like a paper kite.

What had that flower to do with being white,
The wayside blue and innocent heal-all?
What brought the kindred spider to that height,
Then steered the white moth thither in the night?
What but design of darkness to appall?—
If design govern in a thing so small.

Tim Kendall astutely observes the presence of William Blake in *Design*, citing *The Sick Rose* and *The Tyger*. I would add to these another poem from Blake's *Songs of Experience, London*. The ending of Frost's poem, "What but design of darkness to appall?— / If design govern in a thing so small" recalls a London in which "the chimney-sweeper's cry / Every blackning church appalls," playing upon a root meaning of "appall," to whiten or cast a colorless pall. Frost's wickedly lucid sonnet *Design* could be the last Song of Experience in the Blakean sense.

Against all theistic arguments for intelligent design, Frost places his "design of darkness to appall": Blake, an apocalyptic humanist, goes beyond such placement, but the canny Frost knows he must yield to a latecomer's contingencies—like Wallace Stevens in his own generation of poets, Frost writes the poems of our climate. Of their great contemporaries, T. S. Eliot practiced a neo-Christianity that studies the nostalgias, while Hart Crane returned to Blake and Whitman with a fiercely final attempt to write the poems of the American Religion, Orphic and at last suicidal.

Even Frost the arch-poet does not have a more exquisite, more diabolically crafty poem than *Design,* unless it be his ultimate masterpiece, *Directive,* which I will discuss in the next section. Four white entities center *Design:* "a dimpled spider, fat and white," "a white heal-all," "a white piece of rigid satin cloth," and "the white moth." Together they form a white murderous killer-priest, a white altar, and a white victim for a black mass.

Tone here conveys a wicked relish, a gustatory shudder at a witch's breakfast, and a cruel irony in the flower's name, "heal-all." If anything in the poem is askew, the fourth line may be too overt, but Frost compensates with "a paper kite." The last line, though conditional, participates in the rhetorical question of the penultimate one and ends the poem strongly.

After Melville had finished *Moby-Dick,* he wrote that he had written a wicked poem and felt innocent as a lamb. Frost might have said the same about this poem. T. S. Eliot followed Ezra Pound in admiring Frost. I do not know if he ever read *Design* but suspect he would have subjected it also to the castigation he gave Thomas Hardy and D. H. Lawrence in his most revelatory book, *After Strange Gods: A Primer of Modern Heresy.*

Directive

DIRECTIVE, AN EXTRAORDINARY POEM, IS SO RICH THAT READERS RARELY agree as to its meanings. It has a close relation to two ancestor poems, Wordsworth's tale of Margaret in *The Ruined Cottage,* which became Book I of *The Excursion,* and Emerson's genially ironic *Uriel,* sparked by the controversy excited by his address to the Harvard Divinity School.

To Wordsworth, Frost owes "A broken drinking goblet like the Grail." From *The Ruined Cottage:*

> When I stooped to drink
> A spider's web hung to the water's edge,
> And on the wet and slimy foot-stone lay
> The useless fragment of a wooden bowl.
> It moved my very heart.

In Wordsworth's poem, Margaret, pathetic victim of her own hope rather than her despair, benignly gave the water of life to all who passed. She is dead, and the bowl with which she served them has dwindled to a useless fragment. Frost, addressing his directives to himself and to his right readers (as opposed to the "wrong ones" he mentions below), offers only an ambiguous hope to either:

> I have kept hidden in the instep arch
> Of an old cedar at the waterside
> A broken drinking goblet like the Grail
> Under a spell so the wrong ones can't find it,
> So can't get saved, as Saint Mark says they mustn't.
> (I stole the goblet from the children's playhouse.)

> Here are your waters and your watering place.
> Drink and be whole again beyond confusion.

The text from Mark that the poem refers to (4:11–12) is the weirdest in that uncanniest of gospels:

> And he said unto them, Unto you it is given to know the mystery of the kingdom of God: but unto them that are without, all these things are done in parables:
>
>   That seeing they may see, and not perceive; and hearing they may hear, and not understand; lest at any time they should be converted, and their sins should be forgiven them.

In Mark, only the demons know the divinity of Jesus: He himself is uncertain, and his blockhead disciples are puzzled. The author of Mark is a true precursor of the poet who writes *Directive*. To understand Mark or Frost, you have to be daemonic. Robert Frost is what the Bible names a watcher: of places, persons, things, and one's solitary inward self. He does not share Whitman's eros, however intransitive.

There is a frequent harshness in tone that dominates *Directive*, even in its closing lines just cited, which play against Emerson's *Uriel*. Frost's Job, in *A Masque of Reason,* a poem-play that provides a concluding verse 43 to the 42-verse Book of Job, is made to relate Yahweh's reason to that of Emerson:

> Yet I suppose what seems to us confusion
> Is not confusion, but the form of forms,
> The serpent's tail stuck down the serpent's throat,
> Which is the symbol of eternity
> And also of the way all things come round,
> Or of how rays return upon themselves,
> To quote the greatest Western poem yet.
> Though I hold rays deteriorate to nothing:
> First white, then red, then ultra red, then out.

Frost means you to juxtapose this with a quatrain from *Uriel:*

> Line in nature is not found;
> Unit and universe are round;
> In vain produced, all rays return;
> Evil will bless, and ice will burn.

Job's last two lines are Frost's deliberate swerve away from Emerson, yet "then out" is no darker than Emerson's *The Conduct of Life.* What would Emerson have thought could he have read *Directive*? I am more an Emersonian than a Frostian, and that renders the question relevant to me as I embark upon my own reading of *Directive:*

> Back out of all this now too much for us,
> Back in a time made simple by the loss
> Of detail, burned, dissolved, and broken off
> Like graveyard marble sculpture in the weather,
> There is a house that is no more a house
> Upon a farm that is no more a farm
> And in a town that is no more a town.

This monosyllabic backward march is carefully weighed out. The initial line is all monosyllables, the second also except for "simple," an effect repeated in lines five, six (except for "upon"), and seven. This helps produce a kind of parataxis, a biblical style much favored by Walt Whitman, though the Frostian turn is very different.

I am an experiential and personalizing literary critic, which certainly rouses up enmity, but I go on believing that poems matter only if we matter. All criticism of a man's self, said my hero Samuel Johnson, is really oblique praise; it is to show how much he can spare. Frost in *Directive* criticizes himself and his elite readers but only to show how much he and they can spare.

The poem's journey back in time reminds me at eighty-four of the hazard in memorial simplification: Detail is lost. I like to think that such loss is drowsy, but Frost shocks me awake by the hurt "burned, dissolved, and broken off / Like graveyard marble sculpture." After that, house, farm, and town are weathered off into nothingness.

Whether Frost is describing or inventing a home he and Elinor had to abandon is uncertain, but to the poem that scarcely matters. Again, tone is central:

The road there, if you'll let a guide direct you
Who only has at heart your getting lost,
May seem as if it should have been a quarry—
Great monolithic knees the former town
Long since gave up pretense of keeping covered.
And there's a story in a book about it:
Besides the wear of iron wagon wheels
The ledges show lines ruled southeast-northwest,
The chisel work of an enormous Glacier
That braced his feet against the Arctic Pole.
You must not mind a certain coolness from him
Still said to haunt this side of Panther Mountain.
Nor need you mind the serial ordeal
Of being watched from forty cellar holes
As if by eye pairs out of forty firkins.
As for the woods' excitement over you
That sends light rustle rushes to their leaves,
Charge that to upstart inexperience.
Where were they all not twenty years ago?
They think too much of having shaded out
A few old pecker-fretted apple trees.

Defeat is the burden, but the voice directing us possesses authority. What we hear is a spirit "too lofty and original to rage," to quote a later section of the poem. The prouder word here is "original," since the proof of experiential triumph is the poem itself, permanent survivor beyond house, farm, town, "all this now too much for us." Frost is saturnine in contrasting *Directive* to the "cheering song" he will not write:

Make yourself up a cheering song of how
Someone's road home from work this once was,
Who may be just ahead of you on foot
Or creaking with a buggy load of grain.
The height of the adventure is the height
Of country where two village cultures faded
Into each other. Both of them are lost.
And if you're lost enough to find yourself

By now, pull in your ladder road behind you
And put a sign up CLOSED to all but me.
Then make yourself at home. The only field
Now left's no bigger than a harness gall.

That is the most severe humor in all of Frost, so bitter that it becomes something else, comprehending self-mockery, scorn of sociological jargon of "village cultures faded," and the wonderful cartoon perspective of "pull in your ladder road behind you." There is a particularly self-directed cruelty in the reduction of the only remaining field cleared by Frost to a sore inflicted on a workhorse by its harness.

A finer tone enters with the next movement:

First there's the children's house of make-believe,
Some shattered dishes underneath a pine,
The playthings in the playhouse of the children.
Weep for what little things could make them glad.
Then for the house that is no more a house,
But only a belilaced cellar hole,
Now slowly closing like a dent in dough.
This was no playhouse but a house in earnest.

That last line confirms the reader's apprehension that the "children" were Elinor and Robert Frost, playing house in earnest. There is an almost unique poignance, for Frost, in "Weep for what little things could make them glad," countered by the grim brilliance of "slowly closing like a dent in dough."

Tone rises past the earlier irony of "the height of the adventure" to the intensity of an American Sublime:

Your destination and your destiny's
A brook that was the water of the house,
Cold as a spring as yet so near its source,
Too lofty and original to rage.
(We know the valley streams that when aroused
Will leave their tatters hung on barb and thorn.)

That brook of the blessing is a constant image in Frost, though never before so urgent as it is now. We are then led on to the grandest of his conclusions:

> I have kept hidden in the instep arch
> Of an old cedar at the waterside
> A broken drinking goblet like the Grail
> Under a spell so the wrong ones can't find it,
> So can't get saved, as Saint Mark says they mustn't.
> (I stole the goblet from the children's playhouse.)
> Here are your waters and your watering place.
> Drink and be whole again beyond confusion.

Emerson and Frost, both learned classicists, knew that a root meaning of "confusion" was to pour out a libation to the gods. Frost was a profoundly pagan poet, and *Directive* invites its elite readers to a communion with fatal Ananke, the god of contingencies and overdeterminations. This is a cold and clean communion, promising only a Lucretian clarity, a difficult acceptance of the way things are.

V.

WALLACE STEVENS
and T. S. ELIOT

I HAVE WRITTEN ABOUT AND TAUGHT STEVENS MORE THAN ANY OTHER poet except for Shakespeare. I began these pages at dawn on my eighty-third birthday, remembering my close friend Holly Stevens, the poet's only child, who died of cancer in 1992. I helped Holly edit *The Palm at the End of the Mind* and the collected *Letters* and encouraged her to write a memoir of her father, but she declined, saying it would be too painful. A warm and vulnerable person, Holly had reconciled with her father, and they were in harmony long before he died, while Holly did the best she could at sustaining her difficult mother, Elsie.

I met Stevens only once, when I was nineteen and intruded myself into a small audience to whom he read a shorter version of *An Ordinary Evening in New Haven*. It was November 1949, my first visit to Yale and New Haven; I recall disliking both and vowing never to return. From September 1951 until now, I have broken that promise to myself. At a reception after the reading, I sank against a wall, admiring the seventy-year-old poet. I was awed and out of place, uninvited. A future colleague, Norman Holmes Pearson, kindly asked my identity and then pushed a frightened young man over to Stevens, who was standing by himself, drink in hand. Gracious and benign, he spoke to me for about twenty minutes. I recall that our subject was Shelley, whose poetry Stevens knew very well, including the epyllion *The Witch of Atlas*, from which he recited the lines beginning "Men scarcely know how beautiful fire is." Years later, teaching Stevens's mysterious elegy *The Owl in the Sarcophagus*, I recognized an allusion to that stanza in "A diamond jubilance beyond the fire."

I have been reading Stevens since 1943 and teaching and writing about his poetry since 1955, the year of his death. How shall I define the singular elements in his greatness?

This book is a study of the literary daemon, whose place in Wallace Stevens is everywhere, as it is in Dickinson, Emerson, Nietzsche, Shelley, Tennyson, Whitman, Wordsworth—all of them Stevensian precursors. One could add to this list Eliot and Yeats, Stevens's self-chosen adversaries and rivals. Frost and Williams, with whom he had amiable personal relations, might complete the inventory.

Among these, Stevens is the most circuitous, surpassing even Emerson. In Stevens, evasion—a mode inherited from Whitman—becomes an entire rhetoric of defense and discovery. I think (as an instance among many) of *An Ordinary Evening in New Haven*, XXVIII:

> This endlessly elaborating poem
> Displays the theory of poetry,
> As the life of poetry. A more severe,
>
> More harassing master would extemporize
> Subtler, more urgent proof that the theory
> Of poetry is the theory of life,
>
> As it is, in the intricate evasions of as,
> In things seen and unseen, created from nothingness,
> The heavens, the hells, the worlds, the longed-for lands.

Those "intricate evasions" are all but infinite. Poetic masters of evasion include Tennyson and Whitman, though all strong poets elude Freud's reality principle, which would involve making friends with the necessity of dying. The poet-in-a-poet, or daemon, is undying, whatever the stance toward mortality of the woman or man in whom the daemon dwells.

Stevens accepted Freudian reality testing: "Freud's eye was the microscope of potency," he wrote. The daemon in Stevens tells another story, speaking sometimes as the rabbi or "the scholar of one candle," or appearing as "the sun, that brave man," or the roaring lion of poetry, or as Walt Whitman walking along a ruddy shore, singing and chanting, or as a

Quixotic Hidalgo. To ask the question concerning the daemon is to seek an origin of inspiration. Whereas Robert Frost is possessed by an external daemon whose name is Loss, hence the power of *Directive,* Wallace Stevens undergoes possession by the rival daemon of a Supreme Fiction. Frostian unmaking of a diminished thing contrasts antithetically with Stevens's proposing a Supreme Fiction known to be fictive. You can argue that to believe in a fiction known to be untrue *is* to make too much of a diminished thing, but you would then be Frost rather than Stevens.

In 1915, Stevens first approached his project in Stanza VII of *Sunday Morning:*

> Supple and turbulent, a ring of men
> Shall chant in orgy on a summer morn
> Their boisterous devotion to the sun,
> Not as a god, but as a god might be,
> Naked among them, like a savage source.
> Their chant shall be a chant of paradise,
> Out of their blood, returning to the sky;
> And in their chant shall enter, voice by voice,
> The windy lake wherein their lord delights,
> The trees, like serafin, and echoing hills,
> That choir among themselves long afterward.
> They shall know well the heavenly fellowship
> Of men that perish and of summer morn.
> And whence they came and whither they shall go
> The dew upon their feet shall manifest.

"Not as a god, but as a god might be" suggests a Nietzschean fiction, except that Stevens, like J. M. W. Turner and D. H. Lawrence, always starts with the sun in a mode different from Zarathustra's solar trajectory. Sunday is taken back from Christian devotion and returned to paganism, if the high personalism of this dancing ring of men can be called "paganism" at all. Paradise is within them; their lord is the sun, their fellowship their common mortality, and the only evidence for origins and ends alike is in the morning dew.

That is Stevens at thirty-six composing a tentative Keatsian-

Tennysonian version of his "essential poem at the center of things," to quote from *A Primitive Like an Orb*. Thirty-five years later, the seventy-one-year-old master made *A Discovery of Thought:*

> One thinks, when the houses of New England catch the
> first sun,
>
> The first word would be of the susceptible being arrived,
> The immaculate disclosure of the secret, no more obscured.
> The sprawling of winter might suddenly stand erect,
>
> Pronouncing its new life and ours, not autumn's prodigal
> returned,
> But an antipodal, far-fetched creature, worthy of birth,
> The true tone of the metal of winter in what it says:
>
> The accent of deviation in the living thing
> That is its life preserved, the effort to be born
> Surviving being born, the event of life.

Is this clairvoyance still a fiction? What else, prodigious scholar, could it be? Stevens's art makes us more susceptible to nuance, following Whitman yet not too closely, for no other poet could match Whitmanian evasions of "as." Stevens and Eliot as poets have almost nothing in common except covert relations with Whitman's daemonic sublime. Stevens, in *Notes Toward a Supreme Fiction,* speaks of the "hum of thoughts evaded in the mind." That humming in Stevens, as in Whitman, is ultimately the humming of the maternal sea calling out for her castaways to return. Eliot's was a long time of evading Whitman, though he must have known how explicitly *The Waste Land* utilizes *When Lilacs Last in the Dooryard Bloom'd.* Very late he acknowledged Whitman, most interestingly in a London lecture to American soldiers and airmen. So far as I know, the talk remains unpublished, but I read a transcript given to me by the late Yale bibliographer Donald Gallup. Eliot praises Whitman for a perfection in fusing stance and substance. Certain phrases used by Eliot in the speech are close to those in *The Dry Salvages* in *Four Quartets.*

One can argue that Stevens and Eliot are the principal American poets since Whitman and Dickinson. As cogently, one could choose Frost and Hart Crane. Admirers of W. C. Williams, Ezra Pound, Marianne Moore, Robert Penn Warren, and some others might dissent. That the principal poets of a later generation—Elizabeth Bishop, James Merrill, A. R. Ammons, and John Ashbery—are also of such eminence to me seems a likely conclusion.

Stevens felt that *Harmonium* had failed to receive initial acclaim because of *The Waste Land*'s competitive renown. But that was a minor element in his agonistic stance against Eliot, which lasted a lifetime and subtly informed his poetry. Neo-Christianity in the mode of Eliot's *Ash Wednesday* was unacceptable to the seer of poetry as the Supreme Fiction.

The astonishing fecundity of Wallace Stevens in his final twenty years overwhelms Eliot's slender output in his last two decades. It may be a matter of taste to prefer *The Auroras of Autumn* and *The Owl in the Sarcophagus* to *Four Quartets*. The late Hugh Kenner, formidable antiquarian modernist, gaped when I expressed such preference and stiffly repeated his judgment that Stevens was the culmination of the poetics of Edward Lear.

Eliot, who admired Edward Lear (as all of us should), seems closer to the great comic poet of Nonsense (think of Eliot's *Sweeney Agonistes,* a splendid work). Kenner loved Pound and Eliot, and, I think misleadingly, grouped James Joyce with them. In any case, Kenner's religious modernism also led him to high esteem for Wyndham Lewis, whom he preferred to Marcel Proust, as he proudly informed me. Acquaintances at Yale Graduate School, we were never friends, though I came to admire his book *The Pound Era,* and he later surprised me with testy but fair-minded reviews of my books on Yeats and Shakespeare.

Wickedly, I once considered writing a book to be called *The Age of Stevens* but thought better of it and composed instead *Wallace Stevens: The Poems of Our Climate.* I took considerable satisfaction, before I expelled myself from the Yale English Department to become a department of one, in leading a reversal by which Stevens replaced Eliot in the course sequence of the major English non-dramatic poets: Chaucer, Spenser, Milton, Wordsworth, Stevens. I always insisted that Whitman belonged there also, but that was a battle scarcely winnable in the mid-1970s.

This is personal foregrounding but has a relevance to a chapter contrasting Stevens to Eliot. Whitman and Shelley appear favorably by name in Stevens's poetry. Eliot appears, unlovingly, as X. Eliot became Stevens's

English publisher but printed no observations upon the poet of "the marriage of flesh and air."

Endlessly ambivalent toward Eliot, and a lifelong Stevensian, my choice between the two goes back to when I was a child. After all, the figure of wisdom in Stevens is the rabbi, and Eliot had the same use for rabbis as I have for Anglo-Catholic authorities. One does not hear Thomas Stearns Eliot crying out:

> Oh! Rabbi, rabbi, fend my soul for me
> And true savant of this dark nature be.

Charmingly, Stevens juxtaposed himself as "the lion of Juda" with Eliot as one of "the lean cats." The choice of cats is the reader's:

> In the metaphysical streets of the physical town
> We remember the lion of Juda and we save
> The phrase . . . Say of each lion of the spirit
>
> It is a cat of a sleek transparency
> That shines with a nocturnal shine alone.
> The great cat must stand potent in the sun.
>
> —The Auroras of Autumn

> The lean cats of the arches of the churches,
> That's the old world. In the new, all men are priests.
>
> —Extracts from Addresses to
> the Academy of Fine Ideas

Walt Whitman would have approved this declaration. This is followed in *Extracts* by an apotheosis of Eliot as "X, the per-noble master":

> The lean cats of the arches of the churches
> Bask in the sun in which they feel transparent,
> As if designed by X, the per-noble master.
> They have a sense of their design and savor

The sunlight. They bear brightly the little beyond
Themselves, the slightly unjust drawing that is
Their genius: the exquisite errors of time.

I recall an anecdote in which a Boston bluestocking remarks to
Emerson that transcendentalism means "the little beyond"; the sage replies, "Something like that." Eliot dismissed Emerson as "an encumbrance" and wondered why Henry James had not "carved him up." I
murmur that it would be like trying to carve up barbed wire. Emerson,
Thoreau, Whitman, Margaret Fuller, and Dickinson do not take as daemon "the exquisite errors of time." Their genius is to possess and be possessed not by a sense of their own design but by the quest for the face they
had "before the world was made" (Yeats). Eliot, neo-Christian before his
conversion, wants to accept a benign creation, though his extraordinary
poetic sensibility knows otherwise. Waldo and his progeny, from Walt to
Hart Crane, share Melville's famous sense, as expressed by Urania in *After
the Pleasure Party*, that an anarch hand or cosmic blunder broke the vessels
of being and shied the fractions, male and female, through the gates of life.

Rather minimally, Stevens acknowledged Eliot as "an upright ascetic."
Here is Stevens's central polemic against Eliot, *The Creations of Sound*
from *Transport to Summer*:

If the poetry of X was music,
So that it came to him of its own,
Without understanding, out of the wall

Or in the ceiling, in sounds not chosen,
Or chosen quickly, in a freedom
That was their element, we should not know

That X is an obstruction, a man
Too exactly himself, and that there are words
Better without an author, without a poet,

Or having a separate author, a different poet,
An accretion from ourselves, intelligent
Beyond intelligence, an artificial man

> At a distance, a secondary expositor,
> A being of sound, whom one does not approach
> Through any exaggeration. From him, we collect.
>
> Tell X that speech is not dirty silence
> Clarified. It is silence made still dirtier.
> It is more than an imitation for the ear.
>
> He lacks this venerable complication.
> His poems are not of the second part of life.
> They do not make the visible a little hard
>
> To see nor, reverberating, eke out the mind
> On peculiar horns, themselves eked out
> By the spontaneous particulars of sound.
>
> We do not say ourselves like that in poems.
> We say ourselves in syllables that rise
> From the floor, rising in speech we do not speak.

Eliot urged escape from personality yet obstructs by being too exactly himself. He had come, he said, to purify the language of the tribe, as though speech were dirty silence clarified. For Stevens, as with Walt, it is silence made still dirtier. Stevens indicts Eliot profoundly to say of *The Waste Land* that it does "not make the visible a little hard / To see."

But what does it mean to make the visible a little hard to see? Here are two instances from Eliot:

> At the first turning of the third stair
> Was a slotted window bellied like the fig's fruit
> And beyond the hawthorn blossom and a pasture scene
> The broadbacked figure drest in blue and green
> Enchanted the maytime with an antique flute.
> Blown hair is sweet, brown hair over the mouth blown,
> Lilac and brown hair;
> Distraction, music of the flute, stops and steps of the mind
>   over the third stair,

Fading, fading; strength beyond hope and despair
Climbing the third stair.

—Ash Wednesday

The dripping blood our only drink,
The bloody flesh our only food:
In spite of which we like to think
That we are sound, substantial flesh and blood—
Again, in spite of that, we call this Friday good.

—East Coker, from FOUR QUARTETS

Vividness is one of Eliot's clearest poetic gifts, learned partly from Ezra Pound but ultimately from Dante. And yet the greatest of Western poets, Shakespeare and Dante—whenever they so desire—make the visible a little hard to see. Matelda walks in glory by the Pilgrim's side, yet her aura is difficult to envision, while Lear looks up at the heavens and urges them to take his side, because they too are old. How can one show that upon the stage? A daemonic aura or wavering transcendence may be the one mode shared by the authors of *Purgatorio* and *King Lear.*

In the early morning of January 10, 1957, a secret marriage took place in London between Thomas Stearns Eliot, sixty-eight, and his secretary, Valerie Fletcher, thirty. Astonishingly, the marriage flourished until the poet's death on January 4, 1965, after eight years of happiness unique in his otherwise purgatorial life.

I grew up in the age of Eliot, fighting obdurately against it all my days until now. At eighty-four I cease from mental fight, at least against the Eliotics. He was and is a great American poet, very much in the High Romantic tradition of Shelley and Whitman, as he belatedly acknowledged. His literary criticism is another matter, while his social and religious writing was in my view unfortunate. There is also his lifelong anti-Semitism and dislike (and fear) of women to darken his name. Until his final years, he loathed the human condition and was kindled largely by his worship of original sin. You have to be Augustine of Hippo to sustain such a stance, and Eliot possessed that great spirit's tendentiousness but not an intellect so capacious.

I read Lyndall Gordon's *T. S. Eliot: An Imperfect Life* when it appeared in 1998 and have just returned to it. Gordon writes of Eliot with continuous insight and sympathy, emphasizing his enormous sufferings throughout his dreadful first marriage. And yet she presents so extensive a cavalcade of self-concern, prejudice, misogyny, sexual failure, and disgust with the human condition that we would cease to care were Eliot not, at his best, a major poet.

Gordon's Eliot spends his life seeking "the love of God" while scorning "ordinary human affections" until, at sixty-eight, he accepts the love of Valerie Fletcher. "He seemed to suffer from an inability to empathize with suffering outside his own experience," Gordon concludes. Granted the frequent solipsism of strong poets, that is not unusual, yet it may help explain why Eliot's plays are now period pieces.

Eliot's religion professes Anglican orthodoxies, yet the American coloring remained until the close. He strongly misread Hawthorne and Henry James, finding in them advocates of original sin. The creators of Hester Prynne and Isabel Archer have their difficulties with Emerson, but Hester and Isabel are Emersonians and not Eliotic neo-Christians.

Eliot matters now because of a slender body of poetry, *The Waste Land* and *Four Quartets* in particular. He has become a canonical American poet; so are Williams, Pound, and Moore in his generation, but for me he joins our strongest: Whitman, Dickinson, Frost, Stevens, Crane, and those who came later: Bishop, Merrill, Ammons, Ashbery.

All of us live imperfect lives, and I know scarcely anyone foolish enough to censure Eliot's. His prejudices were hardly unique to him, and perhaps major poets ought not to be expected to set moral examples. His neo-Christianity had no trace of compassion for the needy and oppressed, only for himself. Still, that was and is between him and his God, and as a free-thinking Jew I disqualify myself from judgment. Bigots are to be deprecated, yet in darker moments I reflect that anti-Semitism is fundamental to many varieties of Christianity and seems to have been a badge of authentic piety for Eliot. All bad religion is sincere.

Today Eliot's cultural evangelism is an antique: Conservative neo-Christians abound and are remote from classical educations. Dogma does not readily transmember into poetry:

> Those who deny Thee could not deny, if Thou didst not exist; and
> their denial is never complete, for if it were so, they would not
> exist.

That is from the final chorus of *Murder in the Cathedral*. I quoted it once to Allen Tate, when we met at a dinner hosted by Holly Stevens at her house in Wethersfield, Connecticut. The poet-critic and I strained to be well behaved but were antithetical personalities. "What is that clap-trap?" he asked; I avoided telling him, as we already had clashed on Eliot and made peace only by drinking to the memory of Hart Crane, who had been one of his closest friends.

The most useful critical study of Eliot remains Grover Smith's (1956). It concludes rather sadly with the accurate judgment that Eliot can depict only the emotions of his own isolated self. An incantatory genius, he thus remained a true heir of Tennyson and Whitman, not of Dante and Shakespeare. Time will confirm my estimate that Whitman and Tennyson surpass Eliot, as does Shelley, an abiding influence upon him, as upon Stevens and Hart Crane.

At its best moments, *Four Quartets* shows Eliot surmounting his limitations through a problematic fusion of religion and philosophy, pre-Socratic and Indic. Greek traditions do not work as well, here or in *The Waste Land,* as do Sanskrit and Pali texts and their commentaries. The illuminating study remains that of Cleo McNelly Kearns, *T. S. Eliot and Indic Traditions* (1987), which emphasizes that the neo-Christian evangelist preferred Eastern metaphysics to Hindu and Buddhist religious formulations. Wisdom, beyond categories, was Eliot's goal, since his quest for salvation depended altogether upon the incarnation. Kearns makes a tentative distinction between metaphysics in *The Waste Land* and wisdom in *Four Quartets.* I myself detect little wisdom in the latter and not much authentic metaphysics in the earlier poem. Still, she makes her case with restraint and with patience, qualities always difficult for me to manifest. The *Bhagavad-Gita,* which I know only imperfectly through translations, warns against "dark inertia," a malady sadly prevalent in my eighties.

Walt Whitman, contrary to much critical opinion, was the prime begetter of the highly diverse poetry of Stevens, Pound, Eliot, Williams, and Hart Crane. Except for Crane, they denied their "father" but came back to him at the end. It is now a commonplace to recognize Whitman's influence upon Eliot, but that was not the case in my youth and middle years. I recall conversations with—among others—Frank Kermode, R. P. Blackmur, Allen Tate, Louis Martz, F. O. Matthiessen, and Lionel Trilling, in which I met only incredulity when I urged them to read the *Lilacs* elegy and *The Waste Land* side by side.

Whitman contaminates Eliot (and Stevens) rather as Eliot's Pascal was infected by Montaigne. Eliot defended Pascal by saying that to combat Montaigne was like throwing a hand grenade into a fog. Since Walt could not be further from Eliot in personality and human concerns, I surmise that the poet of *Sea-Drift* inhabited the neo-Christian prophet as dusky daemon and dark elder brother. Henry James, a late convert to Whitman, visited wounded British soldiers in World War I London. For Eliot, all of earth was a hospital that he had come to admonish and not to comfort.

Lyndall Gordon surprisingly countenances Eliot as a Hebrew prophet. Though I am grateful to her for helping me partly overcome my dislike of the man, nevertheless that has to be a blemish. Amos and Micah cry out for social justice, and Isaiah would not have found in Thomas Stearns Eliot the shadow of a great rock in a weary land. Walt Whitman is a healer: What shall we call Eliot? At his poetic best, he achieves a rare kind of sublimity in *Little Gidding* and *The Dry Salvages,* yet even they are distracted by a daemonic misprision of the authentic precursors:

> Last season's fruit is eaten
> And the fullfed beast shall kick the empty pail.

> —Little Gidding

To transfer poetic authority, you must persuade the reader that you are augmenting the foundations of poetry itself. Dante beautifully transumes Virgil and Cavalcanti by refounding Rome and pragmatically adding a third testament to the Christian Bible. Eliot is not Dante and cannot altogether make Shelley and Whitman belated and the poet of *Four Quartets* early. Shelley's *The Triumph of Life* intervenes rather than the Dante it revives, and Whitman's *Song of Myself* and oceanic elegies displace ghostly presences Eliot may have preferred, Hamlet's father among them.

STEVENS THOUGHT OF CALLING HIS *COLLECTED POEMS* (1954) BY THE misleading title *The Whole of Harmonium*. Fortunately, he was dissuaded, since his two greatest volumes, *Transport to Summer* (1947) and *The Auroras of Autumn* (1950), are far more representative of his achievement. For me, the whole of his early volume *Harmonium* (1923) is contained in the poem *Tea at the Palaz of Hoon,* a Whitmanian chant I associate with Stevens's more direct tribute to Walt from *Ideas of Order.* Here the two poems are in sequence:

> Not less because in purple I descended
> The western day through what you called
> The loneliest air, not less was I myself.
>
> What was the ointment sprinkled on my beard?
> What were the hymns that buzzed beside my ears?
> What was the sea whose tide swept through me there?
>
> Out of my mind the golden ointment rained,
> And my ears made the blowing hymns they heard.
> I was myself the compass of that sea:
>
> I was the world in which I walked, and what I saw
> Or heard or felt came not but from myself;
> And there I found myself more truly and more strange.
>
>
> In the far South the sun of autumn is passing
> Like Walt Whitman walking along a ruddy shore.
> He is singing and chanting the things that are part of him,
> The worlds that were and will be, death and day.
> Nothing is final, he chants. No man shall see the end.
> His beard is of fire and his staff is a leaping flame.

Stevens playfully suggested Hoon's name as a cipher for the loneliest air of sky and space. To have tea (or write a poem) at the palaz is to share it with the setting sun. Twilight was the moment of *Crossing Brooklyn Ferry* ("Sun-Down Poem" in 1859) and will be again when Stevens walks the beach in *The Auroras of Autumn.*

The skeptic in Stevens questions Hoon in the second tercet, but the daemon replies in the third, where the external "sprinkled," "buzzed," and "swept through" become the mind's "rained" and "blowing" and we receive a declaration worthy of Captain Ahab: "I was myself the compass of that sea."

In a curious way, Stevens was what Goethe asserted himself to be: "the genius of happiness and astonishment." It is the fashion now to regard Stevens as having been very unhappy, but Holly denied that. His marriage was difficult, but no one outside a relationship can judge it. The poetry is delighted and surprised, indeed comic, more often than not. No one else in American poetic tradition, Whitman and Dickinson included, expresses so well that solitary and inward glory few of us can share with others.

Stevens speaks for the solitude at our center:

> There is a human loneliness,
> A part of space and solitude,
> In which knowledge cannot be denied,
> In which nothing of knowledge fails,
> The luminous companion, the hand,
> The fortifying arm, the profound
> Response, the completely answering
>   voice,
> That which is more than anything else
> The right within us and about us,
> Joined, the triumphant vigor, felt,
> The inner direction on which we depend,
> That which keeps us the little that we are,
> The aid of greatness to be and the force.

This, from the late, rather neglected poem *The Sail of Ulysses,* is for me the most heartening aspect of Stevens in my own old age. Poised on the threshold, the poet discerns:

> A life beyond this present knowing,
> A life lighter than this present splendor,
> Brighter, perfected and distant away,
> Not to be reached but to be known,
> Not an attainment of the will

But something illogically received,
A divination, a letting down
From loftiness, misgivings dazzlingly
Resolved in dazzling discovery.

Evasive more than negative, this affirms nothing except our apprehension that our knowing can be Hamlet-like, that our consciousness can be expanded, without deformation, by "a verse, / A passage of music, a paragraph / By a right philosopher." One wants to apply to Stevens himself the final stanza of his tribute to his teacher George Santayana, *To an Old Philosopher in Rome:*

Total grandeur of a total edifice,
Chosen by an inquisitor of structures
For himself. He stops upon this threshold,
As if the design of all his words takes form
And frame from thinking and is realized.

That is one Stevens; there are others. Eleanor Cook, the eminent Canadian scholar of modern poetry, sees them coming together as a poetry of the earth. That seems right to me if you fuse Keatsian celebration with Nietzsche's injunction: "Think of the earth." What would remain, however, is Walt Whitman's passion, in every sense of "passion." Hart Crane sought to reincarnate Whitman, yet Stevens, who needed to keep Walt at a distance, is far closer to him.

I recall the incredulity of the late Frank Kermode half a century ago when I first began to link Whitman and Stevens. Frank regarded that as another of my wild critical adventures, but the indebtedness of Stevens is now clear enough to many besides myself. The surface similarities are few and the temperaments are opposed. What could be less like Stevens than this passage of Whitman?

Whoever you are, now I place my hand upon you, that you be
    my poem,
I whisper with my lips close to your ear,
I have loved many women and men, but I love none better than
    you.

And yet Whitman, even more than Shakespeare, taught Stevens how to hear and express "the hum of thoughts evaded in the mind," the mode of *Notes Toward a Supreme Fiction, The Auroras of Autumn,* and *The Rock.* Emily Dickinson follows Shakespeare in thinking by and through metaphor, while Whitman and Stevens tend to evade even figurative cognition through an intransitive eros. Here is Whitman followed by Stevens:

> A noiseless patient spider,
> I mark'd where on a little promontory it stood isolated,
> Mark'd how to explore the vacant vast surrounding,
> It launch'd forth filament, filament, filament, out of itself,
> Ever unreeling them, ever tirelessly speeding them.
>
> And you O my soul where you stand,
> Surrounded, detached, in measureless oceans of space,
> Ceaselessly musing, venturing, throwing, seeking the
>   spheres to connect them,
> Till the bridge you will need be form'd, till the ductile
>   anchor hold,
> Till the gossamer thread you fling catch somewhere,
>   O my soul.

> Fat girl, terrestrial, my summer, my night,
> How is it I find you in difference, see you there
> In a moving contour, a change not quite completed?
>
> You are familiar yet an aberration.
> Civil, madam, I am, but underneath
> A tree, this unprovoked sensation requires
>
> That I should name you flatly, waste no words,
> Check your evasions, hold you to yourself.
> Even so when I think of you as strong or tired,
>
> Bent over work, anxious, content, alone,
> You remain the more than natural figure. You
> Become the soft-footed phantom, the irrational

Distortion, however fragrant, however dear.
That's it: the more than rational distortion,
The fiction that results from feeling. Yes, that.

They will get it straight one day at the Sorbonne.
We shall return at twilight from the lecture
Pleased that the irrational is rational,

Until flicked by feeling, in a gildered street,
I call you by name, my green, my fluent mundo.
You will have stopped revolving except in crystal.

A *Noiseless Patient Spider* (1868) first appears in Whitman's Washington, D.C., notebook (1862–63) as a vision intimating homoerotic desire. That desire is still present in the revised version, though in the later poem the major emphasis becomes "the bridge" to hereafter. As is customary with Whitman, the verbs are intransitive, as is the eros: "catch somewhere."

In the final canto of the third part of *Notes Toward a Supreme Fiction* (1942), Stevens addresses his fictive bride, the earth, as what the Hebrew prophets called Beulah, "the married land." She is a trope, though humanized—"the fiction that results from feeling"—and Stevens's "fluent mundo," a world flowing with human speech. "Crystal" suggests a poetic revelation in the secular summer night. An eros more intransitive even than Whitman's warms this canto, which evades Stevens's true muse, the fierce old mother in the waves calling her castaways home.

Stevens endlessly attempted to dismiss her, as early as in *Stars at Tallapoosa* in *Harmonium*:

The lines are straight and swift between the stars.
The night is not the cradle that they cry,
The criers, undulating the deep-oceaned phrase.
The lines are much too dark and much too sharp.

The mind herein attains simplicity.
There is no moon, on single, silvered leaf.
The body is no body to be seen
But is an eye that studies its black lid.

Let these be your delight, secretive hunter,
Wading the sea-lines, moist and ever-mingling,
Mounting the earth-lines, long and lax, lethargic.
These lines are swift and fall without diverging.

The melon-flower nor dew nor web of either
Is like to these. But in yourself is like:
A sheaf of brilliant arrows flying straight,
Flying and falling straightway for their pleasure,

Their pleasure that is all bright-edged and cold;
Or, if not arrows, then the nimblest motions,
Making recoveries of young nakedness
And the lost vehemence the midnights hold.

The multiple meaning of "lines" is Whitmanian, stemming more from *As I Ebb'd with the Ocean of Life* than *Out of the Cradle Endlessly Rocking*. In *As I Ebb'd*, Walt, walking the beach in despair, is "seized by the spirit that trails in the lines underfoot." They are his own lines in prior poems and also the wavering lines where beach and sea meet.

Stars at Tallapoosa addresses both its own lines and those "between the stars." Confronting Whitman, Stevens echoes their mutual ancestor Lucretius: "These lines are swift and fall without diverging." The Epicurean vision of the way things are allows for free will through a divergence, the slight swerve or *clinamen* as the atoms fall down through space. In their affirmative moods, Whitman and Stevens favor the *clinamen,* but here the celebrant of *Harmonium* laments the erotic fulfillment that he (and indeed Whitman) never experienced: "young nakedness / And the lost vehemence the midnights hold."

Though he lurks everywhere in Stevens, the presence-by-absence of Walt Whitman is sinuously central in the uneven but sometimes magnificent *Esthétique du Mal,* from *Transport to Summer.* The title, with a twist, alludes to Baudelaire, though Keats and Whitman pervade the sequence, where "evil" means only what it does in them, the necessary pain and suffering of being a natural man or woman living and dying in a natural world.

In 1963 I visited the poet-critic John Crowe Ransom, a gracious presence, as I would have expected. He had read my early book on Blake and was kind enough to find it useful, but we talked about Stevens and *Esthé-tique du Mal,* first printed by him in *The Kenyon Review* (1944). Ransom, an admirer both of Stevens and of Eliot, genially agreed with my impression that the fifteen rather diverse sections of the poem were held together only by an implicit polemic against Eliot.

The glory of the poem is its final section:

> The greatest poverty is not to live
> In a physical world, to feel that one's desire
> Is too difficult to tell from despair. Perhaps,
> After death, the non-physical people, in paradise,
> Itself non-physical, may, by chance, observe
> The green corn gleaming and experience
> The minor of what we feel. The adventurer
> In humanity has not conceived of a race
> Completely physical in a physical world.
> The green corn gleams and the metaphysicals
> Lie sprawling in majors of the August heat,
> The rotund emotions, paradise unknown.
>
> This is the thesis scrivened in delight,
> The reverberating psalm, the right chorale.
>
> One might have thought of sight, but who could think
> Of what it sees, for all the ill it sees?
> Speech found the ear, for all the evil sound,
> But the dark italics it could not propound.
> And out of what one sees and hears and out
> Of what one feels, who could have thought to make
> So many selves, so many sensuous worlds,
> As if the air, the mid-day air, was swarming
> With the metaphysical changes that occur,
> Merely in living as and where we live.

Eliot had published *Four Quartets* in 1943; this is Stevens's riposte at sixty-five to Eliot at fifty-five. One suspects that Stevens saw Eliot, man and poet, as feeling that desire was "too difficult to tell from despair."

That was the burden of *The Waste Land* and still sounds in *Four Quartets*. Stevens also subtly distances himself from his precursors, the heroic naturalists Keats, Whitman, and Nietzsche, adventurers in humanity who supposedly had "not conceived of a race / Completely physical in a physical world." I find that persuasive only as an anguish of contamination. Keats's affirmation that "They seek no wonder but the human face" is untouched by Stevens's critique, nor does it fit well with Whitman's celebrations of "in living as and where we live." Nietzsche is more problematic, though his Zarathustra attempts to be an Emersonian Adam early in the morning.

Beyond the title poem, the opening of a new mode for Stevens in *The Auroras of Autumn* is most strongly marked by *The Owl in the Sarcophagus,* an elegy for Stevens's closest friend, Henry Church. My experience of reading, teaching, and writing about this elegy throughout the years is that its dark difficulties resolve themselves only gradually. They are awesome yet rewarding and perhaps transcend all others in Stevens.

It is clear that Stevens warily keeps in mind *When Lilacs Last in the Dooryard Bloom'd* in this rival to the major American elegy. At a deeper level of poetic consciousness, the Church elegy engages with Whitman's wildest major poem, *The Sleepers,* which seems to me the most prevalent, barely expressed archetype for Stevens, who carries his Keatsian indebtedness more blithely than Whitman does.

A book like this study of the daemonic sublime in our national literature cannot give too much space to close readings of individual poems, but so central to my enterprise is *The Owl in the Sarcophagus* that I will slow down and consider it in some detail.

A dictionary would identify a sarcophagus as a stone coffin—more literally a flesh-eating stone—but that misleads in regard to this elegy. All of earth can seem that negative to Stevens in certain moods, as in the later *Madame La Fleurie:*

> Weight him down, O side-stars, with the great weightings of
>   the end.
> Seal him there. He looked in a glass of the earth and
>   thought he lived in it.
> Now, he brings all that he saw into the earth, to the waiting
>   parent.
> His crisp knowledge is devoured by her, beneath a dew.

Weight him, weight, weight him with the sleepiness of the
    moon.
It was only a glass because he looked in it. It was nothing he
    could be told.
It was a language he spoke, because he must, yet did not
    know.
It was a page he had found in the handbook of heartbreak.

The black fugatos are strumming the blacknesses of
    black . . .
The thick strings stutter the finial gutturals.
He does not lie there remembering the blue-jay, say the jay.
His grief is that his mother should feed on him, himself and
    what he saw,
In that distant chamber, a bearded queen, wicked in
    her dead light.

This dark splendor sets itself against Whitman's motherly muse and
Stevens's invocations of the mother's face in *The Auroras of Autumn,*
both of which attain an apotheosis in "The earthly mother and the mother
of / The dead" in the Church elegy.

Whitman is perplexed and perplexing on the idea of immortality; at
his most impressive he conveys the insight that we will survive only in the
loving memories of our families, comrades, readers. Stevens shared this
mature vision, as we see in these lines from *The Owl in the Sarcophagus:*

I

Two forms move among the dead, high sleep
Who by his highness quiets them, high peace
Upon whose shoulders even the heavens rest,

Two brothers. And a third form, she that says
Good-by in the darkness, speaking quietly there,
To those that cannot say good-by themselves.

Two Whitmanian vistas blend here, the first from *When Lilacs Last in
the Dooryard Bloom'd:*

Then with the knowledge of death as walking one side of me,
And the thought of death close-walking the other side
   of me,
And I in the middle as with companions, and as holding the
   hands of companions,
I fled forth to the hiding receiving night that talks not,
Down to the shores of the water, the path by the swamp in
   the dimness,
To the solemn shadowy cedars and ghostly pines so still.

This fuses with Walt prefiguring his later hospital service in *The Sleepers:*

I stand in the dark with drooping eyes by the worst-suffering
   and the most restless,
I pass my hands soothingly to and fro a few inches from
   them,
The restless sink in their beds, they fitfully sleep.

Whitman perceives himself as making the night journey and beholds "new beings appear." Stevens names these as sleep, peace, and the mother but says they manifest only to an eye opened by imaginative need:

These forms are visible to the eye that needs,
Needs out of the whole necessity of sight.
The third form speaks, because the ear repeats,

Without a voice, inventions of farewell.
These forms are not abortive figures, rocks,
Impenetrable symbols, motionless. They move

About the night. They live without our light,
In an element not the heaviness of time,
In which reality is prodigy.

That prodigal reality is a poem's state of existence: The poem itself is both the one Stevens is composing and the Whitmanian elegies that affect it:

There sleep the brother is the father, too,
And peace is cousin by a hundred names
And she that in the syllable between life

And death cries quickly, in a flash of voice,
Keep you, keep you, I am gone, oh keep you as
My memory, is the mother of us all,

The earthly mother and the mother of
The dead. Only the thought of those dark three
Is dark, thought of the forms of dark desire.

"Keep you" takes the meaning of watch over or protect you. Its triple repetition by the mother of memory matches the dark three forms moving among the dead. To say that the "thought" of these three, being desire, is dark contrasts them with their vista, which shines against darkness. An overt tribute to Henry Church provides an interlude:

II
There came a day, there was a day—one day
A man walked living among the forms of thought
To see their lustre truly as it is

And in harmonious prodigy to be,
A while, conceiving his passage as into a time
That of itself stood still, perennial,

Less time than place, less place than thought of place
And, if of substance, a likeness of the earth,
That by resemblance twanged him through and through,

Releasing an abysmal melody,
A meeting, an emerging in the light,
A dazzle of remembrance and of sight.

The reader might start with "dazzle," which partly takes its root meaning of "vanish" and now means a blinding by excessive light. Church, an amateur but devoted student of philosophy, enters the light of the forms of thought. I think of a fine turn by my late friend Archie Ammons: "Each is accepted into as much light as it will take."

III

There he saw well the foldings in the height
Of sleep, the whiteness folded into less,
Like many robings, as moving masses are,

As a moving mountain is, moving through day
And night, colored from distances, central
Where luminous agitations come to rest,

In an ever-changing, calmest unity,
The unique composure, harshest streakings
    joined
In a vanishing-vanished violet that wraps round

The giant body the meanings of its folds,
The weaving and the crinkling and the vex,
As on water of an afternoon in the wind

After the wind has passed. Sleep realized
Was the whiteness that is the ultimate intellect,
A diamond jubilance beyond the fire,

That gives its power to the wild-ringed eye.
Then he breathed deeply the deep atmosphere,
Of sleep, the accomplished, the fulfilling air.

The *strangeness* of this always startles me. Stevens generally distances himself from grief and other strong affects. Church had been his closest friend, though hardly intimate. Something troubles Stevens's customary reserve, and there is a return of the repressed, here of the ultimate precursors Walt Whitman, identified with the drowned swimmer of *The Sleepers* in "the giant body . . . / As on water," and Shelley, with "A diamond jubilance beyond the fire," alluding to *The Witch of Atlas:*

Men scarcely know how beautiful fire is—
    Each flame of it is as a precious stone
Dissolved in ever-moving light, and this
    Belongs to each and all who gaze thereon.

"The height / Of sleep" in this vision of ultimates is not so much Hamlet's "sleep of death" as it is the Lucretian serenity in regard to death that Stevens shares with Shelley and Whitman. Stevens regarding finalities is haunted by images of flowing and moving mountains: "mountains running like water, wave on wave" in *The Auroras of Autumn*.

"Peace after death, the brother of sleep," below, carries Stevens to an apex of his daemonic counter-sublime:

IV
There peace, the godolphin and fellow, estranged, estranged,
Hewn in their middle as the beam of leaves,
The prince of shither-shade and tinsel lights,

Stood flourishing the world. The brilliant height
And hollow of him by its brilliance calmed,
Its brightness burned the way good solace seethes.

This was peace after death, the brother of sleep,
The inhuman brother so much like, so near,
Yet vested in a foreign absolute,

Adorned with cryptic stones and sliding shines,
An immaculate personage in nothingness,
With the whole spirit sparkling in its cloth,

Generations of the imagination piled
In the manner of its stitchings, of its thread,
In the weaving round the wonder of its need,

And the first flowers upon it, an alphabet
By which to spell out holy doom and end,
A bee for the remembering of happiness.

Peace stood with our last blood adorned, last mind,
Damasked in the originals of green,
A thousand begettings of the broken bold.

This is that figure stationed at our end,
Always, in brilliance, fatal, final, formed
Out of our lives to keep us in our death,

To watch us in the summer of Cyclops
Underground, a king as candle by our beds
In a robe that is our glory as he guards.

Stevens followed Walter Pater's quest for "the finer edge of words," romancing the etymon, as it were. "Peace" in its origins meant a "fastening," as into a covenant. Yet the peace after death, abiding only in our loving memories, is estranged from any covenant with us. It is like the Godolphin Arabian, a stallion of an elite kind, valued by us though uncommon.

Evoking peace after death, Stevens has the huge task of illuminating a state of being that is unknowable to us. He resorts to incisive tropings, akin to the burning bright of Blake's tyger. The emphasis on brilliance, on emitted rather than reflected light, marks this vision as it does Blake's fearful symmetry.

The *otherness* of "peace after death" scarcely could be more severely stressed: "vested in a foreign absolute." Adornment with quasi-oxymorons ("an immaculate personage in nothingness") gives us a figure all but impossible to hold together in a simple image. Primarily, the figuration has emerged from the tradition of poetic elegy from Virgil to the Alexandrians on to the Renaissance and then Romantic exemplars—"Generations of the imagination." These form the robe that is *our* glory as the figure of peace stands watch for us against the terrible Cyclops, evil one-eyed giant who trapped Odysseus and his men in a cave, compounded here with the Hades where the abducted Persephone must abide every winter.

A different tonality enters in Canto V, where the Whitmanian mother exiles trope and the plain sense of an extraordinary reality prevails:

V

But she that says good-by losing in self
The sense of self, rosed out of prestiges
Of rose, stood tall in self not symbol, quick

And potent, an influence felt instead of seen.
She spoke with backward gestures of her hand.
She held men closely with discovery,

Almost as speed discovers, in the way
Invisible change discovers what is changed,
In the way what was ceased to be what is.

It was not her look but a knowledge that she had.
She was a self that knew, an inner thing,
Subtler than look's declaiming, although she moved

With a sad splendor, beyond artifice,
Impassioned by the knowledge that she had,
There on the edges of oblivion.

O exhalation, O fling without a sleeve
And motion outward, reddened and resolved
From sight, in the silence that follows her last
        word—

A self purged of self-consciousness, the mother who is the memory of all the beloved dead utters, through gesture, our deliverance by discovery. She *knows:* the knowledge of death walking one side of the triad with Walt in the midst. Her final word prophesies the phoenix in Stevens's death poem, where the palm at the end of the mind rises in *Of Mere Being:*

The palm at the end of the mind,
Beyond the last thought, rises
In the bronze décor,

> A gold-feathered bird
> Sings in the palm, without human meaning,
> Without human feeling, a foreign song.
>
> You know then that it is not the reason
> That makes us happy or unhappy.
> The bird sings. Its feathers shine.
>
> The palm stands on the edge of space.
> The wind moves slowly in the branches.
> The bird's fire-fangled feathers dangle down.

Contrast to this:

> O exhalation, O fling without a sleeve
> And motion outward, reddened and resolved
> From sight, in the silence that follows her last word—

Difficult to describe, the epiphanies are related: Stevens's final vision is of a shining fashioned by fire and of a dangling-down gesture. The deathly mother's is a fling of outward motion, in a resolution of the visible. Her last word leads to the rest of silence, but Stevens leaves off to the sound of the wind and of the song of the condition of fire.

The Owl in the Sarcophagus concludes with a summa in Canto VI:

> VI
>
> This is the mythology of modern death
> And these, in their mufflings, monsters of elegy,
> Of their own marvel made, of pity made,
>
> Compounded and compounded, life by life,
> These are death's own supremest images,
> The pure perfections of parental space,
>
> The children of a desire that is the will,
> Even of death, the beings of the mind
> In the light-bound space of the mind, the floreate flare . . .

It is a child that sings itself to sleep,
The mind, among the creatures that it makes,
The people, those by which it lives and dies.

"Monsters," in the second line, refers to mythic creatures such as the phoenix, while "mufflings" are carried out here through foldings, robings, stitchings, adornings. "The floreate flare," Stevens's poetic mind in creation, gives us one of his most poignant moments, as the man of seventy becomes a child again:

It is a child that sings itself to sleep,
The mind, among the creatures that it makes,
The people, those by which it lives and dies.

The Auroras of Autumn

MY COPY OF *THE AURORAS OF AUTUMN* SHOWS I PURCHASED IT IN THE Cornell University bookstore on September 11, 1950, the date of publication. At twenty I was a veteran reader of Stevens, but even *Notes Toward a Supreme Fiction* had not prepared me for the title poem of *The Auroras* or for *An Ordinary Evening in New Haven* (though, as mentioned, I had heard the poet read a shorter version of it in November 1949 in New Haven).

By the time I began teaching Stevens at Yale (1955–56), I found that the poem possessed me. I taught it to my Yale discussion group yesterday and was pleased with fresh openings divulged. Since the subject of this book is the American Sublime or Daemonic, *The Auroras of Autumn* has to be as much the center of this book as are *Song of Myself* or *Moby-Dick*.

Uniquely among Stevens's longer meditations, *The Auroras* is a crisis poem, akin to Whitman's *As I Ebb'd with the Ocean of Life* or Wordsworth's *Intimations* ode. Because of marvelous rhetorical control, *The Auroras* conceals (for a time) the intensity of its psychic travail. Certainly the majestic opening can deceive us as to the urgency with which the aging poet of sixty-eight confronts the Northern Lights:

This is where the serpent lives, the bodiless.
His head is air. Beneath his tip at night
Eyes open and fix on us in every sky.

Or is this another wriggling out of the egg,
Another image at the end of the cave,
Another bodiless for the body's slough?

This is where the serpent lives. This is his nest,
These fields, these hills, these tinted distances,
And the pines above and along and beside
  the sea.

"This is" becomes the refrain of the first canto: a Lucretian statement of the way things are. At twilight, summer's end, the poet beholds the evening sky, illuminated by the flashing aurora borealis, coiling and uncoiling, a great serpent of change. Partly the reference is to the constellation Serpens, visible in autumn in the northern sky. I think, though, that Stevens throughout *The Auroras* has Shelley in mind—*Mont Blanc* and *Ode to the West Wind* in particular and *A Defence of Poetry* as well.

Since I published a rather full reading of the poem in a large book on Stevens (1977) and do not desire merely to condense it here, what follows is an appreciation of the poem in one's eighties rather than in one's fifties. I recite the poem frequently to myself, either silently or aloud, depending on whether I am alone. Possession by memory changes your relation to a poem, longer poems in particular. A sense comes of being inside *The Auroras of Autumn,* of internalizing its drama within the self.

I continue teaching the poem each year and am gratified by my students' response to it. Perpetually fresh, it is different each time I hear them recite and interpret it. Stark, near tragic, the poem nevertheless brings so much joy of language and, at last, such exuberance of being that it becomes what Stevens in *The Rock* (1954) calls "the poem as icon":

It is not enough to cover the rock with leaves.
We must be cured of it by a cure of the ground
Or a cure of ourselves, that is equal to a cure

Of the ground, a cure beyond forgetfulness.
And yet the leaves, if they broke into bud,
If they broke into bloom, if they bore fruit,

And if we ate the incipient colorings
Of their fresh culls might be a cure of the ground.
The fiction of the leaves is the icon

Of the poem, the figuration of blessedness,
And the icon is the man. The pearled chaplet of spring,
The magnum wreath of summer, time's autumn snood,

Its copy of the sun, these cover the rock.
These leaves are the poem, the icon and the man.
These are a cure of the ground and of ourselves,

In the predicate that there is nothing else.
They bud and bloom and bear their fruit without
    change.
They are more than leaves that cover the barren rock.

They bud the whitest eye, the pallidest sprout,
New senses in the engenderings of sense,
The desire to be at the end of distances,

The body quickened and the mind in root.
They bloom as a man loves, as he lives in love.
They bear their fruit so that the year is known,

As if its understanding was brown skin,
The honey in its pulp, the final found,
The plenty of the year and of the world.

In this plenty, the poem makes meanings of the rock,
Of such mixed motion and such imagery
That its barrenness becomes a thousand things

And so exists no more. This is the cure
Of leaves and of the ground and of ourselves.
His words are both the icon and the man.

To contrast this with T. S. Eliot's choruses from *The Rock* would be unfair to the neo-Christian ideologue, but this juxtaposition from *Burnt Norton* is not unjust:

> Other echoes
> Inhabit the garden. Shall we follow?
> Quick, said the bird, find them, find them,
> Round the corner. Through the first gate,
> Into our first world, shall we follow
> The deception of the thrush? Into our first world,
> There they were, dignified, invisible,
> Moving without pressure, over the dead leaves,
> In the autumn heat, through the vibrant air,
> And the bird called, in response to
> The unheard music hidden in the shrubbery,
> And the unseen eyebeam crossed, for the roses
> Had the look of flowers that are looked at.

This passage has been much admired and has poetic virtues, though for me they fade when brought up too close to Stevens's extraordinary chant in praise of the iconic poem he composes. In the longest perspective, certain qualities of the two poets may be difficult to distinguish half a century from now. There is a common element in them: the American icon Walt Whitman, embedded so deep they cannot know it. The fiction of the leaves for us is Whitman's, as is the voice of the hermit thrush, image of solitude marking inner American freedom: "And the singer so shy to the rest receiv'd me."

In its final canto, *The Auroras of Autumn* invokes Stevens's image of the rabbi to interpret the poem for us:

> An unhappy people in a happy world—
> Read, rabbi, the phases of this difference.
> An unhappy people in an unhappy world—
>
> Here are too many mirrors for misery.
> A happy people in an unhappy world—
> It cannot be. There's nothing there to roll

On the expressive tongue, the finding fang.
A happy people in a happy world—
Buffo! A ball, an opera, a bar.

Turn back to where we were when we began:
An unhappy people in a happy world.
Now, solemnize the secretive syllables.

Read to the congregation, for today
And for tomorrow, this extremity,
This contrivance of the spectre of the spheres,

Contriving balance to contrive a whole,
The vital, the never-failing genius,
Fulfilling his meditations, great and small.

In these unhappy he meditates a whole,
The full of fortune and the full of fate,
As if he lived all lives, that he might know,

In hall harridan, not hushful paradise,
To a haggling of wind and weather, by these lights
Like a blaze of summer straw, in winter's nick.

The rabbi gets it right the first time: "An unhappy people in a happy world." That fills out a realization from *Notes Toward a Supreme Fiction:*

From this the poem springs: that we live in a place
That is not our own and, much more, not ourselves
And hard it is in spite of blazoned days.

Blazoned days scarcely are recognized until remembered. Stevens urges his wisdom figure to read to us, the congregation, the completed poem *The Auroras of Autumn.* As "the accomplishment / Of an extremist in an exercise," of the old poet who "turns blankly on the sand," it nevertheless confirms the work of the daemon, for that alter ego is precisely one with "the vital, the never-failing genius."

As he aged, the poet in Stevens increasingly became

> A figure like Ecclesiast,
> Rugged and luminous, chants in the dark
> A text that is an answer, although obscure.

There are many such daemonic texts in late Stevens. I join my students in being profoundly moved by *To an Old Philosopher in Rome,* a kind of pre-elegy for an honored former teacher and friend in the spirit. Composed in 1952 (Santayana died later that year, at eighty-eight) by the seventy-two-year-old Stevens, three years before his own death, it refines the American elegiac mode that Whitman invented in *The Sleepers* and the *Sea-Drift* dirges and then perfected in his *Lilacs* threnody for Abraham Lincoln. The Whitmanian accents haunt Stevens's poem, though their daemonic enlargements are tempered by Stevens's wariness of engulfment by a precursor who seems always in the American sunrise.

In an essay of 1948, now available in *The Necessary Angel,* Stevens wrote a scenario for his Santayana celebration:

> Most men's lives are thrust upon them. The existence of aesthetic value in lives that are forced on those that live them is an improbable sort of thing. There can be lives, nevertheless, which exist by the deliberate choice of those that live them. To use a single illustration: it may be assumed that the life of Professor Santayana is a life in which the function of the imagination has had a function similar to its function in any deliberate work of art or letters. We have only to think of this present phase of it, in which, in his old age, he dwells in the head of the world, in the company of devoted women, in their convent, and in the company of familiar saints, whose presence does so much to make any convent an appropriate refuge for a generous and human philosopher.

The mingled influence of Nietzsche and Walter Pater on Stevens is proudly evident in *The Auroras*: Existence is to be justified as "aesthetic value." Santayana, philosopher-poet, makes his long dying into a poem, in the context of devoted nuns who know they tend an unbeliever:

The bed, the books, the chair, the moving nuns,
The candle as it evades the sight, these are
The sources of happiness in the shape of Rome,
A shape within the ancient circles of shapes,
And these beneath the shadow of a shape

In a confusion on bed and books, a portent
On the chair, a moving transparence on the nuns,
A light on the candle tearing against the wick
To join a hovering excellence, to escape
From fire and be part only of that of which

Fire is the symbol: the celestial possible.
Speak to your pillow as if it was yourself.
Be orator but with an accurate tongue
And without eloquence, O, half-asleep,
Of the pity that is the memorial of this room . . .

Stevens's lifetime engagement with "the scholar of one candle"—inspired by an Emersonian trope from *Society and Solitude* ("A scholar is a candle which the love and desire of all men will light")—will go on from this to the very end of his poetic career. Something of Stevens's own daemon, prompted by precursors yet emanating from deepest selfhood, releases from repression the Shelleyan "fire for which all thirst" or "the celestial possible," a secular transcendence that leads on to the magnificent closing stanzas:

It is a kind of total grandeur at the end,
With every visible thing enlarged and yet
No more than a bed, a chair and moving nuns,
The immensest theatre, the pillared porch,
The book and candle in your ambered room,

Total grandeur of a total edifice,
Chosen by an inquisitor of structures
For himself. He stops upon this threshold,

As if the design of all his words takes form
And frame from thinking and is realized.

The "inquisitor of structures," as much Stevens himself as his rabbi Santayana, stops upon "this threshold," returning us to the poem's opening stanzas:

On the threshold of heaven, the figures in the street
Become the figures of heaven, the majestic movement
Of men growing small in the distances of space,
Singing, with smaller and still smaller sound,
Unintelligible absolution and an end—

The threshold, Rome, and that more merciful Rome
Beyond, the two alike in the make of the mind.
It is as if in a human dignity
Two parallels become one, a perspective, of which
Men are part both in the inch and in the mile.

Swerving from Whitmanian enlargement into a narrowing of perspective, the unbelieving Stevens sings for the skeptical Santayana an "Unintelligible absolution and an end." The hushed splendor of cadence is suitable for both these uncompromising aesthetes, sustained by the uncommon daemonism of their common stance.

This is the sublime Stevens I love best, who speaks for the solitude at the center of American being. If you deprecate this as solipsism, then recall Wittgenstein at his most Schopenhauerian in the *Tractatus:* What the solipsist *says* is wrong but what he *means* is right. Thus he leads the way from a mistaken idealism to a logical positivist realism.

This further finding of the self is Whitmanian rather than Emersonian, and for me is expressed most beautifully in Stevens's rather neglected *Chocorua to Its Neighbor,* whose aesthetic splendor I recall disputing in a public discussion with my late if antithetical friend, the formidable Frank Kermode, who thought it very minor Stevens.

Chocorua is a mountain in New Hampshire, where William James had his summer home. Stevens read and admired James, who might have recognized the poem's stance as his own. A lover of Whitman, whose accents hover here, James might have been as moved by Stevens's emphasis as I am:

> To say more than human things with human voice,
> That cannot be; to say human things with more
> Than human voice, that, also, cannot be;
> To speak humanly from the height or from the depth
> Of human things, that is acutest speech.

The mysterious protagonist of this mountain vision is a "prodigious shadow," incarnating freedom and a large sense of the human: "He was not man yet he was nothing else." There is a kind of breathless rapture emanating from the final two stanzas:

> Last night at the end of night and in the sky,
> The lesser night, the less than morning light,
> Fell on him, high and cold, searching for what
> Was native to him in that height, searching
> The pleasure of his spirit in the cold.
>
> How singular he was as man, how large,
> If nothing more than that, for the moment, large
> In my presence, the companion of presences
> Greater than mine, of his demanding, head
> And, of human realizings, rugged roy . . .

This large human form is akin to William Blake's human form divine, a daemon that would be our destiny if we stood alone, but we cannot. I am carried back to an ambivalent poem of crisis, *Anatomy of Monotony*, which Stevens added to the second edition of *Harmonium* (1931):

> If from the earth we came, it was an earth
> That bore us as a part of all the things
> It breeds and that was lewder than it is.
> Our nature is her nature. Hence it comes,
> Since by our nature we grow old, earth grows

> The same. We parallel the mother's death.
> She walks an autumn ampler than the wind
> Cries up for us and colder than the frost
> Pricks in our spirits at the summer's end,
> And over the bare spaces of our skies
> She sees a barer sky that does not bend.

I have memories of Eartha Kitt singing "Monotonous" and varying the word elegantly to "mono-tone-eous." The poem's title in regard to the first stanza makes that suggestion: Aging mother earth and we are children grown old, who die together in this skilled monotone of eleven lines. Astonishingly, the tone is reversed in the poem's remaining stanza:

> The body walks forth naked in the sun
> And, out of tenderness or grief, the sun
> Gives comfort, so that other bodies come,
> Twinning our phantasy and our device,
> And apt in versatile motion, touch and sound
> To make the body covetous in desire
> Of the still finer, more implacable chords.
> So be it. Yet the spaciousness and light
> In which the body walks and is deceived,
> Falls from that fatal and that barer sky,
> And this the spirit sees and is aggrieved.

The poignance of this burned itself permanently into my memory seventy years ago when I was a poetry-haunted boy of thirteen walking about the Jewish East Bronx of 1943. I hear myself involuntarily murmuring it out loud in troubled moments between sleep and wakefulness.

I teach the poem each spring and find students to be smitten by the second stanza and repelled by the first. Stevens was in his early fifties, yet that "so be it" was for him at that age what it is for me thirty years further on. None of my students accept "so be it," nor should they. Monotone of repetition yields for them to "still finer, more implacable chords." If that is deception, they welcome it, since for them the "barer sky" can and should be postponed.

I am moved almost to tears by "The body walks forth naked in the

sun / And, out of tenderness or grief, the sun / Gives comfort." Stevens, like
D. H. Lawrence, never writes less than superbly when roused by the sun, in
this also following Whitman. From start to end, his work is a solar litany.

It commences in *Harmonium* (1923) with *Sunday Morning,* in the
Nietzschean dance-chant of "devotion to the sun, / Not as a god, but as a
god might be." With *Ideas of Order* (1934), the sun becomes a reproach to
an imagination grown recalcitrant, as in *The Sun This March:*

> The exceeding brightness of this early sun
> Makes me conceive how dark I have become,
>
> And re-illumines things that used to turn
> To gold in broadest blue, and be a part
>
> Of a turning spirit in an earlier self.
> That, too, returns from out the winter's air,
>
> Like an hallucination come to daze
> The corner of the eye. Our element,
>
> Cold is our element and winter's air
> Brings voices as of lions coming down.
>
> Oh! Rabbi, rabbi, fend my soul for me
> And true savant of this dark nature be.

The lions represent poetry as a destructive force, while the memorable
closing couplet is the authentic cry of the distressed human: the fifty-two-
year-old Stevens, who returned to composition in 1931 after seven years of
involuntary silence.

Evening Without Angels, only a step beyond this, insists: "Let this be
clear that we are men of sun" and goes on to an immense declaration:

> . . . Evening, when the measure skips a beat
> And then another, one by one, and all
> To a seething minor swiftly modulate.
> Bare night is best. Bare earth is best. Bare, bare,

Except for our own houses, huddled low
Beneath the arches and their spangled air,
Beneath the rhapsodies of fire and fire,
Where the voice that is in us makes a true response,
Where the voice that is great within us rises up,
As we stand gazing at the rounded moon.

Without the sun, Stevens's daemonic voice will not mount up, as it does in his great epiphany of Walt Whitman fused with the autumnal setting sun. In tribute to Walt, the American daemon, Stevens follows deliberately in the Whitmanian mode:

Sigh for me, night-wind, in the noisy leaves of the oak.
I am tired. Sleep for me, heaven over the hill.
Shout for me, loudly and loudly, joyful sun, when you rise.

Live with Stevens's poetry long enough and you can get a sense of somehow dwelling inside particular poems. Sometimes, when I am fortunate enough to sleep as late as 6:00 A.M., I find myself reciting, in ruefully total identification, *The Latest Freed Man:*

Tired of the old descriptions of the world,
The latest freed man rose at six and sat
On the edge of his bed. He said,
             "I suppose there is
A doctrine to this landscape. Yet, having just
Escaped from the truth, the morning is color and mist,
Which is enough: the moment's rain and sea,
The moment's sun (the strong man vaguely seen),
Overtaking the doctrine of this landscape. Of him
And of his works, I am sure. He bathes in the mist
Like a man without a doctrine. The light he gives—
It is how he gives his light. It is how he shines,
Rising upon the doctors in their beds
And on their beds . . ."
             And so the freed man said.

It was how the sun came shining into his room:
To be without a description of to be,
For a moment on rising, at the edge of the bed, to be,
To have the ant of the self changed to an ox
With its organic boomings, to be changed
From a doctor into an ox, before standing up,
To know that the change and that the ox-like struggle
Come from the strength that is the strength of the sun,
Whether it comes directly or from the sun.
It was how he was free. It was how his freedom came.

The charm of this rueful self-portraiture relies upon a saving irony that tempers without negating personal affirmation. Escaping the truth, whatever that be, Stevens beholds the moment's sun at his favorite time of day, the light just before the sun rises above the horizon, "the difficult rightness of half-risen day," as he describes it in his poem *The Rock*.

Haunted in *The Latest Freed Man* as elsewhere by Hamlet's "let it be," Stevens delights in a momentary transcendentalist freedom: ". . . to be, / To have the ant of the self changed to an ox / . . . Come from the strength that is the strength of the sun." Whitman hovers nearby, fended off by gentle irony.

"What spirit have I except it comes from the sun?" might be termed the Stevensian signature of all things. The late Wystan Auden and I were amiable acquaintances but gave up talking to each other about poetry. Shelley, Whitman, and Stevens were unacceptable to him, aesthetically and spiritually, and our common regard for Thomas Hardy made too little difference. He refused to find how subtly they nuanced their most remarkable effects. I cite this because even so humane and gifted a poet as Auden could be blind to figures too distant from his concerns. Through the years I have learned from this to distrust my own initial hesitations in regard to great poets—Alexander Pope and Lord Byron in particular.

Four Quartets

COMPARING WALLACE STEVENS TO THOMAS STEARNS ELIOT IS A DELICATE matter and yet it is necessary in a large study of American literary daemonism. All that these two major Harvard-educated poets possessed in common was their troubled relation to difficult precursors: Shelley, Tennyson, Swinburne, Whitman. I cannot recall any comments by Eliot on Stevens's poetry, though he became its British publisher. Aside from the polemic against Eliot conducted throughout Stevens's poems, there are a scattered number of rather testy remarks in letters and conversations.

Fundamentally, what divides the two poets was spiritual: Eliot longed to believe in the incarnation, while Stevens sought some last remnant of personal nobility, of a possible wisdom, as in the wonderful poem of 1949, *Things of August,* Canto V:

> We'll give the week-end to wisdom, to Weisheit, the rabbi,
> Lucidity of his city, joy of his nation,
> The state of circumstance.
>
> The thinker as reader reads what has been written.
> He wears the words he reads to look upon
> Within his being,
>
> A crown within him of crispest diamonds,
> A reddened garment falling to his feet,
> A hand of light to turn the page,
>
> A finger with a ring to guide his eye
> From line to line, as we lie on the grass and listen
> To that which has no speech,
>
> The voluble intentions of the symbols,
> The ghostly celebrations of the picnic,
> The secretions of insight.

This is a universe away from Eliot's *The Rock:*

> Why should men love the Church? Why should they love her
>   laws?
> She tells them of Life and Death, and of all that they would
>   forget.

She is tender where they would be hard, and hard where
    they like to be soft.
She tells them of Evil and Sin, and other unpleasant facts.
They constantly try to escape
From the darkness outside and within
By dreaming of systems so perfect that no one will need to
    be good.
But the man that is will shadow
The man that pretends to be.
And the Son of Man was not crucified once for all,
The blood of the martyrs not shed once for all,
The lives of the Saints not given once for all:
But the Son of Man is crucified always
And there shall be Martyrs and Saints.
And if blood of Martyrs is to flow on the steps
We must first build the steps;
And if the Temple is to be cast down
We must first build the Temple.

When I was younger, this difference between Stevens and Eliot seemed temperamental and a question of taste. In old age, it becomes a question of remaining time, since I teach, read, and write now against the clock. Is it my personal prejudice only that finds no aesthetic value whatsoever in the devotional verse of T. S. Eliot?

A fairer juxtaposition would be between *The Waste Land* (1922) and *Harmonium* (1923), since that sets Eliot at his full poetic strength against Stevens's initial achievement. Rather than invoke Stevens at his grandest in that volume (*The Snow Man, Tea at the Palaz of Hoon, To the One of Fictive Music*), I choose his first long poem, the somewhat outrageous *The Comedian as the Letter C,* a parodic quest poem ultimately stemming from Shelley's early *Alastor,* whose title means "the avenging daemon." In it, a young poet is stalked to a death by wasting away, unable to get free of "the unavoidable shadow of himself."

The Comedian, an authentically savage performance, helped end Stevens's poetry for nearly seven years (1924–1931) and is at once dreadful and powerful. Rewritten throughout 1922, it is an equivalent to *The Waste Land,* reflecting a crisis both personal and poetic. A Stevens partisan and no lover of Eliot, I bring the two poems together as instances of the American Daemonic Sublime. Because that is the mode of our national bard, I intersperse ancestral passages of Whitman with instances from *The Waste Land* and *The Comedian:*

> In the swamp in secluded recesses,
> A shy and hidden bird is warbling a song.
>
> Solitary the thrush,
> The hermit withdrawn to himself, avoiding the settlements,
> Sings by himself a song. . . .
>
> Then with the knowledge of death as walking one side of me,
> And the thought of death close-walking the other side
>   of me,
> And I in the middle as with companions, and as holding the
>   hands of companions,
> I fled forth to the hiding receiving night that talks not,
> Down to the shores of the water, the path by the swamp in
>   the dimness,
> To the solemn shadowy cedars and ghostly pines so still.
>
> —When Lilacs Last in the Dooryard Bloom'd

> If there were the sound of water only
> Not the cicada
> And dry grass singing
> But sound of water over a rock
> Where the hermit-thrush sings in the pine trees
> Drip drop drip drop drop drop drop
> But there is no water
>
> Who is the third who walks always beside you?
> When I count, there are only you and I together
> But when I look ahead up the white road

There is always another one walking beside you
Gliding wrapt in a brown mantle, hooded
I do not know whether a man or a woman
—But who is that on the other side of you?

—THE WASTE LAND

Out of the cradle endlessly rocking,
Out of the mocking-bird's throat, the musical shuttle,
Out of the Ninth-month midnight,
Over the sterile sands and the fields beyond, where the child
    leaving his bed wander'd alone, bareheaded, barefoot,
Down from the shower'd halo,
Up from the mystic play of shadows twining and twisting as
    if they were alive,
Out from the patches of briers and blackberries,
From the memories of the bird that chanted to me,
From your memories sad brother, from the fitful risings and
    fallings I heard,
From under that yellow half-moon late-risen and swollen as
    if with tears,
From those beginning notes of yearning and love there in
    the mist,
From the thousand responses of my heart never to cease,
From the myriad thence-arous'd words,
From the word stronger and more delicious than any,
From such as now they start the scene revisiting,
As a flock, twittering, rising, or overhead passing,
Borne hither, ere all eludes me, hurriedly,
A man, yet by these tears a little boy again,
Throwing myself on the sand, confronting the waves,
I, chanter of pains and joys, uniter of here and hereafter,
Taking all hints to use them, but swiftly leaping beyond
    them,
A reminiscence sing. . . .

Which I do not forget,
But fuse the song of my dusky demon and brother,
That he sang to me in the moonlight on Paumanok's gray
    beach,
With the thousand responsive songs at random,
My own songs awaked from that hour,
And with them the key, the word up from the waves,
The word of the sweetest song and all songs,
That strong and delicious word which, creeping to my feet,
(Or like some old crone rocking the cradle, swathed in sweet
    garments, bending aside)
The sea whisper'd me.

               —OUT OF THE CRADLE ENDLESSLY ROCKING

. . . A wordy, watery age
That whispered to the sun's compassion, made
A convocation, nightly, of the sea-stars,
And on the clopping foot-ways of the moon
Lay grovelling. Triton incomplicate with that
Which made him Triton, nothing left of him,
Except in faint, memorial gesturings,
That were like arms and shoulders in the waves,
Here, something in the rise and fall of wind
That seemed hallucinating horn, and here,
A sunken voice, both of remembering
And of forgetfulness, in alternate strain. . . .

He was a man made vivid by the sea,
A man come out of luminous traversing,
Much trumpeted, made desperately clear,
Fresh from discoveries of tidal skies,
To whom oracular rockings gave no rest.
Into a savage color he went on.

               —THE COMEDIAN AS THE LETTER C

Palpably, *When Lilacs Last in the Dooryard Bloom'd* is to *The Waste Land* what *Out of the Cradle Endlessly Rocking* is to *The Comedian as the Letter C*. The mothering father, fathering mother, is the elegiac Walt crying out from swamp and sea to his castaways. The patrician Eliot and the elegant Stevens are odd progeny for the Quaker carpenter-journalist to have fostered, and half a century ago it was no surprise that critics as eminent as Tate, Blackmur, Kermode, and Trilling resisted my genealogies. Now, in the second decade of the twenty-first century, the realization of descent is commonplace. Still, it is the *difference* between the ways Eliot and Stevens absorb Whitman that is my concern here.

Is it too much to say that Walt is one of the guises of Eliot's and Stevens's daemon? I think not. Shelley also plays a role for all three: the doomed quester of *Alastor* and *The Triumph of Life* (crucial for Eliot in *Little Gidding*), the elegist of *Adonais,* the prophet of wind, wave, and leaves in the *Ode to the West Wind*. Late statements by Eliot salute Shelley as the poet in English who best captures the accents of Dante and also praise Whitman as a perfect fusion of form and substance, while Stevens's fiction of the leaves compounds Shelley and Whitman.

Stevens's jaunty long poem *The Man with the Blue Guitar* (1937) also has its affinities with Shelley and with Whitman, but I pass on to a final large-scale contrast between Eliot and Stevens, playing *Four Quartets* against aspects of *The Blue Guitar, Notes Toward a Supreme Fiction,* and some works in *Parts of a World*.

The *Quartets* (1943) were composed while Stevens brought forth *The Blue Guitar* (1937), *Parts of a World* (1942), and *Notes Toward a Supreme Fiction* (1942). *Parts of a World* includes, among my favorites, *The Poems of Our Climate, Mrs. Alfred Uruguay,* and *Extracts from Addresses to the Academy of Fine Ideas.*

The *Quartets,* like all Eliot from *Ash Wednesday* (1930) on, center upon the assumption that the incarnation is fact. Flesh and spirit may collide, but the Word is the goal. Stevens, "a dried-up Presbyterian" by his own description, hardly could be further away from Eliot's theocentric cosmos.

I commence with apposite passages from Eliot's *Burnt Norton* and Stevens's *The Man with the Blue Guitar:*

Descend lower, descend only
Into the world of perpetual solitude,
World not world, but that which is not world,
Internal darkness, deprivation
And destitution of all property,
Desiccation of the world of sense,
Evacuation of the world of fancy,
Inoperancy of the world of spirit;
This is the one way, and the other
Is the same, not in movement
But abstention from movement; while the world moves
In appetency, on its metalled ways
Of time past and time future.

—Burnt Norton

Do not speak to us of the greatness of poetry,
Of the torches wisping in the underground,

Of the structure of vaults upon a point of light.
There are no shadows in our sun,

Day is desire and night is sleep.
There are no shadows anywhere.

The earth, for us, is flat and bare.
There are no shadows. Poetry

Exceeding music must take the place
Of empty heaven and its hymns,

Ourselves in poetry must take their place,
Even in the chattering of your guitar. . . .

Throw away the lights, the definitions,
And say of what you see in the dark

That it is this or that it is that,
But do not use the rotted names.

How should you walk in that space and know
Nothing of the madness of space,

Nothing of its jocular procreations?
Throw the lights away. Nothing must stand

Between you and the shapes you take
When the crust of shape has been destroyed.

You as you are? You are yourself.
The blue guitar surprises you.

—THE MAN WITH THE BLUE GUITAR

I have experimented with this juxtaposition in all fairness, sometimes with discussion groups of Yale divinity students. There may be critics who share Eliot's persuasion and could prefer him here on aesthetic grounds alone, but I have encountered no students who do. For Stevens, "the rotted names" certainly include the incarnate word, and the hymns of heaven are emptied out. If you are Saint John of the Cross or Meister Eckhart, then internal darkness, deprivation, destitution do not lack dignity, but is Eliot the peer of Eckhart?

Eliot's *East Coker* is more impressive but perhaps also suffers when brought up too close with *The Poems of Our Climate* and *Mrs. Alfred Uruguay*.

I said to my soul, be still, and let the dark come upon you
Which shall be the darkness of God. As, in a theatre,
The lights are extinguished, for the scene to be changed
With a hollow rumble of wings, with a movement of
       darkness on darkness,
And we know that the hills and the trees, the distant
       panorama
And the bold imposing façade are all being rolled away—

Or as, when an underground train, in the tube, stops too
    long between stations
And the conversation rises and slowly fades into silence
And you see behind every face the mental emptiness deepen
Leaving only the growing terror of nothing to think about;
Or when, under ether, the mind is conscious but conscious
    of nothing—
I said to my soul, be still, and wait without hope
For hope would be hope for the wrong thing; wait without
    love
For love would be love of the wrong thing; there is yet faith
But the faith and the love and the hope are all in the waiting.
Wait without thought, for you are not ready for thought:
So the darkness shall be the light, and the stillness the
    dancing.

                                        —East Coker

There would still remain the never-resting mind,
So that one would want to escape, come back
To what had been so long composed.
The imperfect is our paradise.
Note that, in this bitterness, delight,
Since the imperfect is so hot in us,
Lies in flawed words and stubborn sounds.

                            —The Poems of Our Climate

"The darkness of God" is a dangerous trope to fire off, unless you back it with more than doctrine. "Wait without thought, for you are not ready for thought" startles when brought together with Stevens's "There would still remain the never-resting mind." One notes that "never-resting" is not "restless," and that those who wait without thought, even for devotional illumination, indeed are liable to grow restless. The choice between Eliot and Stevens here is perhaps an issue of temperament.

Four Quartets does become stronger in *The Dry Salvages* and particularly in *Little Gidding*, Eliot's best poem, in my judgment (though my genuine fondness is for *The Hippopotamus*). *The Dry Salvages* returns the poet to his origins in Massachusetts and Missouri and salutes the Mississippi, more in the manner of Hart Crane's *The River* in *The Bridge* than in the spirit of *Huckleberry Finn*. I give a grand passage describing a beacon off the coast of Cape Ann (a scene of Eliot's boyhood) and follow it with Stevens in the polemical, anti-Eliotic *Extracts from Addresses to the Academy of Fine Ideas:*

> The sea howl
> And the sea yelp, are different voices
> Often together heard; the whine in the rigging,
> The menace and caress of wave that breaks on water,
> The distant rote in the granite teeth,
> And the wailing warning from the approaching headland
> Are all sea voices, and the heaving groaner
> Rounded homewards, and the seagull:
> And under the oppression of the silent fog
> The tolling bell
> Measures time not our time, rung by the unhurried
> Ground swell, a time
> Older than the time of chronometers, older
> Than time counted by anxious worried women
> Lying awake, calculating the future,
> Trying to unweave, unwind, unravel
> And piece together the past and the future,
> Between midnight and dawn, when the past is all
>   deception,
> The future futureless, before the morning watch
> When time stops and time is never ending;
> And the ground swell, that is and was from the beginning,
> Clangs
> The bell.

> —THE DRY SALVAGES

What
One believes is what matters. Ecstatic identities
Between one's self and the weather and the things
Of the weather are the belief in one's element,
The casual reunions, the long-pondered
Surrenders, the repeated sayings that
There is nothing more and that it is enough
To believe in the weather and in the things and men
Of the weather and in one's self, as part of that
And nothing more. So that if one went to the
    moon,
Or anywhere beyond, to a different element,
One would be drowned in the air of difference,
Incapable of belief, in the difference.
And then returning from the moon, if one breathed
The cold evening, without any scent or the shade
Of any woman, watched the thinnest light
And the most distant, single color, about to change,
And naked of any illusion, in poverty,
In the exactest poverty, if then
One breathed the cold evening, the deepest
    inhalation
Would come from that return to the subtle centre.

—Extracts from Addresses to
the Academy of Fine Ideas

Eliot for once is refreshingly free of dogma, while Stevens ravishingly believes only in the self's weather. Despite my fierce partisanship of Stevens and distrust of Eliot, the honors here seem to me equally divided. Both poets achieve apotheosis in *Little Gidding* and *Notes Toward a Supreme Fiction:*

And as I fixed upon the down-turned face
That pointed scrutiny with which we challenge
    The first-met stranger in the waning dusk
    I caught the sudden look of some dead master

Whom I had known, forgotten, half recalled
   Both one and many; in the brown baked features
   The eyes of a familiar compound ghost
Both intimate and unidentifiable.
   So I assumed a double part, and cried
   And heard another's voice cry: "What! are
      you here?"
Although we were not. I was still the same,
   Knowing myself yet being someone other—
   And he a face still forming; yet the words sufficed
To compel the recognition they preceded.
   And so, compliant to the common wind,
   Too strange to each other for misunderstanding,
In concord at this intersection time
   Of meeting nowhere, no before and after,
   We trod the pavement in a dead patrol.
I said: "The wonder that I feel is easy,
   Yet ease is cause of wonder. Therefore speak:
   I may not comprehend, may not remember."
And he: "I am not eager to rehearse
   My thoughts and theory which you have forgotten.
   These things have served their purpose: let them be.
So with your own, and pray they be forgiven
   By others, as I pray you to forgive
   Both bad and good. Last season's fruit is eaten
And the fullfed beast shall kick the empty pail.
   For last year's words belong to last year's language
   And next year's words await another voice.
But, as the passage now presents no hindrance
   To the spirit unappeased and peregrine
   Between two worlds become much like each other,
So I find words I never thought to speak
   In streets I never thought I should revisit
   When I left my body on a distant shore.
Since our concern was speech, and speech impelled us
   To purify the dialect of the tribe
   And urge the mind to aftersight and foresight,

Let me disclose the gifts reserved for age
    To set a crown upon your lifetime's effort.
    First, the cold friction of expiring sense
Without enchantment, offering no promise
    But bitter tastelessness of shadow fruit
    As body and soul begin to fall asunder.
Second, the conscious impotence of rage
    At human folly, and the laceration
    Of laughter at what ceases to amuse.
And last, the rending pain of re-enactment
    Of all that you have done, and been; the shame
    Of motives late revealed, and the awareness
Of things ill done and done to others' harm
    Which once you took for exercise of virtue.
    Then fools' approval stings, and honour stains.
From wrong to wrong the exasperated spirit
    Proceeds, unless restored by that refining fire
    Where you must move in measure, like a dancer."
The day was breaking. In the disfigured street
    He left me, with a kind of valediction,
    And faded on the blowing of the horn.

—LITTLE GIDDING

What am I to believe? If the angel in his cloud,
Serenely gazing at the violent abyss,
Plucks on his strings to pluck abysmal glory,

Leaps downward through evening's revelations, and
On his spredden wings, needs nothing but deep space,
Forgets the gold centre, the golden destiny,

Grows warm in the motionless motion of his flight,
Am I that imagine this angel less satisfied?
Are the wings his, the lapis-haunted air?

Is it he or is it I that experience this?
Is it I then that keep saying there is an hour
Filled with expressible bliss, in which I have

No need, am happy, forget need's golden hand,
Am satisfied without solacing majesty,
And if there is an hour there is a day,

There is a month, a year, there is a time
In which majesty is a mirror of the self:
I have not but I am and as I am, I am.

These external regions, what do we fill them with
Except reflections, the escapades of death,
Cinderella fulfilling herself beneath the roof?

—Notes Toward a Supreme Fiction

There is a shared greatness here in two conflicting visions of the American Daemonic Sublime, both composed in 1942. Eliot's, like *The Waste Land,* is a mosaic of highly deliberated echoes and allusions, the most important reflecting Dante, Shakespeare, Milton, Shelley, and Yeats. It is a triumph that these magnificent presences do not overwhelm and flood out the belated poet, as perhaps they sometimes do in *The Waste Land.* Here Eliot attains the mastery of a *magister ludi.*

Stevens employs only Wordsworth's *The Prelude* and Whitman's *By Blue Ontario's Shore,* a remarkable versification of the preface to *Leaves of Grass 1855.* Read deeply side by side, these passages of Eliot and Stevens at their strongest display how totally antithetical each's poetry is in regard to the other's. Stevens, troubled not by Eliot's achievement but by the younger poet's spiritual and critical stance, dismissed him and Ezra Pound together as highly mannered—indeed, lacquered—representatives of what became a fashionable style.

Eliot's limitations, obscured by academic idolatry, are now clear enough. Stevens's have been overemphasized by R. P. Blackmur and others under Eliot's sway. Both poets, however they protested, gave voice to a daemonic isolated self, as did all of our major shapers studied in this book. That Eliot, alone among them, returned to Christianity had no effect upon his self-imprisonment.

This is not a moral matter, nor is Stevens's arrival at a private sense of glory. The choice between them for me—setting aside Eliot's endless anti-Semitism and his contempt for human nature—is a question of originality and freshness of idiom, as well as Stevens's fecundity against Eliot's minimalist sparseness. As I turn now to this superb passage of *Little Gidding*, I must remark that I find its strength and eloquence unsurpassable. Had Eliot written often thus, it would be vain either to praise or blame him. As Dr. Johnson might have observed, all dispraise of Eliot's poetry would show how much he could spare.

Eliot, a professional scholar of philosophy, was deeply versed in the pre-Socratics and thus familiar with ideas of the daemon. His own speculations on poetic influence, like those of Yeats, explicitly rely on the young poet's relation to the daemon. In *Little Gidding*, the ghost, or double, could well be described as Eliot's daemon, equivalent to Whitman's "dusky demon and brother." I suspect the prime model for Eliot's daemon in this poem is not so much Dante's Brunetto Latini as Shelley's Rousseau in *The Triumph of Life*, greatly admired by Eliot throughout his career.

Why Yeats, Shelley's disciple, forms so large a part of the "familiar compound ghost," I have never understood. Eliot recognized Yeats as the arch-poet of the age but knew that Yeats was not an authentic influence upon the self-exiled American. It may be that Yeats stands in for the actual forerunner, a composite of Shelley, Whitman, and Tennyson. Eliot's scholars follow their idol's lead in stating the forerunners to be Dante, Baudelaire, Laforgue, and Pound, yet I take those to be screens, just as Yeats becomes in *Little Gidding*.

The image of a refining fire—Dantesque, Augustinian, Buddhist—also comes from Shelley's burning fountain in *Adonais* by way of Yeats's Byzantine "Condition of Fire." Shelley speaks of "the fire for which all thirst," and Eliot, like Yeats, assimilates it to the dark Heraclitus: All of us "live in each other's death and die in each other's life," a wisdom shared by Eastern metaphysics and Walt Whitman.

Neither Eliot nor Stevens, two remarkably intelligent minds, possessed cognitive originality, a rare quality in major poets: Dante, Shakespeare, Emily Dickinson, and only a few others had it. Eliot turned to the mystics and contemplatives and to F. H. Bradley for cognitive guidance. Stevens tended to employ Nietzsche and William James, who were not congenial to Eliot. Except for Lucretius and Leopardi, strong poets are uneasy with philosophy. Thinking in poetry is something very different, best studied in Angus Fletcher's *Colors of the Mind*.

Among the personae who appear in Eliot's poems, Eliot's "familiar compound ghost" is the most incisive of his thinkers, especially starting with the lines "Let me disclose the gifts reserved for age / To set a crown upon your lifetime's effort." An irony beyond bitterness pierces me now when I chant this negative paean to old age. I wince at the painful rightness of "the laceration / Of laughter at what ceases to amuse" and have to concede that Eliot, toward whom my ambivalence will prolong itself until my deathbed, never wrote more eloquently than in this immortal wound he gave to consciousness.

Loving Stevens's poetry, I conclude this chapter with some relief by turning to the great chant that allows us to hear "the luminous melody of proper sound" (*Notes Toward a Supreme Fiction*). Having published three previous readings of *Notes Toward a Supreme Fiction*, Canto VIII (*It Must Give Pleasure*), I will not reiterate them here. Instead, I want to stand back and ask what it is that renders these twenty-one lines so central in Stevens's work.

Notoriously, Stevens almost always avoids the Whitmanian capital letter "I" and replaces it by "one." But now he uses it nine times in the passage, not in a fiction, as we might expect from him, unless the daemonization of the self has to be considered that, but starting with the direct self-questioning: "What am I to believe?" The good hour "filled with expressible bliss" extends to "a time / In which majesty is a mirror of the self."

What follows, from an Eliotic viewpoint, is blasphemy, but not for those who join Stevens in replacing Yahweh by the god within: "I have not but I am and as I am, I am." The God of Exodus, ordering the reluctant and stammering Moses down into Egypt, states his name by Yahwistic pun: *ehyeh asher ehyeh*. Mistranslated famously as "I am that I am," this more accurately reads: "I will be [present where and when] I will be." When Stevens cries out "I have not," he chooses his own real presence over possession and mounts by the Emersonian stairway of surprise to the American Sublime momentarily shared with Walt Whitman.

Fifty-nine years into the discipline of teaching how to read poetry, I do not know how to choose between Eliot and Stevens at their best, though I am at home in Stevens and always an alien in Eliot's purgatorial cosmos. "It must give pleasure": By that criterion, I leave Eliot to his informed admirers. Many thousands of admirable students have taught me more than I could impart to them. One admonition I tend to give them is: Learn to say of a poet and a poem that she and it touch upon permanence, and we should recognize this. And yet the freedom of reading well permits saying: Despite this achieved splendor, what is most humane in me just does not allow more than a cold admiration. Stevens has helped me to live my life, while Eliot brings out the worst in me. His dogmatism, dislike of women, debasement of ordinary human existence make me furious. His virulent anti-Semitism, in the age of Hitler's death camps, never abated and dangerously fused with his devotional stance of neo-Christianity. I dismiss the exegetes who defend him and Ezra Pound; at best they are misguided, at worst they participate in murderous attitudes toward Jews and Judaism.

We do not read only as aesthetes—though we should—but also as responsible men and women. By that standard, Eliot, despite his daemonic gift, is unacceptable once and for all time.

VI.

WILLIAM FAULKNER
and HART CRANE

WILLIAM FAULKNER

B Y COMMON AGREEMENT, WILLIAM FAULKNER IS THE CANONICAL American writer of prose fiction since the death of Henry James. No one else among Faulkner's contemporaries or in later generations achieved comparable eminence. He shared nothing with Henry James except a relationship to Hawthorne, who, with Melville, Twain, and Eliot, is a vital part of Faulkner's American literary heritage. Honoré de Balzac, Sir Walter Scott, Shakespeare, the King James Bible, James Joyce, and Joseph Conrad are crucial influences on Faulkner as well, but as with all of the writers in this study, what matters most is Faulkner's own daemonic originality. Nothing in him is other than idiosyncratic, yet what I care most for are *As I Lay Dying* (1930) and *Light in August* (1932), astonishing inventions without precedents. Between the two books came a revised *Sanctuary* (1931), composed, according to Faulkner, "in order to make money," though to me it seems a permanent work, one I prefer to *The Sound and the Fury* (1929) and to *Absalom, Absalom!* (1936), grand yet over-schematized narratives.

This in no way suggests limitations, beyond my own as a reader. I know *The Sound and the Fury* almost by heart and sometimes find the stylistic traces of James Joyce distracting, but in the orchestral sonorities of *Absalom, Absalom!*, Thomas Sutpen's saga, I hear only Faulkner's voice at its richest, in the most comprehensive and ambitious of all his superb prose romances. Sometimes I think that I am so overwhelmed by *Absalom, Absalom!* that I cannot take it all in, despite a score or so of readings throughout its panoramas.

The crucial personages I find most memorable in Faulkner are Darl Bundren of *As I Lay Dying* and Lena Grove of *Light in August*. Doubtless it reveals an oddity in me that I add to this list the murderous gangster Popeye of *Sanctuary*. They certainly are a trio: the visionary Darl; the Keatsian harvest girl Lena, who will be light in August when her baby is born; the impotent Popeye, infamous for violating Temple Drake with a corncob.

Most of the American writers studied in this book start with a recognition of the god or daemon within themselves and compose through moving outward: Emerson, Hawthorne, Whitman, Dickinson, Melville, Henry James, Stevens, Frost, Hart Crane. On the other side, Twain, Eliot, and Faulkner begin in the outside world and only gradually encounter inside themselves an affirmation of their outward vision. Twain is found by his daemon only through his Mississippi writings, which give him the new name "Mark Twain." Eliot, resisting his daemon, constructs an antithetical self of critic-philosopher-theologian, but the poetry breaks through nevertheless, High Romantic and daemonic from the start. Faulkner, more than Twain or Eliot, nurtures a new self when he moves from his early, quite bad poetry to prose fiction. The territory all of them light out for is ultimately themselves.

There had been a sense of otherness in Faulkner's verse, a blend of Swinburne and Eliot, but the desire to be different was diffuse and halting. In the early novel (his third) alternately titled *Sartoris* and *Flags in the Dust,* he began to be found by his own daemon.

That daemon belonged to family tradition and particularly to the singular Old Colonel, William Clark Falkner, great-grandfather of the novelist. Colonel Falkner (1825–1889) was almost a parody of the Southern myth: plantation slaveowner, gallant soldier, aggressive lawyer, political opponent of Reconstruction, popular novelist (*The White Rose of Memphis*), and duelist; he was eventually shot to death in the streets by a business associate. In the Civil War, as a Cavalier sporting a knightly black plume, he led the Magnolia Rifles to victory at Manassas, winning the admiration of General J. E. Johnston and of J. E. B. Stuart. The sublimely absurd litany (all factual) goes on: He was a blockade runner and a railroad pioneer, both of which brought him wealth.

The child William Faulkner (who added a "u" to the family name) grew up hearing stories exalting the Old Colonel, an impressive model for personal emulation and a superb stimulus for heroic fiction like *Flags in the Dust* and *The Unvanquished,* in which he becomes Colonel John Sartoris.

The pride, love, and horror of familial connections became Faulkner's decisive tropes for fiction and life alike. This is the burden of his initial breakthroughs into canonical achievement, *The Sound and the Fury* and *As I Lay Dying.* I recall amiable disagreements with Malcolm Cowley and rather sharp ones with Cleanth Brooks when I argued, in some essays and introductions during the mid-1980s, that in Faulkner the ambivalent sufferings and dooms of familial love far outweighed the joy and solace. The common reader of the Compson and Bundren sagas will decide for herself.

Faulkner's fictive fathers are mostly weak and inadequate, while their wives are stronger but deadly cold. Consistently, Faulkner's own care and affection are for the doomed children of these loveless marriages. I am baffled why Faulkner is regarded by some critics as a misogynist. Of the twelve writers considered in this study, only T. S. Eliot shows an unmitigated aversion to female sexuality. Faulkner's Grecian urn is Caddy Compson, the little sister he never had and always desired:

> I said to myself, Now I can write: Now I can make myself a vase like that which the old Roman kept at his bedside and wore the rim slowly away with kissing it. So I, who had never had a sister and was fated to lose my daughter in infancy, set out to make myself a beautiful and tragic little girl.

I once compiled a critical anthology devoted to Caddy Compson and was surprised to find a wealth of published essays on her. She exists in the pages of *The Sound and the Fury* only as a fleeting presence and felt absence in the minds of her three brothers. Indirect representation is a difficult mode for any writer to hazard—short of Dante, Shakespeare, Joyce, Proust, Henry James—and I do not find that Faulkner quite manages it with Caddy Compson. Walt Whitman had a genius for aesthetic concealment and evasion; Faulkner's was more wavering.

We only begin to comprehend Caddy outside her novel, in the remarkable appendix Faulkner contributes to Malcolm Cowley's still essential *The Portable Faulkner* (1946). My own copy of that book, which introduced Faulkner to me, indicates that I purchased it on July 11, 1946, my sixteenth birthday. A year later I went up to Cornell, where a great teacher, William M. Sale, Jr., taught me how to read prose fiction, in courses that included *As I Lay Dying* and *Light in August*. I recall Sale wondering at the effectiveness of Faulkner's overwrought, belated account of his heroine:

> Doomed and knew it; accepted the doom without either seeking or fleeing it. Loved her brother despite him, loved not only him but loved in him that bitter prophet and inflexible corruptless judge of what he considered the family's honor and its doom, as he thought he loved, but really hated, in her what he considered the frail doomed vessel of its pride and the foul instrument of its disgrace; not only this, she loved him not only in spite of but because of the fact that he himself was incapable of love, accepting the fact that he must value above all not her but the virginity of which she was custodian and on which she placed no value whatever: the frail physical stricture which to her was no more than a hangnail would have been. Knew the brother loved death best of all and was not jealous, would have handed him (and perhaps in the calculation and deliberation of her marriage did hand him) the hypothetical hemlock. Was two months pregnant with another man's child, which regardless of what its sex would be she had already named Quentin after the brother whom they both (she and the brother) knew was already the same as dead, when she married (1910) an extremely eligible young Indianian she and her mother had met while vacationing at French Lick the summer before. Divorced by him 1911. Married 1920 to a minor moving-picture magnate, Hollywood, California. Divorced, by mutual agreement, Mexico 1925. Vanished in Paris with the German occupation, 1940, still beautiful, and probably still wealthy too, since she did not look within fifteen years of her actual forty-eight, and was not heard of again.

What is the aesthetic status of this useful, perhaps overwritten summary? Is it part of the novel, or commentary, or personal revelation? As readers we are grateful for it, and that may be enough of a reply.

David Minter, in his biographical study of Faulkner (1980), remarks: "Faulkner assumed that his authentic self was the self variously and nebulously yet definitely bodied forth by his fictions." If Faulkner had not read Giambattista Vico, as Joyce and Yeats did, he still confirmed the Viconian truth "We can know only what we ourselves have made." After *The Sound and the Fury*'s splendor, Faulkner first knew he had been in the place of the daemon.

Like Balzac and Dickens, Faulkner peopled his own cosmos. All three need to be absorbed as seers of *The Human Comedy* but also as tacticians of individual dooms. More than with Hawthorne and Henry James, we do Faulkner violence when we isolate a single narrative and weigh it by itself. Still, I choose *As I Lay Dying, Sanctuary,* and *Light in August* as three daemonic splendors, regretfully turning away from *Absalom, Absalom!,* "Old Man" in *The Wild Palms* (1939), the Snopes saga (*The Hamlet,* 1940 and later volumes), and *Go Down, Moses* (1946 and earlier). Dead before he was sixty-five, Faulkner left his region, his nation, and the world a wealth of story, character, heightened language, and a visionary stance to rival his greatest American precursors: Hawthorne, Melville, and Twain.

I begin with *As I Lay Dying*, since it is not only his most original achievement but takes its place as a prose poem with the most vital American poetry of its time, that of Frost, Stevens, Eliot, and Crane. *Sanctuary,* a deliberate shocker, was drafted before *As I Lay Dying* but was then revised and published after it. Whatever its origins, *Sanctuary* remains radically alive and fiercely memorable. *Light in August,* Faulkner's masterwork, has sustained its freshness for me since first I read it.

As I Lay Dying: DARL

I FIRST READ *AS I LAY DYING* IN 1946, WHEN IT WAS REPUBLISHED IN A single volume with *The Sound and the Fury*. At sixteen I was overwhelmed by the wonderful *strangeness* of the novel: story, form, characters, tone, stance, and above all, Darl Bundren's vision.

Of the book's fifty-nine sections, forty-three are spoken by members of the poor-white Bundren family: Darl narrates nineteen; Vardaman, ten; Cash, five; Dewey Dell, four; Anse, three; Addie and Jewel, one each. Clearly it is Darl's book, and he is for me the most memorable of all

Faulkner's people. Darl, rather than Quentin Compson, is Faulkner's Hamlet: a visionary who is death's ambassador to us, with a sensibility so acute that it touches the frontier of a kind of madness and a detachment so extraordinary that I cannot find an apt name for it. After all, how can we word Hamlet's disinterestedness?

Faulkner quite categorically called Darl insane:

> Who can say how much of the good poetry in the world has come out of madness, and who can say just how much of the super-perceptivity the—a mad person might not have? It may not be so, but it's nice to think that there is some compensation for madness. That maybe the madman does see more than the sane man. That the world is more moving to him. That he is more perceptive. He has something of clairvoyance, maybe, a capacity for telepathy.

This is admirable, yet is Darl clinically psychotic? I would not say that he is but mad north-northwest and returns when the wind blows from the south. He certainly has a relation to reality altogether his own. Is this madness?

> In a strange room you must empty yourself for sleep. And before you are emptied for sleep, what are you. And when you are emptied for sleep, you are not. And when you are filled with sleep, you never were. I don't know what I am. I don't know if I am or not. Jewel knows he is, because he does not know that he does not know whether he is or not. He cannot empty himself for sleep because he is not what he is and he is what he is not. Beyond the unlamped wall I can hear the rain shaping the wagon that is ours, the load that is no longer theirs that felled and sawed it nor yet theirs that bought it and which is not ours either, lie on our wagon though it does, since only the wind and the rain shape it only to Jewel and me, that are not asleep. And since sleep is is-not and rain and wind are *was,* it is not. Yet the wagon *is,* because when the wagon is *was,* Addie Bundren will not be. And Jewel *is,* so Addie Bundren must be. And then I must be, or I could not empty myself for sleep in a strange room. And so if I am not emptied yet, I am *is.*

How often have I lain beneath rain on a strange roof, thinking of home.

Enchantingly difficult, this works like a Hamlet soliloquy, another meditation upon being and presence. Faulkner's fictive meditation "Carcassonne" (1925), a contemplation of the imagination's dilemmas, strongly resembles the disengaged voice of Darl Bundren. Hamlet's meditative questionings as to the *whatness* of man are resumed in Darl's intricate evasions of being. "And so if I am not emptied yet, I am *is*."

As his benign brother Cash the carpenter will say of Darl: "This world is not his world; this life his life."

Because it is neither his world nor his life, Darl sees at the edge of being:

Before us the thick dark current runs. It talks up to us in a murmur become ceaseless and myriad, the yellow surface dimpled monstrously into fading swirls travelling along the surface for an instant, silent, impermanent and profoundly significant, as though just beneath the surface something huge and alive waked for a moment of lazy alertness out of and into light slumber again.

It clucks and murmurs among the spokes and about the mules' knees, yellow, skummed with flotsam and with thick soiled gouts of foam as though it had sweat, lathering, like a driven horse. Through the undergrowth it goes with a plaintive sound, a musing sound; in it the unwinded cane and saplings lean as before a little gale, swaying without reflections as though suspended on invisible wires from the branches overhead. Above the ceaseless surface they stand—trees, cane, vines—rootless, severed from the earth, spectral above a scene of immense yet circumscribed desolation filled with the voice of the waste and mournful water.

Perhaps evoking Revelation 13:1, Darl's vision heralds the flood that will culminate *As I Lay Dying*. Biblical typology, though it matters elsewhere in Faulkner, seems irrelevant to the Bundren saga. Mark Twain's warning about *Huckleberry Finn*—that anyone finding a moral in it would be shot—applies even more forcefully to *As I Lay Dying*. All morality is excluded from the book, where all that matters is what the speakers *see*.

Calvin Bedient got this right back in 1968, unlike the worthy New Critic Cleanth Brooks, who in 1963 had found in Faulkner's amoral narrative a heroic celebration of familial poetry. The Bundrens are a family disaster but then all of life is a dread realm in *As I Lay Dying*. Against that dread, the fiercely clannish Bundrens oppose their desperate pride. Calvin Bedient expressed this with force:

> Like wounded animals that have instinctively found the herb that will cure them, the Bundrens have discovered pride; and each is typical, each is "universal," precisely in bearing, not as an idea but as a fact, the wound of nakedness, the solitary confinement and essential impotency of conscious being.

They come together only to fight back against reality or against one another: Jewel and Darl are enemy half brothers, Jewel an epitome of pride and Darl devoid of it. The terrible mother Addie, who has loved Jewel and rejected Darl, is at the center of this division.

Of the novel's fifty-nine sections, the fortieth is Addie's single monologue. I am tempted to quote all of its seven pages, but instead I give a montage:

> I could just remember how my father used to say that the reason for living was to get ready to stay dead a long time. And when I would have to look at them day after day, each with his and her secret and selfish thought, and blood strange to each other blood and strange to mine, and think that this seemed to be the only way I could get ready to stay dead, I would hate my father for having ever planted me. I would look forward to the times when they faulted, so I could whip them. When the switch fell I could feel it upon my flesh; when it welted and ridged it was my blood that ran, and I would think with each blow of the switch: Now you are aware of me! Now I am something in your secret and selfish life, who have marked your blood with my own for ever and ever.

> "But your living kin," he said. "They'll be different."
>
> "Will they?" I said. "I don't know. I never had any other kind."
>
> So I took Anse. And when I knew that I had Cash, I knew that

living was terrible and that this was the answer to it. That was when I learned that words are no good; that words don't ever fit even what they are trying to say at. When he was born I knew that motherhood was invented by someone who had to have a word for it because the ones that had the children didn't care whether there was a word for it or not. I knew that fear was invented by someone that had never had the fear; pride, who never had the pride. I knew that it had been, not that they had dirty noses, but that we had had to use one another by words like spiders dangling by their mouths from a beam, swinging and twisting and never touching, and that only through the blows of the switch could my blood and their blood flow as one stream. I knew that it had been, not that my aloneness had to be violated over and over each day, but that it had never been violated until Cash came. Not even by Anse in the nights.

Then I found that I had Darl. At first I would not believe it. Then I believed that I would kill Anse. It was as though he had tricked me, hidden within a word like within a paper screen and struck me in the back through it. But then I realised that I had been tricked by words older than Anse or love, and that the same word had tricked Anse too, and that my revenge would be that he would never know I was taking revenge. And when Darl was born I asked Anse to promise to take me back to Jefferson when I died, because I knew that father had been right, even when he couldn't have known he was right anymore than I could have known I was wrong.

And then he died. He did not know he was dead. I would lie by him in the dark, hearing the dark land talking of God's love and His beauty and His sin; hearing the dark voicelessness in which the words are the deeds, and the other words that are not deeds, that are just the gaps in people's lacks, coming down like the cries of the geese out of the wild darkness in the old terrible nights, fumbling at the deeds like orphans to whom are pointed out in a crowd two faces and told, That is your father, your mother.

My father said that the reason for living is getting ready to stay dead. I knew at last what he meant and that he could not have known what he meant himself, because a man cannot know anything about cleaning up the house afterward. And so I have cleaned my house. With Jewel—I lay by the lamp, holding up my own head, watching him cap and suture it before he breathed—the wild blood boiled away and the sound of it ceased. Then there was only the milk, warm and calm, and I lying calm in the slow silence, getting ready to clean my house.

I gave Anse Dewey Dell to negative Jewel. Then I gave him Vardaman to replace the child I had robbed him of. And now he has three children that are his and not mine. And then I could get ready to die.

One day I was talking to Cora. She prayed for me because she believed I was blind to sin, wanting me to kneel and pray too, because people to whom sin is just a matter of words, to them salvation is just words too.

This appalls powerfully when taken in conjunction with the book's title. In Book XI of the *Odyssey,* Odysseus descends into Hades, where Agamemnon cries out against Clytemnestra, who, he says, "as I lay dying," would not close his eyes and mouth so as to allow him decently to enter Hades. Though the title suggests the allusion, it is not clear to me what about Addie is like Clytemnestra, since Faulkner himself declined to find Addie blameworthy in any way.

Though she rejects belief, Addie adheres to the radical Protestant habit of deciding everything for herself. To Faulkner's cold eye, Addie—with her outrageous sadism, death drive, lack of love for her own children, and endorsement of her father's negativity—is no more reprehensible than the rest of us, though many if not most readers might disagree, as do my own students.

I confess that Faulkner's sympathetic yet dispassionate view of Addie hovers outside my ken, but I admire his stoic acceptance. The book astonishes by its veritable apocalypse of fire and flood, heroism and madness, drive beyond the pleasure principle, and its uncanny fusion of farce and pathos. Faulkner, here more than in his other books, bruises the limits of his language in a zest to say what cannot be said, and to see what cannot be seen.

He chooses not to let us see the actual burial of Addie's corpse, since the mad journey *is* the book, and to consider its goal would be a waste of narrative impetus. Faulkner's parody of quest-romance owes much to Eliot's *The Waste Land*, a dominant influence in forming Faulkner's peculiar sensibility. *Sanctuary* is also profoundly Eliotic. Faulkner and Hart Crane, who may never have read each other, both attempted to transume Eliot's stance and style into modes of heroic action, Melvillean in Faulkner, Whitmanian in Crane. The shadow of *The Waste Land* nevertheless hovers over both *As I Lay Dying* and *The Bridge*.

When Darl desperately sets fire to the Gillespie barn in an effort to incinerate Addie's remains and thus end the dreadful journey, his enemy half brother, Jewel, saves the corpse and its enclosing coffin by an act of remarkable courage. Darl narrates it in one of Faulkner's marvelous epiphanies:

> "Jewel!" Dewey Dell cries; "Jewel!" It seems to me that I now hear the accumulation of her voice through the last five minutes, and I hear her scuffling and struggling as pa and Mack hold her, screaming "Jewel! Jewel!" But he is no longer looking at us. We see his shoulders strain as he upends the coffin and slides it single-handed from the saw-horses. It looms unbelievably tall, hiding him: I would not have believed that Addie Bundren would have needed that much room to lie comfortable in; for another instant it stands upright while the sparks rain on it in scattering bursts as though they engendered other sparks from the contact. Then it topples forward, gaining momentum, revealing Jewel and the sparks raining on him too in engendering gusts, so that he appears to be enclosed in a thin nimbus of fire. Without stopping it overends and rears again, pauses, then crashes slowly forward and through the curtain. This time Jewel is riding upon it, clinging to it, until it crashes down and flings him forward and clear and Mack leaps forward into a thin smell of scorching meat and slaps at the widening crimson-edged holes that bloom like flowers in his undershirt.

Enclosed in a nimbus of flame, Jewel rides his mother's coffin as Ahab in Fedallah's boat rides the vortex of Moby Dick to a final destruction. Somewhere in Faulkner's daemonic consciousness, Addie's coffin is associated with Queequeg's, which at the end saves Ishmael alone from the *Pe-*

quod's immolation. Faulkner, in 1927, in response to the book editor of the *Chicago Tribune*'s question of what book he wished he'd written, chose *Moby-Dick*, stating unforgettably that he envied Ahab his death: "a sort of Golgotha of the heart become immutable as bronze in the sonority of its plunging ruin."

Darl's final monologue is too painful for me to go on rereading. Incarcerated in a state madhouse, this most poignant consciousness in Faulkner is reduced to a drone of one "yes" after another.

Faulkner exalted courage, yet his exemplars of that virtue do not persuade me. The wounds he chronicles in his protagonists can be unbearable, but that belongs to his own courage as a writer.

Sanctuary: POPEYE

I THINK FAULKNER SAID HE WOULD WANT MICKEY MOUSE TO PLAY POPeye should *Sanctuary* ever be filmed. In 1961, a travesty came forth with Lee Remick as Temple Drake and Yves Montand as one Candy Man, a lustful Cajun who rapes and exploits the blue-eyed Remick. Popeye flickers by in a flash, and the movie is an unfortunate venture throughout.

Sanctuary is a nightmare narrative in the spirit of the Jacobean dramatists: John Webster, John Ford, Cyril Tourneur, Thomas Middleton. The genre is marked by sudden violence, mournful eloquence, deathly eros, and sadomasochistic ecstasies. Temple Drake, under the ministrations of Red, the impotent Popeye's surrogate, becomes a furnace of insatiable lust while continuing to be a judge's daughter: selfish, unjust, untruthful, reverting to respectability when it is in her interest.

Popeye—as Faulkner's casting suggestion of Mickey Mouse shows—is a brilliant cartoon, hardly a person, and yet he is *Sanctuary*'s daemon: The book is his. He looks rather like some aspects of *The Wizard of Oz*'s Tin Man. A prominent Memphis mobster, raking profits from gambling, moonshine, and prostitution, Popeye is beyond affect, as his execution will show:

> While he was on his way home that summer they arrested him for killing a man in one town and at an hour when he was in another town killing somebody else—that man who made money and had

nothing he could do with it, spend it for, since he knew that alcohol would kill him like poison, who had no friends and had never known a woman and knew he could never—and he said, "For Christ's sake," looking about the cell in the jail of the town where the policeman had been killed, his free hand (the other was hand-cuffed to the officer who had brought him from Birmingham) fin-icking a cigarette from his coat.

"Let him send for his lawyer," they said, "and get that off his chest. You want to wire?"

"Nah," he said, his cold, soft eyes touching briefly the cot, the high small window, the grafted door through which the light fell. They removed the handcuff; Popeye's hand appeared to flick a small flame out of thin air. He lit the cigarette and snapped the match toward the door. "What do I want with a lawyer? I never was in— What's the name of this dump?"

They came for him at six. The minister went with him, his hand under Popeye's elbow, and he stood beneath the scaffold praying, while they adjusted the rope, dragging it over Popeye's sleek, oiled head, breaking his hair loose. His hands were tied, so he began to jerk his head, flipping his hair back each time it fell forward again, while the minister prayed, the others motionless at their posts with bowed heads.

Popeye began to jerk his neck forward in little jerks. "Psssst!" he said, the sound cutting sharp into the drone of the minister's voice; "pssssst!" The sheriff looked at him; he quit jerking his neck and stood rigid, as though he had an egg balanced on his head. "Fix my hair, Jack," he said.

"Sure," the sheriff said. "I'll fix it for you;" springing the trap.

Faulkner's narration here is as affectless as Popeye and is high art. *Sanctuary,* perhaps because of its author's ambivalence toward it, remains undervalued. Popeye is more than a grotesque: He crosses the frontier of myth and establishes a new mode of parodistic farce, one exploited after Faulkner by Nathanael West, Flannery O'Connor, and Thomas Pynchon. *Miss Lonelyhearts, The Violent Bear It Away,* and *The Crying of Lot 49* sail in *Sanctuary*'s wake, permanent works of parodistic frenzy, akin just as *Sanctuary* is to the Jacobean extravaganzas of John Webster, Cyril Tourneur, Thomas Middleton, and John Ford. Popeye's ancestors can be searched out in *The White Devil, The Atheist's Tragedy, The Revenger's Tragedy,* and *'Tis Pity She's a Whore.*

Sanctuary parodies detective fiction, a genre Faulkner yearned to master. I can think of only a few hard-boiled detective stories as brutal as *Sanctuary.* Faulkner summed it up as a book "about a girl who gets raped with a corn cob." Impotent Popeye inducts Temple Drake with that gesture. Faulkner shows a grudge against Temple, but I would dispute feminist contentions that this indicates a profound misogyny. Ruby Lamar, the martyred Lee Goodwin's common-law wife, is a rather admirable character, and there are others scattered in his pages.

This is not to say that Temple Drake finally is any less depraved than the murderous Popeye. Horace Benbow, the observing character in the book, totally pervades the original version of *Sanctuary,* splendidly edited for us by Noel Polk, who provides us with a necessary guide to the textual labyrinths of Faulknerian revision.

Polk rightly calls the initial *Sanctuary* Horace Benbow's Gothic nightmare as much as it also is a repressed element in William Faulkner. As Polk remarks, the reader needs to experience both versions of the novel, since Faulkner's achievement hovers in the space between them. Horace's childhood traumas (and Faulkner's?) lurk throughout the original text.

We are reminded by Polk that in Faulkner's cosmos the mothers dominate and badger, though none as terribly as Addie Bundren of *As I Lay Dying.* The fathers are weak, evasive, and in a sense impotent. Like Polk, I prefer the first *Sanctuary,* because the image of Faulkner's voice is evident more consistently. One hears his *duende,* the daemonic tonality of his genius, at its most astonishingly free, and where else except in Darl Bundren do we encounter it so wonderfully?

Faulkner himself did not see anyone in *Sanctuary* as evil: For him, even Popeye is "another lost human being." All of the protagonists—Temple, Horace, Popeye, Goodwin, Ruby—end in a condition of total emotional indifference, a despair so total that to name it apathy or nihilism seems inadequate. Popeye, quickest of killers, is content to be hanged by a hick hangman for a murder he did not commit. It does not matter to him. Does it to the reader?

That is Faulkner's art, that we do care. Why? We never get inside Popeye's mind, whatever it be. Violated Temple has very little mind, while poor Horace Benbow has more than he can accommodate. What is it about *Sanctuary* that gives aesthetic value a chance to get started?

Faulkner started out writing bad poems influenced by *The Waste Land* but became a great novelist under the influence of Dostoyevsky. Even a casual reader might note the similarities of crime, trial, and judgment between *Sanctuary* and Dostoyevsky's *Crime and Punishment* and *The Brothers Karamazov*. Metallic Popeye is no Smerdyakov, but the two murderers hang—Popeye for a killing he did not commit and Smerdyakov at his own hands. Svidrigaïlov and Raskolnikov, and Ivan and Mitya Karamazov, scarcely resemble Horace Benbow and Lee Goodwin, while Katerina Ivanovna and Grushenka are yet more remote from Temple Drake and Ruby Lamar, but it is the situations of false accusations and injustice that Faulkner absorbs and transforms throughout *Sanctuary*.

It was courageous of Faulkner to echo *The Brothers Karamazov* in particular. Freud perhaps overhailed the book by calling Dostoevsky's masterpiece the greatest Western novel, but it strongly contends with Cervantes, Tolstoy, Balzac, Stendhal, Flaubert, Proust, Joyce, Mann, Lawrence, or anyone else. *Sanctuary*, authentic Gothic shocker, cannot be placed in such company.

Dostoyevsky also haunts *The Sound and the Fury*, though less cogently. One cannot say that Faulkner's allusive overtones enhance aesthetic value in *Sanctuary*, but they supply literary context. A fiercely nationalistic (and anti-Semitic) Russian Orthodox believer, Dostoyevsky exalts Alyosha and handles Ivan very darkly, though with novelistic fairness. The theocentric universe of *The Brothers Karamazov* contrasts with the Gnostic wasteland of *Sanctuary*, which is set—like most of Faulkner's great phase of 1927 through 1930—in what Gnostic ancients termed the *kenoma*, the cosmological emptiness into which we have been thrown.

Contra Cleanth Brooks, there is little "residual Christianity" in Faulkner, nor does Faulkner accept T. S. Eliot's vision of evil. Faulkner reverses biblical typology—indeed, subverts it—with the single exception of that late disaster, *A Fable*. If there is a god in him, it is the stranger or alien god of the Gnostics, who wanders in the interstellar spaces or else is buried deep within the rock of the self. Like most of our Southern writers, Faulkner is no Emersonian, yet Emerson's American religion of self-reliance is relevant to Faulkner's great books of 1927 to 1932. Not that

Faulkner's fictive people of those years are self-reliant: How can lost souls, who wait in vain for their doom to life, manifest any confidence in their own daemons? The survivors in *Sanctuary*—Ruby, Temple, Horace—are as dead as Goodwin and Popeye.

Sanctuary, particularly in its original version, will prove to be a permanent work. Though it is set in Faulkner's self-generated county, by now, after eighty years, it has contaminated reality, and not just in the American South and Southwest.

Light in August: JOE CHRISTMAS

LIGHT IN AUGUST WAS COMPOSED BETWEEN 1931 AND 1932. IN 2013 THE novel retains its power, sweep, terror, and the perpetual relevance of great art. Of the protagonists, whose novel is it: Joe Christmas's? Lena Grove's? Gail Hightower's? Joanna Burden, Byron Bunch, Percy Grimm, Doc Hines, Simon McEachern, and the Armstids surround the central figures. Yet Faulkner's narrative voice—very different from those of the speakers of *As I Lay Dying* and *Sanctuary*—outweighs even those of Joe Christmas and Lena. It is a remarkably varied tonal instrument, as in the contrast between the novel's opening and close:

> Sitting beside the road, watching the wagon mount the hill toward her, Lena thinks, "I have come from Alabama; a fur piece. All the way from Alabama a-walking. A fur piece." Thinking *although I have not been quite a month on the road I am already in Mississippi, further from home than I have ever been before. I am now further from Doane's Mill than I have been since I was twelve years old.*
>
> She had never even been to Doane's Mill until after her father and mother died, though six or eight times a year she went to town on Saturday, in the wagon, in a mailorder dress and her bare feet flat in the wagon bed and her shoes wrapped in a piece of paper beside her on the seat. She would put on the shoes just before the wagon reached town. After she got to be a big girl she would ask her father to stop the wagon at the edge of town and she would get down and walk. She would not tell her father why she wanted to walk in in-

stead of riding. He thought that it was because of the smooth streets, the sidewalks. But it was because she believed that the people who saw her and whom she passed on foot would believe that she lived in the town too.

When she was twelve years old her father and mother died in the same summer, in a log house of three rooms and a hall, without screens, in a room lighted by a bugswirled kerosene lamp, the naked floor worn smooth as old silver by naked feet. She was the youngest living child. Her mother died first. She said, "Take care of paw." Lena did so. Then one day her father said, "You go to Doane's Mill with McKinley. You get ready to go, be ready when he comes." Then he died. McKinley, the brother, arrived in a wagon. They buried the father in a grove behind a country church one afternoon, with a pine headstone. The next morning she departed forever, though it is possible that she did not know this at the time, in the wagon with McKinley, for Doane's Mill. The wagon was borrowed and the brother had promised to return it by nightfall.

Then what? What did she do then?

Nothing. Just sitting there, riding, looking out like she hadn't ever seen country—roads and trees and fields and telephone poles— before in her life. She never saw him at all until he come around to the back door of the truck. She never had to. All she needed to do was wait. And she knew that

Him?

Sho. He was standing at the side of the road when we come around the curve. Standing there, face and no face, hangdog and determined and calm too, like he had done desperated himself up for the last time, to take the last chance, and that now he knew he wouldn't ever have to desperate himself again He continues: "He never looked at me at all. I just stopped the truck and him already running back to go around to the door where she was sitting. And he come around the back of it and he stood there, and her not even surprised. 'I done come too far now,' he says. 'I be dog if I'm going to quit now.' And her looking at him like she had known all the time what he was going to do before he even knew himself that he was going to, and that whatever he done, he wasn't going to mean it."

" 'Ain't nobody never said for you to quit,' she says." He laughs, lying in the bed, laughing. "Yes, sir. You can't beat a woman. Because do you know what I think? I think she was just travelling. I don't think she had any idea of finding whoever it was she was following. I don't think she had ever aimed to, only she hadn't told him yet. I reckon this was the first time she had ever been further away from home than she could walk back before sundown in her life. And that she had got along all right this far, with folks taking good care of her. And so I think she had just made up her mind to travel a little further and see as much as she could, since I reckon she knew that when she settled down this time, it would likely be for the rest of her life. That's what I think. Setting back there in that truck, with him by her now and the baby that hadn't never stopped eating, that had been eating breakfast now for about ten miles, like one of these dining cars on the train, and her looking out and watching the telephone poles and the fences passing like it was a circus parade. Because after a while I says, 'Here comes Saulsbury' and she says,

" 'What?' and I says,

" 'Saulsbury, Tennessee' and I looked back and saw her face. And it was like it was already fixed and waiting to be surprised, and that she knew that when the surprise come, she was going to enjoy it. And it did come and it did suit her. Because she said,

" 'My, my. A body does get around. Here we ain't been coming from Alabama but two months, and now it's already Tennessee.' "

Lena Grove, a never-resting benign force, moves on with a biblical sense of the Blessing, in shattering contrast to the death drive of Joe Christmas and his Joanna Burden, and of Hightower, Grimm, and everyone else except the humorous and helpful Armstids. Faulkner gives her the opening and closing visions, framing the violence, hatred, self-destructive drive of the rest of the novel. Faulkner's esteem for her is palpable and clearly redeems much of the misogyny that feminists assert to be his stance.

Except for *As I Lay Dying,* I take *Light in August* to be Faulkner's finest aesthetic achievement. It tends to defeat criticism, perhaps because the false touchstone of "unity" is applied to it. The sagas of Joe Christmas, Hightower, and Lena are separate stories, and the links between them are minor. But narrative power sustains all three recitals, and each is aided by juxtaposition with the others. The existence of Joe Christmas is a continuous nightmare, while Hightower dwells in an unreal dream, and Lena moves on like the natural process she both exemplifies and enhances.

So intricate is the plot of *Light in August* that I find it helpful to note its more labyrinthine and sinuously elaborate aspects. As Lena travels to Jefferson, she sees a burning house in the middle distance. Only later will we learn that this is Joanna Burden's house, torched by Joe Christmas, who has murdered her.

Byron Bunch, who falls in love with Lena at first glance, is Hightower's friend. The two represent polarities of being, though both are humane and decent persons. Byron lives in reality, Hightower in a Tennysonian dream of the past and all its illusions. Civil War legends of his grandfather— a daring raid or an ignoble immolation by shotgun while chicken-stealing—mingle with bizarre memories of his wife's infidelity and his subsequent expulsion by his parish congregation. These also are gilded by dream-distancing. It is not until Hightower delivers Lena's baby that he encounters reality. This leads to his culminating attempt to save Joe Christmas from a lynch mob of the Ku Klux Klan, akin to Byron Bunch's beating by Lucas Burch, Lena's perpetually illusive despoiler.

Light in August is the book of Joe Christmas, a man neither black nor white, decent nor evil, who is doomed by his region, upbringing, and election as a born, total victim. His symbolic relation to Jesus Christ has nothing to do with redemption or divinity but only with the exemplary status of Jesus as infinite sufferer.

Faulkner's sympathy with Joe Christmas is not shared by the reader, because the novelist renders the outcast in terms that are antipathetic: Christmas is murderous, vicious to all women as such, and loathes his own sexual desires while abominating theirs. He *is* the death drive beyond the pleasure principle and contaminates Joanna Burden with what becomes her own northern Puritan version of the same destructive malady.

Is he a tragic protagonist? Not in the Shakespearean sense: He is a more complex cartoon than Popeye but a caricature nevertheless. For tragic, almost Shakespearean figures in Faulkner, you turn to Darl Bundren and Quentin Compson, who possess consciousness, while Thomas Sutpen seems to me precariously balanced between Marlovian caricature and Shakespearean inwardness.

And yet there seems no end to Joe Christmas; like Darl Bundren, he intimates no limits. Faulkner has managed to catch in Joe something permanently American, not just Southern. Not knowing yet fearing personal "blackness," Christmas in one sense is the American everyman, wondering just who or what he or she is or madly fearing madness, murderous impulses, suicide, lovelessness, or the curse of sundered parentage. I never will understand Cleanth Brooks on Faulkner. Somehow that archetypal Southern critic thought Faulkner exalted both supposed community values and family cohesiveness. *Light in August* acutely shows the malign influence of both Mississippi social mores and family romance.

And yet the novel is Faulkner's richest in the novelty of its tonalities and human stances. Balancing Christmas and the increasingly deranged Joanna, and the dubious grouping of Lucas Burch, McEachern, and Doc Hines are the book's extremes: the Nazi stormtrooper-in-advance, Percy Grimm, who murders and mutilates Joe Christmas; the benignly deluded Hightower; Byron Bunch; and, above all, there is Lena Grove, the unfallen Eve of an otherwise desolated world.

Indeed *Light in August* is the book of Joe Christmas; and yet whenever I recall it, I think first of Lena. Her relevance to the book has been questioned but not by any deep reader of Faulkner. Her serene presence contributes to what can be termed Faulkner's "ecstasy of the ordinary," curious moments that are secular epiphanies.

Like his ancestor Melville in *Moby-Dick* and his disciple Cormac McCarthy in *Blood Meridian*, Faulkner alternates violent action with a quietism akin to that which calms Melville's "tornadoed Atlantic of my being." There are in Faulkner uncanny moments of listening, as if his narrative art sought a still center, where racial and personal violence, and the agonies of copulation and dying, could never intrude.

HART CRANE

White Buildings: URBAN PURGATORIO

PRAISE FOR AN URN

THE CRY OF THE OCEAN IS HEARD IN STEVENS AND IN ELIOT BUT MUTED, in covert echo of Whitman. Hart Crane, consciously braiding together Melville and Whitman, returns to their diapason of water. It is as though his Orphic resignation is enriched by them at a very high cost of confirmation, darker for the life than for the work.

Crane's capacity for absorbing American precursors extends to Dickinson and to Eliot: Your gift had to be prodigal to *survive* such wealth. Hart Crane at seventeen had a unique voice, refined by endless revision until his death in 1932. Whitman's image of voice is what he named "the tally"; Crane's is the most traditional of such images—the wind:

> And so it was I entered the broken world
> To trace the visionary company of love, its voice
> An instant in the wind (I know not whither hurled),
> But not for long to hold each desperate choice.

Whitman's verbs are intransitive; so was his eros, directed "To You, Whoever You Are." Crane's verbs seek and briefly find too many objects. So did his eros. The tally counts the voices of the mockingbird and the hermit thrush, fusing them with Walt's and those of night, death, the mother, and the sea. Turning into the wind, Hart's words vault the sea, the prairie's dreaming sod, transmembering the image of poetic election into a knowing myth.

Crane's profound continuities with Romantic tradition emerge strongly in the elegy *Praise for an Urn*. Ernest Nelson, a painter whom the young poet knew in Cleveland, where he grew up, was killed by a reckless driver in December 1921. Crane's memorial followed soon after:

It was a kind and northern face
That mingled in such exile guise
The everlasting eyes of Pierrot
And, of Gargantua, the laughter.

His thoughts, delivered to me
From the white coverlet and pillow,
I see now, were inheritances—
Delicate riders of the storm.

The slant moon on the slanting hill
Once moved us toward presentiments
Of what the dead keep, living still,
And such assessments of the soul

As, perched in the crematory lobby,
The insistent clock commented on,
Touching as well upon our praise
Of glories proper to the time.

Still, having in mind gold hair,
I cannot see that broken brow
And miss the dry sound of bees
Stretching across a lucid space.

Scatter these well-meant idioms
Into the smoky spring that fills
The suburbs, where they will be lost.
They are no trophies of the sun.

Pierrot, the gentle clown figure of commedia dell'arte, fuses in Nelson with Gargantua, exuberant titan of the will in Rabelais. The poem's lasting power is in its final two stanzas. Crane's ultimate loss is conveyed by the highly original trope "And miss the dry sound of bees / Stretching across a lucid space." That is a metaphor for Nelson's consciousness, his amiably ironic serenity.

The last stanza is Crane at his best: the idioms—the poem's own language—mingle with Nelson's ashes. Superbly, the ultimate line plays against the close of Keats's *Ode on Melancholy:*

I

No, no, go not to Lethe, neither twist
　Wolfs-bane, tight-rooted, for its poisonous wine;
Nor suffer thy pale forehead to be kiss'd
　By nightshade, ruby grape of Proserpine;
Make not your rosary of yew-berries,
　　Nor let the beetle, nor the death-moth be
　　　Your mournful Psyche, nor the downy owl
A partner in your sorrow's mysteries;
　　For shade to shade will come too drowsily,
　　　And drown the wakeful anguish of the soul.

II

But when the melancholy fit shall fall
　Sudden from heaven like a weeping cloud,
That fosters the droop-headed flowers all,
　And hides the green hill in an April shroud;
Then glut thy sorrow on a morning rose,
　Or on the rainbow of the salt sand-wave,
　　Or on the wealth of globed peonies;
Or if thy mistress some rich anger shows,
　　Emprison her soft hand, and let her rave,
　　　And feed deep, deep upon her peerless eyes.

III

She dwells with Beauty—Beauty that must die;
　And Joy, whose hand is ever at his lips
Bidding adieu; and aching Pleasure nigh,
　Turning to poison while the bee-mouth sips:
Ay, in the very temple of Delight
　Veil'd Melancholy has her sovereign shrine,
　　Though seen of none save him whose strenuous tongue

> Can burst Joy's grape against his palate fine;
> His soul shall taste the sadness of her might,
> And be among her cloudy trophies hung.

The "bee-mouth" may well have suggested to Crane the dry sound of bees. Keats's quester ends up as another glorious victim of Melancholy, taken here as the muse. The "cloudy trophies" of the souls of poets like Shelley, Keats, and Hart Crane will be exhibited as among our triumphs. Crane believed his own elegy for Ernest Nelson would be lost, not being one of the trophies of the Sun God. Fortunately, his pessimism has proved mistaken with regard to his stronger poems, including this one.

POSSESSIONS

I BEGAN READING HART CRANE IN THE LIBRARY ON MY TENTH BIRTH-day. For my twelfth birthday, July 11, 1942, my sisters pooled together their money and bought me my own copy of *The Collected Poems of Hart Crane,* the first book I ever owned. Today I commence writing what will have to be farewell to my personal favorite among all poets, ancient and modern. A reader's passion for a poetry he scarcely understood when first encountered has augmented over seven decades into an instrument or touchstone for judging and appreciating all of American poetry.

Crane deliberately fused his American precursors into the refiner's fire of his style and stance. Whitman, Melville, Dickinson, Poe, Eliot, and Stevens join Blake, Shelley, Keats, and Hopkins among his strong forebears, as do Shakespeare, Marlowe, Donne, and Rimbaud. Yet so daemonic was Hart Crane's gift, so possessed by a vision of poetry's power to transform self and cosmos, that this formidable tradition scarcely daunted him.

Rimbaud's "It can only be the end of the world, advancing," from *Illuminations,* was chosen by Crane as the epigraph to his first volume, *White Buildings* (1926). Though Rimbaud's oblique slantings figure in Crane's earlier lyrics, the apocalyptic sentiment is alien to him. Clearly, though, even those first lyrics show a rich unchurched spirituality that can cross over into a desire for finalities.

Increasingly, I have learned to immerse myself in the appreciation of *Possessions,* a savage masterpiece that explores Crane's nightly descent

into the hell of Avernus as he ventures into homoerotic cruising on the
streets of Greenwich Village:

Witness now this trust! the rain
That steals softly direction
And the key, ready to hand—sifting
One moment in sacrifice (the direst)
Through a thousand nights the flesh
Assaults outright for bolts that linger
Hidden,—O undirected as the sky
That through its black foam has no eyes
For this fixed stone of lust . . .

Accumulate such moments to an hour:
Account the total of this trembling
    tabulation.
I know the screen, the distant flying taps
And stabbing medley that sways—
And the mercy, feminine, that stays
As though prepared.

And I, entering, take up the stone
As quiet as you can make a man . . .
In Bleecker Street, still trenchant in a void,
Wounded by apprehensions out of speech,
I hold it up against a disk of light—
I, turning, turning on smoked forking spires,
The city's stubborn lives, desires.

Tossed on these horns, who bleeding dies,
Lacks all but piteous admissions to be spilt
Upon the page whose blind sum finally burns
Record of rage and partial appetites.
The pure possession, the inclusive cloud
Whose heart is fire shall come,—the white
    wind rase
All but bright stones wherein our smiling plays.

"Stone" antithetically plays between slang for the male genitalia and the "white stone" of Revelation 2:17:

> He that hath an ear, let him hear what the Spirit saith unto the churches; To him that overcometh will I give to eat of the hidden manna, and will give him a white stone, and in the stone a new name written, which no man knoweth saving he that receiveth *it*.

What unknowable name will be inscribed on the stone Crane takes up to replace "this fixed stone of lust"?

My students, who find the poem a triumph of negative exaltation, tend to question the plural title *Possessions*. Crane overtly includes a single "pure possession" that Revelation names as Jesus Christ but that the poet himself declines to disclose. The initial possession is by insensate lust, "undirected as the sky."

No other poem by Hart Crane so powerfully presents daemonic suffering under the sway of the drive to sexual assuagement (not fulfillment). I think of Dante's "stony" sestina to the Lady Pietra and of Shakespeare's Dark Lady sonnets when I recite *Possessions,* a poem searingly eloquent enough to be worthy of that company. Shakespeare's "desire is death" could be Crane's epigraph, generations before the plague of AIDS. Whitman held back from embracing his daemon, the "dusky demon and brother" of the *Sea-Drift* elegies. Crane, beyond Whitman as American Orphic poet, walks Bleecker Street, desperately fused with his daemon, who perhaps will find a new name or perish instead.

Why does the poem begin "Witness now this trust!"? Crane does not *trust* in the white stone of Revelation. His only faith is in writing the next poem, the only relational event he ever can trust. In this he is the heir of Whitman and of Dickinson. The stone is his tally, an image of voice counting up a thousand nights of undirected lust and counting down to his self-destruction.

The poem's unfolding depends upon verbs and nouns of enumeration: "sifting," "a thousand nights," "accumulate," "account the total," "tabulation," "medley," "blind sum," "record." Crane's burden is to make his dark poem light, lest it become little more than a countdown to Avernus. Recalling and yet transuming the infernal cities of Blake, Baudelaire,

Dickens in *Our Mutual Friend,* and T. S. Eliot, *Possessions* enters a literary space that at first may seem too anguished to allow aesthetic response.

Pater defined the High Romantic as "strangeness added to beauty." In *Possessions,* an estrangement is compelled to take on a marvelous interplay between the Greek daemonic, which was always an image, and the Hebrew prophetic daemon, which was a voice. Angus Fletcher has emphasized the alienation between image and voice in Shelley and in Whitman. Walt's tally is thus an image of voice, while Hart Crane gives you the voice of an image. The fleshly "bolts that linger / Hidden" transmute into "still trenchant in a void, / Wounded by apprehensions out of speech." That recalls the voice of Whitman's hermit thrush, his "song of the bleeding throat" in the *Lilacs* elegy.

When Crane concludes with Revelation's white stone, the daemonic image is dominant, but a ghostly remnant of the image of voice abides.

Crane, an immensely sophisticated craftsman, was never more knowing than in *Possessions.* All the poem's images are wound together into one negative tally or image of wounded voice. The "trust" ("Witness now this trust!") is in his own art to fuse phallic image with achieved poem. Yeats said that he sought an image, not a voice, but Crane, in the American tradition, rarely could settle between the two; and then, like Whitman and Stevens, he proclaims the voice is great within us that rises up.

The conversion of "this fixed stone of lust" begins when Crane, a night-walker on Bleecker Street, holds it "up against a disk of light" (a streetlamp perhaps) and has the horrific vision of himself being roasted on the spit of the city's whirling skyscrapers:

> I, turning, turning on smoked forking spires,
> The city's stubborn lives, desires.

These become a bull's horns upon which the poet is gored, and then the bleeding wonderfully becomes the composition of *Possessions:* "piteous admissions to be spilt / Upon the page." The horns, too, are the "thorns of life" upon which Shelley falls and bleeds in his ode to the uncontrollable "Destroyer and Preserver," the "wild West Wind."

Crane mounts to an American sublime in the three final lines, where "the pure possession" radiantly replaces the possessive drive of lust. Moralizing is thrown aside by apocalypse or total self-revelation. Hart Crane plays upon his own name in the "heart" of fire, the image extending itself to the white wind of *Possessions* that will rase everything but the bright stones of the new name and "our smiling plays."

The daemonic image of the stone yields to the secret newly named stone; the negative tally ("blind sum") takes fire, and the voice of the white wind burns away all but the newness. Why is this persuasive? Crane is not preaching Christ: He hymns, as he will in *The Bridge,* a god unknown since he knows only the hymn, the next poem to be written, if that he can.

PASSAGE

THIS IS ONE OF CRANE'S DARKEST MEDITATIONS, AKIN TO *POSSESSIONS* and to *The Tunnel* in *The Bridge.* It moves boldly from Wordsworth's *Immortality* ode to Whitman's *As I Ebb'd with the Ocean of Life* and ends by contextualizing Whitman and Crane himself in the High Romantic cosmos of Blake, Coleridge, and Shelley. All this allusiveness does not negate Crane's quest, to achieve the American epic which strongly accepts its own hazardous path.

The opening quatrain has haunted me since childhood:

> Where the cedar leaf divides the sky
> I heard the sea.
> In sapphire arenas of the hills
> I was promised an improved infancy.

Though inland—like Wordsworth in the *Immortality* ode, having a vision of children playing upon the shore—Crane "was promised an improved infancy," but Crane intends this in a radically American sense, as Adam early in the morning. Freud remarked that it was all over for each of us by the first birthday. Crane intends the opposite: There is deep pathos in his phrase "an improved infancy."

Passage is an agon with the *Sea-Drift* cosmos of Crane's prime poetic father, Walt Whitman, who invented the American Shore Ode. It is dangerous to wrestle Walt at the shore's edge, because the shores of America are his.

Crane achieves not victory but transmemberment:

The evening was a spear in the ravine
That throve through very oak. And had I walked
The dozen particular decimals of time?
Touching an opening laurel, I found
A thief beneath, my stolen book in hand.

"Why are you back here—smiling an iron coffin?"
"To argue with the laurel," I replied:
"Am justified in transience, fleeing
Under the constant wonder of your eyes—."

He closed the book. And from the Ptolemies
Sand troughed us in a glittering abyss.
A serpent swam a vertex to the sun
—On unpaced beaches leaned its tongue and drummed.
Memory, committed to the page, had broke.

This recalls and seeks to transume an extraordinary encounter between Whitman and his daemon, or "real Me," in *As I Ebb'd with the Ocean of Life:*

O baffled, balk'd, bent to the very earth,
Oppress'd with myself that I have dared to open my
    mouth,
Aware now that amid all that blab whose echoes recoil upon
    me I have not once had the least idea who or what I am,
But that before all my arrogant poems the real Me stands
    yet untouch'd, untold, altogether unreach'd,
Withdrawn far, mocking me with mock-congratulatory
    signs and bows,
With peals of distant ironical laughter at every word I have
    written,
Pointing in silence to these songs, and then to the sand
    beneath.

I perceive I have not really understood any thing, not a single
    object, and that no man ever can,

Nature here in sight of the sea taking advantage of me to
    dart upon me and sting me,
Because I have dared to open my mouth to sing at all.

"These songs" would be a copy of *Leaves of Grass* that Walt holds. Crane instead has had *his* book stolen from him by his own dusky daemon and dark brother. *Passage* was written late in 1925 and appeared in Crane's first published collection, *White Buildings,* in 1926.

Poetic agon is the argument with the laurel, or Crane's usurpation from both Whitman and Eliot. The serpent who swims a vertex (or vortex) to the sun suggests a Shelleyan trope and prophesies the beach scene in Stevens's *The Auroras of Autumn.* Crane's vortex plays against the one created by the *Pequod* as it sinks and the whirlpool in the *Death by Water* section of *The Waste Land.*

The unpaced beaches record Whitman's absence, while the juxtaposing of fountains and ice suggests Coleridge's *Kubla Khan.* Crane's own passage to a new poetic abandons the memory of his precursors, adopting a rhetoric of breaking to deal with the broken world.

REPOSE OF RIVERS

CRANE COMPOSED *REPOSE OF RIVERS* IN 1926 BEFORE LEAVING FOR THE Isle of Pines in the Caribbean to continue work on *The Bridge.* He was able to place the poem in *White Buildings,* where its excellence vies with *Possessions* and the *Voyages* sequence.

The incarnation of the poetical character crucial to the Romantic Sublime takes place in the scene of instruction in *Repose of Rivers.* Crane chooses *Moby-Dick* and *Song of Myself* as his poem's allusive starting points because he stands upon the threshold of his *annus mirabilis* and wishes his strongest American precursors to aid his own quest. Sexual orientation and poetic maturation are allied here: Whitman's love of comrades and the Ishmael-Queequeg "marriage" are part of the forerunners' role.

Once I ventured the interpretation that Crane's "How much I would have bartered!" in *Repose of Rivers* intimated an exchange of "nature for poetry," but that was simplistic. Who is to define "nature"? King Lear's "nature" is antithetical to Edmund the Bastard's, and Allen Tate's and

Yvor Winters's conviction that their friend Crane's sexual orientation was unnatural is now of little interest. Crane was scarcely happy in his homo-eroticism but would have been unhappier still as a lover of women. He had been a battleground upon which his selfish and stupid parents pursued their narcissistic motives, thus rending his psyche: His mother, highly neurotic and immature, whose beauty faded quickly, and his business magnate father couldn't get along almost from the start, and they sought to alienate each other from their child. So intense was his daemonic genius that he survived to become a great poet, but his self-destructiveness became the cost of that confirmation.

Crane is fiercely subtle, even for him, in blending his voice with that of the river:

> The willows carried a slow sound,
> A sarabande the wind mowed on the mead.
> I could never remember
> That seething, steady leveling of the marshes
> Till age had brought me to the sea.

In Chapter 58 of *Moby-Dick*, the right-whales feed on brit:

> As morning mowers, who side by side slowly and seethingly advance
> their scythes through the long wet grass of marshy meads; even so
> these monsters swam, making a strange, grassy, cutting sound . . .

A sarabande is a slow, stately Spanish dance of past centuries. The poem being visionary and scarcely natural, phantasmagoria is every-where: rivers that speak, winds that dance, mammoth turtles slow in cruel coition and destroyed by the sun's heat. Crane's likely source was *The Encantadas* in Melville's *Piazza Tales*, but there is a clear parallel in D. H. Lawrence's tortoise poems in *Birds, Beasts, and Flowers*.

In the following stanza, "flags, weeds" suggests Whitman in *Song of Myself*, as does the poet's incestuous entry into the mothering waters. Whitman merges with the mother in the hermit thrush's song of death in the *Lilacs* elegy:

> Flags, weeds. And remembrance of steep alcoves
> Where cypresses shared the noon's

Tyranny; they drew me into hades almost.
And mammoth turtles climbing sulphur dreams
Yielded, while sun-silt rippled them
Asunder . . .

How much I would have bartered! the black gorge
And all the singular nestings in the hills
Where beavers learn stitch and tooth.
The pond I entered once and quickly fled—
I remember now its singing willow rim.

The cypress traditionally represents erotic suffering, while the willow is the emblem of mourning and also the signature of Orpheus. Crane employs the "alcoves"/"almost" pararhyme to intensify the hazard of heterosexual incest: "the pond I entered once and quickly fled." Anyone who has watched the violent courtship of beavers will appreciate "stitch and tooth."

The slow sound of the willows swells into the pond's singing willow rim and preludes the poem's superb resolution:

And finally, in that memory all things nurse;
After the city that I finally passed
With scalding unguents spread and smoking darts
The monsoon cut across the delta
At gulf gates . . . There, beyond the dykes

I heard wind flaking sapphire, like this summer,
And willows could not hold more steady sound.

The city is at once Hart Crane's New York and the Mississippi's New Orleans, as it will be in the extraordinary close of *The River* in *The Bridge*. The stinging rancidity of the homoerotic "scalding unguents spread and smoking darts" is poetically offset by the Shelleyan and Orphic close of the last two lines.

The flaking of the sapphire sky is at once an Orphic breaking and a Shelleyan showering of the azure of vision. As Langdon Hammer noted, this is apocalyptic, another falling away of nature. *Repose of Rivers* shares the stance of Blake and of Shelley and is worthy of them.

AT MELVILLE'S TOMB

CRANE WROTE THIS SUPERB TRIBUTE TO HERMAN MELVILLE IN October 1925 and printed it in *White Buildings*, where it is placed just before
the six *Voyages*. Melville's "tomb" is the ocean and *Moby-Dick* but also
the primal abyss below the waves.

> Often beneath the wave, wide from this ledge
> The dice of drowned men's bones he saw bequeath
> An embassy. Their numbers as he watched,
> Beat on the dusty shore and were obscured.
>
> And wrecks passed without sound of bells,
> The calyx of death's bounty giving back
> A scattered chapter, livid hieroglyph,
> The portent wound in corridors of shells.
>
> Then in the circuit calm of one vast coil,
> Its lashings charmed and malice reconciled,
> Frosted eyes there were that lifted altars;
> And silent answers crept across the stars.
>
> Compass, quadrant and sextant contrive
> No farther tides . . . High in the azure steeps
> Monody shall not wake the mariner.
> This fabulous shadow only the sea keeps.

Several of my departed friends, lovers alike of Melville and of Crane,
requested that this poem be read at their final services. It is a last word for
Melville, Hart Crane, and all readers who share their tragic vision of materialism in matters pertaining to death.

Crane's control is a miracle of firmness and restraint in this very formal
lyric. Like Hamlet, Melville is death's ambassador to us. The "numbers"
refer to the dice into which the sea has rendered the bodies of the drowned
men but also to Crane's metric. "Calyx" is at once a vortex of a sinking
ship, like Ahab's *Pequod*, and also a cornucopia. The Greek word "calyx,"

which refers to a flower's outer whorl, also meant a chalice or drinking vessel. John Irwin, the great authority on the image of hieroglyphics in the American Renaissance, reminds us that tattooed Queequeg is himself a hieroglyphic, but so are Ahab and his entire book. The White Whale and livid Ahab become the largest of daemonic hieroglyphics.

With the "coil" and "lashings," we are still in the world of *Moby-Dick,* where both refer to the mode of Ahab's death. The "frosted eyes" are those of the floating Ishmael gazing up at the constellation Ara (the altar), while the silent answers are from the constellations Cetus (the whale) and Argo Navis (the boat *Argo*).

In a dramatic moment in *Moby-Dick,* Ahab destroys his quadrant, a navigational device, while later in the novel the *Pequod*'s compass suffers reversal. Crane, in a letter to Harriet Monroe, remarked that instruments like the compass, quadrant, and sextant have extended concepts of space in the imagination so that now metaphorically they have expanded the boundaries of both the seen and unseen.

The poet's monody will not wake Melville the mariner, since neither the author of *Moby-Dick* nor of *The Bridge* believes in resurrection. What remains is a fabulous shadow both of Ahab and his crew and of Hart Crane himself, another drowned man whom only the sea keeps.

VOYAGES

Voyages II

I OMIT COMMENT ON VOYAGES I—AS PLEASING AS IT IS, IT NEEDS NO explication. But Crane's *Voyages II* is the equivalent in the twentieth century of Coleridge's *Kubla Khan* in the nineteenth: an absolute cognitive music caught in a single lyric with immense reverberation. I memorized both poems long ago, before I comprehended either, and only now is my appreciation flowering into full clarity.

Sea change, a great Shakespearean trope, haunts both *The Waste Land* and *Voyages*. Crane, in his love for Emil Opffer, the Danish merchant mariner with whom he had a short but passionate relationship, suffers sea change even as the poet overhears his own poem and tallies his losses. Ecstatic celebration of mutual passion ebbs with an ebb of the ocean of life.

Following in the wake of Shelley, Crane also discovers that love and the means of love are irreconcilable.

Shelley's *Alastor,* or *The Spirit of Solitude,* composed in 1815 when he was twenty-three, is a young poet's remorseless quest to unite with a dream woman. Narcissistic and solipsistic, he is haunted by his daemon, a nemesis who is an avenging spirit. Voyaging in a little shallop down the shores of Asia Minor, the poet wastes away into death. Crane takes from *Alastor* a unity of "sleep, death, desire" and the poet's voyage, which becomes the slow, rocking movement of the boat carrying the lovers through "adagios of islands." *Voyages I,* composed earlier, introduces the menace of its final line: "the bottom of the sea is cruel." Until then it weaves together the children playing upon the shore from Wordsworth's *Immortality* ode and Whitman's fantasia of the twenty-nine bathers from *Song of Myself,* with Crane in the role of the female twenty-ninth bather. In *Voyages II,* we inhabit a different world, Hart Crane's heterocosm. Though it is a realm of total sexual fulfillment, the daemonic sense of loss floods the poem, foretelling total surrender to death.

Crane loads every rift with ore (the agonistic advice of Keats to Shelley in a letter that suggests Shelley's poetry is being composed too profusely and hastily) and achieves a rhetorical richness that rivals Coleridge, Shelley, Keats, and Tennyson. The poem's surge of erotic ecstasy is carried by a rhapsodic intensity beyond anything created earlier by the American Orphic poet, whose muse is not so much Emil Opffer as it is Crane's own daemon, potential divinity but also the guilt of the slayers of Dionysus.

Voyages II returns us to Melville's tomb, at once the ocean and the language of *Moby-Dick:*

> —And yet this great wink of eternity,
> Of rimless floods, unfettered leewardings,
> Samite sheeted and processioned where
> Her undinal vast belly moonward bends,
> Laughing the wrapt inflections of our love;
>
> Take this Sea, whose diapason knells
> On scrolls of silver snowy sentences,
> The sceptered terror of whose sessions rends
> As her demeanors motion well or ill,
> All but the pieties of lovers' hands.

And onward, as bells off San Salvador
Salute the crocus lustres of the stars,
In these poinsettia meadows of her tides,—
Adagios of islands, O my Prodigal,
Complete the dark confessions her veins spell.

Mark how her turning shoulders wind the hours,
And hasten while her penniless rich palms
Pass superscription of bent foam and wave,—
Hasten, while they are true,—sleep, death, desire,
Close round one instant in one floating flower.

Bind us in time, O seasons clear, and awe.
O minstrel galleons of Carib fire,
Bequeath us to no earthly shore until
Is answered in the vortex of our grave
The seal's wide spindrift gaze toward paradise.

In "The Spirit-Spout" chapter of *Moby-Dick,* "all the waves rolled by like scrolls of silver; and, by their soft, suffusing seethings, made what seemed a silvery silence." The mark of Melville is strong throughout: *Moby-Dick* is the American epic "of rimless floods, unfettered leeward-ings."

The Tennysonian "samite sheeted and processioned," with its silken aura of the Lady of the Lake, clashes with the "undinal vast belly" of the sea bending moonward, seeking a lover who might give her a soul. Punning on "wrapped" and "rapt," Crane implicitly begins the sea's negative judgment of the lovers, whose inflected tonalities of passion are mocked.

Nevertheless, Crane remains bold: "Take this Sea." Its rush of sound "knells" on scrolls that are sentences of death, delivered by an authority whose supposed benignity instead "rends" in sessions of "sceptered terror" the bodies of the lovers yet cannot end the pieties of their joined hands.

After the knelling come the "bells," which perhaps came about from a story Emil Opffer told Crane about the lost city of Port Royal, Jamaica, which was sucked into the sea following a great earthquake in 1692. Crane was excited at the legend which claimed that standing on the shore one still could hear sunken church bells ringing, tolling with the tide—a story

Crane assimilated with the legend of lost Atlantis. That he refers to San Salvador instead of Jamaica is another of Crane's brilliant transpositions, as legend also had it that Columbus first set foot in the New World on the coast of San Salvador.

Two stanzas into this lyric of implication, I stand back to ask: What has Crane subtly left out? This is not the mothering sea of Walt Whitman but the estranging element in Herman Melville.

In Hart Crane's gnosis—as in Melville's—the sea is part of the broken world, the universe of death. *Voyages II,* in its desire to celebrate (though unable to prolong) Crane's authentic love, has to exercise the poet's power of mind over the universe of death. Can it? Is it so exercised? The sea's demeanors capriciously can motion well or ill, but I dissent from John Irwin, Crane's best critic, when he speaks of the sea's sympathy for the lovers. Like its lover the moon, the sea is time and destroys love and lovers.

Against time and the sea, Crane sets one of his best-known tropes: "adagios of islands." At once the reference is to the slow, rocking motion of a small boat as it winds through islets, the sexual exchange between the lovers, and also an assertion against the rapid pace that will end them.

The sea becomes a clock, compelling haste. Yet it is sleep, death, desire, and not the sea, that will fail and become false. A closing prayer asks for the lovers to be covenanted "in time" yet only to be reprieved long enough to achieve both clarity and awe, in Emily Dickinson's sense of her love for Judge Otis Lord.

The *Pequod*'s fate is invoked again in "the vortex," the conceptual image of whirlpool that will end Crane and his lover in the yearning glance of *Moby-Dick*'s young seals seeking their lost mothers, a paradise unknown. But why the Melvillean "spindrift" for spray? The lovers, like the bereft seals, will receive an answer but only one indistinctly seen through spray.

The harmonies of *Voyages II* are deliberately at odds with its implicit sense of destruction. Yet Crane's rhetorical art achieves an apotheosis that even he could not often match.

Voyages III, IV, V

A LONG ACQUAINTANCE WITH THE SIX *VOYAGES* WILL SHOW HOW DIVERSE they are. Where the second is celebratory though shadowed, the third moves toward a sublime Shakespearean sea change:

Infinite consanguinity it bears—
This tendered theme of you that light
Retrieves from sea plains where the sky
Resigns a breast that every wave enthrones;
While ribboned water lanes I wind
Are laved and scattered with no stroke
Wide from your side, whereto this hour
The sea lifts, also, reliquary hands.

And so, admitted through black swollen gates
That must arrest all distance otherwise,—
Past whirling pillars and lithe pediments,
Light wrestling there incessantly with light,
Star kissing star through wave on wave unto
Your body rocking!
        and where death, if shed,
Presumes no carnage, but this single change,—
Upon the steep floor flung from dawn to dawn
The silken skilled transmemberment of song;

Permit me voyage, love, into your hands . . .

Voyages III, IV, V have traces in them of sonnet form with attached codas. They are very different poems—from one another and from the celebratory *II*. You can chart *III* by its transitive verbs: "bears," "retrieves," "resigns," "enthrones," "wind," "laved," "scattered," "lifts," "admitted," "arrest," "wrestling," kissing," "rocking," "shed," "presumes no carnage," "flung," "permit." The verbs attest to a lyric of "infinite consanguinity" between lovers. Shelley was the master of the mode of a transitive eros that vanishes only momentarily into its object, and he, more than Whitman, is an undersong in *Voyages*.

The lovers swim together, and the estranging sea—for a time only—serves a religious function to preserve the holy relics of eros. But then the coda divides in three: coition, transmemberment (Crane's coinage), and a final gesture of grace, lover to lover.

Crane's transumptive style, turning his belatedness into earliness, is at its strongest in this coda of Shakespearean eloquence. Muted by presages of the end of love, nevertheless the great style is subtler in *Voyages IV*:

> Whose counted smile of hours and days, suppose
> I know as spectrum of the sea and pledge
> Vastly now parting gulf on gulf of wings
> Whose circles bridge, I know, (from palms to the severe
> Chilled albatross's white immutability)
> No stream of greater love advancing now
> Than, singing, this mortality alone
> Through clay aflow immortally to you.
>
> All fragrance irrefragably, and claim
> Madly meeting logically in this hour
> And region that is ours to wreathe again,
> Portending eyes and lips and making told
> The chancel port and portion of our June—
> Shall they not stem and close in our own steps
> Bright staves of flowers and quills today as I
> Must first be lost in fatal tides to tell?
>
> In signature of the incarnate word
> The harbor shoulders to resign in mingling
> Mutual blood, transpiring as foreknown
> And widening noon within your breast for gathering
> All bright insinuations that my years have caught
> For islands where must lead inviolably
> Blue latitudes and levels of your eyes,—
>
> In this expectant, still exclaim receive
> The secret oar and petals of all love.

A poem of the lover's momentary return, it delays the opening octaves with full force until the final two lines result in a stretching of syntax beyond limits. "Whose" becomes an unanswered question, and what Crane wants, he fears he cannot know: the reality of a renewable love.

The sea's spectrum changes constantly, and the parting gulf is unlikely to be bridged by circles even of white immutability. "From palms to the severe" takes two antithetical words into a fresh field of meaning, while the "chancel port and portion" becomes in itself a severe poem. The chancel is the part of a church where the altar rises, while the port/portion play suggests the law of the sailor Opffer's life: always to set forth on the next voyage.

The lovers constituted a closing "round one instant in one floating flower," a union repeated in a darker tone, one that causes Crane to "be lost in fatal tides." Occultly, the signature of all things inscribes the incarnate word of the poetic *Logos,* a process the harbor "shoulders" as the waters of the Atlantic mingle with those of the East and Hudson rivers.

In this shouldering, Opffer's blue eyes are reduced to "latitudes and levels." Rather desperately, Crane abuses syntax by crying out that expectation is negatively fulfilled yet "still exclaim receive" the token of allure: petals of mutual enclosure and a talismanic "secret oar," an emblem of guidance now rendered into an ultimate promise.

After this difficult battle against inevitable erotic loss, Crane accepts his fate in *Voyages V,* a poem whose splendor matches that of *Voyages II:*

> Meticulous, past midnight in clear rime,
> Infrangible and lonely, smooth as though cast
> Together in one merciless white blade—
> The bay estuaries fleck the hard sky limits.
>
> —As if too brittle or too clear to touch!
> The cables of our sleep so swiftly filed,
> Already hang, shred ends from remembered stars.
> One frozen trackless smile . . . What words
> Can strangle this deaf moonlight? For we
>
> Are overtaken. Now no cry, no sword
> Can fasten or deflect this tidal wedge,
> Slow tyranny of moonlight, moonlight loved
> And changed . . . "There's

Nothing like this in the world," you say,
Knowing I cannot touch your hand and look
Too, into that godless cleft of sky
Where nothing turns but dead sands flashing.

—"And never to quite understand!" No,
In all the argosy of your bright hair I dreamed
Nothing so flagless as this piracy.

              But now
Draw in your head, alone and too tall here.
Your eyes already in the slant of drifting foam;
Your breath sealed by the ghosts I do not know:
Draw in your head and sleep the long way home.

This is one of Crane's supreme lyrics, unlike any other in its resigned erotic wisdom. "Meticulous" carries a touch of its finer edge or root meaning of "fearful." The elegance of *Voyages V* appears to rule out bitterness or even regret. Its tone is so steeped in rhetorical negativity that it is very difficult to describe. The dominant trope is "piracy," a word Crane transmembers into freedom for the erotic pirate Opffer and a Shakespearean detachment (as in the sonnets) for the poet.

Crane's care at employing personal pronouns establishes the forms of farewell. "Our sleep" and "we / Are overtaken" yield to "you say" before "I" first appears in "I cannot touch your hand" and then in the further negations "I dreamed / Nothing" and "I do not know." What remain are "your head, alone" and "your breath sealed."

At once bereft and dispassionate, Crane creates his most rigorously unified lyric, where almost every figuration in the first twenty lines explores the *topos* of piracy: "one merciless white blade," "cables . . . so swiftly filed," "cry" and "sword," "dead sands flashing," "argosy," "flagless." This makes the coda persuasive and nobly forlorn:

              But now
Draw in your head, alone and too tall here.
Your eyes already in the slant of drifting foam;

Your breath sealed by the ghosts I do not know:
Draw in your head and sleep the long way home.

This generous yielding-up of love and loss to the drifting foam and the long voyage to a destination that is not oneself is the reverberation of Shakespearean richness and strangeness. Crane perhaps is most himself as rhapsode; this too is part of his splendor.

Voyages VI

THE WANING OF LOVE SO CLEARLY LIMNED IN *VOYAGES V* IS THE START-ing point of the sequence's brilliant final lyric, one of Crane's major transumptions of literary tradition. Eight swiftly flowing Orphic quatrains evoke Ezekiel, Revelation, Ovid, Shakespeare's *Richard III*, Marlowe and Chapman's *Hero and Leander*, Milton's *Samson Agonistes*, Keats's *Endymion*, Poe's "The Conversation of Eiros and Charmion," Pater's *Renaissance*, and Eliot's *Gerontion*. All these are subsumed and transmuted in the fire of Crane's acknowledgment of erotic loss.

Neither celebratory nor elegiac, *Voyages VI* is another instance of Crane's rhetoric of breaking, his *via negativa*. Working by inference and implication, he identifies himself with blinded Oedipus, Tiresias, and Samson and with the dismembered Dionysus and Orpheus.

Wordsworth and Coleridge sought to transform experiential loss into imaginative gain. Crane, like Shelley and Keats, declined that venture. *Voyages VI* is in the mode of *Alastor* and *Endymion:* daemonic quests for failure, but failure with a difference.

In *Cutty Sark,* composed soon after, Crane introduces the Old Man of the Sea, who is based on Glaucus in Ovid and *Endymion*. The opening stanza of *Voyages VI* refers to him:

Where icy and bright dungeons lift
Of swimmers their lost morning eyes,
And ocean rivers, churning, shift
Green borders under stranger skies.

Glaucus preserves the bodies of drowned lovers, with the implicit promise of a secular resurrection lifting them from their bright captivity.

In the next verse a voyaging shell—both an auditory seashell and a small oared boat—suggests apocalyptic overtones as an early sun becomes a ship, recalling Whitman's "and a kelson of the creation is love":

> Steadily as a shell secretes
> Its beating leagues of monotone,
> Or as many waters trough the sun's
> Red kelson past the cape's wet stone;

Ezekiel 43:1–2 records Yahweh's voice "like a noise of many waters," a trope borrowed by Revelation 1:14–16 to describe the Second Coming. Crane's reaction to this new dawn inextricably fuses images of rebirth with those of the torments of blinding and splintering:

> O rivers mingling toward the sky
> And harbor of the phoenix' breast—
> My eyes pressed black against the prow,
> —Thy derelict and blinded guest
>
> Waiting, afire, what name, unspoke,
> I cannot claim: let thy waves rear
> More savage than the death of kings,
> Some splintered garland for the seer.

Like D. H. Lawrence (whom he admired), Crane invokes the immortal phoenix, whose five-hundred-year cycle ends on a funeral pyre that gives birth to another phoenix. But Crane, the fiery poet, finds the fate of the blinded seers Oedipus and Tiresias. Though he cannot claim the name of Orpheus, Crane will become, like Shakespeare's *Richard II,* a Dionysiac sacrifice.

Another movement of Crane's voyage evokes Pater's vision of Botticelli's *Birth of Venus:*

> Beyond siroccos harvesting
> The solstice thunders, crept away,
> Like a cliff swinging or a sail
> Flung into April's inmost day—

Creation's blithe and petalled word
To the lounged goddess when she rose
Conceding dialogue with eyes
That smile unsearchable repose—

Uncannily, Crane has introduced in this last line the blinded Samson of Milton, another victim of Eros. At the end of *Samson Agonistes,* the Hebrew chorus famously declares: "all is best, though we oft doubt / What the unsearchable dispose / Of highest Wisdom brings about." "Unsearchable dispose" transmutes into "unsearchable repose," as the poem moves from Yahweh to Aphrodite. That adds the role of ruined Samson to Crane's erotically bereft Orphic identity. What remains is the much-misread conclusion of *Voyages VI:*

Still fervid covenant, Belle Isle,
—Unfolded floating dais before
Which rainbows twine continual hair—
Belle Isle, white echo of the oar!

The imaged Word, it is, that holds
Hushed willows anchored in its glow.
It is the unbetrayable reply
Whose accent no farewell can know.

"Fervid" is called into question by the "white echo of the oar." "Covenant" recedes because "the imaged Word" remains unspoken. In the early ecstasy of his love for Emil Opffer, Crane had cried out: "I have seen the Word made flesh." Betrayal and farewell cannot touch the "imaged Word," but only because it constitutes a dialogue of one.

The Bridge

PAUL VALÉRY OBSERVED THAT "NO POEM IS EVER FINISHED; IT IS ABANdoned." *The Bridge* is a prime instance: The versions published in 1930, first by Harry and Caresse Crosby's Black Sun Press in Paris and then, somewhat revised, by Liveright in New York City, are and are not Crane's

American Supreme Fiction, in sequence with *Moby-Dick, Song of Myself, Walden, The Waste Land,* and then with later works by Stevens, Williams, Merrill, Ammons, Ashbery.

So endlessly did Crane revise that to speak of his received texts is itself a kind of fiction. Astute exegetes disagree as to what constitutes *The Bridge,* some arguing that the 1926 manuscripts of the poem are more persuasive than later ones. I gradually have adopted this vista, first developed in long conversations after 1973 with Kenneth Burke, my rhetorical mentor, who had been Crane's friend and admirer and who also found the 1926 *Bridge* to be superior to subsequent revisions. Kenneth remarked that Hart Crane incarnated the genius of American rhetoric: metamorphic and restless. What could be called the Matter of America, an epic theme, was bound to dissolve for Crane, who was all too aware that little remained to celebrate in Walt Whitman's mode or in Emerson's optative mood.

But like the High Romantics—Wordsworth, Shelley, Keats—Crane in 1926 apprehended all summer long his new role of lyrical self-chronicler bearing testimony of election to what in his death poem *The Broken Tower* he called "the visionary company," taking the phrase from Walter Pater's fragment *Gaston de Latour.*

The fact and image of Brooklyn Bridge have been deprecated by Allen Tate and others since as an arbitrary, Whitmanian synecdoche for American hope. I met Tate several times, through the good offices of our mutual friends Holly Stevens, R. W. B. Lewis, and Robert Penn Warren. I was grateful to Tate for such fine poetic meditations as *The Mediterranean* and *Aeneas at Washington* yet was unhappy with his Eliotic literary criticism.

Tate was glad enough in the 1970s to express his abiding affection for Crane's memory but was reluctant to discuss *The Bridge,* an ambivalence I honored. Once, though, at a dinner given by Holly Stevens, he suddenly extolled *To Brooklyn Bridge* as being inevitable in its phrasing. With *Voyages II, Repose of Rivers,* and *The Broken Tower, To Brooklyn Bridge* is for me a touchstone for American Romantic poetry.

After Crane's marvelous summer of 1926, *To Brooklyn Bridge* became a breakthrough to a nine-canto version of *The Bridge* that is the poem at its most coherent: I agree with Edward Brunner that Crane might have kept to this sequence, except that I love other cantos and cannot yield them up:

1. *Proem: To Brooklyn Bridge*
2. *Ave Maria*
3. *Cutty Sark*
4. *Three Songs*
5. *Southern Cross*
6. *National Winter Garden*
7. *Virginia*
8. *The Dance*
9. *The Harbor Dawn*

The four others that I love are

10. *Van Winkle*
11. *The Tunnel*
12. *Atlantis*
13. *The River*

Unlike Brunner, who found *Atlantis* weak, I have loved its high song since childhood and will give it a very comprehensive reading here. I dissent most, however, from Brunner on *The River*, to me an immensely varied and great poem in all respects. I vote therefore in favor of Crane's final ordering of *The Bridge*, with two reservations. The first is, I would be glad to exclude *Cape Hatteras*, *Indiana*, and *Quaker Hill*, all unworthy of Crane. The second, more positive suggestion is to read the poem in the order of its composition.

1. *Atlantis*, 1923–1926
2. *Ave Maria*, March 1926
3. *National Winter Garden*, 1926
4. *Van Winkle*, 1926
5. *The River*, July 1926–July 1927
6. *The Tunnel*, Autumn 1926
7. *Proem: To Brooklyn Bridge*, January 1927
8. *The Harbor Dawn*, Spring 1927
9. *Cutty Sark*, April 1927
10. *The Dance*, Summer 1927

11. *Southern Cross,* 1927

12. *Virginia,* September 1929

Omit the three poems Hart Crane composed in alcohol and despair:

1. *Cape Hatteras,* 1927–1929

2. *Quaker Hill,* Autumn 1929

3. *Indiana,* Autumn 1929

That final three I cut when I study *The Bridge* with my students; composed from 1923 to 1929, our *Bridge* opens with the organ tonalities of *Atlantis* and ends with the charming song *Virginia.* I sometimes imagine printing a volume in that shape to enjoy the new perspectives that would open up. What are the aesthetic consequences of such a sequence?

Northrop Frye remarked that certain great poets—Dante and Shakespeare for example—followed a rhythm of development, while others—such as Cavalcanti and Marlowe—simply unfolded. Wallace Stevens developed, while Hart Crane unfolded. The order of composition for the unfolding seems to me crucial in this *Bridge.*

The poem's protagonist is Crane as the quester searching for what he knows cannot be found, Walt Whitman's dream of an America that never was, prodigal with the love of comrades. The poet begins with a vision of America as the lost Platonic Atlantis, an absolute music hymned as the wanderer crosses Brooklyn Bridge, whose implicit leap binds together our national past and future.

Crane next wrote *Ave Maria,* in which a Whitmanian Christopher Columbus invokes the Virgin Mother Mary to bless his New World voyages. It delights me that the robustly boisterous *National Winter Garden* followed, evoking a famous New York City burlesque house where Mary Magdalene bumps and grinds a dark salvation for us.

After that lively juxtaposition, Crane's daemon gave him *The River,* a tribute to the Mississippi akin to the rivering voice of the superb lyric *Repose of Rivers,* also composed in 1926. Not the muse but Hart Crane's agile rage to order belatedly compiled the five-part "Powhatan's Daughter" sequence that moves from *The Harbor Dawn* and *Van Winkle* meditations on to *The River* and *The Dance,* to conclude sentimentally with the unfortunate *Indiana*. This scheme, partly influenced by William Carlos Williams's *In the American Grain*, in my judgment takes away more from *The Bridge* than it awards.

Crane's *annus mirabilis* was 1926–27; he spent from May to early October of 1926 year in the Caribbean Isle of Pines, which he associated with the happiest of his childhood memories. After writing *The River*, he went on to the dark splendor of *The Tunnel*, a descent to Avernus that breaks into dawn in New York Harbor after a night's sojourn in the subway. Then only could he compose the superb *To Brooklyn Bridge* and the radiant *The Harbor Dawn*. Set free momentarily to be found by his daemon, Crane gave birth to *Cutty Sark* and *The Dance*, brilliant inventions that were followed by *Southern Cross*, *The Bridge*'s true conclusion, with *Virginia* a gracious envoi.

Hart Crane's daemon knows how it is done and creates an epic of Pindaric odes, lyrics, meditations, and supernal longings without precedent. The letters of Crane remind me of those of John Keats, inextricably mingling the life and the poetry. Both poets ultimately rely upon their balance between personal daemon and strong precursors; for Keats these were Shakespeare, Milton, and Wordsworth; for Crane, the most important were Whitman, T. S. Eliot, and surprisingly Shelley, far more than Rimbaud.

The universalism of Keats has a Shakespearean element informing it; Crane, despite his authentic triumphs, cannot stand with Keats, but no twentieth-century American poet can, Frost and Stevens included. Only twenty-five, John Keats died, as Hart Crane departed at thirty-two. Keats desperately wanted to live, but tuberculosis ended him. Crane desperately refused more life. Years of pondering this, and of reliance upon skilled biographers like John Unterecker and Paul Mariani, have not persuaded me that I understand Crane's terrible decision.

Something wholesome in the man as in the poetry and letters intimates a healing power implicit in the last, great death poem, *The Broken Tower*. John Irwin and others have related Crane's figurations of the writer's death to Freud's trope of the death drive in "Beyond the Pleasure Principle." From 1970 through 1985, I attempted to complete a large study of Freud, to be called *Transference and Authority*, but my own gathering ambivalence toward Freud's work finally defeated me. A huge unfinished manuscript rests abandoned up in my attic, testifying to what I no longer seem to know. "The poets were those before me," Freud remarked, perhaps thinking of Goethe, yet Shakespeare was Goethe's truest forerunner as he was Freud's.

Crane hardly ever mentions Freud: There is nothing in him like Stevens's "Freud's eye was the microscope of potency" and no direct admission akin to Stevens's "The mother's face, the purpose of the poem, fills the room." Stevens, like Keats, made peace with the daemon of poetry. Hart Crane, like Blake and Shelley and their disciple Yeats, chose the place of the daemon.

I turned first to Freud in 1965, when I experienced a middle-of-the-journey crisis. But I also became an Emersonian, and at every crossroad I chose him over Freud. Kenneth Burke several times told me that Crane read Emerson but absorbed him more fully from Kenneth's generous discourses upon the American Plato. As a wise older friend and mentor to me, Burke told me to give up the Freud book and stay with the poets. Kenneth himself had no difficulty in holding Freud and Emerson together, yet he sympathized with disciples of less amplitude than himself.

I return to the ordering of *The Bridge* following Burke's suggestion that the poem quested for Hart Crane's "bride" in the bridge. After the Pindaric fireworks of *Atlantis,* the epic evokes contrary images of a woman in *Ave Maria* and *National Winter Garden. Van Winkle, The River,* and *The Tunnel* mostly forsake any nuptial quest, but then it returns in all that follow: *To Brooklyn Bridge, The Harbor Dawn, Cutty Sark, The Dance, Southern Cross, Virginia.*

As he indicated in his "Powhatan's Daughter" rubric, *The River* also is an epithalamion. The surprising poem in Crane's daemonic sequence is *The Tunnel,* chosen for publication in *The Criterion* by T. S. Eliot, always an acute editor, who accurately saw in the poem both an influence of *The Waste Land* as well as a tribute to and dissent from it.

Crane's subway daemon brings home a mother to her golden-haired children and resurrects the poet himself as a new Lazarus to his own harbor dawn, with intimations of an aubade that does not arrive. Crane as the American Orpheus suffers a *sparagmos* as rival traditions flow together.

There is no Eurydice in Crane's Orphism, a truncation of Emerson's more optimistic prophecy of the fate of the Orphic poet in America. Hart Crane's ascent from the subway may darkly prophesy the failure of his quest at bridging his own past and future. And yet this is a knowing failure at variance with his own tradition: the Shelleyan search for an epipsyche—a soul within a soul—carried on by Emily Dickinson, and the Whitmanian refusal to surrender on the love of comrades.

ATLANTIS

HOWEVER WE ORDER *THE BRIDGE*—AND I WILL GO ON SOON TO contrast Crane's final choice with my arguments for his compositional flow—Crane's endurance of his own era cannot be its governing theme and value. Like *Song of Myself, Moby-Dick, The Adventures of Huckleberry Finn,* it must vindicate itself as an achievement sustained by its own linguistic, cognitive, and imaginative power.

Crane's impulses, like his design, were normative in *The Bridge.* Love is celebrated as marriage: Woman and man, man and man; space and time are reconciled. More than Whitman, Crane is inclined away from the world of night, death, the mother, and the sea. "Sleep, death, desire"—the ancient Gnostic formulation of our fall into the mirror of space and time—are not his gods.

Like Herman Melville, Crane rightly held *King Lear* to be a limit of imaginative literature in the West. Ahab compounds the White Whale with the forces of chaos.

The whiteness of the whale is the matchless trope for the American dread that origin and end will turn into one figure only: original formlessness and the void.

Crane's quest for origins joins itself to one of the major aspects of Anglo-American Romantic tradition: the assertion of the power of the poet's mind over a universe of death. Coleridge, echoing Milton, proclaimed that as Wordsworth's program. Emerson, guided initially by Coleridge, gave this an American twist taken up by Whitman: America need not be a cosmos spent in the past, but itself could be a poem in our eyes. Eliot's break with Emerson, whose essays he called an encumbrance, became acute in *The Waste Land,* against which Stevens, Aiken, Williams, and Hart Crane fought back with more positive visions of the American Sublime.

Yet Crane's agon with Eliot was equivocal; more than Eliot's style and "perfection of death" (Crane's phrase) contaminated *White Buildings* and *The Bridge.* Eliot admired Crane's poetry, particularly *The River* and *The Tunnel.* He slyly appreciated the allusion to *The Waste Land* in *The Tunnel,* and I think John Irwin is accurate in noting Eliot's subtle reference to Crane as "the builder of bridges" in the opening lines of *The Dry Salvages,* nine years after Crane's death by water.

Like Eliot, who was High Romantic against the grain, Crane reverted to the powerlessness of the mind over a universe of death. Crane's New York City is quite as dark and agonizing as Eliot's London. The erotic suffering and humiliation searingly expressed in Crane's *Possessions* and *O Carib Isle!* far transcend those affects in any poem by Eliot. Fundamentally, Crane, who urges Whitmanian vistas, is most himself in dramatizing a universal malaise.

And yet that is not an adequate description of his poetry. Rather, his poetry is exultant hymn-making to a god unknown, in the manner and mode of Shelley. Crane and Shelley were beings divided between head and heart. Strong alike in despair and transcendental hope, both Pindaric rhapsodes soar above the universe of death into a kind of neo-Platonic ecstasy of the celebration and possible fulfillment of desire. *Atlantis* is very close to *Adonais,* and the *Voyages* to *Alastor.*

Eliot at the close returned to Shelley, commending *The Triumph of Life* as being closer to Dante than anything the poet of *Four Quartets* could write. This is rather like late Eliot's turn to Whitman as a maker who had achieved perfect balance between form and content.

For decades I have circled round the question: What actually is the goal of Crane's quest in *The Bridge?* Kenneth Burke's suggestion finally seems to me right: Hart Crane, lifelong homosexual—except for his final, doomed affair with Peggy Baird Cowley, estranged wife of Malcolm Cowley—sought his bride in the vaulting movement of Brooklyn Bridge. The search of Crane's brief American epic is for a composite of Eve, the Virgin Mary, Mary Magdalene, and the Whitmanian mother who is also night, sleep, death, and the sea. Or, as my friend A. R. Ammons phrased it, "an image for longing."

One reason I prefer Crane's order of composition to his formal structuring is that the pattern of unfolding rather than imposing clarifies this pilgrimage to the bridge-as-bride. *Atlantis,* a Pindaric ode with elegiac overtones, celebrates Brooklyn Bridge as a prime way to the lost city, whose glory and catastrophe were recounted by Plato in *Critias* and *Timaeus.*

Crane begins *Atlantis* with an epigraph from a third Platonic dialogue, the *Symposium:* "Music is then the knowledge of that which relates to love in harmony and system." Like Plato's writing, Crane's *The Bridge,* including *Atlantis,* is a hymn to love, both human and cosmic.

The twelve octaves of *Atlantis,* begun in 1923, were burnished by Crane for six years and achieve inevitable phrasing. In labyrinthine ways, *Atlantis* contains and condenses all of *The Bridge.* It is also an energetic agon with two precursors, Shelley and Whitman. The Shelley of propulsive force is recalled throughout: There are echoes of *Prometheus Unbound* and *Ode to the West Wind* and of *Adonais* in particular. Whitman as a forerunner generates more anxiety for Crane, here and elsewhere.

Though Whitman is not mentioned in *Atlantis,* he pervades the poem. Shelley's *Adonais* is an elegy for John Keats, yet it becomes a premonitory threnody for Shelley himself. *Atlantis* is a lament for Walt Whitman and for his vision of the United States as being in itself the greatest poem. Unlike T. S. Eliot, against whom Crane's struggle was for his own style, the agon with the prophetic Walt is darker, more profound, and far more anxious. How much had *Song of Myself* left for *The Bridge* to originate?

I emphasize again that Hart Crane, who never finished high school, is a severe and acute literary critic in his poems as much as in his letters. He preceded most critics in the 1920s in appreciating the greatness of Whitman, Melville, Dickinson, and Stevens, and his genius gave him an extraordinary range and skill at employing the full ensemble of Western literary rhetoric without any formal study of it. Kenneth Burke told me that Crane understood the nature of rhetoric far better than any other poet he knew.

Lee Edelman's *Transmemberment of Song* (1987) remains the only useful study of Crane's rhetorical art. Like Wallace Stevens, Crane affirmed that the final belief was to believe in a fiction that you labored upon while knowing it was not true. Rhetoric is both defense and persuasion. The rhetoric of Crane and of Stevens, like that of Yeats and Lawrence, is High Romantic in its defense against the age and in the persuasion that fictions supreme enough can renovate the spirit.

Of the twentieth-century High Romantics, all of whom descended from Shelley, Crane is closest to the poet of *Prometheus Unbound* and

The Triumph of Life in the speed of his making and unmaking of trope. Stevens and Yeats also are masters of unmaking, yet they show more constancy to certain figurations—Stevens to the sun "not as a god, but as a god might be," Yeats to his phases of the moon.

Crane's one supreme fiction is Brooklyn Bridge, not as a god or daemon is but as it might be, a bridge to Atlantis, to Walt Whitman, to a desired America. Neo-Platonists would have understood Crane's purposes as a kind of theurgy, a strengthening of the daemon or calling a god into existence. The Kabbalists practiced theurgy so as to heighten the powers of the covenantal God. Their binding was akin to Crane's bridging.

Atlantis in its final version is as formal a masterpiece as *Adonais,* with Crane's octaves matching Shelley's Spenserian stanzas in measured eloquence. The first of Crane's dozen octaves introduces almost all of the figurations to come:

> Through the bound cable strands, the arching path
> Upward, veering with light, the flight of strings,—
> Taut miles of shuttling moonlight syncopate
> The whispered rush, telepathy of wires.
> Up the index of night, granite and steel—
> Transparent meshes—fleckless the gleaming staves—
> Sibylline voices flicker, waveringly stream
> As though a god were issue of the strings. . . .

Crane walks Brooklyn Bridge at night, gazing upward at its architecture. The common experience undergoes transfiguration through the rhetoric of the High Romantic sublime's key metaphor, the Aeolian harp, crucial in Coleridge and in Shelley. But who or what is the god born out of the bridge's taut music? In the eighteenth-century myth of the birth of the poetical character, Apollo is reborn as a youth with flashing eyes and floating hair, the young poet as a god. Moving from William Collins's odes on through Coleridge's *Kubla Khan*, the figure at last becomes Stevens's youth rushing down the mountain of vision in *Mrs. Alfred Uruguay.*

"Hart Crane" himself must be the answer: Orpheus revives through and by the bridge's music. Emerson had prophesied an Orphic poet for America: Crane answered the call. Eric Dodds, discoursing to me on the daemon, traced its lineage to Orpheus, about whom we know little. A personal friend of Yeats, Eliot, and Auden, Eric read Crane when I gave him *The Collected Poems* but confessed he could barely understand the phrasing and worried that ecstasy was replacing intellect, a misjudgment I met also in Malcolm Cowley, who had known Crane.

Atlantis rises in continual ecstasy from octave to octave but Crane's rigorous intellect is always in play. By the autumn of 1929, Crane was an alcoholic, hence *Cape Hatteras, Indiana,* and *Quaker Hill,* bad poems that Crane knew were unworthy of *The Bridge.* The second octave of *Atlantis,* in its weaving together of the poet's discernment and his rhapsodic glory, is a glory of American poetry.

> And through that cordage, threading with its call
> One arc synoptic of all tides below—
> Their labyrinthine mouths of history
> Pouring reply as though all ships at sea
> Complighted in one vibrant breath made cry,—
> "Make thy love sure—to weave whose song we ply!"
> —From black embankments, moveless soundings hailed,
> So seven oceans answer from their dream.

The bridge transmembers from Aeolian harp to Ahab's *Pequod:* Recall Starbuck defying a sea storm: "Let the Typhoon sing, and strike his harp here in our rigging." "Cordage" puns on "chord," while "weave" is prophetic of "towering looms" in the fourth octave, *Moby-Dick* again being the source. Ishmael refers to the "Loom of Time," while Melville remembers Thomas Carlyle's "Loom of Time" in *Sartor Resartus,* itself taken from Carlyle's version of Goethe's *Faust.* Crane, aware of all this, employs such *materia poetica* as ore for the refiner's fire of his vision. Primarily, he wants us to follow and accept the transformations of Brooklyn Bridge into a wind harp, a ship, and at last a woman, the only bride he ever can possess.

Love is the driving force of *Atlantis:* The word begins in the Platonic epigraph and is repeated four times in the poem. How is such love to be defined? In Crane it seems more Shelleyan than Platonic or Christian, particularly since *Adonais* can be overheard throughout *Atlantis.* Shelley called love a total going out from our nature into the nature of another, which Crane believed he had experienced with Emil Opffer in 1924: "I have seen the Word made flesh," he wrote. The relationship gave him *Voyages* but no enduring solace, confirming his place in the Romantic tradition in which imaginative gain too often is founded upon experiential loss.

Walt Whitman celebrates love—of comrades, of marriages, of strangers—yet his own actuality was self-gratification. Hart Crane's "long-scattered score of broken intervals" is best portrayed in the desperate *Possessions*. It is poignant that the quest of *The Bridge* is for a bride who might as well be Shelley's Platonic white radiance of eternity. Gently yet with plangency, Crane concentrates this whiteness as emanating from the anemone, the Ovidian emblem of the slain Adonis. "Anemone," the spring flower of the annual revival of Adonis, means "daughter of the wind," of Aeolus.

Unlike the tradition of a blank whiteness that culminates in Wallace Stevens's *The Auroras of Autumn*, "white" for Crane was the transparence of his vision. *White Buildings* took its title from Crane's lyric *Recitative:* "And gradually white buildings answer day." The proem *To Brooklyn Bridge* sings of "white rings of tumult," a good generic description of Crane's prevalent trope.

The drafts of *Atlantis* make clearer Crane's reliance upon Shelley's "white radiance of Eternity" in *Adonais,* whose "dome of many-coloured glass" stains that radiance. Crane terms the bridge a "synoptic foliate dome," a description excised from the final version, perhaps because the reference to Shelley is so palpable.

I have taught *Adonais* and *Atlantis* together and been moved by students' responses to both the similarities and the differences. Unlike Whitman and Crane, Shelley did not regard his poems as bridge-building. Whitman, not Shelley, is in Crane's mind as he writes and revises, yet his rhetorical mode is Shelley's, who with Marlowe and Shakespeare could match and overgo even Crane's rhetorical speed, drive, and figured complexity.

Despite this, Crane's rhetorical art is different from that of anyone else in the language or from Rimbaud's in French. In 1928 he discovered Gerard Manley Hopkins, but by then his own style was fully formed, though it is provocative to compare his reaction to Walt Whitman with Hopkins's strong sense of an affinity to that poet. What my students and other readers initially find difficult in Crane is his intense word-consciousness, his continual effort to break and bruise the limits of his diction in what I would call a gnosis, a way of knowing attained through language that negates, evades, and at last achieves controlled extravagance, a measured wandering beyond limits.

Extravagance—in Whitman, Stevens, and Crane—touches the sublime by propounding Supreme Fictions: Whitman, one of the American roughs; Stevens, the great lion standing potent in the sun; Crane, Brooklyn Bridge as harp, ship, and bride.

Crane's rhetorical negativity is omnipresent: He abuses metaphor until it hardly can be called that. Like Whitman and Stevens (whom he admired), he is agile at evasion, fighting off old definitions, rotting names, and darkening lights.

Kenneth Burke first told me to read Crane as a pioneer in the rhetoric of religion. Like Whitman, Crane was not a Christian but an exemplar of the American Religion, our extraordinary emulsion of Orphism, Gnosticism, and seventeenth-century Enthusiasm.

The drafts of *Atlantis,* from February 1923 through August 1926, are a remarkable aid to the apprehension of the final text. Until the version sent to Waldo Frank in January 1926, only a few phrases and lines suggest the coming American Sublime, and even the lines to Frank are frequently clumsy. Over the years I have studied all of the Crane manuscripts (at Ohio State, Columbia, Yale, and other libraries) and am always surprised at the extent to which his finished texts are against the grain, as it were, so unlike his superb letters, which have a tone of total clarity. They remind me of the experience of reviewing Walter Pater's letters, which similarly have not an iota of his famous style. Crane's unique and difficult greatness as a poet came from an uncompromising revisionary effort to found a new idiom for American visionary poetry.

Technically, Crane's relation to that tradition depends upon the trope of transumption, explored in Angus Fletcher's *Allegory,* my *A Map of Misreading,* and John Hollander's *The Figure of Echo.* Transumption uniquely is the trope-undoing trope, making itself early and its precursors belated. Crane works in order to make it appear as if he were the poetic ancestor of Whitman, Melville, and Eliot—and not a swimmer in their wake.

Fletcher suggests "threshold" or "liminal" for such a poetics, and Crane, who saluted "new thresholds, new anatomies," could have agreed.

The quest of *The Bridge*—and of *Atlantis* in particular—is to render *Song of Myself* and *The Waste Land* legatees of Crane, not his forerunners. *Atlantis* is a threshold neither to the myth of a democratic America nor to a myth of cultural and religious decline. It is the starting point of a daemonic romance, an ultimate internalization of a quest that fulfills itself uselessly, as much a knowing parody of a purely fictive goal as is Robert Browning's great monologue, *Childe Roland to the Dark Tower Came.*

Why did Crane, aware of this American defeat, compose *The Bridge?* His critical contemporaries—Tate, Winters, Cowley, Edmund Wilson, and the others—got this wrong, possibly because of T. S. Eliot's primacy. Even William Carlos Williams misunderstood Crane's intentions. Part of the problem is that Crane, in order to win the patronage of the financier Otto Kahn, wrote several letters making his enterprise seem positive. In truth, *The Bridge* is darker than *The Waste Land,* since Crane scarcely would end by urging us, through Indic wisdom, to give, sympathize, and so achieve self-control. Eliot resorts to Saint Augustine and to the Buddha's Fire Sermon. Crane hopes that his poetry will become part of a secular Word that will not die, but his deepest reply to Whitman and to Eliot is an outcry to New York City, its towers and its bridges:

> Kiss of our agony Thou gatherest
> > O Hand of Fire
> > > gatherest—

As in *White Buildings* and in parts of *The Bridge,* there is also a simpler, more direct, poignant lyrical poet in Crane, who does not enter *Atlantis.* I think of poems I treasure: *Sunday Morning Apples, Praise for an Urn, Repose of Rivers,* and several poems and passages in *The Bridge,* though not the most sublime.

Increasingly, my experience of *Atlantis* has been an awareness of the shadows darkening it, even when the poem is most ecstatic, in the eighth octave, my favorite since I was a child:

> O Thou steeled Cognizance whose leap commits
> The agile precincts of the lark's return;
> Within whose lariat sweep encinctured sing
> In single chrysalis the many twain,—

Of stars Thou art the stitch and stallion glow
And like an organ, Thou, with sound of doom—
Sight, sound and flesh Thou leadest from time's realm
As love strikes clear direction for the helm.

I frequently cite this to students as a prime instance of the American Sublime. Ruskin might have been startled by the aggressive "pathetic fallacy" of Brooklyn Bridge's cognizance, a knowing that is its leap of covenant between past and future. The finer edge of the word "commits" is its meaning of trusting in the covenant, while "precincts" is a path toward "encinctured," from the same root meaning "encircling." Despite its heroic rapture, this crucial octave is dark with excessive light, since love and death share a common doom.

John Irwin emphasizes "the lark's return" in the eighth octave as an allusion to Shelley's *To a Skylark*. I would take this further, since in my judgment *Song of Myself* and *The Waste Land* actually influence Crane less profoundly than do *Alastor, Adonais,* and Shelley's most prominent lyrics. Shelley is a great pioneer in making the visible a little hard to see. In *To a Skylark*, the bird flies so high that we cannot view him but can only hear his song as if it were disembodied. The lark's return in *Atlantis* marks a covenant between Crane and Shelley. Yet this is a binding together of two skeptical idealists who know that love and the means of love, and good and the means of good, are irreconcilable. I am echoing Shelley's *The Triumph of Life,* but it could be Crane's *The Broken Tower.* From the start, Crane knew that poets were twisted with the love of things irreconcilable. That may be why the eighth octave invokes a "lariat sweep" and "stallion glow," the stars being those of the constellation Pegasus, the winged horse of poetry.

Knowing I will not again write about Crane, I ask why I find the steeled-cognizance octave so inexhaustible to meditation? In a heraldic sense, it is Hart Crane's blazon, and the meaning of "cognizance" becomes "recognition," a badge of self-identity. Brooklyn Bridge and its poet alike fix emblazoned zones and fiery poles, arranging, deepening, enchanting night. Crane, in the shadow of his bridge, chants it also as harp, ship, death, and the bride he cannot in this life embrace. All daemonic, belated romance wants to fail in its own manner and not in the cast-off garments of precursor works. *The Bridge,* like *Alastor* and *The Waste Land,* is clarified by

Robert Browning's superbly negative dramatic monologue *Childe Roland to the Dark Tower Came*. Crane never mentions Browning and probably never read him, but that scarcely matters. He shares Shelley as forerunner with Browning and Eliot.

The Bridge attempts to be a brief epic on the model of *Song of Myself*; a daemon diverts it to the mode of Romantic quest, on the model of *Alastor* and *Endymion*. Wallace Stevens, admired by the young Crane in 1919 as "a man whose work makes most of the rest of us quail," composed *Notes Toward a Supreme Fiction* in 1942, a decade after Crane's death. *Notes* is Stevens's *Song of Myself*, a brief epic stressing the content of poetic vision. *The Bridge* centers on the poet's relation to his own vision, an emphasis that fosters quest-romance, as it did in *The Waste Land* and Crane's own *For the Marriage of Faustus and Helen*. The internalization of quest-romance is necessarily its daemonization, reliant upon the poet's stance toward death, even as any trope whatsoever depends upon a stance in regard to a properly literal meaning.

AVE MARIA; NATIONAL WINTER GARDEN

IN MARCH 1926, CRANE BEGAN TO COMPOSE *AVE MARIA*, A STRONG YET rather neglected section of *The Bridge*. Like *Atlantis*, the poem is in packed octaves of intense invocation. But *Ave Maria* is Crane's only dramatic monologue, chanted by a resolute Christopher Columbus. The monologues of Browning and Tennyson are Crane's ultimate model for *The Bridge* as mediated by Eliot and Pound. *Ave Maria* fuses Whitman and Eliot with no trace of the poet of *Childe Roland*, relying particularly on Whitman's autobiographical *Prayer of Columbus*.

At the heart of *Ave Maria* is Crane's subtle allusion to Isaiah the prophet:

> —Rush down the plenitude, and you shall see
> Isaiah counting famine on this lee!

The reference is to Isaiah 5:11–15:

> Woe unto them that rise up early in the morning, that they may follow strong drink; that continue until night, till wine inflame them!

And the harp, and the viol, the tabret, and pipe, and wine, are in their feasts: but they regard not the work of the Lord, neither consider the operation of his hands.

Therefore my people are gone into captivity, because they have no knowledge: and their honourable men are famished, and their multitude dried up with thirst.

Therefore hell hath enlarged herself, and opened her mouth without measure: and their glory, and their multitude, and their pomp, and he that rejoiceth, shall descend into it.

And the mean man shall be brought down, and the mighty man shall be humbled, and the eyes of the lofty shall be humbled:

Peter Cole astutely notes that here, halfway through *Ave Maria,* Crane turns against the hubristic ambition of the conquering or questing vision (Columbus's, Europe's, Crane's) and calls for the prophetic corrective of charity.

Isaiah knits the poem together, clarifying a Columbus who is a High Romantic quester and not a conquistador. As Crane seeks lost Atlantis, this Shelleyan Columbus is persuaded he has found "Cathay ... the Chan's great continent." Once Isaiah has inspired a plenitude of charity, *Ave Maria* is freed into Crane's rhetoric of internalized power:

> O Thou who sleepest on Thyself, apart
> Like ocean athwart lanes of death and birth,
> And all the eddying breath between dost search
> Cruelly with love thy parable of man,—
> Inquisitor! incognizable Word
> Of Eden and the enchained Sepulchre,
> Into thy steep savannahs, burning blue,
> Utter to loneliness the sail is true.
>
> Who grindest oar, and arguing the mast
> Subscribest holocaust of ships, O Thou
> Within whose primal scan consummately
> The glistening seignories of Ganges swim;—
> Who sendest greeting by the corposant,
> And Teneriffe's garnet—flamed it in a cloud,

Urging through night our passage to the Chan;—
Te Deum laudamus, for thy teeming span!

Of all that amplitude that time explores,
A needle in the sight, suspended north,—
Yielding by inference and discard, faith
And true appointment from the hidden shoal:
This disposition that thy night relates
From Moon to Saturn in one sapphire wheel:
The orbic wake of thy once whirling feet,
Elohim, still I hear thy sounding heel!

White toil of heaven's cordons, mustering
In holy rings all sails charged to the far
Hushed gleaming fields and pendant seething
        wheat
Of knowledge,—round thy brows unhooded now
—The kindled Crown! acceded of the poles
And biased by full sails, meridians reel
Thy purpose—still one shore beyond desire!
The sea's green crying towers a-sway, Beyond

And kingdoms
                naked in the
                        trembling heart—
Te Deum laudamus
                        O Thou Hand of Fire

As in Emily Dickinson, God is addressed here as "Inquisitor!" This God is creator and destroyer, manifested by the fire of the corposant and of earthly life. The sounding heel of the Elohim is heard again, and the questing explorer and poet can cry out: "still one shore beyond desire!" In a leap forward to the end of *The Tunnel*, Crane exclaims: "O Thou Hand of Fire." The Virgin's charity and that fire mark the limits of Hart Crane's knowing quest for what cannot be found.

Soon after *Ave Maria*, Crane countered its apparently Catholic temper by the splendidly rancid *National Winter Garden:*

Outspoken buttocks in pink beads
Invite the necessary cloudy clinch
Of bandy eyes. . . . No extra mufflings here:
The world's one flagrant, sweating cinch.

And while legs waken salads in the brain
You pick your blonde out neatly through the smoke.
Always you wait for someone else though, always—
(Then rush the nearest exit through the smoke).

Always and last, before the final ring
When all the fireworks blare, begins
A tom-tom scrimmage with a somewhere violin,
Some cheapest echo of them all—begins.

And shall we call her whiter than the snow?
Sprayed first with ruby, then with emerald sheen—
Least tearful and least glad (who knows her smile?)
A caught slide shows her sandstone grey between.

Her eyes exist in swivellings of her teats,
Pearls whip her hips, a drench of whirling strands.
Her silly snake rings begin to mount, surmount
Each other—turquoise fakes on tinselled hands.

We wait that writhing pool, her pearls collapsed,
—All but her belly buried in the floor;
And the lewd trounce of a final muted beat!
We flee her spasm through a fleshless door. . . .

Yet, to the empty trapeze of your flesh,
O Magdalene, each comes back to die alone.
Then you, the burlesque of our lust—and faith,
Lug us back lifeward—bone by infant bone.

After the Virgin Mary, the Magdalene: Crane's gusto makes me wonder
as to the bisexuality partly concealed by his notorious career of intercourse with an entire generation of seafarers.

WITH VAN WINKLE's ADMONITION TO RIP—"AND HURRY ALONG, VAN Winkle—it's getting late!,"—the ambience is set for *The River,* a Cranean masterwork that battles any sense of belatedness.

Mark Twain is mentioned in Crane's letters but only as author of the ribald *1601,* and I wonder if the poet of *The River* ever read *Huckleberry Finn*'s Mississippi episodes. Crane certainly read William Carlos Williams's *In the American Grain* (1925) and employs it throughout *The Bridge,* particularly in the quatrains that conclude *The River.*

A very diverse poem, held together by its drive back and down to origins—the poet's and the land's—*The River* is as somber as it is powerful.

Crane allies his childhood to the hobo-trekkers and other outcasts who are nomads of rails and the river:

> Behind
> My father's cannery works I used to see
> Rail-squatters ranged in nomad raillery,
> The ancient men—wifeless or runaway
> Hobo-trekkers that forever search
> An empire wilderness of freight and rails.
> Each seemed a child, like me, on a loose
>   perch,
> Holding to childhood like some termless play.
> John, Jake or Charley, hopping the slow freight
> —Memphis to Tallahassee—riding the rods,
> Blind fists of nothing, humpty-dumpty clods.

That final line, reductive and nihilistic, immediately is mitigated:

> Yet they touch something like a key perhaps.
> From pole to pole across the hills, the states
> —They know a body under the wide rain;
> Youngsters with eyes like fjords, old reprobates
> With racetrack jargon,—dotting immensity

They lurk across her, knowing her yonder breast
Snow-silvered, sumac-stained or smoky blue—
Is past the valley-sleepers, south or west.
—As I have trod the rumorous midnights, too.

The Bridge quests for a bride, the American Eve for the American Adam.
John Irwin rightly emphasizes Goethe's *Faust: Part Two*, as a prime source
of Crane's visionary search. With a key supplied by Mephistopheles,
Faust descends to the abyss of the mothers, a quasi-Platonic realm suggested to Goethe by his reading of Plutarch. The Faustian key that brings
back Helen of Troy—clearly phallic in Goethe—suggests the key touched
by Crane's derelicts, who know the Whitmanian mother that is the American landscape.

Few effects, even in Hart Crane, are stronger and more moving than
this one. It preludes what I find to be the most exciting transition in American literature, when the poet modulates from a final octave that belongs
to the hobo world, centering on the death of the mythic vagabond Dan
Midland, to the first of eight exalted quatrains describing the Mississippi
River's descent to the gulf:

Yes, turn again and sniff once more—look see,
O Sheriff, Brakeman and Authority—
Hitch up your pants and crunch another quid,
For you, too, feed the River timelessly.
And few evade full measure of their fate;
Always they smile out eerily what they seem.
I could believe he joked at heaven's gate—
Dan Midland—jolted from the cold brake-beam.

Down, down—born pioneers in time's despite,
Grimed tributaries to an ancient flow—
They win no frontier by their wayward plight,
But drift in stillness, as from Jordan's brow.

"Down, down—" is an allusive tribute to William Carlos Williams's
account of the Spanish explorer Hernando De Soto's watery burial, so
strongly stated in Williams's *In the American Grain*:

> Down, down this solitary sperm, down into the liquid, the
>   formless, the insatiable belly of sleep . . .

As in the quatrains, a dark negativity belies the stately flow of the verse. The wayward plight of the waters is akin to the situation of the hobo-trekker. And yet the daemonic ecstasy of Crane's rhapsodic gift sustains *The River*'s final movement, equivocal as it must be:

> You will not hear it as the sea; even stone
> Is not more hushed by gravity . . . But slow,
> As loth to take more tribute—sliding prone
> Like one whose eyes were buried long ago
>
> The River, spreading, flows—and spends your dream.
> What are you, lost within this tideless spell?
> You are your father's father, and the stream—
> A liquid theme that floating niggers swell.
>
> Damp tonnage and alluvial march of days—
> Nights turbid, vascular with silted shale
> And roots surrendered down of moraine clays:
> The Mississippi drinks the farthest dale.
>
> O quarrying passion, undertowed sunlight!
> The basalt surface drags a jungle grace
> Ochreous and lynx-barred in lengthening might;
> Patience! and you shall reach the biding place!
>
> Over De Soto's bones the freighted floors
> Throb past the City storied of three thrones.
> Down two more turns the Mississippi pours
> (Anon tall ironsides up from salt lagoons)
>
> And flows within itself, heaps itself free.
> All fades but one thin skyline 'round . . . Ahead
> No embrace opens but the stinging sea;
> The River lifts itself from its long bed,

Poised wholly on its dream, a mustard glow
Tortured with history, its one will—flow!
—The Passion spreads in wide tongues, choked and slow,
Meeting the Gulf, hosannas silently below.

Crane triumphs poetically even though nothing is affirmed. Pentecostal imagery, "choked and slow," ensues without purpose, but with a plangency and a yearning memorable beyond all measure.

In the compositional order, Crane's daemon knew how it was done and follows *The River* with the descent into hell of *The Tunnel*.

THE TUNNEL

AFTER THE PENTECOSTAL PASSION AND HOSANNAS THAT CONCLUDE *THE River,* the daemon responds with the painful and superb *The Tunnel,* Crane's Virgilian journey into Avernus. The labyrinth, crucial in epic descents from Virgil through Borges, is the central image in Crane's nightmare ordeal exploring the subway. A constant rider of the New York City underground in my far-off youth, I find my own dread of it renewed every time I reread or teach *The Tunnel*.

Virgil's Book VI, with its poignant reunion of Aeneas and his father Anchises, might be the model for Crane's uncanny encounter with Poe, as John Irwin surmises, but the feeling-tone is so utterly different that I doubt it. Under Eliot's influence, Crane found his paradigm in Dante's meeting with his teacher and precursor, Brunetto Latini.

One of the summits of Crane's art, his Poe fantasia centers a vision that acknowledges *The Waste Land* and then transcends it:

Our tongues recant like beaten weather vanes.
This answer lives like verdigris, like hair
Beyond extinction, surcease of the bone;
And repetition freezes—"What

"what do you want? getting weak on the links?
fandaddle daddy don't ask for change—IS THIS
FOURTEENTH? it's half past six she said—if

you don't like my gate why did you
swing on it, why *didja*
swing on it
anyhow—"

And somehow anyhow swing—

The phonographs of hades in the brain
Are tunnels that re-wind themselves, and love
A burnt match skating in a urinal—
Somewhere above Fourteenth TAKE THE EXPRESS
To brush some new presentiment of pain—
"But I want service in this office SERVICE
I said—after
the show she cried a little afterwards but—"

Whose head is swinging from the swollen strap?
Whose body smokes along the bitten rails,
Bursts from a smoldering bundle far behind
In back forks of the chasms of the brain,—
Puffs from a riven stump far out behind
In interborough fissures of the mind . . . ?

And why do I often meet your visage here,
Your eyes like agate lanterns—on and on
Below the toothpaste and the dandruff ads?
—And did their riding eyes right through your side,
And did their eyes like unwashed platters ride?
And Death, aloft,—gigantically down
Probing through you—toward me, O evermore!
And when they dragged your retching flesh,
Your trembling hands that night through Baltimore—
That last night on the ballot rounds, did you,
Shaking, did you deny the ticket, Poe?

The heterosexual jargon of the swinging on her gate as a trope of intercourse yields to Crane's dark homoerotic wit: "And somehow anyhow

swing—" and to the memorable rancidity of: "a burnt match skating in a urinal," a deprecation of male-female passion. We may wince, but the representation of Poe restores us to admiration of Crane's genius at what Emerson termed "surprise."

The prior "swings" prepare for Poe's head "swinging from the swollen strap." Crane affirms the popular legend that an intoxicated Poe was dragged from polling place to polling place on election night in a ballot-stuffing scam in Baltimore, until he died. Mere fact denies this, but Crane was poetically right to expand upon the myth.

The ineffable Edgar Poe (whose verse is of a badness not to be believed) plagiarized Lord Byron's *Darkness* in writing *The City in the Sea,* a New York City apocalypse in which "Death looks gigantically down." Crane improves this but evidently felt its aesthetic dignity.

It is thrillingly precise that the daemonic Crane proceeds to address the subway and New York City as a daemon in many guises:

> And does the Daemon take you home, also,
> Wop washerwoman, with the bandaged hair?
> After the corridors are swept, the cuspidors—
> The gaunt sky-barracks cleanly now, and bare,
> O Genoese, do you bring mother eyes and hands
> Back home to children and to golden hair?
>
> Daemon, demurring and eventful yawn!
> Whose hideous laughter is a bellows mirth
> —Or the muffled slaughter of a day in birth—
> O cruelly to inoculate the brinking dawn
> With antennae toward worlds that glow and
>   sink;—
> To spoon us out more liquid than the dim
> Locution of the eldest star, and pack
> The conscience navelled in the plunging wind,
> Umbilical to call—and straightway die!

Crane thus returns to his home overlooking Brooklyn Bridge. For me, the supreme epiphany of his life's work concludes *The Tunnel:*

O caught like pennies beneath soot and steam,
Kiss of our agony thou gatherest;
Condensed, thou takest all—shrill ganglia
Impassioned with some song we fail to keep.
And yet, like Lazarus, to feel the slope,
The sod and billow breaking,—lifting ground,
—A sound of waters bending astride the sky
Unceasing with some Word that will not die . . . !

A tugboat, wheezing wreaths of steam,
Lunged past, with one galvanic blare stove up the
    River.
I counted the echoes assembling, one after one,
Searching, thumbing the midnight on the piers.
Lights, coasting, left the oily tympanum of waters;
The blackness somewhere gouged glass on a sky.
And this thy harbor, O my City, I have driven under,
Tossed from the coil of ticking towers. . . . Tomorrow,
And to be. . . . Here by the River that is East—
Here at the waters' edge the hands drop memory,
Shadowless in that abyss they unaccounting lie.
How far away the star has pooled the sea—
Or shall the hands be drawn away, to die?

Kiss of our agony Thou gatherest,
               O Hand of Fire
                 gatherest—

New York City is now invoked as "the Daemon." The "Hand of Fire" gathering the sum of Crane's creative agony is also each of his own hands. What is the song he has failed to keep? It can only be the high Pindaric of *The Bridge,* his heroic effort to achieve "some Word that will not die."

When his hands "drop memory," they assume the role of Milton's fallen angels, in a line worthy of *Paradise Lost:* "shadowless in that abyss they unaccounting lie." Even if they choose to "be drawn away, to die," Crane emulates Nietzsche in giving his last kiss to the abyss.

TO BROOKLYN BRIDGE

READERS ARE SO ACCUSTOMED TO SEEING *TO BROOKLYN BRIDGE* AS A proem, or opening dedication, that it can be initially startling to realize how differently it works in the compositional sequence. It was written in January 1927, just after *The Tunnel* and directly before *The Harbor Dawn*. A daemonic Hand of Fire traces a path from the quester "searching, thumbing the midnight on the piers" through the dawn and on to night again, "under thy shadow by the piers," and then on to another dawn awakening, with Crane in his room overlooking Brooklyn Bridge. More inwardly, the movement is an ascent from Hades through "prayer of pariah, and the lover's cry," on to the waking dream of union with an unknown woman.

However contextualized, *To Brooklyn Bridge* is one of Crane's aesthetically perfect lyrics, standing with *Voyages II, Repose of Rivers,* and *The Broken Tower.* Its eleven quatrains echo Blake yet are more in the mode of the Spanish mystical poet John of the Cross, whom Crane had not read:

> O harp and altar, of the fury fused,
> (How could mere toil align thy choiring strings!)
> Terrific threshold of the prophet's pledge,
> Prayer of pariah, and the lover's cry,—
>
> Again the traffic lights that skim thy swift
> Unfractioned idiom, immaculate sigh of stars,
> Beading thy path—condense eternity:
> And we have seen night lifted in thine arms.
>
> Under thy shadow by the piers I waited;
> Only in darkness is thy shadow clear.
> The City's fiery parcels all undone,
> Already snow submerges an iron year . . .
>
> O Sleepless as the river under thee,
> Vaulting the sea, the prairies' dreaming sod,
> Unto us lowliest sometime sweep, descend
> And of the curveship lend a myth to God.

It is astonishing how Crane, addressing his bridge, invokes the diction and drive of a Catholic baroque mystic to adumbrate a vision of his personal transcendentalism, with its superb apotheosis of the American Sublime. I recite these three final stanzas to myself several times a day, because they capture so well the theurgy of Gnostic traditions: Hermetic, neo-Platonic, Kabbalistic.

Crane relies on his own *Atlantis* for the trope of Brooklyn Bridge as an Aeolian harp and as giving birth upon its altar to a God unknown. The evocation of Michelangelo's *Pietà,* where the Virgin Mary holds her crucified son upon her lap with one of her hands beneath his armpit, as if she could raise him, is a poetic absolute in "and we have seen night lifted in thine arms." Audaciously, that transmembers Brooklyn Bridge into God's bride, lending thus of its curveship "a myth to God," who badly needs one.

The dark night of the soul of Saint John of the Cross, where the poet seeks God as his beloved, in the mode of the Song of Songs, has a fit companion in Crane's vigil under the shadow of the bridge. Master of trope, Crane surpasses himself in "the City's fiery parcels all undone." Envision, as he does, the towers of Manhattan ablaze with light, as though you'd unpacked gifts and the wrappings unfolded into points of flame. "An iron year" of suffering vanishes into the snow, and Crane utters the prayer of the pariah he was to become for many in 1929 through 1932.

The poet who had prophesied "new thresholds, new anatomies" and who had sought to memorialize the lover's cry renders instead the cry of the human lowliest, hoping only for the accolade of anonymity.

Like "the chartered Thames" of Blake's *London,* the bay waters shed by the seagull are "chained," while the bridge, like Blake's sunflower, counts the steps of the sun. Keats is subtly invoked through his faith in the unspent motion of power-in-reserve.

Crane, when asked to select his best lyric, once chose *To Brooklyn Bridge* and *Voyages II* and *VI.* This judgment was similar to his sense that *The Dance* was as good as he could do. Beyond his darkening consciousness, he could not have anticipated what must be his greatest poem, *The Broken Tower,* written in Mexico from December 1931 to January 1932, before he plunged to his death-by-water on April 27, 1932, just thirty-two years and nine months old.

THE HARBOR DAWN

TO BROOKLYN BRIDGE CONCLUDES WITH BOTH BRIDGE AND RIVER addressed as "Sleepers." Composed directly afterward, *The Harbor Dawn* commences with Crane waking fitfully from a dream:

> Insistently through sleep—a tide of voices—
> They meet you listening midway in your dream,
> The long, tired sounds, fog-insulated noises:
> Gongs in white surplices, beshrouded wails,
> Far strum of fog horns . . . signals dispersed in veils.
>
> And then a truck will lumber past the wharves
> As winch engines begin throbbing on some deck;
> Or a drunken stevedore's howl and thud below
> Comes echoing alley-upward through dim snow.
>
> And if they take your sleep away sometimes
> They give it back again. Soft sleeves of sound
> Attend the darkling harbor, the pillowed bay;
> Somewhere out there in blankness steam
>
> Spills into steam, and wanders, washed away
> —Flurried by keen fifings, eddied
> Among distant chiming buoys—adrift. The sky,
>
> Cool feathery fold, suspends, distills
> This wavering slumber. . . . Slowly—
> Immemorially the window, the half-covered chair
> Ask nothing but this sheath of pallid air.

Here as elsewhere, I find that Crane's own marginal commentary and the "Powhatan's Daughter" rubric take more away from an exquisite poem than they restitute.

Lee Edelman reads the "tide of voices" as ancestral: Whitman's above all in the "beshrouded wails" of the maternal sea. That is suggestive though secondary to actual sounds: "And if they take your sleep away sometimes / They give it back again."

The beauty of Crane's harbor dawn is in its minute particulars. So profuse are these that the tropes conveying them are relatively subdued: "gongs in white surplices," "soft sleeves," "pillowed," "blankness," "cool feathery fold," "sheath of pallid air." In how many other places in his poetry is he so untroubled?

Crane has slept and waked alone but from a dream of love:

> And you beside me, blessèd now while sirens
> Sing to us, stealthily weave us into day—
> Serenely now, before day claims our eyes
> Your cool arms murmurously about me lay.

Though the sunlight causes the window to grow blond slowly, the poem in an earlier version contained "a shadow bloomed aloud" in sleep. John Irwin thinks this the shadow of Columbus, yet I suggest that Crane's daemon, who next composed *Cutty Sark,* saw this as the garrulous Old Man of the Sea who dominates that marvelously inventive fantasy.

CUTTY SARK

CRANE, IN A LETTER TO OTTO KAHN, PATRON OF *THE BRIDGE,* CALLED *Cutty Sark* a fugue. It is something wilder, though it does blend several voices playing against one another.

Glaucus—of Keats's *Endymion* rather than Ovid's Glaucus—is *Cutty Sark*'s Old Man of the Sea. Crane's old salt, whom he encounters in the South Street Seaport, is considerably livelier than Keats's calmer version.

> I met a man in South Street, tall—
> a nervous shark tooth swung on his chain.
> His eyes pressed through green glass
> —green glasses, or bar lights made them
> so—
>
>   shine—
>   GREEN—
>
>   eyes—

stepped out—forgot to look at you
or left you several blocks away—

in the nickel-in-the-slot piano jogged
"Stamboul Nights"—weaving somebody's nickel—sang—

O Stamboul Rose—dreams weave the rose!

Murmurs of Leviathan he spoke,
and rum was Plato in our heads . . .

The "green" emphasis tells us that the tall man resembles Glaucus, a fisherman changed into a greenish sea-god. Something recalcitrant in Crane's companion resists mythic identifications:

"It's *S. S. Ala*—Antwerp—now remember kid
to put me out at three she sails on time.
I'm not much good at time any more keep
weakeyed watches sometimes snooze—" his bony hands
got to beating time . . . "A whaler once—
I ought to keep time and get over it—I'm a
Democrat—I know what time it is—No
I don't want to know what time it is—that
damned white Arctic killed my time . . ."

O Stamboul Rose—drums weave—

Ala is Latin for "bird's wing," and Crane's derelict mariner then associates voyaging with the image of flying. "Cutty Sark" is a witch's flight costume in Robert Burns's serio-comic poem *Tam o'Shanter*, where Tam comes upon a nocturnal orgy of witches and warlocks. Greatly moved by a young witch named Nannie and her exuberant dancing, he roars out, "Weel done, Cutty-Sark," referring to the short shift, her only garment.

Crane weaves throughout a song by Sigmund Romberg from a 1922 musical, *The Rose of Stamboul,* varying it until Atlantis rises up, displacing "O Stamboul Rose—dreams weave the Rose!" with "Atlantis Rose drums wreathe the rose."

In their drinking bout, the former whaler and Crane have brooded on Plato's myth of Atlantis and on Melville's *Moby-Dick,* cited when the old seaman shouts: "—that spiracle!" The reference is to the breathing hole behind a sperm whale's head, as Platonized in *Moby-Dick*'s Chapter 85, "The Fountain."

Cutty Sark achieves the sublime in its final third:

I started walking home across the Bridge . . .

Blithe Yankee vanities, turreted sprites, winged
                                        British repartees, skil-
ful savage sea-girls
that bloomed in the spring—Heave, weave
those bright designs the trade winds drive . . .

> *Sweet opium and tea, Yo-ho!*
> *Pennies for porpoises that bank the keel!*
> *Fins whip the breeze around Japan!*

Bright skysails ticketing the Line, wink round the Horn
to Frisco, Melbourne . . .
                                        Pennants, parabolas—
clipper dreams indelible and ranging,
baronial white on lucky blue!

Perennial-*Cutty*-trophied-*Sark*!

Thermopylae, Black Prince, Flying Cloud through Sunda
—scarfed of foam, their bellies veered green esplanades,
locked in wind-humors, ran their eastings down;

> *at Java Head freshened the nip*
> *(sweet opium and tea!)*
> *and turned and left us on the lee . . .*

Buntlines tusseling (91 days, 20 hours and anchored!)
                                        Rainbow, Leander

(last trip a tragedy)—where can you be
Nimbus? and you rivals two—

a long tack keeping—

Taeping?
Ariel?

From *The Harbor Dawn*, Crane's daemon leads us to the South Street Seaport while reserving the image of America as desired bride for *The Dance*, next in the compositional sequence. Though the rose image in *Cutty Sark* provides a reminder of the trope of questing, Crane was wary of any unqualified acceptance of the High Romantic internalization of quest-romance. The last movement of *Cutty Sark* therefore intends a more severely aesthetic fulfillment of Crane's desire. As the disciple both of Pater and Nietzsche, Crane believed we possess poetry lest we perish of the truth.

This lyric celebration of the vanished romance of the clipper ship may be the unique instance in which Crane relaxes the poetic will. For once, the rhetoric refuses breaking and negation. The nostalgia for the clipper ships is its own glory. Here, at least, Crane joins himself to Pater at his strongest:

Every one who aims at the life of culture is met by many forms of it, arising out of the intense, laborious, one-sided development of some special talent. They are the brightest enthusiasms the world has to show: and it is not their part to weigh the claims which this or that alien form of genius makes upon them. But the proper instinct of self-culture cares not so much to reap all that those various forms of genius can give, as to find in them its own strength. The demand of the intellect is to feel itself alive. It must see into the laws, the operation, the intellectual reward of every divided form of culture; but only that it may measure the relation between itself and them. It struggles with those forms till its secret is won from each, and then lets each fall back into its place, in the supreme, artistic view of life. With a kind of passionate coldness, such natures rejoice to be away from and past their former selves, and above all, they are jealous of that abandonment to one special gift which really limits their capabilities.

—THE RENAISSANCE

THE DANCE

ONE OF CRANE'S TRIUMPHS, *THE DANCE* CONTINUES THE MARCHING quatrains that conclude *The River* but in a different tonality, with a more personal urgency.

At *The Dance*'s center are two allied gnomes: "Lie to us,—Dance us back the tribal morn!" and "I could not pick the arrows from my side." Dark as these are, *The Dance* is a positive venture into a world of perpetually renewed quest, though Crane knows all quest is fated to fail.

Crane's pleasure in his own mastery informs *The Dance* with an exuberance of being that overwhelms its ostensible emphasis on the martyrdom of the winter king Maquokeeta, in his death dance. The questing poet fuses with the Native American sacrifice and so is transmembered into the dancer. This doubling enhances the poem's power and helps explain why Crane called it the "fiery core" of *The Bridge* and the best thing he had done.

So swiftly does *The Dance* move that I am surprised to note its length of twenty-six quatrains. It opens like an idyll:

> The swift red flesh, a winter king—
> Who squired the glacier woman down the sky?
> She ran the neighing canyons all the spring;
> She spouted arms; she rose with maize—to die.
>
> And in the autumn drouth, whose burnished hands
> With mineral wariness found out the stone
> Where prayers, forgotten, streamed the mesa sands?
> He holds the twilight's dim, perpetual throne.
>
> Mythical brows we saw retiring—loth,
> Disturbed and destined, into denser green.

Greeting they sped us, on the arrow's oath:
Now lie incorrigibly what years between . . .

There was a bed of leaves, and broken play;
There was a veil upon you, Pocahontas,
    bride—
O Princess whose brown lap was virgin May;
And bridal flanks and eyes hid tawny pride.

The archetypal American dream of beauty, Pocahontas has had many lovers and yet is virgin. Deftly doubling, the poet enters as alternative protagonist:

I left the village for dogwood. By the canoe
Tugging below the mill-race, I could see
Your hair's keen crescent running, and the blue
First moth of evening take wing stealthily.

What laughing chains the water wove and threw!
I learned to catch the trout's moon whisper; I
Drifted how many hours I never knew,
But, watching, saw that fleet young crescent die,—

And one star, swinging, take its place, alone,
Cupped in the larches of the mountain pass—
Until, immortally, it bled into the dawn.
I left my sleek boat nibbling margin grass . . .

I took the portage climb, then chose
A further valley-shed; I could not stop.
Feet nozzled wat'ry webs of upper flows;
One white veil gusted from the very top.

O Appalachian Spring! I gained the ledge;
Steep, inaccessible smile that eastward bends
And northward reaches in that violet wedge
Of Adirondacks!—wisped of azure wands,

Over how many bluffs, tarns, streams I sped!
—And knew myself within some boding shade:—
Grey tepees tufting the blue knolls ahead,
Smoke swirling through the yellow chestnut glade . . .

I recall attending Martha Graham's *Appalachian Spring* in the mid-1940s and admiring her performance to Aaron Copland's music. If my memory is correct, she had suggested the Cranean title to him. Crane, with his appreciation of Isadora Duncan, would have been an appropriate viewer for Graham. His own dance pulsations carry these stanzas into an ecstasy of the American Sublime.

The sublime of Longinus and of Edmund Burke *astonished*. Emerson's American Sublime *surprises,* though the astute Burke speaks of *suddenness,* and Emerson emulates the praxis of Longinus and Burke by making quotation the road to sublimity. Burke's emphasis on *power* is enhanced by Emerson, for whom life and literature alike depend upon potential. Hart Crane learned from Emerson what Nietzsche also learned: that power resides in transition, in the new moment of eloquence.

In an astonishing transition, Crane moves from the joyous "Appalachian Spring" to the death dance of the Sachem, who has been the lover of Pocahontas, interpreted by Crane as the legendary American Eve. Joining in the dance, Crane becomes the martyred shadow:

Spears and assemblies: black drums thrusting on—
O yelling battlements,—I, too, was liege
To rainbows currying each pulsant bone:
Surpassed the circumstance, danced out the siege!

And buzzard-circleted, screamed from the stake;
I could not pick the arrows from my side.
Wrapped in that fire, I saw more escorts wake—
Flickering, sprint up the hill groins like a tide.

I heard the hush of lava wrestling your arms,
And stag teeth foam about the raven throat;
Flame cataracts of heaven in seething swarms
Fed down your anklets to the sunset's moat.

O, like the lizard in the furious noon,
That drops his legs and colors in the sun,
—And laughs, pure serpent, Time itself, and
     moon
Of his own fate, I saw thy change begun!

And saw thee dive to kiss that destiny
Like one white meteor, sacrosanct and blent
At last with all that's consummate and free
There, where the first and last gods keep thy
     tent.

Why a rain dance becomes a fiery and tortured death seems inexplicable except in the context of Native American defeat by our national exploitation and decimation of their men, women, and culture. *The Dance* eloquently concludes by granting them an imaginative triumph of endurance:

High unto Labrador the sun strikes free
Her speechless dream of snow, and stirred again,
She is the torrent and the singing tree;
And she is virgin to the last of men . . .

West, west and south! winds over Cumberland
And winds across the llano grass resume
Her hair's warm sibilance. Her breasts are fanned
O stream by slope and vineyard—into bloom!

And when the caribou slant down for salt
Do arrows thirst and leap? Do antlers shine
Alert, star-triggered in the listening vault
Of dusk?—And are her perfect brows to thine?

We danced, O Brave, we danced beyond their farms,
In cobalt desert closures made our vows . . .
Now is the strong prayer folded in thine arms,
The serpent with the eagle in the boughs.

SOUTHERN CROSS; VIRGINIA

THE DANCE WAS COMPOSED IN THE SUMMER OF 1927. IN ITS AFTERGLOW, Crane wrote *Southern Cross* in August 1927 and *Virginia* in September 1929, the month before the stock market crashed, precipitating the Great Depression. He had begun *Cape Hatteras* in 1927 and desperately revised it in 1929, the year that gave him *Indiana* and, in the autumn, *Quaker Hill*. You can love Crane's poetry and still refuse to suffer the hysteria and hyperbole of *Cape Hatteras,* the sentimental bathos of *Indiana,* and the nasty social attitudes of *Quaker Hill* (which are not even Crane's!).

The daemon ends *The Bridge* with the negative sublimity of *Southern Cross* and the grace note of *Virginia.* Crane's ambivalences toward what A. R. Ammons called "an image for longing" are explicit in *Southern Cross,* an envoi to his lifelong quest for "the mercy, feminine, that stays / As though prepared."

The Southern Cross is a constellation of four main stars, visible in the Southern Hemisphere. Crane employs it as an emblem for a dead Christianity, presented without nostalgia but with a full awareness of the void that remains:

> I wanted you, nameless Woman of the South,
> No wraith, but utterly—as still more alone
> The Southern Cross takes night
> And lifts her girdles from her, one by one—
> High, cool,
>   wide from the slowly smoldering fire
> Of lower heavens,—
>   vaporous scars!
>
> Eve! Magdalene!
>   or Mary, you?
>
> Whatever call—falls vainly on the wave.
> O simian Venus, homeless Eve,
> Unwedded, stumbling gardenless to grieve
> Windswept guitars on lonely decks forever;
> Finally to answer all within one grave!

And this long wake of phosphor,
                                iridescent
Furrow of all our travel—trailed derision!
Eyes crumble at its kiss. Its long-drawn spell
Incites a yell. Slid on that backward vision
The mind is churned to spittle, whispering hell.

I wanted you . . . The embers of the Cross
Climbed by aslant and huddling aromatically.
It is blood to remember; it is fire
To stammer back . . . It is
God—your namelessness. And the wash—

All night the water combed you with black
Insolence. You crept out simmering, accomplished.
Water rattled that stinging coil, your
Rehearsed hair—docile, alas, from many arms.
Yes, Eve—wraith of my unloved seed!

The Cross, a phantom, buckled—dropped below the dawn.
Light drowned the lithic trillions of your spawn.

Repeated readings reveal both the aesthetic splendor and painful revulsion of this tense lyric meditation. Personified as a desired woman, the Southern Cross begins as "no wraith" but a triad of Eve, Magdalene, and the Virgin Mary. Yet at poem's end, this Eve has become "wraith of my unloved seed," and the Cross only a phantom of darkness. Still, this is a poem of Oedipal heterosexual desire, in which "homeless Eve" cannot be reduced to Grace Hart Crane, Crane's difficult mother. The "whispers antiphonal in azure swing" that conclude *Atlantis* are replaced by "whispering hell," while Venus is invoked as "simian."

To temper this negativity, Crane ended *The Bridge*—as I read and teach it—with *Virginia,* a skilled variation upon two of Grimms' fairy tales, "Rapunzel" and "Rumpelstiltskin":

O Mary, leaning from the high wheat tower,
    Let down your golden hair!

High in the noon of May
On cornices of daffodils
The slender violets stray.
Crap-shooting gangs in Bleecker reign,
Peonies with pony manes—
Forget-me-nots at windowpanes:

Out of the way-up nickel-dime tower shine,
                    Cathedral Mary,
                                  shine!—

When I hobble down Bleecker Street, I sometimes juxtapose the lovely wordplay of "peonies with pony manes" with the "still trenchant in a void" of *Possessions*. For me, it is a good way to conclude *The Bridge* that I love, reread, and teach.

The Broken Tower

IN *VOYAGER* (1969), HIS DISTINGUISHED BIOGRAPHICAL STUDY OF CRANE, John Unterecker quotes Lesley Simpson, a friend of the poet during his tumultuous year in Mexico:

I was with Hart Crane in Taxco, Mexico, the morning of January 27, this year, when he first conceived the idea of "The Broken Tower." The night before, being troubled with insomnia, he had risen before daybreak and walked down to the village square. . . . Hart met the old Indian bell-ringer who was on his way down to the church. He and Hart were old friends, and he brought Hart up into the tower with him to help ring the bells. As Hart was swinging the clapper of the great bell, half drunk with its mighty music, the swift tropical dawn broke over the mountains. The sublimity of the scene and the thunder of the bells woke in Hart one of those gusts of joy of which only he was capable. He came striding up the hill afterwards in a sort of frenzy, refused his breakfast, and paced up and down the porch impatiently waiting for me to finish my coffee. Then he seized my arm and bore me off to the plaza, where we sat in the shadow of the church, Hart the while pouring out a magnificent cascade of words. It was . . . an experience I shall never forget.

Simpson recently had heard Crane, in a resonant voice, chant aloud the entire *Bridge.* There are, alas, no recordings of Crane's performances: They would enhance our ability to master his difficulties. Though *The Broken Tower* fuses so many echoes and allusions into its swift, unfractioned idiom, its elegy for the poetic self achieves memorable clarity.

As he ceaselessly revised, Crane changed the manuscript version from "Those stark / Black shadows in the tower" to "shadows in the tower" in his opening stanzas:

> The bell-rope that gathers God at dawn
> Dispatches me as though I dropped down the
>   knell
> Of a spent day—to wander the cathedral lawn
> From pit to crucifix, feet chill on steps from hell.
>
> Have you not heard, have you not seen that corps
> Of shadows in the tower, whose shoulders sway
> Antiphonal carillons launched before
> The stars are caught and hived in the sun's ray?

The image of a broken tower begins in English with Chaucer's *The Knight's Tale,* where Saturn as the God of Time proclaims his sway:

> Min is the ruine of the highe halles,
> The falling of the towers and of the walles.

Spenser directly anticipates Crane in Book I, Canto II, of *The Faerie Queene:*

> The old Ruines of a broken tower . . .

Milton's *Il Penseroso* created the Hermetic image of "some high lonely tower" of meditation, which influenced Shelley's *Prince Athanase:*

His soul had wedded Wisdom, and her dower
Is love and justice, clothed in which he sate
Apart from men, as in a lonely tower.

Yeats, haunted by Shelley's image, employs it frequently, including in his book of the daemon, *Per Amica Silentia Lunae:* "the ringers in the tower have appointed for the hymen of the soul a passing bell."

Crane's sacred book was *Moby-Dick,* and he read widely elsewhere on Melville. *The Piazza Tales,* now most esteemed for "Benito Cereno" and "Bartleby, the Scrivener," also contains "The Encantadas," which influences both *Repose of Rivers* and *O Carib Isle!,* while "The Bell Tower" affects *The Broken Tower.* Melville's allegory examines the fate of Bannadonna; the visionary architect is destroyed by his mechanical sexton slave Talus, who rings the titanic bell of a three-hundred-foot tower: "So the bell was too heavy for the tower. So the bell's main weakness was where man's blood had flawed it."

One of the fragments shored against Eliot's ruins as he concludes *The Waste Land* are the words from the French poet Gérard de Nerval's poem *El Desdichado,* "*la tour abolie,*" while earlier the poem gives us its own ruined towers:

And upside down in air were towers
Tolling reminiscent bells, that kept the hours
And voices singing out of empty cisterns and exhausted wells.

Though in anguish and suicidal despair, Crane keeps to his lifelong program of so transuming his wealth of forerunners as to make them seem belated and himself their ever-early if sacrificial displacement:

The bells, I say, the bells break down their tower;
And swing I know not where. Their tongues engrave
Membrane through marrow, my long-scattered score
Of broken intervals . . . And I, their sexton slave!

Oval encyclicals in canyons heaping
The impasse high with choir. Banked voices slain!

Pagodas, campaniles with reveilles outleaping—
O terraced echoes prostrate on the plain! . . .

After the supreme eloquence of his poetic gift breaking down his whole
sense of being, unable to sustain his own daemonic inspiration, Crane
relegates *Moby-Dick* and *The Waste Land* to "heaping / The impasse high
with choir," recalling Captain Ahab saying of the White Whale: "he heaps
me."

Crane then surpasses himself:

> And so it was I entered the broken world
> To trace the visionary company of love, its voice
> An instant in the wind (I know not whither hurled)
> But not for long to hold each desperate choice.

> My word I poured. But was it cognate, scored
> Of that tribunal monarch of the air
> Whose thigh embronzes earth, strikes crystal Word
> In wounds pledged once to hope,—cleft to despair?

More than a half century ago, I published a book on Romantic poetry
called (after Crane) *The Visionary Company.* Many years later, I read
Walter Pater's unfinished novel *Gaston de Latour* and tracked Crane's
presence before me in Chapter I:

> Seen from the incense-laden sanctuary, where the bishop was as-
> suming one by one the pontifical ornaments, La Beauce, like a
> many-coloured carpet spread under the great dome, with the white
> double house-front quivering afar through the heat, though it
> looked as if you might touch with the hand its distant spaces, was
> for a moment the unreal thing. Gaston alone, with all his mystic
> preoccupations, by the privilege of youth, seemed to belong to both,
> and link the visionary company about him to the external scene.

Crane's poignant longing to be "healed, original now, and pure,"
quoted in the verses below, is consonant with Pater's scene. "My word I

poured," but Apollyon, Revelation's blending of Satan and Apollo, scores with a hand of fire all of Crane's poetry, with its record of rage and partial appetite.

In loving desperation, Crane turns to his first and only woman, the sleeping Peggy Baird Cowley:

> The steep encroachments of my blood left me
> No answer (could blood hold such a lofty tower
> As flings the question true?)—or is it she
> Whose sweet mortality stirs latent power?—
>
> And through whose pulse I hear, counting the strokes
> My veins recall and add, revived and sure
> The angelus of wars my chest evokes:
> What I hold healed, original now, and pure . . .

The open question "is it she?" was soon answered negatively, but the brief relationship nevertheless is tenderly conveyed. The two final stanzas achieve Crane's last sublimity:

> And builds, within, a tower that is not stone
> (Not stone can jacket heaven)—but slip
> Of pebbles,—visible wings of silence sown
> In azure circles, widening as they dip
>
> The matrix of the heart, lift down the eye
> That shrines the quiet lake and swells a tower . . .
> The commodious, tall decorum of that sky
> Unseals her earth, and lifts love in its shower.

"Slip / Of pebbles" transmembers the slip of finely ground clay employed in pottery-making into the mingling of female and male sexual fluids, reminding us of the red clay of Adam's creation. A tribute to the close of Wallace Stevens's *Sunday Morning* can be heard in the "extended wings" that cunningly "dip / The matrix of the heart."

For his final image, Crane turned to Dante, *Paradiso*, Canto 14:

Qual si lamenta perché qui si moia
per viver colà sù, non vide quive
lo refrigerio de l'etterna ploia.

Whoever laments that here we must die in order to live up
   above does not see that the refreshment of the eternal
   shower is here.

Perhaps the spiritual force of Dante was too strong for Crane to sub-sume, yet he is yearning rather than asserting. His dying music was worthy of the greatness of his daemonic gift.

THE PLACE OF THE DAEMON
IN THE AMERICAN SUBLIME

Hart Crane's Achievement

CONCLUDING THIS BOOK, I EXPERIENCE THE PATHOS OF YIELDING further discussion of poets I have loved for seventy years and more. A recent three-month delay was involuntary, with a protracted illness followed by an accident. These last weeks I sometimes find I idle myself out of a reluctance to conclude.

Whitman, Emerson, Melville, Dickinson, and Stevens I have loved incessantly but not with the passion Hart Crane's poetry goes on evoking in me. Sometimes I reflect upon this love with puzzlement. I have noted already that my mentor Kenneth Burke, who composed verse throughout his long life, once persuaded me that my own lack of desire to write poems was related to loving Crane's work.

I came to Crane simultaneously with Blake and with Shelley, sensing affinities and also the Blakean and Shelleyan influence upon the American High Romantic. Crane's eminence is of their order. His critical gifts were remarkable; like Blake and Whitman, he was an autodidact and a stubborn thinker for himself.

Literary love, like any other eros, is inexplicable in regard to origins. Certain figures—Shakespeare and Dante—are too large to be loved. Poetry that capacious contains us. Stevens and Crane, unlike Whitman, are not that large: I can love their poetry with a growing awareness after many decades that I may yet fully apprehend it. *The Auroras of Autumn* and *The Bridge* open fresh vistas as I continue studying and teaching those poems, yet these vistas have limits, as the openings to vision in the *Commedia, Hamlet,* and *King Lear* do not.

Song of Myself is so shape-shifting a poem that it shuttles between what Stevens called fresh down-pouring of the sun, which I learn to follow, and elliptical leaps whose difficult pleasures can hint at those of Dante and Shakespeare. Stevens received from Whitman the Emersonian conviction that poetry imparts wisdom as well as pleasure. Emerson's American scholar of one candle awakened no response in Whitman but haunted Stevens, where the figuration of the rabbi blended into the scholar.

Crane's poetry seeks only the wisdom of the poets whose trust is in words. Extra-poetic credences are not relevant to his vision. Late in his brief career, he encountered the work of Gerard Manley Hopkins and reacted with enthusiasm, as though the Keatsian stylist in the Jesuit poet was all that mattered.

Walter Pater, whom I have taken as a critical ideal all my life, was Hopkins's tutor at Oxford and inspired the young poet to dispute his teacher's secularization of the epiphany into "the privileged moment" of aesthetic vision. Hopkins sought to restore the Christian context and yet remained a Keatsian-Paterian poet.

The influence of Pater upon Hart Crane was extensive and deep, as indeed it was upon W. B. Yeats, James Joyce, Virginia Woolf (tutored by one of Pater's sisters), and nearly all major Anglo-American writers of the earlier twentieth century. T. S. Eliot professed to find Pater much diminished, but this was defensive. Wallace Stevens's critical prose is Paterian, and his poetry frequently echoes the aesthetic critic.

Crane seems to have read much of Pater: *The Renaissance, Greek Studies, Plato and Platonism,* and, surprisingly, the lovely fragment of the unfinished *Gaston de Latour.* What Crane took most crucially from Pater is summed up in the 1868 "Conclusion" to *The Renaissance:*

> We have an interval, and then our place knows us no more. Some spend this interval in listlessness, some in high passions, the wisest, as least among "the children of this world," in art and song. For our one chance lies in expanding that interval, in getting as many pulsations as possible into the given time. Great passions may give us this quickened sense of life, ecstasy and sorrow of love, the various forms of enthusiastic activity, disinterested or otherwise, which

come naturally to many of us. Only be sure it is passion—that it does yield you this fruit of a quickened, multiplied consciousness. Of this wisdom, the poetic passion, the desire of beauty, the love of art for art's sake, has most; for art comes to you professing frankly to give nothing but the highest quality to your moments as they pass, and simply for those moments' sake.

William Butler Yeats, in his Paterian reverie *Per Amica Silentia Lunae* (1917), recalled that his prime precursor, Shelley, had characterized our minds as "mirrors of the fire for which all thirst" and reacted with a Gnostic outcry: "What or who has cracked the mirror?" Yeats says the closest a poet can come to an answer is to turn to his daemon until he discovers his true self "in the place where the daemon is, until at last the daemon is with me." That is Crane's answer also.

Pater defined Romantic poetry as adding strangeness to beauty. Owen Barfield amended this to "it must be a strangeness of *meaning*," and then added:

> It is not correlative with wonder; for wonder is our reaction to things which we are conscious of not quite understanding, or at any rate of understanding less than we had thought. The element of strangeness in beauty has the contrary effect. It arises from contact with a different kind of *consciousness* from our own, different, yet not so remote that we cannot partly share it, as indeed, in such a connection, the mere word "contact" implies. Strangeness, in fact, arouses wonder when we do not understand: aesthetic imagination when we do.

At several luncheons with Barfield in London in the 1950s, I discussed Crane with him (introducing the poet, whom he had not previously read), and he remarked on how different Crane's consciousness was from that of most poets. I demurred, because for me Crane isolates and clarifies poetic sensibility in what is still our time.

No other American poet of his eminence invested herself or himself in their work so severely as Crane did. William Empson once told me that he had experienced a late conversion to Hart Crane because the American Orphic poet showed that poetry had become "a mug's game." If Crane somehow composed the next poem, he could go on living; if not, not.

The ultimate meaning and value of Crane's best poetry transcends such extremity, yet this is part of the shadow haunting *The Bridge*. Hart Crane is the most ambitious of American poets, though Whitman is a close second. Crane's daemon and Whitman's "real Me" carry on Emerson's American Religion: post-Christian, Gnostic, Enthusiastic, Orphic.

Shelley remarked that the function of the sublime was to persuade us to abandon easier for more difficult pleasures. Hart Crane, the American Shelley, locates the meaning and value of his own poetry in just that quest.

In some respects Crane is the most difficult of all American poets, but that is part of his greatness. To read him properly, you need to enhance your awareness of sound and sense in his diction, syntax, and cognitive music. In doing so you will learn to read Shakespeare better.

I conclude by expressing a lifelong sense of personal gratitude to Hart Crane, who addicted me to High Poetry. He taught me that my own daemon desired that I read deeply, appreciate, study, and clarify my response to his work. In doing so, my long education began and is ongoing.

Acknowledgments

MY PRIME OBLIGATIONS ARE TO MY EDITOR AND PUBLISHER, Celina Spiegel, to whom I am happy to return after so many years away. I am as always greatly indebted to my devoted agents and friends of thirty years, Glen Hartley and Lynn Chu. Isabelle Napier, by her devotion, skill, and endless labor, made this book possible by transmuting my various manuscripts into the continuity that allowed it to go upon her computer. As my text shows throughout, I am always under the influence of my close friend Angus Fletcher, for the last two-thirds of a century.

A Note on Sources

THESE ARE THE PRIMARY EDITIONS CONSULTED FOR THE BOOK'S TWELVE major authors.

Bloom, Harold, ed. *Mark Twain* (Bloom's Modern Critical Views). New York: Chelsea House, 2006.

Bloom, Harold, ed. *Robert Frost* (Bloom's Modern Critical Views). New York: Chelsea House, 2003.

Crane, Hart. *Complete Poems and Selected Letters.* Edited by Langdon Hammer. New York: Library of America, 2006.

Dickinson, Emily. *The Poems of Emily Dickinson.* Edited by R.W. Franklin. Cambridge, Mass.: Belknap Press of Harvard University Press, 1999.

Eliot, T. S. *Complete Poems and Plays 1909 to 1950.* New York: Harcourt Brace & Company, 1952.

Emerson, Ralph Waldo. *The Annotated Emerson.* Edited by David Mikics. Cambridge, Mass.: Belknap Press of Harvard University Press, 2012.

Emerson, Ralph Waldo. *Emerson's Prose and Poetry.* Selected and edited by Joel Porte and Saundra Morris. New York: W. W. Norton, 2001.

Faulkner, William. *As I Lay Dying* (Norton Critical Edition). Edited by Michael Gorra. New York: W. W. Norton, 2010.

Faulkner, William. *Novels 1930–1935.* Edited by Joseph Blotner and Noel Polk. New York: Library of America, 1985.

Frost, Robert. *Collected Poems, Prose & Plays.* Edited by Richard Poirier and Mark Richardson. New York: Library of America, 1995.

Hawthorne, Nathaniel. *Collected Novels.* Edited by Millicent Bell. New York: Library of America, 1983.

Hawthorne, Nathaniel. *Tales and Sketches.* Edited by Roy Harvey Pearce. New York: Library of America, 1982.

James, Henry. *Tales of Henry James* (Norton Critical Edition, 2nd ed.). Selected and edited by Christof Wegelin and Henry B. Wonham. New York: W. W. Norton, 2003.

James, Henry. *The Wings of the Dove* (Norton Critical Edition, 2nd ed.). Edited by J. Donald Crowley and Richard A. Hocks. New York: W. W. Norton, 2003.

Melville, Herman. *Moby-Dick* (Norton Critical Edition, 2nd ed.). Edited by Hershel Parker and Harrison Hayford. New York: W. W. Norton, 2001.

Stevens, Wallace. *Collected Poetry and Prose.* Edited by Frank Kermode and Joan Richardson. New York: Library of America, 1997.

Stevens, Wallace. *The Palm at the End of the Mind.* Edited by Holly Stevens. New York: Knopf, 1971.

Twain, Mark. *A Connecticut Yankee in King Arthur's Court* (Norton Critical Edition). Edited by Allison R. Ensor. New York: W. W. Norton, 1982.

Twain, Mark. *Adventures of Huckleberry Finn* (Norton Critical Edition, 3rd ed.). Edited by Thomas Cooley. New York: W. W. Norton, 1999.

Twain, Mark. *Pudd'nhead Wilson; and Those Extraordinary Twins* (Norton Critical Edition, 2nd ed.). Edited by Sidney E. Berger. New York: W. W. Norton, 2005.

Whitman, Walt. *Leaves of Grass and Other Writings* (Norton Critical Edition). Edited by Michael Moon. New York: W. W. Norton, 2002.

Whitman, Walt. *Leaves of Grass.* Boston: Thayer and Eldridge, 1860. http://www .whitmanarchive.org/published/LG/1860/

Index

ABOUT THE AUTHOR

HAROLD BLOOM is a Sterling Professor of
Humanities at Yale University and a former
Charles Eliot Norton Professor at Harvard.
His more than forty books include
*The Anxiety of Influence, Shakespeare:
The Invention of the Human, The Western
Canon,* and *The American Religion.* He is a
MacArthur Fellow, a member of the
American Academy of Arts and Letters,
and the recipient of many awards and
honorary degrees, including the American
Academy of Arts and Letters' Gold Medal
for Belles Lettres and Criticism,
the Catalonia International Prize, and
Mexico's Alfonso Reyes International Prize.
He lives in New Haven, Connecticut,
and in New York City.

ABOUT THE TYPE

This book was set in Sabon, a typeface designed by the well-known German typographer Jan Tschichold (1902–74). Sabon's design is based upon the original letter forms of sixteenth-century French type designer Claude Garamond and was created specifically to be used for three sources: foundry type for hand composition, Linotype, and Monotype. Tschichold named his typeface for the famous Frankfurt typefounder Jacques Sabon (c. 1520–80).